GENDER in AFRICAN
PREHISTORY

I dedicate this book to my nephews and nieces—Danny, Lauren, Sammy, and Julia Kent. I hope that by understanding gender in the past, they will be able to better understand gender today and in their futures, regardless of its cultural construction in Western society.

Susan Kent

GENDER in AFRICAN
PREHISTORY

Edited by
Susan Kent

ALTAMIRA
PRESS

A division of Sage Publications, Inc.
Walnut Creek • London • New Delhi

For information address:

AltaMira Press
A Division of Sage Publications, Inc.
1630 North Main Street, Suite 367
Walnut Creek, CA 94596
explore@altamira.sagepub.com

SAGE Publications Ltd.
6 Bonhill Street
London EC2A 4PU
United Kingdom

SAGE Publications India Pvt. Ltd.
M-32 Market
Greater Kailash 1
New Delhi 110 048
India

PRINTED IN THE UNITED STATES OF AMERICA

Library of Congress Cataloging-in-Publication Data

Gender in African prehistory / edited by Susan Kent.
    p. cm.
    Includes bibliographical references and index.
    ISBN 0-7619-8968-4. — ISBN 0-7619-8967-6 (pbk.)
    1. Sex role—Africa. 2. Prehistoric peoples—Africa. 3. Africa—Antiquities.
4. Archaeology—Africa. I. Kent, Susan, 1952– .
GN861.G46   1998
305.3'096—dc21   97-33728
                                      CIP

98 99 00 01 02 03 10 9 8 7 6 5 4 3 2 1

Production by Labrecque Publishing Services
Editorial Management by Joanna Ebenstein
Cover Design by Joanna Ebenstein

Table of Contents

■ *Part One* ■

Introduction

Chapter One

Gender and Prehistory in Africa

Gender in archaeology has become a fashionable topic, a decade later than when it was first popular in cultural anthropology. This is almost two decades after gender research became common in other social science disciplines. Environmental reconstructions, however, remain popular and have been emphasized in archaeology over the past 30 to 40 years. Many archaeologists spend their time studying paleoenvironments and extant environments, in contrast to studying sharing, gender, stratification, and other facets of culture (e.g., Erlandson 1994; Kelley 1995). Although environments, depending on one's theoretical orientation, may affect culture, they are not themselves culture. Environments may be modified by humans, yet they are not created by them in the sense that culture is. Culture, on the other hand, is not only created and perpetuated by humans, it is also modified by them. *Gender in African Prehistory* is a book about past cultures. Some of its authors present more environmental data than others, but each chapter deals primarily with how gender is expressed in the archaeological record and why patterns change through time.

As a result of the emphasis on environmental reconstructions over the past three or four decades, we archaeologists have come a long way in determining paleoenvironmental factors on both the macro- and microscopic levels. Had we spent as much time, money, and effort on studying gender and sociopolitical organization, we probably would have as much knowledge about prehistoric gender relations as we currently have about ancient environments. *Gender in African Prehistory* is the first book that exclusively attempts to examine gender using the African archaeological record. While the geographical region covered in this volume is limited to Africa, the time periods, the topic of gender, the methods, and the theoretical orientations are not limited to that continent.

Why Gender?

While the sex of individuals is a basic biological division among humans, gender is the cultural construction of that division. That is, humans use their conceptions of gender to define and categorize the biological sexes. Individuals understand and legitimize their perceptions of sex through their conceptualization of gender and gender relations. Gender is imbued in almost every facet of culture found in all modern human societies (we cannot be sure about archaic humans or earlier hominids). Although recognized by most archaeologists as an important organizing principle of culture, gender has historically not been well studied in archaeology. However, the situation is changing with the publication of a variety of books that examine gender (e.g., Claassen 1991; Claassen and Joyce 1997; Gero and Conkey 1991; Nelson 1997; Walde and Willows 1991; Wright 1996). With few exceptions, some including authors in this book, the lack of focus on gender is particularly noticeable in the research of African prehistory. Archaeology in Africa has concentrated more on reconstructing paleoenvironments, locating and understanding the earliest hominids, analyzing faunal remains and lithic artifacts, and studying the exploitation of economic resources. The dearth of gender research, again with the exception of many of the following authors, seems particularly conspicuous when compared to archaeology conducted on other continents. *Gender in African Prehistory* attempts to fill this void. The book provides methods and theories for delineating and discussing prehistoric gender relations while understanding their change through time, endeavors that are relevant to all geographic areas and time periods.

Gender is defined here as the interaction between females and males as constructed by culture. Women and men are viewed as reacting to and interacting with one another, even in those societies with complementary and nonoverlapping gender divisions of labor. To some anthropologists gender means women. However, women today and in prehistory never operated in isolation from men. There often are facets of culture that exclude one sex, like secret societies or the use of space, but even those are in response to how men and women interact overall. Often such exclusion is important in defining separate gender roles; that is, they are a reaction to one another. In fact, femininity can best be understood in opposition to masculinity and vice versa. Thus, the activities of both men and women are essential to the understanding of gender and, when possible, both are examined in the following chapters. For some authors, it was necessary that they revise basic assumptions concerning the role of each sex in the activities that contributed to the archaeological record before analyzing site data (e.g., Segobye, Chapter 12). For others, data already collected had to be reanalyzed in light of questions concerning gender (Stahl and Cruz, Chapter 11). These new analyses and revised thinking made writing the chapters a stimulating challenge, leading the authors to think in new directions. Thus, this book was exciting to write and, I hope, is exciting to read.

Gender in African Prehistory includes sites ranging geographically from Egypt to South Africa and from Ghana to Tanzania. Time periods discussed vary from the Stone Age (Parkington, Chapter 2; Kent, Chapter 3; Wadley, Chapter 4; Casey, Chapter 5; and Barich, Chapter 6) to the period just prior to colonialization (Stahl and Cruz, Chapter 11; Hall, Chapter 13). Its authors approach the study of gender from a variety of theoretical orientations, ranging from processualism to postmodernism, political economy, and feminist criticism. I believe that the inclusion of multiple theoretical perspectives promotes a more holistic view of gender than any one view can provide by itself.

Congruent with emphasizing the importance of multiple ways of viewing the past, four distinguished archaeologists discuss the implications of the chapters. The four enhance the book by approaching the topic from very different backgrounds. Hassan (Chapter 14) is an Africanist archaeologist whose research experience spans the period from prehistoric, relatively noncomplex societies to the most complex society on the African continent, the ancient Egyptian civilization. He examines sociopolitical, cognitive, and environmental change through time. Bar-Yosef and Belfer-Cohen (Chapter 15) work in the contiguous Middle East. They study change through different time periods, concentrating on Mesolithic Natufians and the following Neolithic period. They bring a perspective from an adjacent culture area, along with an interest in gender studies, the transition to sedentism, and the shift to agriculture. The research areas of Nelson (Chapter 16) include women and power in Asian prehistory, particularly Korea and China, in addition to the North American Southwest. Her work focuses on gender and sociopolitical organization in complex societies, and her feminist orientation adds an important dimension from which to view the various chapters. The diverse expertise of these authors allows them to present varied and insightful commentaries that, together with the other chapters, complete the book.

While 20th-century archaeology has emphasized function, physical environment/ecology, and materialism, I predict that the 21st century will focus more on holistic approaches to the study of past societies that explicitly integrate gender with sociopolitical organization and other facets of culture (also see Hassan, Chapter 14). Such a shift in inquiry will provide a more full and realistic view of the past. It will be a time of examining data in new ways without forsaking empirical verification, as well as a time of emphasizing culture over the physical environment while not ignoring the basic constraints imposed by the environment. Moreover, the 21st century will be a time of gaining important insights by incorporating the diversity of cross-cultural data into archaeological explanations and understandings without resorting to the problematic use of analogies (noted also by Hassan, Chapter 14). The exploration of gender in African prehistory by the contributors to this book represents a beginning from which to embark on the challenge of 21st-century archaeology.

Why Not Just Women?

Gender is the cultural overlay that determines who are included in the categories girls, women, and "feminine" and in their male counterparts, boys, men, and "masculine." That is, gender defines what it means to be a woman or a man in a particular society and the kind of behavior and thought that is considered to be feminine or masculine. Gender likewise determines whether there are more than two genders present. The possibility of more than two genders with only two biological sexes and the presence of institutionalized homosexuality in some societies underscore the fact that biology has little to do with gender beyond creating a fundamental division (though MacLean, Chapter 9, attributes biological reasons for certain gendered activities). It is difficult, if not impossible, to understand women without also understanding men. The fact that most earlier archaeology did neglect women led to misconceptions not only of women, but also of men and gender in general. Because my definition of gender includes both women and men interacting and/or reacting to one another, I encouraged this volume's authors to include discussions of both, as is exemplified by most of the following chapters.

Perhaps the most common mistake resulting from studies that emphasize one sex over the other is perpetuating a stereotyped view of gender, one often based on Western precepts. No one sex is more important to know about than the other. I think it is relatively safe to say that in all societies both sexes contribute to the archaeological record in one way or another. Therefore it is important to study both.

Gender As Culture

I find it paradoxical that while many archaeologists see gender as a cultural construct (Joyce and Claassen 1997, and others), a number of archaeologists perceive gender relations and roles as universal in nature, that is, as biological rather than cultural. Although men in prehistory are often viewed as prominent in social, religious, economic, and political affairs, Damm (1991) cautions archaeologists against assuming that because "men are dominant in the present day society, they are portrayed as dominant also in the past, usually by both men and women."

The underlying theoretical orientation of an archaeologist influences the interpretations of gender in the archaeological record. Interpretations depend on an individual's assumptions and perceptions of gender in the present. To examine just one example in detail, Hayden (1992b:35) states that he does not understand how some women can question the universality of the sexual division of labor or why some try to deny its presence: "there is little general doubt that this patterning of gender behavior [man the hunter and woman the gatherer] is the expression of a fundamental principle of organization of hunter/gatherer societies . . ." and this provides "some of the best foundations that can be hoped for modeling prehistoric gender behavior." He also writes that "shell, bone or horn crafts [are] exclusively performed by men in traditional societies the world over" and that there is "an almost universal role of women scraping and preparing hides in societies without specialists" (1992:35). Therefore, he concludes that it is valid to assume that lithic tools, such as handaxes and bifaces, "should be primarily and perhaps exclusively associated with male tasks" (1992b:35). Moreover, such patterns "may even imply that the cross-cultural preponderance of hunter/gatherer males in public forums and in dealings with non-local groups may be an extension of the division of labor . . ." (Hayden 1992b:35). The question is, how valid are these statements? Do all societies have tasks, space, and tools that are exclusively male or female? For those who answer yes, the opposition of women and men is taken as the natural order, one with deep biological roots (Maurer 1991).

Some archaeologists think that gender is basically isomorphic among cultures (as an example, women are equated with house interior and private, as contrasted with men, who are exterior and public; Pearson and Richards 1994). Cross-culturally, men are perceived as seeking power in most facets of culture, economic wealth, and political or public influence. Others believe that women cross-culturally are viewed as domestic, subordinate to men, and culturally conservative (Moore 1994; Nelson 1997). As noted in Gifford-Gonzalez's Chapter 7, men are assumed to be the agents responsible for technologically or aesthetically complex artifacts (including lithics and ceramics), for technological breakthroughs, or for change in sociopolitical organization. Gifford-Gonzalez contends that most models of pastoral societies perceive women's work as only marginally important, if that much, to production, trade, and social life. She states that in pastoralist societies, anthropologists tend to report what the men do—and what the men do is what is defined as important. But, if gender is a cultural construction, by definition it cannot be universal because it must vary by culture, just as kinship and political organizations vary.

I suggest that gender is one of the organizing devices of culture, along with age and kinship. Therefore, concepts of gender and gender interaction should be as diverse as are the different cultural interpretations of kinship known ethnographically. Other archaeologists see gender as a means for societies to organize sexuality (e.g., Claassen 1992a). However, gender in some societies has little or nothing to do with sexuality or even with the biological sexes. Sexuality permeates gender in Western and other cultures, but I question its universality as a function of gender. If culture specifies what categories and attributes define each gender, then prehistoric and historic conceptions of gender must be seen within the perspective of a diverse array of cultures. Although not accepted by all archaeologists, most cross-cultural research demonstrates the cultural variability of gender in opposition to universal gender roles (Kent 1984, 1990a, in press). Perhaps unintentionally, some researchers perceive men and women, maleness and femaleness, as reflections of Western cultural norms (Kent in press; Moore 1994). Such a perspective stereotypes gender in accordance with the images of Western conceptions of male and female behavior. This is why some archaeologists have criticized attempts to examine gender prehistorically and particularly cross-culturally (e.g., Conkey and Spector 1984). We know that archaeologists who claim that only or even primarily men hunt and make lithic or shell tools are incorrect, as noted by Costin (1996). Cross-cultural studies elucidate the fascinating diversity of gender roles currently present, and no doubt the range was even more diverse prehistorically before the encroachment of Western society.

Highly egalitarian, mobile foragers can be characterized as having an extremely flexible gender division of labor in which both sexes can or do participate in conducting various tasks (Barnard and Widlok 1996; Guenther 1996; Kent 1996a). For example, Agta and Chipewyan women hunt big game using the same weapons as men (Estioko-Griffin and Griffin 1981; Brumbach and Jarvenpa 1997). Tiwi women also regularly hunt and when they were girls were taught hunting skills along with the boys (Goodale 1971). Basarwa (Bushmen, San) women routinely engage in manufacturing shell crafts, women in some Basarwa groups regularly trap and hunt small animals, both men and women cook meat and wild plants, both butcher and distribute meat, and men scrape and prepare hides and clothing, though not exclusively (Kent 1993b, 1995, 1996b, n.d.). Another example is Chipewyan female hunters who own their own knives (Brumbach and Jarvenpa 1997:30). At least some of the lithic bifaces archaeologists uncover were probably used as knives in the past (Brumbach and Jarvenpa 1997:30). Men regularly collect wild plants in many highly egalitarian societies. Lee (1979) calculated that as much as 40 percent, or almost half, of all gathering is done by Basarwa men. It is ironic that the Basarwa, often considered to be the archetypical hunter-gatherers past or present, undermine many universalist assumptions.

As a result of universal assumptions about gender, lithics (except for scrapers) are often defined as males' tools, and grinding stones as females' (see Gero 1991). This is patently not true, for grinding stones are also used by men in many cultures to grind nonfood plants and minerals (Bruhns 1991). Men also weave and make pottery in a number of societies around the world (Rice 1991; Bruhns 1991). I believe it is better to be a little more indefinite about examining gender in prehistory than it is to use inaccurate or biased inferences. Similar universal gender convictions are not held solely by male archaeologists, but are promoted also by women who were taught by men to use Western idealized stereotypes of gender.

Some ethnoarchaeologists and ethnographers do not recognize the impact of restricting their informants to only males or to only females. Others fail to take into account the biases male Western ethnographers, explorers, and colonialists had about gender, biases that unintentionally influenced their interpretations of non-Western societies. These biases have perpetuated the myth of stereotyped and rigid divisions of labor cross-culturally (Lane 1994–1995). For example, male Westerners perceived matrilineal Navajo men as the important actors in decision making. During contact and beyond, male North American government officials would not consider asking a woman for permission to go on her land, or to make a decision about her herd of animals. In many societies with varying amounts of egalitarianism, men from patriarchical societies forced indigenous men to be the public spokesperson for a group, to make decisions that were binding for the group, and to interact with foreigners by simply not talking to women nor taking what women said as important (as occurred at Kutse, Botswana, where I work). No wonder there is a widespread assumption that men are leaders, represent public consensus, and so on! Westerners and men from other patriarchical societies did not allow the women to have such roles. Stereotyped behaviors are still being forced onto non-Western societies. For example, Western AID agencies in some developing countries are introducing wage-earning development projects that separate male and female work that is incongruous with the indigenous culture. Western-inspired development programs implemented among the Basarwa, for example, often unintentionally emphasize or exclude one sex, depending on whether the program centers on wild plants or animal products (Kent 1995). By providing differential access to wage-earning projects, the programs foster a rigid gender division that undermines the Basarwa flexible division of labor while mirroring Western gender stereotypes.

Biased Concepts of Gender

Because one's own culture seems innate or "normal," both male and female researchers sometimes are not aware that they are applying Western gender concepts to non-Western societies. Particularly misleading is the use of historical records written mostly by men and later read by male or female anthropologists who do not take into account the profound effects of contact and culture change. Anthropologists or colonial officials often strengthen male leadership, status, and economic positions within local patriarchal societies by making laws or policies that enhance men's ability to control resources and to dominate women, simply by making laws or policies that parallel Western customs (Lane 1994–1995:58). Several anthropologists (Gifford-Gonzalez, Chapter 7; Stahl and Cruz, Chapter 11; Nelson, Chapter 16; Fratt 1991) have discussed the distortions in the ethnographic record written mostly by Western males who exclusively or primarily talked to male informants. Claassen (1997:73) notes that many gender studies conducted in North America, and particularly those concerned with Plains archaeology, "assume that historic sex roles were present in the past." Once archaeologists assume this, they also assume that gender is universal and unchanging. The extreme impact of culture change in indigenous populations brought about by Westerners profoundly altered most facets of culture, including gender. Westerners gave indigenous men political, social, and economic resources and power while basically ignoring the women (see Fratt 1991; Prezzano 1997:94–98). The increase in hostilities brought about by Westerners' intervention with non-Western societies also often elevated male prestige through increased warfare.

Prezzano (1997) recognizes the fallacy of accepting historic accounts of gender at face value. She writes that "The influx of disease and trade goods significantly altered the [Iroquois] political base of extra-village activities in the colonial period and are thus poor indicators of the traditional place of household [and gender] politics in fueling change [through time] in sociopolitical organization" (1997:98). Using contemporary accounts of non-Western societies ahistorically or out of the context of cross-cultural research distorts our understanding of the past. However, we cannot dismiss all historic and ethnographic observations of non-Western cultures; doing so would undermine our understanding of non-Western societies, past or present. We need to critically evaluate the validity of observations before accepting them. We need to ask who made the observations, why, and how.

A different type of fallacy has also originated from the uncritical use of data. Some anthropologists contend that contemporary hunter-gatherer societies are not valid for examining models of forager behavior because the group does not live up to the anthropologists' conceptions of what a specific society "should" look or act like (e.g., Wilmsen 1989; Wilmsen and Denbow 1990). Does the presence of a few trade goods at a site imply that a society has forsaken its cultural autonomy to imitate a culture seen by archaeologists as superior because of its use of domesticates or more complex sociopolitical organization? Consider the erroneous interpretations a future archaeologist would make about the number of objects made in Asia that late 20th-century North Americans possess. Using a similar line of reasoning as that espoused by Wilmsen and Denbow (1990) and others who claim that the Basarwa have not been culturally autonomous for centuries, if not millennia, it might be concluded that North Americans adopted Asian cultural beliefs out of envy of Asia's superior high technology or the opportunity to gain access to Japanese-designed cars, televisions, VCRs, and the like. We should not assume that throughout prehistory most small-scale societies were envious of more sociopolitically complex societies with a higher level of technology. Such societies may have traded together, but small-scale groups were not necessarily interested in abandoning their culture for that of the newcomers. Archaeologists need to be aware of the assumptions behind arguments they posit as valid for the past, such as Wilmsen and Denbow's (1990) view of migrating Bantu-speaking pastoralists seducing and dominating indigenous hunter-gatherer populations circa 2,000 years ago in southern Africa.

We also need to test the reliability of observations to ensure that they are not idiosyncratic and therefore misleading to infer as valid for a group. An example is Nisa, an unusual Ju/'hoansi woman, whose life and beliefs do not represent that of other Ju/'hoansi women (for example, she trapped and hunted, Shostak 1981). Whereas women in other Basarwa groups can and routinely do trap and hunt small animals, Ju/'hoansi women do not (Kent n.d.). Because of Nisa's nonrepresentative ideas on Ju/'hoansi culture, she is not an appropriate source of knowledge about hunting among Ju/'hoansi women. Single informant accounts of their culture are useful only in combination with interviews and observations of other members of the group. Whatever the gender of the ethnographer, it is crucial to interview both females *and* males during fieldwork. Men may not perceive women the same way that women do and vice versa (also see Lane, Chapter 10).

As Lane (Chapter 10) states, forms of gender representation that are present today in Western or non-Western societies are not necessarily accurate portrayals of past social realities. This makes it essential that we view ethnographic and ethnohistorical observations critically and contextually, taking into account the change of a culture through time. We can explore the factors that encourage or discourage specific gender conceptions and behavior, such as the relationship between gender equality and the amount of egalitarianism and hierarchies present in a culture, without resorting to simplistic ethnographic analogies. Analogies presume that certain behaviors were present in the same way in the past as today, whereas ethnoarchaeological modeling only assumes that relationships structure behavior similarly, such as the relationship among sociopolitical complexity, gender segregation of space, and material culture.

My experiences in Africa provide one illustration of how to take into account both culture change through time as well as male-dominated interpretations of societies. In 1987, when I first went to the Kalahari there was only one known community of full-time foragers still exclusively using traditional hunting weapons and techniques (Tari Madondo, National Museum and Art Gallery of Botswana: 1987 personal communication). They continued this way of life because of historical circumstances. To facilitate my study of culture change in the Kalahari (focusing on the impact of sedentarization), I read widely comparative ethnographies written by both males and females in the 1950s, 1960s, and early 1970s. During those decades various groups of Basarwa, mostly Ju/'hoansi and G/wi, were also still primarily hunters and gatherers (Draper 1975a, 1976; Lee 1968, 1969, 1972, 1979, 1982; Marshall 1976; Silberbauer 1981). I examined the more recent research conducted among these same Basarwa groups, in order to understand how aspects of culture change, including sedentarization, affected them (Draper and Cashdan 1988; Draper and Kranichfeld 1990; Lee 1993b). I then compared my own observations with those of the other ethnographers.

Draper (1975a,b, 1992) recorded pronounced differences between women's autonomy and status among nomadic and sedentary Ju/'hoansi. The drop in women's authority and prestige was attributed to the shift to sedentism, along with some influence from neighboring patriarchal Herero Bantu-speakers with whom they were closely interacting. I studied gender among the Kutse Basarwa (composed of G/wi and G//ana), in some cases asking similar interview questions as had Draper. My observations and interview answers were quite different from Draper's. They were more similar to descriptions of nomadic full-time hunter-gatherers than to the initial sedentary Ju/'hoansi groups (Kent 1995). My work indicated that sedentism by itself does not cause gender inequality. Instead, aggregation, particularly when combined with sedentism, is the culprit (Kent 1995, n.d.a). This finding has profound implications for the study of the origins of gender inequality in the past and offers an example of using the ethnographic record critically and contextually while providing archaeologically relevant information for model-building and testing.

My research suggests that gender segregation of activities varies by cultures' sociopolitical organization (Kent 1990a, 1996a, in press). Costin (1996:134) also suggests that the segregation of production either by men or by women is associated with complex societies where gender differences are usually pronounced and segregated. She found that craft specialization in complex societies is often gender specific, but not necessarily conducted by women. According to Costin (1996:121) cross-cultural studies of craft production in complex societies show that "the actual allocation of tasks is remarkably idiosyncratic when considered on a worldwide basis." Others, such as Nelson (Chapter 16), believe that gender differentiation and stratification are not necessarily associated with sociopolitical complexity, though not all the authors writing in this volume concur (e.g., Bar-Yosef and Belfer-Cohen, Chapter 15). Discovering the underlying factors that influence gender equality in the past and present is one of the most exciting projects facing archaeologists. Failing to acknowledge the diversity in gender relations will only hamper our attempts to understand equality and to comprehend why changes occur through time and space.

Most archaeologists would agree that subsistence, architecture, mobility patterns, and sociopolitical organization, as examples, are variable through time. However, these same archaeologists sometimes see gender as timeless. The tiresome dichotomy of "man the hunter; woman the gatherer" has been used to model prehistoric gender relations, as noted in the following chapters. We know that culture forms an integrated whole or system. We also know that gender is culturally constructed. If other parts of culture change through time, then surely so must gender. For example, returning to the historic period of North America, many Native Americans' behavior and material culture changed radically. If these facets of culture changed, then gender also must have at least been impacted. The historic record can be best used to test how much and in which way gender relations changed in various prehistoric societies. Historic views of gender also allow archaeologists to develop non-Western-centric models of gender that can be used to understand archaeological patterning. This is what I try to do in Chapter 3, what Schmidt does in Chapter 8, and what Hall does in Chapter 13.

If we want to understand culture change, we need to understand the social dynamics of both sexes. Even in the most patriarchical, patrilineal, patrilocal societies known historically or today, men do not necessarily contribute significantly more to the archaeological record than women, nor are women in any way unimportant. In patriarchical societies, men expend much energy and resources to maintain their hierarchies, economic sources, purity, and status that, from their perspective, allow them to control women. Thus women are as important as men in understanding any society, past or present. In theory, if women were not present, patriarchical societies would not have to segment their architecture to cloister them, maintain their own differentiated space, have elaborate secret rituals, need tools that only they can use, defend against or create feuding and warfare over women, and so on. In my opinion, and probably that of most readers, the key is to study men and women *together.*

In sum, there currently is much evidence disproving the idea that all societies organize males and females similarly—that is, not all societies emphasize the differences between the sexes or rank them hierarchically in terms of power, dominance, domesticity, status, and so on. Archaeologists who assume that a rigid division of labor characterizes all modern human societies run the risk of projecting their Western beliefs onto the archaeological record. Moreover, they jeopardize the neutrality of their interpretations as well as others' ability to assess those interpretations. However, those researchers who come to the archaeological record with the concept of diversity in gender, ethnographically and prehistorically, will be able to develop models that enhance our understanding of the relations between males and females in different societies and at different times. Models of gender interaction then can be tested empirically with archaeological data.

The Many Views of Gender Research

As the reader of this volume will discover, not all its authors agree with one another. Far from being a flaw, I see this as a *strength* of the book, because archaeologists are still learning about gender and what causes its variation among societies. It is too premature in our understanding of gender for everyone to agree with a particular paradigm or theoretical perspective of how gender operates in different types of societies. At this point we can distinguish between studies of gender that are Western-centric, male-biased, biologically deterministic, or otherwise flawed, but other than the extremes, we have much more research to conduct before determining which perspectives are most productive.

The various contributors to the book have come to the study of gender in very different ways. The genesis of my own work on gender began after I conducted research in several culturally different contemporary societies. From this began my interest in gender, which ultimately led to this book, *Gender in African Prehistory.* The ethnoarchaeological studies I began in 1978, made me realize how simplistic and unsophisticated were many archaeologists' perspectives on gender. Most prominent were assumptions that in all societies males equal power, prestige, and spatial segregation—while females equal domesticity, subordination, and their own, usually technologically or aesthetically inferior, tools. I certainly observed such a dichotomy among the Euroamericans I studied (Kent 1984). However, the dichotomy was mitigated by status among the Salish-speaking Northwest Coast Indians and was not present among the Navajo Indians I observed. I was aware of similar gender dichotomies present among Arabic, Japanese, and other non-Western, highly complex societies. Later, cross-cultural studies of why anthropologists often consider hunting and meat to be more important than gathering made me aware of many anthropologists' unglamorous views of women's work (described in Kent 1989a). The only conclusion that one could draw from the literature was that women led extremely boring, repetitive lives that stood in sharp contrast (according to the writers) to the exciting, risky, and generally more interesting lives of men. Women were "burdened" with child care (a concept, I suggest, that is probably most appropriate to Westerners, who perceive raising children as a burden; child care is not necessarily thought of the same way in other societies). Sadly, according to some researchers, as the result of a biological constraint on women's time and efforts, they could not participate in the supposedly more stimulating, politically important, and socially valued activities of men (Kent 1989a).

A cross-cultural study of the correlation among gendered space and tools, function-specific space and tools, and the sociopolitical organization of societies revealed a great diversity in gender relations that was influenced by the sociopolitical system of a group (Kent 1990a,b). This ethnographically documented variability was not recognized or applied to most archaeologists' interpretations of the past use of space or objects, though the concept of variability was usually incorporated in interpretations of prehistoric sociopolitical organizations.

My understanding of gender continued to evolve and continued to diverge from that written by many archaeologists. In 1987, I began my first research season among the highly egalitarian Basarwa at Kutse. Some of my views of gender were either not appropriate or not conscious (see Kent 1993b, 1995). For example, I interviewed both women and men on the same issues, only to find that what I had been taught about males and females was not appropriate in all societies. I found myself making implicit assumptions about males and females that prompted individuals to ask "why do you say [or think, or ask] that?" I discovered that more of my assumptions than I realized were Western assumptions about the nature of gender, a topic I explored over the next nine field seasons at Kutse.

About the same time, gender was beginning to be examined more intensively by archaeologists. I was concerned that many Western assumptions that stereotyped gender were being applied to past non-Western societies. The "universalist" belief of a biologically determined or influenced division of labor was basically Western culture's conception of gender. My fieldwork showed the assumption was far from universally present. The even more common belief that all societies past and present separate male and female activities, material culture, and space also was not supported by my fieldwork, which indicated a rich diversity in gender that was culturally determined, and therefore culturally variable. This cultural diversity was even present within groups having similar economies, such as hunter-gatherers. The increase in gender studies of the past by archaeologists led to differences in the approach and theoretical orientations that, as noted by Nelson (Chapter 16), varied by continent. Considering the diversity of cultures and gender found today in Africa, it is interesting that archaeologists have tended to regard prehistoric African gender relations as similar to their own society's concepts. When a non-Western view of prehistoric gender relations is sought, many archaeologists rely on a single ethnography of a contemporary group, such as the Bantu Central Cattle Pattern, or on androgynous interpretations of the past.

I have described my personal odyssey that led to the development of *Gender in African Prehistory*. All of the following authors have their own individual odyssey that has led them to study gender. Most view gender as being variable through time and, at least partially, as being integrated symbolically in the behavioral expression of culture (e.g., Schmidt, Chapter 8; Lane, Chapter 10; Segobye, Chapter 12; Hall, Chapter 13). The chapters attest to the methodological rigor connected with examining gender in prehistory. As noted by Nelson (Chapter 16) and Gifford-Gonzalez (Chapter 7), gender research requires better, not worse, archaeology than that often practiced today.

My quest to understand gender relations in the past has not ended with the publication of this book. Instead, my knowledge of gender has further developed in its sophistication as I incorporated the valuable insights provided by reading the following chapters. I believe archaeologists of the 21st century will pursue the study of gender, stratification, symbolism, ideology, and other facets of culture known to influence relations between people and will begin to discard the Western-centric or environmental models so popular, but yet potentially so misleading, that are common in the archaeology of the 20th century. I fervently hope readers interested in Africa and beyond will be able to incorporate the knowledge of the diversity of gender in African prehistory and what dynamics influenced the construction of gender through time. Ultimately, studies such as those represented in this book and in emerging studies of gender throughout the world will force archaeologists to rethink the prehistory of *all* the continents.

Acknowledgments

I would like to thank Sarah Nelson, Lyn Wadley, Fekri Hassan, and Cheryl Claassen for useful suggestions on a rough draft of this chapter. However, all errors are my responsibility alone.

■ *Part Two* ■

Perspectives of Gender from the African Archaeological Record

Chapter Two

Resolving the Past

Gender in the Stone Age
Archaeological Record of the Western Cape

Resolution

Engendering the archaeological record or the prehistoric past requires that we ask and attempt to answer a number of difficult questions. Most specifically we may ask who collected the shellfish, who painted the rock paintings, and who made the stone artifacts we record and collectively regard as "the record." Was it men, was it women, was it both, was it some men or some women, or was it anyone who could? More generally we may wonder what it was like to have been a man, a woman, or perhaps an old woman, in some particular prehistoric time and place. And it follows from this that we should wonder how male, female, or other roles were maintained, challenged, and changed in social situations where men and women held different agendas, enjoyed differential access to status and power, and may have led very different lives. In short, engendering the past is a search for resolution in the social dimension and an attempt to reflect the experiences of different categories of person. It is a parallel endeavor to the resolution of space and time that, when taken together, offer a resolved and therefore meaningful past.

During the heyday of ecological archaeology the relations that were considered significant were those between people and their natural environment (for a critique see Mazel 1987). Although the environment was conceived of as complex and as incorporating many interactive components such as rainfall, soils, vegetation, and resources, society was often depicted as unified and simple, apparently devoid of internal structure or divisions. Not surprisingly society, incorporating undifferentiated "people," generated no latent energy for change, no contradictions to be accommodated; explanations, consequently, focused on environmental or climatic change. Coincident with, and in fact necessary for, a shift to an interest in social explanations for changing archaeological signatures has been the recognition that past societies were far from simple. Thus, the recognition of interest groups with conflicting objectives or competitive visions allows the engine of change to be situated in the social as well as the natural environment. This shift has meant that "people" now have to be resolved into men and women, young and old, initiated and uninitiated, relatives by blood and by marriage, stone tool makers, bead makers, dancers, and painters. I view gender as a component of this interest in greater resolution.

The problem is, clearly, how to achieve the resolution of person, how to recognize the roles of and rules for women or men at particular times in the past. For me it is not simply a matter of problematization, a stage that has been effectively achieved very largely through the momentum of the feminist movement (Conkey and Spector 1984; Gero and Conkey 1991). It now appears to be an issue of method, a need to operationalize our understanding of the roles of men and women by relooking at archaeological evidence through gender-sensitive eyes. My suggestion here is that to find gender, the culturally defined roles of men and women, requires first that we find men and women. It is hard to disentangle the specific question "who collected shell-fish?" from the more general "what was it like to have been a woman?" or the issue "how were gender relations constructed, perceived, and changed?"

To pursue this agenda I describe some work being done by archaeologists interested in the history of Stone Age precolonial people in the Western Cape of South Africa. The intention is not to claim that the arguments are conclusive, or even persuasive, but rather to illustrate an approach to seeing men and women in the distant past as actors in a social as well as an environmental arena. My thread is the argument that there is a consistency among very different kinds of evidence, written and material, about gender relations among Southern African hunter-gatherers (often referred to as San, Basarwa, or Bushmen) for the past few millennia, but that this becomes elusive when we look back as far as the terminal Pleistocene. I suggest three sources, from which men and women are clearly visible: ethnographic texts, rock art images, and buried human skeletons. I refer also to some less well-anchored speculations drawn from other parts of the archaeological record such as stone tools and faunal remains. Although spatial patterns in archaeological remains may relate to gendered behavior, I agree with Kent (this volume) that most patterns reflect the distribution of activities rather than gendered space.

Ethnography

Ethnographic accounts of former hunter-gatherer communities in the Kalahari (among them Katz 1982; Lee 1979; Marshall 1976; Silberbauer 1981; Tanaka 1976) obviously contain direct observations of men and women and have been a popular entry point for Western Cape archaeologists interested in various technological and social issues including gender (as examples see Parkington 1972, 1977, 1984, 1988, 1996; Solomon 1989, 1992, 1994). This is not unreasonable because it is widely believed that there are strong genetic, linguistic, and cognitive links between 20th-century people of the Kalahari and late precolonial communities of the Western Cape. More pertinently, perhaps, we have observations made by early travelers and early settlers on the lives and behaviors of hunter-gatherer and pastoralist groups that survived into the 17th or even 19th centuries in the Western Cape, albeit often as dispossessed and subordinate communities (see, for example, the reports in Barrow (1801–04); Sparrman (1785); Thunberg (1795–96)). Even more direct references to the lives of men and women come in the form of the 19th-century accounts of life in the Karoo region of the South African interior collected by Wilhelm Bleek and Lucy Lloyd (Bleek 1924, 1931, 1932a,b, 1933a,b, 1935, 1936; Lloyd 1911). These /Xam people were former hunter-gatherers who were being incorporated into colonial society as farm laborers. It is not the intention here to deny the usefulness of ethnographic or historic observations for suggesting explanations of archaeological remains. Quite the contrary, the implication is that gender roles may not have changed much in the last thousand years before colonialism. Perhaps the problem, though, is well made by returning to some of the questions posed earlier. Who painted, who collected shellfish, who made stone tools? In the Kalahari and the Karoo the answer is, simply but obviously, *no one does any longer*. Historical and ethnographic accounts incorporate changes resulting from colonial intervention, so that some behaviors had disappeared prior to reliable observations and others had changed.

What, then, does it mean to be informed by the ethnography, more specifically on the issue of gender? Women emerge as the gatherers of plants, providers of carbohydrates, collectors of the major components of the diet; as the makers of ostrich eggshell beads; as the singers and clappers but not normally the dancers at healing dances; as potential "owners" of water holes and central figures in the maintenance of group identity; as users and maintainers, but perhaps not makers, of digging sticks and perforated weight stones; as closely identified with domestic space and duties but not so with wider-scale political roles. Men, by contrast, are meat providers, being solely responsible for the hunting of large game with the bow and poisoned arrows, though this may happen rarely and contribute occasional bounties rather than regular fare. Men also manufacture most hunting and gathering gear, engage in dance and trance more frequently than women at healing occasions, are more likely perpetrators of violence against both men and women, and emerge in interactions with farmers and administrators as spokespersons for former hunter-gatherers.

So much for the economics and technology, but Megan Biesele's work (1993) on the expressive culture of Kalahari Ju/'hoansi has revealed the deep and pervasive role of gender relations in the language and oral traditions of such groups. What emerges is a complex metaphorical framework whereby men and women articulate the tensions of gender relations, incorporating and focusing on the roles of "man the hunter" and "woman the childbearer." Encapsulated in the belief system of n!ao (n!ow in Lorna Marshall's [1957] usage), the economic and procreational levels are conflated so that a common language for sex and hunting is used. McCall (1970) has aptly noted that men "hunt" women as they hunt large game. Equivalents are noted between the penis and the arrow, the semen and the poison, the blood of the kill and the blood of birth. It is also apparent from Biesele (1993) and other texts that these tensions characterize the relations only of adult and sexually active men and women. Girls before first menstruation and boys before their first large game kill—in each case the first shedding of blood—do not engage in the metaphorically phrased struggle, and older men and women—after the last shedding of killing or menstruating blood—are less antagonistically related. These tensions find expression in the notion that harm enters society through women, especially women who are, or expect to be, menstruating, who thus are disqualified from becoming healers and must adopt the supportive role of clapping and singing at the healing dances.

Nor is such a framework limited to the Kalahari of the mid-20th century, though it is best reported here. Clearly the comments of /Xam Bushmen of the 19th century Karoo to Lucy Lloyd and Wilhelm Bleek reflect a version of n!ao belief, although the word is never used. Thomas's (1950) northern Namibian (then South West African) observations from the first half of the 20th century and Qing's comments to Orpen (Orpen 1874) may be taken to imply a widespread set of beliefs that framed gender relations through the perceived equivalence of hunting and sex. These beliefs also include the creation of hunters and husbands at male initiation and prey and wives at female first menstruation rituals (Parkington 1996). A man has two wives, his human wife and his eland or gemsbok mate animal. There is, thus, a direct link between the technology of the bow and poisoned arrows, the economics of the division of labor between man the hunter and woman the gatherer, carnivore and herbivore, and the generalized gender roles of aggressive man and supportive woman.

It is obviously tempting to simply import these wonderfully detailed scenarios into our reconstructions of Western Cape late prehistory. But it is important for us to question whether we are learning much about the past by this form of analogical reasoning (Wylie 1982). Even a brief focus on the question of shellfish gathering may persuade us that we are not. There are many changes in the archaeological record of shellfish gathering in the Western Cape during the Holocene. The volumes of shell midden recorded per unit time vary enormously, as do the sizes, numbers, and placement of sites (Buchanan 1988; Jerardino and Yates 1996; Parkington et al. 1988). The frequencies of different shellfish targets also vary considerably and include periods of undoubted focus on either limpets or mussels as well as periods where more diverse sets of shellfish were gathered. There are some Holocene millennia missing from the coastal archaeological record, suggesting the possibility of a lengthy cessation of shellfish gathering on any scale. The density and range of artifacts and animal bones in shell-dominated deposits also varies, as does the extent to which the animal bones point to seasonally restricted collecting times. All of this points to a far from stable strategy of shellfish gathering and an almost certainly variable relationship between coastal visits and overall settlement systems. Reliance on the ethnography might lead us to assume that shellfish collecting is invariably the task of women, whereas this may have been quite variable through the millennia.

Clearly the ethnographic and early traveler accounts provide ideas and detailed scenarios that can be used to formulate hypotheses about past situations. Testing such hypotheses, in this instance ones about male and female roles, requires that we build arguments to link men and women with component parts of the changing patterns of evidence we call the archaeological record. Where, though, is the check on our constructed history? Obviously ethnography alone does not produce a past, so information from these sources needs to be linked to material traces of past systems. We may not have to penetrate far back into the prehistory of the Western Cape before we have to envisage scenarios quite different from those seen and partially described by travelers and ethnographers.

Rock Art

For many viewers the most beautiful rock art images in the Western Cape, and certainly among those into which the most obvious efforts to incorporate natural detail have gone, are the magnificent paintings of large game, most often the eland. These animals are the most likely to have been killed by men with bows and poisoned arrows and they remind us of the "hunter and his gemsbok wife" (Thomas 1950) or the special relationship between the creator mantis/kaggen and his eland (Bleek 1924). The focus on these animals, to the almost complete exclusion of shellfish, plant foods, and small game such as tortoises that could have been collected by women, encourages us to begin to see the art as part of the same expressive vocabulary as Marshall and Biesele have recorded as n!ao in the Kalahari.

Human figures are far more frequently painted than animal figures in the corpus of Western Cape rock art. As a residual art, however, many of the human figures are not readily diagnosed as those of men or women, and instead have to be recorded as of indeterminate sex. My view, not shared by all researchers (Solomon 1996), is that almost all human figures were intended to be read unambiguously as either men or women, and quite probably particular categories of men or women, more specifically related to differences in age and initiation. The regular depiction of penises on men and buttocks on women draws attention to the sexual potential of these people and underlines the relationship between the paintings and sexual tensions and metaphors. Men are painted with recognizable penises not because they walked and hunted naked, but surely because the painter intended the viewer to be able to distinguish between different categories of person, between men and women, and between younger and older men and women. If we are right, then, here is a finely resolved component of the Western Cape archaeological record that allows us to assess the roles, associations, and references implied by male and female human figures.

Constraining the potential of this situation, and certainly limiting the range of gender interpretations, is the social context and both the ritual and symbolic intent of the painters and the painting (Lewis-Williams 1981, 1993; Lewis-Williams and Dowson 1989, 1994; Vinnicombe 1976). No doubt the paintings are far from a simple visual ethnography and refer more directly to the socially constituted roles of men and women, rather than attempting to illustrate the range of activities and contributions made by them. There are clear patterns reflecting distinctions intentionally drawn by the painters between depictions of men and women, and these are of direct relevance to gender roles and relations. The association of men with bows and, less often but no less unambiguously, women with weighted digging sticks, is entirely consistent with ethnographic accounts, as is the observation that most groupings of humans are either predominantly men or women and seldom include both. Men with the finger-spread clapping convention have never recorded on survey. These features of the painted record can be taken as meaning that the society of the painters was similarly structured along gendered lines and shared many of the gendered roles with that of modern Kalahari groups.

In the Western Cape there are many more depictions of men than of women, in some subregions as many as five or seven times as many (Manhire 1981; Van Rijssen 1980). Most of the large groupings of human figures, certainly those with more than 10 figures, are processional and best interpreted as dances—most likely the dancing associated with initiation events for young men or first menstruation events for young women (Parkington and Manhire 1991). Many paintings, including processional ones, and especially those dominated by men, include conventions that are reliably associated with trance, either the occasion of a healing dance or the geometric forms experienced by shamans during an altered state. The initiation events and the shamanistic references clearly link the paintings with custom and belief as expressed in Kalahari and Karoo ethnographies (Yates and Manhire 1991; Yates et al. 1985).

Consistent metaphorical associations between women and the kinds of large game animals hunted by men with bows and arrows are found in recent Kalahari expressive culture, specifically among the Ju/'hoansi (Biesele 1993; McCall 1970), 19th-century Karoo stories (Bleek 1924), and Western Cape rock paintings (Parkington 1996). The paintings, as Solomon has noted (1989, 1992, 1994), relate explicitly, and perhaps primarily, to gender and sexual relations and should continue to be the focus of any research that attempts to uncover the history of gender in Southern African hunter-gatherer society. It is, thus, extremely important to try to date rock paintings so that archaeologists can actively derive changes in subject matter, which may constitute a unique record of the maintenance, challenge, and change in relations between men and women. The paintings at the moment express detailed resolution of place and person, but not of time, with the result that the detection of change through this evidence is difficult or impossible. Recent dates for buried painted wall slabs in the Western Cape (Jerardino and Yates 1996) of over 3,000 years imply that the association of male and female identities with hunting and procreation respectively may be valid for at least much of the later Holocene.

Burials

Buried human skeletons, if dated directly, are easily the most resolved component of the archaeological record. Not only can time, place, and person be derived from appropriate analysis, but also some resolution of the age of the person can be gained. What this means is that any associated grave goods, any pathologies, any inferences from anatomy, tooth wear, or injury, and any measurement of trace element or isotopic composition refer to a specific, individual man or woman. There can be little doubt that here lies the most significant potential for establishing patterned differences between men and women at particular times in the past—differences that could provide the basis for gendered interpretations of diet, health, injury, and general behavior.

In the Western Cape the most promising work so far in this direction is that of Judy Sealy and her colleagues in the analysis of stable carbon and nitrogen isotopes (Sealy and van der Merwe 1985, 1986, 1987, 1988; Sealy et al. 1987; Lee Thorp et al. 1989), trace elemental composition (Gilbert et al. 1994; Sealy and Sillen 1988), and tooth wear and tooth pathology patterns (Gilbert et al. 1994) among dated human skeletons, most of them from the coastal strip. Although there is much discussion about the translation of stable carbon isotope readings into specific dietary profiles (Parkington 1986, 1988, 1991), and though the effects of pregnancy and lactation on bone signal turnover are poorly understood as yet, the patterns of male and female isotope values must potentially reflect differences between the diets of men and women as well as shifts in those differences through time.

Interestingly, the most pronounced separation of male and female carbon isotope values, though still perhaps not strictly statistically significant, is that of skeletons dated to between 2,000 and 3,000 years ago (Lee Thorp et al. 1989). Before this time there are relatively few observations, and after it the values for men and women are clearly indistinguishable. What is interesting about this particular millennium is that it is marked in the archaeological record of at least part of the Western Cape coast by the accumulation of "megamiddens," very large shell accumulations opposite rocky shorelines with extremely low densities of artifacts and animal bones and showing little evidence of domestic features (Buchanan 1988; Jerardino and Yates 1997; Parkington et al. 1988). This is a reassuring convergence of evidence from the archaeological and archaeometric records and implies some connection between the formation of megamiddens and the level of difference between the diets of men and women, more specifically a higher marine food intake by men.

The meaning of the megamidden phenomenon has been and remains controversial. My position is as follows (Henshilwood et al. 1994). The very large volumes and extraordinarily low densities for any materials other than shell and charcoal in the megamiddens (Buchanan 1988) stand in stark contrast with equivalent values for either cave or open site localities in earlier or later millennia (Parkington et al. 1992). One interpretation for this, but not the only one, is that the megamiddens are the residue of logistically planned visits to appropriate rocky shore localities where shellfish, specifically mussels, were gathered, dried, and accumulated for transport elsewhere, leaving only modest evidence for domestic behavior in massive shell and charcoal heaps. Because of the temporal correlation with a more marked differentiation between the stable carbon isotope values of men and women, and because the protein of shellfish would unquestionably be reflected in the carbon isotope values of the collagen measured, it is tempting to identify men as making up the logistical shellfish parties. Regular, if short, visits to shellfish colonies might have exposed men to higher intakes of marine foods than women, even if the dried shellfish were subsequently shared equally among all band members.

Conventionally, the Kalahari hunter-gatherers are not seen as "logistical" in Binford's (1980) sense, because they move people to resources rather than the opposite. They practice residential rather than logistical mobility. Thus, the shellfish drying and transportation scenario suggested here departs from ethnographic practice in proposing logistical trips to the coast involving spending some days away from a home base. But Kalahari men are occasionally away from camp for a few nights when hunting, whereas women are much less likely to stay away. Logistical parties of male shellfish processors are consistent with some aspects of ethnographic practice. It remains to be shown why such behavior characterized this particular millennium and why there was such a need for protein resources when terrestrial alternatives must surely have existed. It is also clear that, at present, the information derived from the buried human skeletons, while interesting and important, remains somewhat detached from that derived from the rock art and makes little direct reference to gender.

Stone Tools and Faunal Remains

Most Holocene stone tools in the Western Cape, as elsewhere in much of Southern Africa (Deacon 1984b), are made on small flakes or bladelets struck from single- or multi-platformed cores made of fine-grained raw materials such as silcrete, chalcedony, or quartz. A variety of small scrapers, backed pieces, and drills are made from these blanks, and residual cores are often included in the assemblages. These cores weigh only a few tens of grams and even when capable of producing tens or dozens more flakes would have been easily carried around in a bag for ad hoc use by a stone tool maker. For the most part, then, the assemblages are microlithic and the conventional reduction sequence involves the production of small flakelets and bladelets suitable for mounting or hafting. It is extremely unfortunate that this pattern of toolmaking did not survive long enough to be reliably reported by early travelers, so that we do not know definitively who made the tools.

In these Holocene assemblages there is another tool type, an adze, that was conventionally made on a much larger flake and that was used for woodworking, to judge by both microwear observations (Binneman and Deacon 1986) and wood shaving associations (Mazel and Parkington 1981). Many adzes have been made on older flakes, some of them dating from the Middle Stone Age (Anderson 1990; Kaplan 1987), and were not specifically struck for the purpose. This can be easily seen from the patination difference between the bulbar surface of the adze and the adze retouch or utilization scars. It is quite likely that Later Stone Age stone tool makers recognized Middle Stone Age sites as useful sources of large, fairly rectangular flakes suitable for mounting as adzes. Cores capable of producing a few dozen adze flakes on demand would have weighed several kilograms and would not have been easily transported. The production of adzes thus completely bypasses the conventional stone tool production sequence and in fact does not require any initial involvement in flaking. This is interesting in light of our argument that the primary, but not only, use for the adze would be for making and maintaining wooden digging sticks of the kind recorded in both ethnography and rock art as associated with women. Bows, once made, need almost no maintenance, but digging sticks need to be made and sharpened regularly (Vincent 1985a).

It is obviously possible that men made adzes as often as they made scrapers or drills, simply recognizing the advantages of raiding a Middle Stone Age site for large blanks over carrying heavy cores, even if such large cores were available. For that matter, women may have made all stone tools, though general ethnographic patterns may make that unlikely. The point is, though, that we have suggestive but not conclusive evidence that links plant food collecting, digging stick use and maintenance, woodshavings and adze frequencies, and women's work with a circumvention of (read "challenge to"?) the mainstream procedure of stone tool making. Whether this implies some tension between men and women emerging in the toolmaking and tool using arena is difficult to say.

In the terminal Pleistocene, stone artifact making patterns were markedly different; adzes much rarer, less patterned, and more frequently made of quartz; and woodworking not necessarily restricted to adzes (Binneman in press; Parkington and Yates in press). The fit between ethnographically recorded patterns and the archaeological record of this time is so far only examinable at Elands Bay Cave, a fairly large cave that currently lies some 200 meters from the shore in the base of a prominent ortho-quartzite cliff. In the terminal Pleistocene it experienced (if caves can be said to experience) a dramatic change of place as the sea level rose from its maximum low of about minus 120 meters at 20,000 years ago to a high of about plus 3 meters some 6,000 years ago, shifting the coastline some 30 to 35 kilometers east. The deposits of the cave contain a very diverse reflection of this change in the form of variable depositional volumes per unit time and a dramatically variable assemblage of artifactual and foodwaste debris. The argument I have put forward (Parkington 1988, in press) is that the nature of cave occupation changed through this time from one characterized by brief but regular visits by male hunting parties to one of longer visits by complete groups of hunter-gatherers once the shoreline had advanced to within exploitable distance of the cave. The evidence I used for what is at least in part a gender argument is as follows.

Shellfish are almost entirely absent from deposits predating 11,000 years ago but dominate all subsequent levels. With the appearance of shellfish, the densities of tortoise bone and ostrich eggshell fragments per unit volume, and thus by extrapolation, per unit time, increase extraordinarily, while the densities of stone tools, but not bone tools, decrease substantially. Bone tools, including bone beads, as well as ostrich eggshell beads, including many unfinished examples, increase after 11,000 years ago, adding to the impression of extraordinary diversity of materials, artifacts, and foodwaste after that time. Burials are unknown before 11,000 years ago, though five were found, including a newborn child, to have occurred between then and 8,000 years ago.

Although greater space would allow a more sophisticated or nuanced presentation, the pattern is for pre-11,000-year-old levels to be fairly rich in mammal bone and an expediently produced quartz-based stone tool assemblage, with modest amounts of tortoise bone and very small numbers of ostrich eggshell fragments. Shellfish, ostrich eggs, and tortoises, all slow-moving or stationary targets not inconsistent with the ethnographic contributions of women, either first appear or peak at 11,000 years ago along with evidence for an across-the-board increase in manufacturing activities in bone and shell. Longer periods are spent at the site, and occasional deaths in residence result in a modest but noticeable pulse of burials. It seems inescapable that at 11,000 years ago the proximity of the shoreline prompted people to begin to use the site as a home base, but does the absence of arguably collected food and arguably female (on ethnographic grounds) activities imply the absence of women beforehand? Other variables such as preservation and the relatively smaller size of our pre-11,000-year-old sample are hard to eliminate, and supporting evidence from other contemporary sites is not yet available. Closure is some way off, but enough evidence is at hand to make it likely that settlement strategies were then more logistical, settlement patterns more dispersed, and gender relations less likely to have remained static.

Terminal Pleistocene settlement patterns in the Cape have been envisaged as involving large group sizes, large "territorial" ranges (Deacon 1976), and infrequent but large-scale movements, contrasting with the Kalahari-style small group residential mobility of the Holocene. If there is any truth in these speculations, there are enormous implications for the roles of men and women, as well as for marriage rules and consequent residential and affinal arrangements. As an educated guess, the length of residential stay would be inversely proportional to the importance of plant foods in the diet, unless some form of storage or food manipulation was practiced, because large parties of women radiating out from one location would soon exhaust local edible plant foods. At Elands Bay Cave the terminal Pleistocene bone tool assemblage is very substantial but includes not a single example of the bone point or linkshaft forms of the later Holocene. Although others disagree with this suggestion (Deacon 1984b; Wadley Chapter 4 this volume), I take this to imply that bow and arrow technology was either nonexistent or radically different at that time. Certainly the density and assemblage composition of terrestrial animals change markedly at about 9,000 years ago, in what I take to be a major shift in settlement strategy. If it is accepted that terminal Pleistocene hunters were operating without the bow and poisoned arrow, then the metaphorical links between hunting and sex could not have existed, at least not as articulated in ethnographic record. Moreover, the remarkable linguistic parallel drawn between the dying eland and the trancing shaman could also not have existed. There is an enormous difference between an eland slowly succumbing to the effects of poison and an eland felled by rapid loss of blood from a heavy arrow or spear wound. Poison, in other words, is crucial to both the technological and the expressive dimensions of recent Kalahari and late precolonial gender relations.

These attempts illustrate the chronological limitations of currently known and ethnographically documented gender roles even as they urge us to envisage and articulate terminal Pleistocene arrangements quite alien to recent Kalahari practice. But they do suggest that there is some connection between the technological, social, and political spheres that can be approached cautiously with archaeological evidence such as stone tools and faunal remains. If the more distant past is to be engendered, archaeologists need to be innovative and imaginative in the ways they relate arguments to evidence. Women may still have made beads and collected plants in the terminal Pleistocene but "what it was like to have been an old woman" may not have resembled the experiences of a recent San grandmother.

Conclusion

"Knowing the past" may be an ambitious goal, in that the closure of an argument through controlled experiment and the ability to focus on one variable at a time are not strictly possible. Archaeological knowledge is a form of triangulation from the territory of the relatively well known into the frontier of the relatively poorly known. Unlikely scenarios can be identified as such, but competitive explanations are likely to coexist for long periods and critical evidence is scarce. The aim is to link ethnographic and historic eyewitness accounts with empirical observations from archaeological excavations, viewing all such evidence as *capta* (things taken) rather than *data* (things given), thus recognizing the active agency of the archaeologist (Chippindale 1991).

In recent times Southern African hunter-gatherers have constructed a system of belief, n!ao, that mediates sexual relations by grafting some culturally generated rules onto some biological facts. Whereas childbirth is the realm of women, the hunting of large game is constructed as the realm of men. In an effort to underline the significance of both and to firm up this division of real and symbolic labor, women are likened to the large game animals such as eland, linguistic usages blur the difference between enjoyment of the two "meats," and women are culturally defined as bringing bad luck to the hunt. Precisely when women are capable of conceiving, they are forbidden to touch the arrows of hunters, husbands are encouraged to focus on one or other wife (meat) at a time, and everyone makes as much, if not more, fuss over the death of an eland as over the birth of a child. A man's identity is so intensely invested in his hunting ability that he would never consider leaving camp without his bow and a quiver full of poisoned arrows.

The success of this system may be judged from the comments of several anthropologists about the relative egalitarian nature of San society, where women often rise to positions of leadership, are identified as the "owners" of n!ores (territories), and have substantial influence on social issues. In the issues of violence, contacts with external groups, and dominance on ritual occasions such as the public healing dance, men retain far greater power and influence. The basis of male–female relations, however, is clearly the notion of complementarity, whereby men and women have notional equality by performing parts of various tasks with socially constructed status, respect, or value. Competition between men and women is diffused by humorous exchanges from separately defined positions.

Tracking this system back into undocumented prehistory is a great challenge. The Holocene archaeological record generally supports an economic division of labor, but not unambiguously so. Technological continuities such as the making of ostrich eggshell beads; wooden digging sticks with perforated stone weights; reed, bone, and sinew arrows; ochreous paint; vegetable mastics; and fibrous string and cord are *suggestive* of behavioral continuities, but no more. Burials so far have proven relatively mute on issues of gender, though there are hints that changes in food consumption patterns may be accessible. Stone tools have no documented pedigree and thus can only with imagination be used to construct gender profiles. My assessment of the material from Elands Bay Cave (Parkington in press) is that there are substantial changes in settlement at almost exactly 9,000 years ago. At least the coastal component of settlement changes from relatively long periods of cave use, perhaps combined with longer moves between a smaller set of residential locations, to much shorter visits with many more sites used in a seasonal round. My sense is that this change is a barrier through which it would be dangerous to push ethnographically or historically derived patterns of behavior. It is quite likely that terminal Pleistocene hunter-gatherers related to one another in ways that do not easily fit into Kalahari models.

It is the rock art that has the greatest potential to extend back in time our understanding of gender and sexual relations. The choice of subject matter, the conventional emphasis on the male hunter, the large game animals, the sexual attributes of adult men and women, and the absence or rarity of copulation or kill scenes all imply a reference to the roles of and rules for adults rather than to the depiction of their activities. The absence of paintings of plants, shellfish, or other small game that are more properly gathered than hunted is supportive of this position, but the large number of paintings of small bovids, not n!ao animals, suggests that other explanations have a place. It may be prudent to admit that we will probably never have a satisfactory explanation for many paintings, either because the images are residual or because the meanings are not recoverable without textual parallels.

This does bring up the issue of the dating of the paintings, without which we are incapable of constructing a history of image choice, convention, or emphasis. Despite cries of chronocentrism (Lewis-Williams 1993), we certainly suffer from not knowing the age of the paintings we study. It is quite likely, for example, that the paintings we see in the Western Cape are much older than those we see in the Drakensberg and also that many of the anecdotally noted differences relate to differences in social context and both external and internal social relations. Women are notably rarer in the Drakensberg than in the Western Cape (Lewis-Williams 1981; Manhire 1981), while therianthropes are arguably more common. It is very unlikely that any of what we see in either region was painted in the terminal Pleistocene, which means that any help in reconstructing gender relations that we can get from the rock art is inapplicable to these earlier times.

Chapter Three

Invisible Gender—Invisible Foragers

*Hunter-Gatherer Spatial Patterning and
the Southern African Archaeological Record*

Many archaeologists who study gender tend to assume that most cultures have gender relations similar to their own. As a result, they miss the fascinating diversity that is present in the different ways people organize gender: differentiated, stratified, hierarchical, or none of these. Gender relations are often inferred from examining the use of space and material culture at a site, the topic of this chapter. Archaeologists need to know when gender-specific areas are *not* present in a society as well as when they are. At times, archaeologists should *not* expect to find spatial, architectural, or material cultural segregation based on gender. Why do we expect that all groups used sex-specific loci or material culture when we do not expect that all groups throughout time had rigid stratification? Using several databases, I attempt to examine artifact distributions and spatial patterning purported to be evidence of gendered space at Late Stone Age, Early Iron Age, and Late Iron Age sites in southern Africa.

Discerning Gender in the Archaeological Record: Model Before Methods

Archaeologists who assume that a rigid division of labor characterizes all modern human societies risk projecting their Western beliefs onto the archaeological record. If a researcher instead approaches the archaeological record with the concept that diversity is present in gender relations both ethnographically and prehistorically, models of gender interaction can be tested with archaeological data. Based on a model formulated from cross-cultural research, I suggest that sociopolitical complexity influences gender differentiation and stratification, or its lack. Therefore, contemporary or prehistoric foragers who are highly egalitarian tend not to have a rigid division of labor that would be visible archaeologically or ethnographically. This model is unlike ethnographic analogy, which, as Stahl and Cruz (Chapter 11) and Nelson (Chapter 16) point out, is inappropriate for most archaeological interpretations because analogies ignore variability and history. I would add that analogy ignores prehistory as well. My use of ethnographic data here is quite different. I look at cross-cultural relationships and what influences those relationships, rather than using an analogy that assumes that how one society defines gender is appropriate for how all societies define it. My own ethnographic work shows that hunter-gatherers have very different concepts of gender, dependent on the complexity of their sociopolitical organization. Ethnographically consistent relationships, not ethnographic analogies, are imperative if we are to achieve archaeological understanding, because they allow archaeologists to see the full diversity of non-Western cultures. Ethnoarchaeological research reveals that the amount of sociopolitical complexity in a society influences the amount of differentiation and stratification present, including that of gender.

The differences between analogy and what I am referring to as ethnoarchaeology, while seemingly subtle, are actually crucial to interpretation. The use of ethnographic analogy assumes that contemporary and past societies are the same, so knowing how a specific modern group thinks or behaves will inform archaeologists studying specific prehistoric groups. Ethnoarchaeology, in contrast to ethnographic analogy, does not assume that groups are similar. Instead it looks at cross-cultural ethnographies to gain insights into how people organize themselves according to their cultural categories and how this varies across different types of societies. Ethnoarchaeology is concerned with relationships among culture, behavior, and material culture as well as with what conditions the relationships. Therefore, the fact that modern Basarwa (Bushmen or San) behave in a specific way is irrelevant for archaeology, except to expose fallacies of over-generalization (e.g., whether or not Ju/'hoansi, or !Kung, women hunt). However, the Basarwa provide an extremely valuable example of how highly egalitarian small-scale societies operate in general (examples are the relationship between the flexibility of a gender division of labor and the gender use of space, the conception of gender and its influence on behavior, the interaction between males and females and the use of gendered material culture, and so on). Understanding gender in prehistoric, highly egalitarian societies without first understanding it in the Basarwa or another highly egalitarian contemporary society can lead to a Western-centric or otherwise fallacious view of these societies, past or present.

Ethnoarchaeological cross-cultural research indicates that a consistent relationship exists between the rigidity of a division of labor that influences the use of space and objects by gender and a society's sociopolitical complexity. It is the relationship between the gender division of labor and the sociopolitical organization that I am testing with archaeological data. I am not, however, applying whatever a sample of societies happens to suggest is a common theme in the gender division of labor.

The cross-cultural model has been discussed in detail in several publications and is only briefly described here (e.g., Kent 1990a,b, 1991a, 1996a, in press, n.d.). The tenets of the model are as follows:

1. Behavior is not biologically determined; therefore, gendered behavior is neither biological nor universally the same across cultures.

2. The manufacture and use of cultural material is not biologically determined. For instance, pottery does not necessarily denote women's activities nor do lithic tools denote men's activities.

3. Gender, behavior, and cultural material are directly influenced by the way in which a society's culture is organized, particularly its sociopolitical system.

4. Societies that divide or stratify their sociopolitical organization also divide or stratify their division of labor, economics, architecture, material culture, and use of space. The opposite is the case for societies that do not stratify their sociopolitical system.

If we can demonstrate that prehistoric foragers were highly egalitarian, we can postulate that they did not have a rigid division of labor. More sociopolitically complex societies—whether foragers, farmers, or pastoralists—partition space, material culture, activities, politics, and status by gender. The gender of people using activities and the built environment in these societies becomes more visible because they are more commonly segregated by gender as societies increase in complexity. Such societies divide their universe into more compartments (which is why they are referred to as *complex*—they have more parts). Complex societies tend to have both sex-specific and function-specific activity areas as well as architectural features because men's and women's tasks are less likely to overlap in function than occurs in less complex groups. Gender-specific jobs are present because the differences between men and women are emphasized more than they are in less complex societies. As a result, functionally discrete activities are performed by one sex at a locus not usually frequented by the other sex. Researchers are able, therefore, to discern male from female space and to distinguish activity areas by function of the tasks performed there.

The problem with this view is that not all societies have gender-specific behavior expressed in the use of activity areas. Gendered behavior that is not ethnographically visible (that is, the absence of a pronounced sexual division of labor and therefore an absence of gendered artifacts or space) is also not archaeologically visible. This poses a dilemma for the archaeologist: how can a model be assessed and validated with invisible or negative data? That is, how does one demonstrate the *absence* of patterns?

How Do We Interpret the Invisible?

Much literature and entire debates have been devoted to the issue of archaeological visibility. One example is the "Kalahari debate" in which so-called revisionists argue that all modern Basarwa are only "degraded" pastoralists occupying the lowest niche in the Bantu-speaking Batswana hierarchy. They base their argument partially on the absence of a continual record of hunter-gatherer sites in the Kalahari (Wilmsen 1989; Wilmsen and Denbow 1990). Even though other anthropologists working in the Kalahari have exposed numerous and serious mistakes, misinterpretations, and inaccuracies in their claims (Lee and Guenther 1991, 1993; Harpending 1991; Kent

1992a), the revisionist position is often adopted uncritically by anthropologists working with small-scale societies around the world (e.g., Headland and Reid 1991).[1]

The most compelling critiques against the Wilmsen-Denbow position are those written by individuals not connected in any way to the Lee (Harvard University Project) group or the Wilmsen-Denbow group. My analysis is only one example (Kent 1992a, 1996a); others include Blurton-Jones, O'Connell, and Hawkes 1996. However, perhaps the best study thus far is by Sadr (1997), who presents a thorough and systematic examination of the contested archaeological sites that Wilmsen (1989), Wilmsen and Denbow (1990), and Denbow (1990b) use to support their claims. Sadr questions Wilmsen and Denbow's view of encapsulated hunter-gatherers dispossessed of their culture and forced into a marginalized, serflike relationship with Bantu-speakers as far back in time as the Early Iron Age. Based on the Late Stone Age/Early Iron Age archaeological record, Sadr (1997:111) concludes that there is little evidence for the degraded relationship with Bantu-speakers envisioned by the "revisionists." Instead, autonomous hunter-gatherers probably did exist into historic times. Sampson (1997: personal communication) also casts doubts on the Wilmsen-Denbow premise based on the numerous historic documents describing foraging people in the interior of South Africa (e.g. Dunn 1873, 1931; Neville 1996; Rudner 1979, among many others).

Wilmsen (1989) and Wilmsen and Denbow (1990) argue that if foragers were not intimately and profoundly affected by Iron Age pastoralists, there should be sites that demonstrate it. Such sites should have an absence of objects that Wilmsen and Denbow consider pastoralist in origin. There should be a continuous record of sites occupied by foragers that spans the last 2,000 years during which pastoralists are thought to have been in southern Africa. But such sites do not exist. Denbow wrote that negative evidence of a continuous foraging way of life "should therefore be taken for what it is—*no evidence at all*" (Denbow 1990a:124; original emphasis). We, as archaeologists, need to evaluate Denbow's assertion. Exactly what can be expected to be visible in the archaeological record, and why? Furthermore, how can we turn negative data into positive interpretations, or is this even possible?

As noted, gender segregation of tasks, areas, roles, status, and the like, cross-culturally co-occurs with stratification and/or hierarchies in various facets of culture. In other words, gender stratification does not automatically occur in all societies. Societies that segregate individuals by status, age, occupation, and wealth also segregate labor, material culture, and the use of space by gender. We can examine site structure and artifacts to determine the likelihood of segregation of any kind, with gender as our focus (Kent 1984, 1989a, 1990a,b, 1996a). Particularly important for this type of analysis is the spatial patterning of objects and features within a site and use-wear studies of artifacts indicating whether or not tools are multipurpose. Some archaeologists are comfortable making large inferential leaps when the subject is economics or the environment, but are not willing to make small inferential arguments about gender, even when it is appropriate (Conkey and Gero 1991). In other words, they use different standards when evaluating inferences of paleoenvironments versus past gender relations. The following is an examination of the inferences needed to study gender in southern African prehistory.

Brooks and Yellen (1987) examined the type of sites archaeologists can potentially discern in the Kalahari archaeological record. They concluded that the typical mobile hunter-gatherer habitation camp would, in most cases, not be visible archaeologically. However, sites do occur in the archaeological record. The primary kinds of sites archaeologically recognizable are reoccupied special activity sites, such as hunting blinds reused many times by men (Brooks and Yellen 1987). I would extend their argument to include rockshelters and similar multicomponent sites reoccupied over time, in addition to sites with large concentrations of refuse, such as shell middens.[2] Occasionally a site is well preserved and/or visible due to particular environmental or historic circumstances (e.g., Seacow Valley, South Africa, Sampson 1988). However, sedentary camps are usually more visible than those of mobile groups because of their more durable architecture and associated features, larger accumulations of artifacts and refuse, more permanent storage facilities, and so forth (Kent 1991b, 1993a).

The paucity of habitation sites occupied by hunter-gatherers throughout the Kalahari does not necessarily indicate an absence of occupation by full-time foragers. It simply means that nomadic foragers' sites were not preserved and are therefore not visible (Kent 1990c). In addition, systematic foot surveys for sites have not been conducted for much of the Kalahari, compounding the problem of locating sites (Sadr 1997: personal communication). The dearth of visible hunter-gatherer sites in the Kalahari, for example, has given Iron Age sites in the northern Kalahari a disproportionate importance in the cultural history of the area. Since Basarwa sites tend not to be discernible in the archaeological record, sites occupied by the more sedentary pastoralists and farmers may be misinterpreted as acculturated Basarwa or sites with mixed ethnic groups. In either of these cases, usually the foragers are seen as disadvantaged in comparison to the pastoralist/farmers. One may mistakenly assume that there were no autonomous foragers for decades or longer because there are few foraging sites that postdate the arrival of the Bantu-speakers and other migrating peoples. Forager sites that predate the arrival of Bantu-speakers tend to be located in rock shelters with extraordinary preservation. These sites were often reoccupied many times, enhancing their archaeological visibility, or have large accumulations of durable refuse, as exemplified by shell middens. We do not know how many Late Stone Age open-air, autonomous forager, single occupation sites remain invisible.

Wadley (Chapter 4) suggests that Late Stone Age foragers had aggregation/dispersal mobility patterns similar to Kalahari Ju/'hoansi. If so, the aggregation phase occurred during the dry season when foragers occupied rockshelters or pan (clay-lined shallow depressions) margins. During this season, foragers were stationary for several months at a time. Aggregation sites, which also were occupied longer, are more archaeologically visible than are dispersed sites. A number of studies show that architectural durability and material culture frequency depend on how long people think they will occupy a camp; the longer the anticipated habitation, the more permanent the built environment (Kent 1991b, 1993a). Archaeologists cannot ignore differential preservation and visibility of sites of highly mobile societies who lack animal transportation (Kent 1992a).

Even if Early Iron Age farmers and pastoralists who were more dependent on water for their crops and stock appropriated the pans with water year-round, thereby "encouraging" foragers to live in small dispersed camps during the winter dry season, it does not necessarily follow that foragers became destitute fringe populations. Nor does the presence of a few Iron Age objects mean that foragers gave up their culture for the Bantu-speakers' culture. The presence of wild faunal remains at Iron Age sites, likewise, does not mean that foragers provided the meat or were in a client/serf relationship with the Bantu-speakers. Many Bakgalagadi families today hunt, as their ancestors probably also did in the past. I argue that most foragers during the Iron Age were not dependent on the farmers/pastoralists, even if they had to change their dry season mobility pattern or spend less time at pans that contained year-round water. In fact, the ethnic group probably most impacted by the incursion of the Bantu was the indigenous Khoi pastoralists who had to share water resources and grazing land with the newcomers. Foragers were probably not displaced or affected as much by the appearance of the new Bantu arrivals as were indigenous herders.[3]

The implication, then, is that many of the Late Stone Age sites excavated by archaeologists in southern Africa are palimpsests of repeated occupations that occurred over long periods of time. Because the perishability of material culture and the site structure are linked to mobility patterns, camps at which inhabitants plan relatively long occupations are more visible than camps at which a short occupation was anticipated (Kent 1991b; Kent and Vierich 1989). Consequently, Bantu-speakers' camps with longer occupations are more visible and therefore more prevalent in the archaeological record. The frequency of Iron Age pastoralist camps has led some archaeologists to conclude erroneously that there were no autonomous foragers present when, in fact, foragers may even have been the most populous group. It also would be easy to falsely conclude that sedentary people were dominant in a region when they were not—only their sites were better preserved through time than the foragers' camps, and therefore are more detectable today.

What Is Gendered Space?

In my opinion, application of the labels "women's activity area" or "gender segregated space" should be reserved for loci that are primarily or solely used by women and not used by both sexes or by men for similar or dissimilar activities. Wadley (in press b; Chapter 4, this volume) interprets formal activity areas and possible gender segregation at the Late Stone Age Jubilee rockshelter based on a view of a sexual division of space thought to characterize contemporary Ju/'hoansi spatial patterning. While perhaps this view is correct, we need much more data to evaluate her interpretation. It is true that traditional Ju/'hoansi (though not other Basarwa groups) divide the hearth in front of a hut into male and female sides. However, they do so only during specific times—on formal occasions such as a marriage, or in the evening when people talk and sit around their hearth before going to bed (Kent n.d.). During the day both men and women sit at either side of the hearth. Because of this, debris from men's and women's daytime activities overlap and obscure any material culture patterning that may accumulate during the evenings. The disturbance of such patterning might be further influenced by the actions of children, who, if they are prepubescent, are often seen as neuter (Lane, Chapter 10). The space is only situationally gender-specific for a few hours a day; the rest of the time it is not. Therefore, Ju/'hoansi evening segregation of hearth space probably would not be visible archaeologically. However, as I show below (and as Hall, Chapter 13, demonstrates), gendered activity areas are visible at later sites in the late Iron Age.

Nonetheless, the Ju/'hoansi custom should have little bearing on the interpretation of the use of hearth space at Jubilee because there is no evidence to suggest that the occupants' customs were identical to the Ju/'hoansi of the mid-20th century, in contrast to the G/wi and other Basarwa groups that do not segregate hearth space by gender. The problems with direct analogies like this one are the implicit inference that the Ju/'hoansi are the descendants of the Jubilee occupants, and the implicit assumption that the Ju/'hoansi descendants have not changed their spatial patterning for thousands of years. We need evidence for such inferences. We cannot automatically assume, without explicit support from the data, that all societies divide space either by gender or by task function. We still need to use it as one of what should be a number of competing hypotheses to test. And, in fact, cross-cultural data show that not all societies separate space and activities by gender. The majority of societies that do so are the more sociopolitically complex ones (Kent 1990a, 1991a).

Spatial Patterning of Activities at Hunter-Gatherer Sites

Taking site preservation into account, what can be said about gendered space at Late Stone Age sites in southern Africa? If the aforementioned ethnographically derived model is valid, we should be able to make predictions about differences between prehistoric pastoralists' and hunter-gatherers' sites. Although most camps occupied by nomadic Late Stone Age hunter and gatherers are probably not visible, as noted by Brooks and Yellen (1987) and Kent (1990c), a few multiple occupation sites located in areas that enhance preservation, such as rockshelters, have been identified. These sites allow us to examine gender and activity spatial patterning (e.g., Wadley Chapter 4, this volume, and elsewhere).

According to the model presented above, camps occupied by highly egalitarian foragers should be spatially undifferentiated by gender or by activity area function. The spatial patterning of objects and features in and out of activity areas should be redundant. In contrast, the sociopolitically more complex Iron Age agropastoralist sites should exhibit some differentiation of activities.

Dunefield Midden Site

Dunefield Midden is one of the best examples of spatial archaeology in southern Africa. The shell midden site, located on the western Cape coast of South Africa, was investigated by Parkington and students and preliminarily analyzed (Parkington et al. 1992; Henshilwood 1990; Reeler 1992). The excavation strategy is novel. Large horizontal areas were uncovered, allowing for the analysis of spatial patterning. C^{14} dates suggest a single winter occupation for the northern part of the site approximately 650 years BP (Parkington et al. 1992:63). The following discussion is based on my interpretations of the descriptions presented in Parkington et al. 1992 and Henshilwood 1990.

Dunefield Midden consists of three to four focal hearths probably representing separate living areas. These areas may have been associated with a windbreak or hut, along with two or three hearths that were likely used as auxiliaries. Most modern Basarwa, Bakgalagadi, and other camps with more than three or four people will have auxiliary hearths not associated with a windbreak or hut. These hearths are used when the wind blows from a direction such that the current windbreak does not provide protection. The hearths are also used to accommodate large numbers of visitors when necessary. It is a mistake for archaeologists to equate each hearth with a windbreak or hut, and therefore with an individual family or other resident unit. In other words, not every hearth should be used to determine site population. Two roasting pits were also identified at the site (Figures 3.1 through 3.5).

While final analyses and report have not been published, there are distributions of objects that provide interesting preliminary evidence of patterning at a single Late Stone Age occupation. Most of the very small faunal remains (bones from tortoises, fish, rock lobsters, snakes, and birds) tend to be distributed around the hearths (Figure 3.1). Small faunal remains are associated with hearths at which the animals were probably consumed by humans and the bones consumed, or at least investigated, by canids (dogs or jackals). Small bones elsewhere on the site can be explained by dislocation from trampling and by canids. The presence of scavenging canids and their influence in displacing faunal remains is clearly indicated by the presence of rock lobster mandibles in carnivore coprolites.

Larger bones include those of seal, eland, and small- to medium-sized bovids (e.g., duiker, steenbok). These bones are scattered more than are the smaller bones, suggesting that unlike the very small bones, dogs or jackals may have removed them away from hearths probably to avoid competition with other canids waiting near the hearths for a bone to be tossed their way (Figure 3.2). Figure 3.3 shows that voluminous refuse from processing molluscs is primarily located in the midden that is separate from the living area around the habitation hearths (Henshilwood 1990; Parkington et al. 1992).

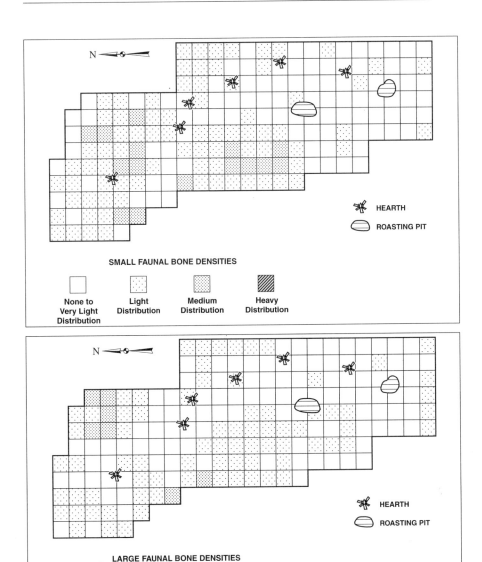

Figure 3.1 (top). Distribution and density of small faunal remains at the Dunefield Midden Site, including snake, tortoise, bird, fish, and lobster.

Figure 3.2 (bottom). Distribution and density of medium to large faunal remains at the Dunefield Midden Site, including eland, seal, steenbok, and other small to medium size bovids.

No scale is presented here because the data are still preliminary and most appropriately show relative object distributions. Data are modified from Henshilwood 1990 and Parkington et al. 1992.

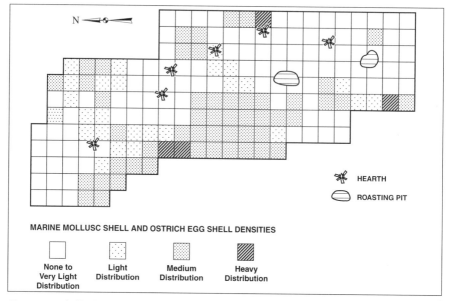

Figure 3.3. Shell refuse distribution and densities at Dunefield Midden Site. No scale is presented because the data are still preliminary and most appropriately show relative object distributions. Data are modified from Henshilwood 1990 and Parkington et al. 1992.

The one-meter units south and west of the hearths did not contain much shell refuse, bones of any sized animals, or artifacts (Figures 3.1 through 3.5). These areas may have been a communal path on which people went from hearth to hearth. Any objects located there would have been displaced by trampling. Alternatively, the back wall of shelters may have faced west-southwest, with activities oriented toward the opening of the structures. The southern- and northern-most hearths tend, instead, to have more objects located south and west of them and, though speculative, may have been hearths not associated with a windbreak or hut.

Artifacts include ceramic sherds, various lithic tools and debris, and ostrich egg-shell beads. Except for the ostrich eggshell beads, artifacts are scattered around and between the hearths. The most dense frequencies of artifacts occur near the hearths, which unquestionably indicate activity areas (Parkington et al. 1992; Henshilwood 1990). Reeler (1992:71) suggests that lithic tool manufacturing and use, as well as food processing (inferred by the presence of lithic debitage and tools or sherds), occurred at separate hearths, indicating functionally specific activity loci. However, extrapolating from Henshilwood's figures (1990), lithics and sherds were found together at hearths, with the one exception at which debitage was located but no sherds were. Lithic tools occurred without much debitage (fewer than 11 pieces per meter) at three hearths and were present with light distributions (12–49 pieces per meter) at three other hearths (Figures 3.4 and 3.5). I agree with the excavators that tool manufacturing and retouch

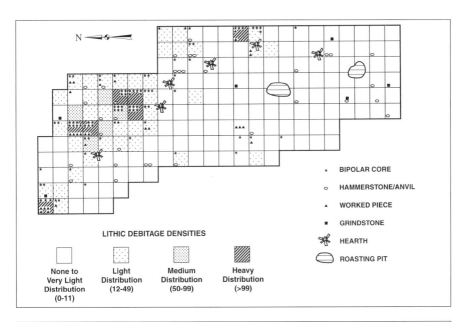

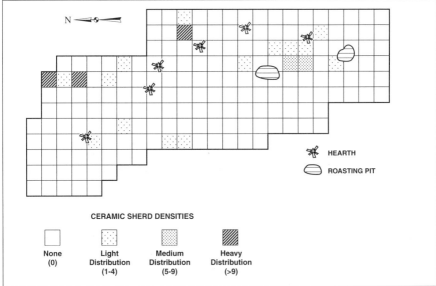

Figure 3.4 (top). Distribution and density of lithic artifacts at the Dunefield Midden Site.

Figure 3.5 (bottom). Distribution and density of ceramic sherds at the Dunefield Midden Site.

No scale is presented because the data are still preliminary and most appropriately show relative object distributions. Data are modified from Henshilwood 1990 and Parkington et al. 1992.

probably occurred, at least at the latter hearths with the slightly higher density of debitage, if not also at the former. The excavators and I disagree that the hearths were used solely or primarily for tool reduction or resharpening and therefore can be interpreted as a specific tool manufacturing activity area.

One reason I do not think the hearths represent a function-specific activity area is that all were located approximately one meter or closer to a light or heavier ceramic sherd distribution, with one exception. The exception, the eastern-most hearth, had lithic artifacts located nearby, but no ceramics. One must remember, however, that people are more likely to sit on very small debitage in a sandy matrix than they are to do so with ceramic sherds, which tend to be larger and tend to be swept to the margins of an activity area. Therefore, we should not expect sherds to be located as close to hearths as debitage to indicate the use of ceramics at an area. Moreover, except for night or very cold days, people do not always sit within one meter of a hearth. Observations of vastly different groups, from Navajos to Basarwa and on, indicate that people use hearths as focal points for activities, but they tend to sit and perform activities anywhere from around one to three meters from the hearth. Even the apparently "anomalous" eastern-most hearth is within three meters of sherds. The distribution of lithics supports my view of the use of space at a hearth. Debitage and tools located two to three meters away from hearths indicate that people do not always sit within one meter of a hearth. The heaviest concentrations of debitage are often several meters away from any hearth where the activity is thought to have occurred (Figure 3.4). If this is true for lithic distributions, it must also be true for ceramics.

The second reason I do not think that any of the hearths were task-specific lithic reduction loci is the distribution of faunal remains. Every hearth has very small faunal remains located in or near it, which, like the tiny lithic debitage, are less likely to be dispersed by post-depositional agents. At the least, food consumption occurred at every hearth, if not also cooking. Therefore, the hearths cannot be labeled as function-specific. Note that the distribution of objects around these hearths differs considerably from hearths in the latter part of the Late Iron Age where task- and gender-differentiated space probably did occur (as is discussed below).

Dunefield Midden clearly shows the presence of activity areas, including lithic manufacturing, cooking and eating, and other tasks, focused around hearths. Even though not all archaeologists would agree, including some of the site's excavators, the site does not, in my opinion, exhibit evidence of either gendered space or activity function-specific areas. Beyond the roasting pits perhaps used solely for cooking and the middens used for the dumping of refuse, I also do not see any function-specific areas (e.g., see Reeler 1992:74–76 for an argument for functionally discrete loci; Parkington 1997: personal communication, also believes at least one hearth represents a stone tool function-specific area). Activity areas definitely occur near the hearths, as noted above, but I find no conclusive data that indicate that any were segregated by the particular types of tasks performed or by the gender who performed the tasks.

Both Wadley (Chapter 4) and Casey (Chapter 5) caution that lithic debitage and tools cannot be automatically interpreted as having been produced or used by males and, in fact, ethnographic data from southern Africa to Ethiopia, as well as Asia and North America, suggest that stone tools or their modern equivalents were used by both men and women (Brumbach and Jarvenpa 1997; Brandt 1996; Casey, Chapter 5, this volume; Gero 1991; O'Brien 1990).

While again not all agree, I do not see evidence for task function-specific activity areas merely because one hearth area has lithic objects but not ceramic ones. That only means to me that a pot did not break there, but it is difficult to infer that a pot also was never used at that locus. More convincing would be if all or the vast majority of the hearths that contained lithic debris did not contain ceramics and vice versa. That kind of spatially separated activity patterning by task function or by gender is not, in my opinion, present in the Dunefield Midden data as it has been reported thus far, though further analyses may change this view. Instead, in my opinion, the data suggest that, within the living areas, artifacts are scattered around hearths where apparently many types of activities occurred conducted by both men and women.

In sum, we can see that with fine-grained excavation techniques and analyses, it is possible to distinguish activity areas at forager sites. While separate activity areas are readily discernible at the Dunefield Midden site, based on artifact distributions, I suggest that none was differentiated by gender or by function of the activity performed there.

Other Hunter-Gatherer Sites in Southern Africa

Researchers at various hunter-gatherer sites in southern Africa have studied spatial patterning and attempted to delineate function-specific and gender-specific areas. For example, Deacon (1996) associates hearths with women's tasks at a 19th-century site possibly inhabited by the family of one of Bleek and Lloyd's informants in the 1870s. Drawing from Bleek and Lloyd's informant interviews, Deacon (1996) interprets the association of grinding stones with hearths as indicating that women worked next to the hearths. Anvils, probably used by both women and men, were found next to hearths and on the edge of the site. Deacon interprets the patterning as evidence of gender-differentiated space (1997: personal communication). The distribution of anvils "provides some indication of the gender division of labour with women using them for some tasks near the hearth and men using them in areas away from the women and the hearth" (Deacon 1996:267).

The antiquity of such gender segregation in activities, if indeed this is gender segregation, is difficult to assess since a pattern of men working away from hearths and women working at hearths has not been observed by ethnographers studying 20th-century Basarwa in the Kalahari or in other highly egalitarian societies of which I am familiar. However, much cultural diversity exists among different groups of Basarwa today and no doubt did among hunter-gatherers in the past as well. From the distribution of the artifacts alone, and without the information provided by

Bleek's informants, I suggest that gender-segregated work areas, if present, would have been most difficult to discern at Deacon's sites.

Other researchers describe separate female-associated ostrich eggshell bead manufacturing areas at Late Stone Age sites. For example, the majority of ostrich eggshell bead fragments at the Goergap rockshelter (South Africa) are located at the rear of the site (van der Ryst 1996:83, 87). The high densities of beads and eggshell debris, presumably from their manufacture, in the back of the rockshelter "show that this activity had a clear spatial restriction" (van der Ryst 1996:83). The majority of grooved stones and polished bone artifacts are also located at the rear of the rockshelter (van der Ryst 1996:87). There is little doubt that ostrich eggshell beads were manufactured at or near this locus. Nonetheless, the presence of polished bone objects also at this locus may imply that the area was multifunctional, even if one of the activities performed there was restricted to that location. Artifact distributions at sites in rockshelters are difficult to interpret. The enclosed space confines activities, the distribution of artifacts, and refuse areas. The next, perhaps more difficult question to answer is whether ostrich eggshell bead manufacturing also occurred at a spatially discrete area at open-air sites.

The spatial patterning of two interesting South African hunter-gatherer rockshelter sites, Rose Cottage and Jubilee, suggests similarities with other Late Stone Age hunter-gatherer sites (Wadley in press a,b). According to their excavator, the faunal analysis, artifacts and their density, and the extent of the occupation area all suggest that both Jubilee Shelter and Rose Cottage were winter aggregation sites, based on the traditional Ju/'hoansi settlement pattern (Wadley in press a,b). A variety of activities were probably conducted by both men and women, adults as well as children, around the hearths at the two sites. Areas were identified for bead making, bone point manufacturing, lithic reduction, and plant processing (Wadley in press a,b). At Jubilee Shelter, ostrich eggshell beads and debris were uncovered on one side of a hearth. On the opposite side of the same hearth were broken shafts of polished bone. Wadley (in press b) interprets the spatial patterning of objects around the hearth as a formal use of space at Jubilee that may imply gender segregation. She also suggests that the positioning of grinding stones in the back of the Rose Cottage shelter might indicate a discrete women's food processing area (Wadley in press a). However, it also is possible, though difficult to test, that the locus was a storage area where the objects, when not in use, were put out of the way. Modern G/wi and G//ana hunter-gatherers, as just one example, place bulky grinding stones beside a windbreak fence or hut wall rather than store them near a hearth where people sit and interact. Among contemporary Kalahari foragers, grinding stones are brought to the hearths when in use and are left at the windbreak or hut wall when not in use. Whether the same pattern occurred in the past is very difficult to assess. Even if it does, the contemporary patterning of space does not mean that the Late Stone Age hunter-gatherers also did the same. All it means is that we cannot assume *a priori* that grinding stones are found at the locus that they were used—whether they are located where used (or where stored) has to be determined with data.

Walker (1995:53) hypothesizes that the large rockshelters in the Matopos of Zimbabwe occupied by Late Stone Age hunter-gatherers were used for ritual gatherings and may have been divided into male and female areas around a ceremonial center. However, he does not present any information on the spatial positioning of the artifacts or why the site should be so divided. He also does not state what he bases his interpretation on or reasons for Late Stone Age foragers to segregate space into male and female areas. Without such information, it is very difficult to know how to interpret his suggested layout and division of space by men and women or why the rockshelter would be partitioned by the sex of the occupants.

As Wadley (Chapter 4, this volume) notes, several anthropologists refute the myth that stone knappers everywhere equal males (e.g., Casey, Chapter 5, this volume; Brandt 1996; O'Brien 1990; Gero 1991). Her interpretation that stone tool manufacturing and/or use was conducted by both men and women is justified, as well as a nice break in the time-honored belief that lithics were only, or even primarily, made and used by men. Despite the paucity of observations of stone tool use in southern Africa, ethnographic observations of the metal or plastic equivalents among contemporary hunter-gatherers indicate that stone tools were *not* necessarily made or used solely by men (discussed in Chapters 1, 4, and 5, this volume). Not all archaeologists agree—Parkington thinks that men may have made many, but not all, stone tools in the Late Stone Age of southern Africa (1997: personal communication; Chapter 2, this volume). While Parkington also states that the gender(s) making stone tools must be demonstrated by evidence (1997: personal communication), there is no archaeological evidence of which I am aware indicating that only men made or used stone tools. We do have ethnographic evidence of both genders using tools, including stone scrapers in various African societies (e.g., Brandt 1996). If one is to speculate about whether stone tools and debitage should be attributed to one gender or the other, it seems prudent either to consider stone tools as nongender-specific objects as I propose, or to assume that we will never be able to determine the gender of Late Stone Age users of lithic tools, since both could have made and used them. However, I personally see no reason, archaeologically or ethnographically, to suggest that men exclusively used or made lithic artifacts during the Stone Age. In other words, I do not see lithic tools, or their refuse from manufacturing, as gendered artifacts. However, many researchers, including some authors in this book, would disagree.

While the above detailed spatial studies allow us to see women in prehistory, making some of the invisible visible, the studies do not, in my opinion, indicate the presence of gender-segregated or function-specific activity areas at Late Stone Age hunter-gatherer sites in southern Africa. Is the same true for Early Iron Age pastoralist sites?

Cultural Differences Between Stone Age
Hunter-Gatherers and Iron Age Farmers/Pastoralists

The differences between the cultures of prehistoric agropastoralists and hunter-gatherers are considerable. Women's status is usually thought to be higher in mobile hunter-gatherer societies than in farming or pastoral ones. This assumption is based on cross-cultural studies, but why differences exist—if in fact they do—is usually left unexplained. Comparing groups of Basarwa (Ju/'hoansi, G/wi, and G//ana and Nharo), I suggest that regardless of their economic focus, societies that are regularly aggregated for several months or more, particularly if also stationary during that time, tend to have incipient differentiation in their culture, often expressed by the presence of an informal leader/arbitrator.

The cross-culturally consistent relationship among human social interactions, aggregation, and mobility explains the variability in gender differentiation and status among various historic and modern Basarwa groups (Kent n.d.). Human relationships and interactions create the need for a mediator of either gender. That is, the nature of human social relationships in aggregated situations makes necessary an arbitrator who can solve interfamily disputes. Because people go to the person to solve disputes, the arbitrator is viewed politically and socially as slightly different from the other members of the group; the person has a different status than others. This difference in status is concomitant with increased differentiation throughout the culture, including a more differentiated gender division of labor (Kent 1997). Human sociality, then, creates a situation where one or several individuals are differentiated as a leader. The need for such a leader is not caused by, but rather is exacerbated by, a sedentary pattern of mobility. When a group is both aggregated and stationary, it has a greater need for a political leader to arbitrate disputes than a group that is more mobile (Kent 1989b). When sociopolitical differentiation begins to emerge, as with the presence of an informal leader, other realms of culture, including gender, also become differentiated. That is, males and females become seen as increasingly different, though not necessarily as superior or inferior until differentiation is accompanied by stratification.

For example, G/wi and G//ana have no leaders, only situational advisors, and just minimal gender differentiation. During the winter, they are stationary but not aggregated. The Ju/'hoansi, in contrast, are both aggregated and stationary during the winter. Leadership is present among the Ju/'hoansi, but ephemeral. Gender is more differentiated among the Ju/'hoansi than among the G/wi and G//ana. Women are much more restricted in Ju/'hoansi society and do not usually hunt, trap, butcher, distribute meat, or touch men's hunting equipment, whereas G/wi and G//ana women are allowed to do all these activities (they cannot touch men's equipment only if they are menstruating). Unlike G/wi or G//ana myths, Ju/'hoansi myths express antagonism against the sexes, which results in a balance of power between women and men (Biesele 1993). I suggest the major factor affecting the differences between Ju/'hoansi and G/wi and G//ana gender relations is that the former are aggregated while stationary and therefore the need of a mediator, while the latter are aggregated while mobile without such a need for political differentiation. Because parts of culture are integrated, differentiation in the political realm affects differentiation in other realms, including social status, gender, and others. Now we need to test whether this association among gender, social differentiation, and sedentism and aggregation is valid for southern Africa prehistory—or whether this relationship is valid only for the contemporary forager groups. But to answer this, we first need to know if there are differences between forager and nonforager sites.

Mazel (1989:141–142) proposes, on the basis of the prehistory of the Thukela Basin in South Africa, that the Early Iron Age farmers/pastoralists who first migrated to southern Africa from the north had good relations with the indigenous hunter-gatherers living there. Interaction probably was based on trade. "Items historically associated with hunter-gatherers, such as worked bone, stone tools, OES [ostrich eggshell] pieces and beads are found on farming community sites, whilst farming community decorated pottery and iron ore have been recovered from Mbabane Shelter" (Mazel 1989:141). Early Iron Age villages exchanged goods and interacted with one another as well as with the local hunter-gatherers "who possessed a quite distinct culture and economy" (Maggs 1980:139). Bollong and Sampson (1996) note that while Khoi herders did intrude into the upper Seacow Valley, South Africa, they did not displace the resident hunter-gatherers (Bollong and Sampson 1996). Perhaps archaeologists have become so enamored with Wilmsen's (1989) proposition that herders and autonomous hunter-gatherers cannot coexist without one group losing its cultural identity that it has diverted attention from the people probably most impacted by the incoming Bantu-speaking herders—the Khoi herders who had to compete with the Bantu-speakers for the same environment and resources.

Certainly the fact that Early Iron Age hunter-gatherer sites are discernible from pastoralist/farmer sites indicates that some, if not most or all, cultural autonomy was preserved during the Early Iron Age and likely far beyond to the present. Sadr (1997:109) shows that there is no evidence of social or economic changes in hunter-gatherer material culture at the same archaeological sites that Wilmsen and Denbow claim demonstrate that hunter-gatherers were forced into working as client-herders 2,000 years ago. Many sites, including "the pivotal site in Denbow and Wilmsen's argument about Bushman encapsulation, show hardly any material change from its oldest to youngest levels" (Sadr 1997:109). Other sites in Botswana show equally little change that would indicate a transition to serfdom. Hunter-gatherers during the Iron Age were not Stone Age foragers, any more than are modern hunter-gatherers. However, in my opinion, the foragers maintained a distinct cultural autonomy from the farmers/ pastoralists. Both groups obviously were in contact with one another, and relations between foragers and herders probably varied from group to group by geographical area and time periods. Parkington et al. (1986:317) concur: "we subscribe to the view that the appearance of pastoralism involved an influx of new people and that some communities continued to pursue an almost exclusively hunter-gatherer existence long after pastoralists intruded." Wadley (Chapter 4) also expresses doubt that foragers were controlled or dominated by agropastoralists during the Early Iron Age. The intrusion of Europeans into southern Africa created unprecedented tensions between groups, made some groups extinct, and plunged others into poverty. I suggest that it is erroneous to use an analogy from historic pastoralist/forager relations after one hundred or more years of contact with Europeans who were determined to alter, if not exterminate, mobile groups that proved difficult to govern or exploit. I have yet to see convincing evidence that the same patterns occurred over such a large area at the same magnitude before the arrival of Europeans.

Contrasts: Spatial Patterning of Activities at Early and Late Iron Age Sites

Since Iron Age pastoralists planned on staying longer at their camps than hunter-gatherers, their sites are more archaeologically visible. Constructed of durable materials, including clay, dung, and stones, Iron Age architecture is more identifiable than the ephemeral grass windbreaks and huts at hunter-gatherer sites. The few Early Iron Age sites that have been excavated appear to diverge significantly from Late Iron Age sites (for specifics, see Lane, Chapter 10, and Segobye, Chapter 12). Apparently, internal house space during the Early Iron Age, unlike the Late Iron Age, was not differentiated (Lane, Chapter 10; Hall, Chapter 13).

Compared with Late Iron Age pastoralists' villages, Early Iron Age (pre-AD 1300) populations at the oldest pastoralist/farmer sites were smaller and less socio-politically complex, though more complex than those present during the Late Stone Age. In Botswana during this time, there is little evidence of either the hierarchical sociopolitical system or the rigid gender roles that characterize many modern Bantu-speaking groups, though changes occurred during the later Early Iron Age (Denbow 1982, 1984). Site structure and spatial patterning at many Early Iron Age sites elsewhere in southern Africa support this interpretation (Lane, Chapter 10; Mazel 1989).

One difficulty with interpreting Early Iron Age sites is that excavators have failed to record artifacts and features systematically (particularly the plotting of objects) in such a way as to determine fine-grained spatial interpretations, as is possible with Late Stone Age sites. Not only are artifacts not provenienced in the published materials on Early Iron Age sites, but house interior features and artifacts are similarly not published (Lane, Chapter 10). Relatively small sections of Early Iron Age sites have been excavated, making inferences on spatial patterning, gender, and other topics difficult to posit (Lane 1994/95). However, the evidence of Early Iron Age settlements that is available strongly suggests important differences from both Late Stone Age and Late Iron Age sites in the use of space, gender, and other facets of culture, behavior, and site layout (Lane, Chapter 10, details the differences between Early Iron Age and Late Iron Age sites). Despite these differences and in the absence of specific spatial data, some archaeologists speculate that the Early Iron Age kitchens and other areas were gender-specific for women, based on an analogy with modern Bantu-speakers' use of space.

Spatial patterning at Early Iron Age sites may indicate discrete activity areas, unlike highly egalitarian, mobile hunter-gatherer sites. However, without knowing the spatial patterning of individual artifacts in context with features, I believe in exercising caution when interpreting an area as male- or female-specific. Archaeologists have suggested that the front and back areas around huts, kitchens, and other activity areas were used or thought of differently based on an invididual's gender (e.g., Walker 1995; Greenfield and Jongsma 1996; Huffman 1996b,c; and others). Again, until there are detailed studies as the one by Parkington et al. (1992), we are constrained in what we know about Iron Age women or men and the spatial patterning of their activities.

Since additional early Late Iron Age sites have been excavated, we can infer more about gendered space. During the Late Iron Age, there is a notable change during the early and late periods. Clear evidence of spatial differentiation between the animal corral and the habitation hut occurs. Moreover, some sites appear to be divided spatially into a front and a back area (Evers 1984). The front courtyard usually contains a formal food preparation area/kitchen, implying a function-specific locus (Evers 1984). A South African Late Iron Age pastoralist site surveyed but not excavated revealed a stone wall encircling huts within (Taylor 1984). What may have been courtyards surrounded the circular huts. Grinding stones were found on the surface in the open areas between houses (Taylor 1984). Grain storage platforms were present and a large corral probably was used for cattle, in contrast to smaller ones that probably were for goats and/or sheep (Taylor 1984).

Late Iron Age sites do indicate the presence of differentiation that is consistent with their "simple" chiefdom level of sociopolitical organization (Hall, Chapter 13). Differentiation is visible on intervillage, intravillage, and household levels, and in the sociopolitical organization as well (Denbow 1986; Huffman 1996c). Early Late Iron Age villages were small sites, occupied relatively briefly, composed of loose circles of huts situated around a corral (Hall, Chapter 13). They lack evidence of spatial differentiation outside the huts, though inside hut artifact and feature distributions indicate a female (left) and male (right) division, in addition to a sacred/private and profane/public division (Hall, Chapter 13). With the emergence of complex chiefdoms during the late Late Iron Age circa AD 1300 to AD 1500, camp gender differentiation becomes marked and rigid both in and outside huts. Bounded, discrete gender- and function-specific activity areas are visible in the compound area (Hall, Chapter 13). Hut interiors appear to have been partitioned by function and perhaps by gender (see Chapter 13). Other very late Late Iron Age sites also show evidence of activity area differentiation (e.g., Parkington and Cronin 1979).

Portions of Iron Age sites excavated in Botswana also indicate spatial segregation like that seen at South African Late Iron Age sites. An adult male and a female were found buried in two adjacent corrals at the Late Iron Age portion of Modipe Hill

(Pearson 1995). That both burials occurred in corrals is interesting in that archaeologists usually associate corrals more with men than women (Huffman 1996c and elsewhere). Both adults had grave goods buried with them, and a four- to six-year-old child was interred with the male (Pearson 1995). We need much more data to determine whether these separate interments represent a spatial, and therefore cognitive, differentiation between the sexes, where adult males and females were buried separately when possible. If such differences existed between the sexes, why was a women buried in what is assumed to be "male" space? Was "male" space not as restrictive as it is today among many Bantu-speakers? Alternatively, did social status override gender differences and, if so, then were gender differences important only within a single sociopolitical class and not between? According to Lane (1997: personal communication), status did supersede gender, a factor not acknowledged in the Central Cattle Pattern model where space is gender-segregated without regard to status. In sum, we find that a few discrete, task-differentiated activity areas may be present at some Early Iron Age sites. Still, excavations have not been specifically geared to collect spatial information, so interpretations are difficult to posit. Gender- and function-specific areas are definitely visible and more common at Late Iron Age sites, increasing in frequency through time.

Differences Between Iron Age and Stone Age Site Excavations

Why are Iron Age sites generally excavated so differently from Stone Age sites? One reason might be the greater size and number of objects located at Iron Age sites. As a result, systematic excavation of Iron Age sites requires many resources in terms of funding, time, and workers. Another reason may be the popularity of the Central Cattle Pattern model. Huffman (1982) adapted ethnographic observations of the spatial patterning of contemporary Bantu-speakers' compounds to formulate the Central Cattle Pattern. The Central Cattle Pattern has since been applied to Early and Late Iron Age sites (Lane, Chapter 10, Segobye, Chapter 12, and Hall, Chapter 13, this volume, discuss the model). A number of archaeological interpretations of Iron Age sites are influenced by the Central Cattle Pattern model or based on a modification of it, which is used to identify differentiated space by gender at sites (e.g., Evers 1984; also see Lane, Chapter 10).

Spatial patterns are not derived from the distribution of artifacts or features, but are assumed to exist, based on their presence in the model. Without detailed plotting of artifact distributions and wide-scale horizontal excavations, it is not possible to interpret the spatial patterning at a site. Nor is it possible, therefore, to interpret the presence of gendered divisions of space or how public and private areas were used. Instead, archaeologists postulate the presence of these divisions based on contemporary Batswana and related groups' division of compounds and houses, implicitly assuming that there has been no change through time. Although excavation techniques at Early Iron Age sites in southern Africa may be changing (Hall 1996:

personal communication), some archaeologists, such as Lane (1997: personal communication), see a number of such sites still being interpreted based on the Central Cattle Pattern model.

Huffman (1996c) writes that his model should be used as a base from which to test archaeological data. He cautions against assuming that the pattern remains static through time. Nonetheless, there are archaeologists who, because of the model, expect gender and function spatial divisions to be present, rather than testing the model to see if the data support their presence. Even if the data are ambiguous or missing, some archaeologists fall back on the Central Cattle Pattern model to justify the presence of gender spatial divisions. Both Lane (Chapter 10) and Segobye (Chapter 12) outline differences between the Central Cattle Pattern model and the spatial patterning of Early Iron Age sites, including the use, distribution, and meaning of pits and the location of iron smelting activity areas in the center of settlements. Lane (Chapter 10) describes the many differences between Early Iron Age, Late Iron Age, and the ethnographically observed Bantu compounds, demonstrating the model's inappropriateness for interpreting Early Iron Age habitations (as have others, Segobye 1993). It is crucial to test the validity of the Central Cattle Pattern model before assuming its validity in order to determine if prehistoric, protohistoric, and contemporary agropastoralist gender and spatial patterns are the same or have changed through time.

Discussion: Visibility of Gender
Among Foragers and Farmers/Pastoralists

Some archaeologists may be so interested in finding gendered space that they interpret relatively small differences in artifact densities, distributions, or spatial locations as signifying gender and/or functionally discrete areas. Actually, gender-specific activities are not as common as many archaeologists assume they are. Ethnographically known small-scale noncomplex societies, regardless of economic orientation, do not consistently segregate space or architecture by gender or by activity function (see Kent 1990a,b, 1991a,b). I suggest the same is true for small-scale prehistoric societies. Because a locus shows a high frequency of flakes or debitage does not make it solely a lithic manufacturing area, particularly if other objects, such as faunal remains or ceramic sherds, are located nearby. Neither does the presence of sherds at a locus make it a food preparation or a women's area—perhaps the area was used to store pots, dump broken vessels, or conduct other activities.

Male and female and function-specific work areas are much more common in more-complex societies where there is a strict division of labor and partitioning of space by gender. Archaeological sites from the complex societies that emerged during the later Late Iron Age and Historic Period in southern Africa, such as the Great Zimbabwe, exhibit numerous examples of the use of function-specific loci and gendered space (e.g., Huffman 1996a,c; Parkington and Cronin 1979; Hall, Chapter 13).

Few anthropologists have explicitly investigated what constitutes gendered space and what women's or men's activity areas should look like. We need to define "gendered space" and explain what a gender-specific locus is. Do archaeologists mean an area used only by, or primarily by, women and not by men at all? Archaeologists may apply the label *gendered space* to indicate the presence of women at an area, not to imply the exclusive use of an area either by women or by men, which is actually what the term suggests. There are archaeologists who identify an area containing pots and grinding stones as a female work area. I agree that such an area may signify the presence of women in prehistory, assuming that the tools were used primarily by women and not by men to grind tobacco, paints, medicinal plants, or other non–food processing activities. But I disagree that the area was necessarily gender-specific or a women's food processing area. There needs to be evidence that the locus was not used for activities by men. If men also used the area to sit, sleep, eat, or perform other activities, it by definition cannot be a gendered space or a women's area. Rather, it is a multipurpose, non-sex-specific locus at which food processing was one task performed. An example is the diffuse distribution of lithic flakes at Rose Cottage Cave, which Wadley (Chapter 4) identifies as being used for a variety of activities by both males and females (a similar interpretation of flakes in Ghana is made by Casey, Chapter 5).

Wadley (Chapter 4) interprets my chapter here as lacking optimism for archaeologists to be able to recognize gender in the spatial patterns at Stone Age sites, but I disagree. I actually am quite optimistic about finding the presence of women (and men) at sites and about discerning gendered space at some sites, as at Late Iron Age agropastoralist sites. I do not think gender-specific areas can be found at all sites because I believe that not all people throughout time segregated space into gender-specific areas. Based on the model of the relationship between sociopolitical complexity and egalitarianism, including gender equality, I do not think that Stone Age peoples divided activity areas by gender, nor did they use gender-specific tools. I interpret Wadley's description of the Rose Cottage Cave data as supporting my position—there were no activity areas or tools used exclusively or primarily by one sex. Instead, lithics were probably used by males and females throughout the site. Are lithics used by both females and males to be considered gendered objects? And are activity areas used by both men and women to be labeled gendered space? In other words, we need to define the signatures of gender-restricted space and tools. My understanding of a gendered object is that it is used primarily by men or primarily by women, but not by both. Flakes probably were used by both men and women so, until we have data that suggest otherwise, they cannot be an example of a gendered artifact, nor can their presence mark the location of a gender-specific locus. Is the disagreement that Wadley and I have one of definitions (what gendered objects and gender space imply) or one of concepts (the presence or absence of tools or areas used primarily by one gender at Late Stone Age sites)?

Not many researchers have systematically recorded the kinds and distributions of gender-associated objects at ethnographically known activity areas. I have recorded the objects located in contemporary Navajo Indian hogans, though not in as detailed a manner as I would have liked. My observations of object location in the United States, as in Africa, allow us to see what gendered space should look like archaeologically, at least for one society. In general, the object patterning among the Navajos is not similar to patterning at sites where archaeologists have interpreted gender-specific activity areas.

In the traditional Navajo hogan, male and female space is separated by use, rather than by physical partitions such as walls. The northeast quarter of a hogan is primarily used by women, the southeast by men. Women more commonly go into the men's area than vice versa. For instance, I observed the male head of the household enter the women's area only once for a brief period over more than 45 days of continuous observations, including both days and nights (I lived with household members and slept in their hogan). He retrieved a tool, and then returned to the male area of the hogan to use it. Men's and women's objects are consistently located in the areas designated as male or female space (Figure 3.6). Other areas are neither men- nor women-specific, and artifact use and ownership generally reflect this absence of gender spatial division—that is, male and female objects are stored together in these areas.

While food preparation among the Navajos is primarily done by women, and therefore performed in the female-restricted northeastern portion of the hogan, the area is only gender-specific and not function-specific. Other women's activities take place there, such as weaving baskets, eating, talking, and entertaining. Because a range of activities occur at this locus, it cannot be designated a food preparation area (i.e., a function-specific area). The occurrence of sex-specific areas and the absence of function-specific areas can be seen in the distribution of objects in the hogan. Female-specific tools are consistently located in the women's half of the hogan, male-specific objects in the men's half (Figure 3.6). This patterning also is unlike any of the areas described at Late Stone Age sites. Archaeologists infer both gender- and function-specific loci, including women's food preparation areas, at many Late Stone Age sites, based on the presence of one or two female-associated artifacts.

I also observed the use of space in a nontraditional Navajo family's hogan located a few kilometers from the traditional family described above. The nontraditional Navajos no longer follow the Blessingway ceremonialism and, as a result, the hogan is not divided into men and women's space. During 35 days of continuous observations I saw no area used in a way that could be called gender- or activity function-specific. Objects and activities associated with women occurred throughout the hogan, as did men's objects and activities. Figure 3.7 illustrates the spatial patterning of objects and use areas in a dwelling in which there is no gender- or function-specific activity areas. The distribution of women's and men's objects is visibly different from their distribution in the hogan with gendered space (Figure 3.6).

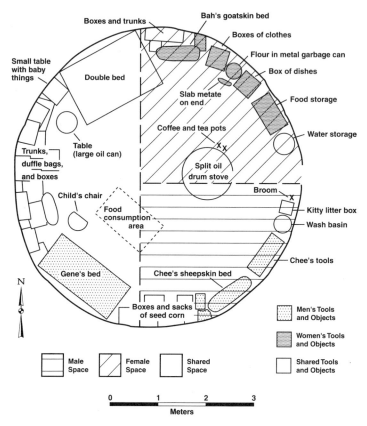

Figure 3.6. Spatial patterning of gendered space in a traditional Navajo hogan (adapted and modified from Kent 1984).

The nature of the distribution of female- or male-specific objects in dwellings that are divided by gender appears to be cross-culturally consistent. Huts occupied today by the Mpondo Bantu speakers of southern Africa, for example, are cognitively divided into male and female areas (left is equated with males and right with females; Davison 1988:105–106). Although a detailed inventory of objects was not made, observations indicate that items associated with males occur primarily on the left side of huts and those with females on the right (Davison 1988). This pattern in Africa is congruent with the traditional Navajo use of hogans I observed, in that gender-specific objects are located in the appropriate male or female portion of a structure. Note, however, that this is not similar to many areas interpreted as gender-specific at Late Stone Age sites that have only one or two artifacts associated with one gender or the other.

The presence of a single or few objects inferred to be associated with women does not make an area gendered or sex-specific. For example, the nontraditional

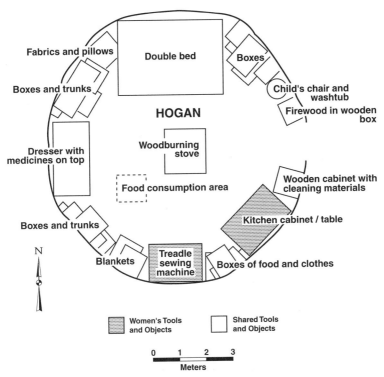

Figure 3.7. Distribution of objects along the wall of a nontraditional Navajo family's hogan in which space was not partitioned by gender (modified from Kent 1984).

hogan (Figure 3.7) has several areas along the wall where women's items are stored, despite the lack of any gender division of space. An archaeologist might be tempted to interpret the southeastern portion of the wall as a women's area because of the presence of women's objects. However, men also used the area for various activities. It was not a gender-segregated locus; in fact, there were no areas in or outside the hogan associated primarily with one sex or the other. Is the same true for the patterning of objects noted at the Flat and Grass Bushmen historic camps, Goergap, Jubilee, Rose Cottage, Dunefield Midden, and other sites?

The variations in spatial patterning at hunter-gatherer and pastoralist sites clearly indicate different cultures, architecture, and use of space between Stone Age and Iron Age groups. According to most excavators, relatively recent Late Iron Age and historic pastoral sites reveal functionally differentiated (often also gender-specific) activity areas. Patterning during the Early Iron Age cannot be determined until more spatially oriented excavations are conducted, using techniques that allow researchers to determine the presence or absence of gender- or function-specific areas. Based on what has been excavated and what is known about Late Iron Age pastoralist sites, the use of space appears to have differed substantially from the indigenous hunter-gatherer pattern.

Gender spatial separation is invisible at both Late Stone Age sites and Early Iron Age sites, but for different reasons. It cannot be discerned at Stone Age sites because, I suggest, the foragers did not organize their culture into male and female divisions. Not all societies segregate space, tools, tasks, and the like, by gender. Cross-culturally, space is divided by gender when gender itself is conceptually separated with rigid divisions of labor, gender-specific tools and tasks, and a sociopolitical organization that encourages or requires segregation, be it by gender, age, status, or another factor. If there are no male-female segregated tasks or ideology that promotes gender differentiation, then why would there be gendered space in which male or female activities predominate? In contrast to Late Stone Age sites, some gendered space may have been used at Early Iron Age sites, but it remains invisible because artifacts and features at the sites are not provenienced with sufficient detail to permit spatial and gender analyses. Excavators who rely on ethnographic analogy more than data to support their interpretations of gendered space at Late Stone Age and Early Iron Age sites must assume, with little evidence, that space has been organized the same way for the past 2,000 or more years.

Conclusions

What does the ability to state conclusively that men sat here and women there at a prehistoric site tell us about gender during the Stone Age or after it? We cannot study change in gender relations through time using analogies, because the very use of an analogy implies that there was no change. If change had, in fact, occurred, the analogy would no longer be appropriate. Cross-culturally valid ethnographic or ethnoarchaeological models that detail why a particular relationship or behavior occurred can lead to an understanding of gender relations through time. It is important that archaeologists not merely assume that modern gender relationships are identical to the past without positing a reason why such relations remained static through time.

Some archaeologists are comfortable in pronouncing that men worked or stayed in one area and women in another, based on very little evidence or on a modern analog when the same people would never think of doing this with environmental data or for paleoenvironmental reconstructions. Most archaeologists would prefer to base their paleoenvironmental reconstructions on soil samples, pollen profiles, and macrobotanical and faunal remains than on speculation or descriptions of current environments. Why should gender studies be any less rigorous (also see Gifford-Gonzalez, Chapter 7)? The only way I know to study gender in prehistory, without resorting to using a simple analogy, is to investigate artifact spatial distributional patterning and densities, architectural partitioning, and site features. This cannot be accomplished with merely a few test pits or by excavating a few trenches. Areas at which activities routinely occurred, including gendered space, require large horizontal excavations of sites and detailed measurement of artifact proveniences. However, even detailed excavations will not, by themselves, provide information on gender-segregation and its change through time. A model of gender relationships is necessary that frames one's theoretical orientation, such as the model presented above. The cross-cultural model does not presuppose that gender differentiation occurs in all societies in all time periods. It shows that gender relations vary in different types of cultures with different amounts of stratification. Gender segregation occurs in those societies with slight to more sociopolitical differentiation and is common in societies with hierarchies. Gender segregation of space does not occur in all modern human societies, nor does it occur randomly in a culture. There is a reason for the use of both gender-segregated and function-segregated space. That reason is based on how a culture is organized—with or without differentiation, with or without hierarchies, and so on.

While most forager sites are invisible (that is, not archaeologically visible), because of their ephemeral nature and poor preservation, those identifiable sites that have been excavated do not indicate the use of gendered (or function-specific) space. I propose that many Stone Age sites have been excavated with sufficient detail to delineate discrete activity areas, if any such areas had been segregated by gender or task. Significant for examining gender in the southern African record is that various artifact types at the Dunefield Midden site are clustered near the focal hearths, but not in any way that could be construed as patterned gender-specific (or function-specific) loci. In other words, if they were present, partitioning by gender or activity function would be archaeologically visible in the patterning of artifacts and features at the Dunefield and other Late Stone Age sites in southern Africa. Since such areas have not, in my opinion, been conclusively discerned at these sites, I interpret Late Stone Age foragers as not having partitioned space or material culture into male and female domains. If the same highly controlled excavation techniques used to investigate Late Stone Age sites were conducted at Early Iron Age sites, I suggest that some spatial segregation of loci may be present. So while many Early Iron Age sites are visible, gendered space is invisible because most have not been excavated with enough detail to discern activity areas differentiated by function or gender. I am reluctant to plot ethnographic analogy onto archaeological data for the distant past without the evidence to support or refute its validity. Instead, some artifactual patterning or feature distributions must be present to support claims that an area was divided into, for instance, male and female space. By contrast, observations of Navajo Indian hogans indicate that artifact patterning *can* indicate male-female segregated areas.

Gendered space may have been used at Early Iron Age sites, but its invisibility, at least to me, is a consequence of excavation techniques. Hall (Chapter 13) characterizes the earlier Late Iron Age sites as not having as much gender spatial or architectural segmentation as the later sites have. He describes a change through time wherein space becomes increasingly segmented with more identifiable function- and gender-discrete areas. He also suggests that the increase in architectural compartmentalization of space during the later part of the Late Iron Age coincides with increasing male control over females in various facets of their lives. Late Iron Age sites are segregated space by both gender and activity function. The segregation is visible without the use of the ethnographic Central Cattle Pattern analogy. Unlike before, features, such as stone walls, enclosed women and their activities during the later Late Iron Age. I agree with Hall (Chapter 13, 1997: personal communication), who states that men were manipulating space to indicate their differences from and superiority to women.

I believe there has to be enough data that all point to the identification of a locus as gender- or function-specific before it can be so defined. At the Navajo hogan in which space was segregated by gender, male-oriented objects are not found on the woman's side nor vice versa, even though exceptions no doubt occur. What archaeologists refer to as possibly gendered space appears more similar to the distribution of objects in the nontraditional hogan, in which space was not divided by gender, than it is to the traditional hogan in which space was divided by gender. In the nontraditional hogan there were a few areas that contained only or primarily female-associated objects, but there was no patterned spatial division of any kind. Is this similar to the patterning at Late Stone Age sites?

Unlike many archaeologists, I do not think that all societies separate space by gender or function. As a result, I do not go to the data expecting to find differentiated space. I also do not feel despair when the artifacts and features do not support evidence of segregated loci. I have shown that most southern African Late Stone Age sites have been well documented with good horizontal and vertical control; the archaeological methods are generally excellent. Therefore, the fact that I do not see any compelling evidence that suggests gendered space (space used primarily by one sex) does not, in my opinion, indicate that the sites were not excavated with enough detail. I propose that Late Stone Age foragers did not use gender segregated space as many archaeologists believe they did. Stone Age foragers did not, I posit, conceptualize space in that way, even if later Iron Age villagers did.

Acknowledgments

I am most grateful to Christopher Henshilwood, Lyn Wadley, Jeanette Duncan, and Thomas Huffman, all of whom sent unpublished materials. I could not have written the chapter without their assistance. I also appreciate helpful comments made by Lyn Wadley, John Parkington, Paul Lane, Simon Hall, Diane Gifford-Gonzalez, Karim Sadr, Garth Sampson, Sarah Nelson, and Barbara Barich. However, none is to be blamed for problems with the chapter; all errors are strictly mine alone. Linda Fondes provided valuable editorial comments. The Old Dominion University graphics department drafted the figures.

Notes

1. I suggest that the rush to accept the revisionists' position results from the world systems and political economy orientations currently influential in cultural anthropology. These are heavily influenced by Westerners' new appreciation of a global economy and world environment. Although these both exist in the 20th century, they were not necessarily present in the past. Unfortunately, scholars often fail to examine the ideas of contemporary society and how they influence their discipline's theoretical orientations. The result is the uncritical acceptance of questionable theories that support transient popular ideas.

2. However, the Central Kalahari Basarwa, unlike the Ju/'hoansi (!Kung) or other Kalahari foragers, do not use hunting blinds, so even these would be absent for sites historically occupied by G/wi.

3. It is possible that one or two ethnic groups occupied better pasture areas containing more water. They probably differed economically, sociopolitically, and in other ways from the majority of Late Stone Age hunter-gatherer groups. This is true for contemporary and historic Tuya Basarwa who live along the Nata River, as opposed to the G/wi and Ju/'hoansi Basarwa who occupy areas of little interest to prehistoric and historic pastoralists (i.e., without the technology to drill boreholes). Differences among hunter-gatherer groups were probably as diverse prehistorically in southern Africa as in Botswana. So even if one or two groups were displaced or disrupted by incoming pastoralists, that does not mean that all ethnic groups were similarly. Again, I think hunting and gathering populations survived in many areas in southern Africa until the incursion of Europeans (also see Sadr 1997). Even a few groups in Botswana and Namibia survived to the late 20th century in areas not of interest to colonialists and other Westerners.

Chapter Four

The Invisible Meat Providers

Women in the Stone Age of South Africa

Introduction

Gendered interpretations are not new to Stone Age archaeology. For many years, archaeologists uncritically labeled Stone Age man as "man the hunter," "man the butcher," "man the meat provider," and "man the tool maker." Since cultural development is often considered to be linked to technological development, the unspoken assumption was that man was the agent of change. This left woman as the passive bearer of children and collector of plant food, so it is not surprising that Stone Age woman went almost unnoticed in the archaeological record. She was often absent from archaeological reports except where she was mentioned in her capacity as "woman the plant food gatherer." Such gender stereotypes illustrate an androcentric and ethnocentric view of gender roles; they trivialize the division of labor and, indeed, social relations. I shall show that these gender stereotypes are inappropriate when applied to modern hunter-gatherer people and that they are almost certainly inappropriate for people in the past.

The old gender assumptions have had a stifling effect on interpretation of social behavior. It is only since 1984, with the publishing of Conkey and Spector's seminal paper, that self-conscious gender studies have been undertaken. Gender centers on social values invested in sexual differences; gender relations are an integral part of social theory (Gilchrist 1991:498) and cannot be ignored by anyone wishing to make social interpretations of the past. The new generation of gender studies has concentrated on looking afresh at old issues (Moore 1994:6–7), and new critiques are made from gendered perspectives without seeking gender attribution (Dobres 1995a).

Organization of the Hunt

The "man the hunter" interpretation of the Stone Age came about through the use of androcentric ethnographic accounts. In the 1970s Murdock and Provost (1973:207) claimed that hunting was one of the most obviously gender segregated activities in hunter-gatherer ethnography, and their argument was so persuasive that contradictory reports of gender equality in some hunter-gatherer societies were generally disregarded as aberrant or idiosyncratic. However, since the 1970s, reports of hunter-gatherer gender equity have increased and the stereotype of "man the hunter" has begun to be deconstructed. I begin to do so here by examining some of the ethnographically recorded variability in the way that meat is obtained. In so doing I am aware of the problems associated with the use of ethnographic analogy (see Gifford-Gonzalez, Chapter 7) but, due to space limitations, I concentrate on examples from southern Africa and draw on selected ethnographies from elsewhere to illustrate specific points about, for example, the organization of labor and exploitation of resources. Additional hunter-gatherer ethnographies from around the world could be drawn on to expand my arguments.

The best-known exception to the male-only hunting rule is that of the Agta women of the Philippines who are known to hunt occasionally with bow and arrow (Estioko-Griffin and Griffin 1981). Chipewyan and Tiwi women also hunt big game regularly and, like the Agta women, they use the same weapons as men (see Kent, Chapter 1). The Mbuti net hunters of Zaire include women in the hunt, yet men and women do not perform the same role. Men hold the nets and spear the prey while women drive the game and act as beaters (Ichikawa 1983:58). This cooperative form of hunting with a large number of personnel is highly productive (Ichikawa 1983:63). Women and children also take part as beaters in Begbe, an unpoisoned arrow hunt, and they drive the duiker in the same way as in the net hunt (Harako 1976). Begbe takes place only in the dry season when interband cooperation is observed.

Among the Inupiat of Alaska, women are seen as pivotal to the hunt and ritually attract animals, thus being classed as hunters (Bodenhorn 1990). One successful Inupiat hunter said, "I'm not the great hunter, my wife is!" (Bodenhorn 1990:61). He was referring to his wife's ability to attract animals through her generous behavior rather than to her ability to shoot with a rifle (Bodenhorn 1990:62). Nonetheless, some Inupiat women are skilled with rifles, are good at paddling, and may take their place in whaling crews or on hunts with their spouses (Bodenhorn 1990:60). What is really important is that it is not necessary for a woman to accompany her husband on the hunt in order to be regarded as a hunter: women's activities such as sewing, butchering, and meat sharing are all classed by Inupiat as hunting skills (Bodenhorn 1990:65).

Basarwa women at Kutse, in Botswana, may also accompany their husbands on the hunt and, conversely, men may spend much time gathering plant food with their wives or collecting firewood or water (Kent 1995:521; 1996b:130). Kutse women and men manufacture snares, and meat caught in these belongs to the person who made or owns the snare (Kent 1995:518). Bow and arrow hunting and spear hunting, on the other hand, are restricted to men (Kent 1995:518), though, unlike some other Basarwa groups, there is no restriction on a woman touching a bow and arrow (providing that she is not menstruating) or using a man's knife or spear for cutting

(Kent 1995:520). Furthermore, women occasionally use digging sticks to kill small animals and will check their husband's traps when men are away from the settlement. Women regularly butcher small animals and may also butcher animals such as springbok when men are busy (Kent 1995:520). Thus the concept of "man the hunter" and "woman the gatherer" has a fuzzy boundary at Kutse (Kent 1995:520). The majority of Kutse activities are not gender linked; therefore, most tools are not associated with only one sex: digging sticks and spears, for example, are not exclusively women's and men's tools, respectively. Although men use spears most often for hunting, women may use spears for stirring food and as knives (Kent 1995:525).

The Ju/'hoansi (previously known as !Kung) of the Kalahari use a wider range of meat-getting techniques than the Basarwa at Kutse: bow and poisoned arrow hunting, large-group spear hunting on foot, spear hunting with the use of pit-traps, spear hunting on horseback, snaring, running down small game, and scavenging game killed by lions. Most Ju/'hoansi bow and arrow hunting, spear hunting, and hunting by snares takes place in the dry/hot and dry/cold seasons, and hunted meat is scarce at other times of year (Wilmsen and Durham 1988:63). Rain and dew fall from November to May, the wet season, and the dampness causes the sinew parts of bows, arrows, and spears, as well as the cordage of snare lines, to malfunction (Lee 1979:208; Wilmsen and Durham 1988:70, 72). In addition, prey are dispersed and spoor obscured during this wet season (Wilmsen and Durham 1988:72).

Ju/'hoansi archers hunt successfully either in small groups or as individuals because hunting with a poisoned arrow relies on stealth, surprise, and a good aim. Ju/'hoansi women are specifically barred from bow and arrow hunts and they do not participate in butchering animals (Draper 1975b; Marshall 1976:97, 287). Though they are not present at the hunt, Ju/'hoansi women contribute considerably to hunting success because they observe game movements and the condition of the veld when they collect plant foods, and they supply hunters with this valuable information (Draper 1975b).

Spear hunting on foot by large groups of hunters is no longer practiced by Ju/'hoansi, though Lee (1979:234) described an elephant hunt as it was recounted to him:

> They set grass fires on one side and the people came in on the other side. The dogs worry it, then when it raises its ears the people throw in their spears one after another. They didn't put poison on their spears. They just gathered many men together to throw their spears.

Lee comments that the spear hunt on foot requires the coordination of many people and suggests that this is no longer possible among 20th-century Ju/'hoansi.

The use of pit-traps was observed ethnographically at !Gi in Botswana (Brooks 1984). Animals caught in the traps were dispatched with spears. The pit-trap and spear technique may have been widespread earlier this century because it was also used by the Batwa, of Lake Chrissie in Mpumalanga, who no longer exist as a distinct cultural group (Potgieter 1955:22). The hunters excavated pit-traps for game, and then formed rows in the veld and frightened approaching game driven there by other band members.

Modern conditions have brought changes to Ju/'hoansi hunting patterns. Traditional bow and arrow hunting, for example, has been largely replaced by spear hunting where hunters have obtained horses. Ju/'hoansi men of /Xai/Xai (Cae Cae) now ride horses and throw metal-tipped spears for eland hunting and use dogs and spears for warthog and carnivore hunting (Wilmsen 1989:230–231), as do the ≠Kade of the central Kalahari (Osaki 1984). These modern spear hunts, which are viable even for solitary hunters, are efficient because the equestrian hunter hunts half as frequently as the archer on foot yet obtains almost two and a half times as much total return (Wilmsen and Durham 1988:78; Wilmsen 1989:252). The ≠Kade use the new hunting techniques to facilitate changing social relations. Meat ownership has moved from the owner of the weapon to the owner of the horse, thereby enhancing the wealth and status of those men with access to a cash economy. ≠Kade men sell some of their hunted meat, while the horse owners have the potential to become a wealthy elite relative to the non-horse-owning ≠Kade. The ≠Kade changes are linked to circumstances brought about by the demographic shift to a massive settlement of some 500 people. The ≠Kade demographic change was, in turn, brought about through contact with pastoralists and villagers, and also through the availability of store-bought foods and a regular supply of borehole water.

Snaring of animals is also a highly productive means of obtaining meat. Rope snares, made of plant fiber, are most often used by Ju/'hoansi for catching antelope and game birds. A noose is made from the rope and this is attached to a sapling that acts as a spring. The device is activated by a wooden trigger (Lee 1979:142). Most of the steenbok, duiker, and birds captured by Ju/'hoansi are taken in snares (Wilmsen and Durham 1988:71) that are most often set by old men and young boys whose mobility is limited (Lee 1979:207). Nisa, the unusual Ju/'hoansi female interviewed by Shostak, reported that Ju/'hoansi women and girls set snares (Shostak 1981:91) and that she (Nisa) had also run down and killed animals such as steenbok and small kudu (Shostak 1981:94, 102). Nisa was, however, an atypical Ju/'hoansi woman and should perhaps not be considered representative of her group (Kent, Chapter 1). Although Ju/'hoansi women and girls often collect tortoise, snakes, lizards, and birds (Lee 1979:235), they are not reported to have set snares by anyone other than Nisa.

Scavenging of animals killed by lion or other predators is also an important meat source (Wilmsen and Durham 1988:71). Women spend much time in the veld, and they sometimes come across dead animals and alert the other camp members to their find (Shostak 1981:93, 101).

This brief review of selected ethnography confirms that the stereotype of "man the hunter" and "man the meat provider" is flawed. It is true that men generally reserve the right to handle weapons (though Kent [1995] observed a Kutse woman firing her husband's bow at a springbok that wandered into camp), but it is *not* universally true that women are excluded from playing an active role in the hunt or the meat quest. In the Mbuti example, women are indispensable to the hunt even though they do not deal the death blows. In the Kalahari example we see that the regular meat supply is provided by methods other than hunting with weapons, that is, by snaring and collecting, and we find that it is often old men, children, and women who bring this meat back to camp. Women at Kutse set traps for small game and collect small creatures. Thus Basarwa men are not the only meat providers and, by the same token, Basarwa women are not the only plant food providers. Out of 116 person-days of gathering, 21.5 were performed by Ju/'hoansi men (Lee 1979:262).

Among the Inupiat, women are regarded as more important to the hunting process than men, even where their contribution is restricted to sewing items that are needed for the hunt. Given this wealth of evidence it is clear that the interpretation of women as nonhunters or as exclusively plant providers is largely a western construct and has little to do with hunter-gatherer perceptions. There is a tendency for westerners to define hunting as exclusively the killing of large game with weapons such as bow and arrow or spear, but many hunter-gatherer societies regard the meat quest in a broader light (Casey, Chapter 5; Kent, Chapters 1, 3).

The hunter-gatherer ethnography described here displays considerable variability in the details of gender relationships, and it is clear that change has occurred this century, not only in hunting techniques employed, but also in the organization of labor. While the modern hunter-gatherer change has been fueled by, for example, contact with pastoralists, farmers, white settlers, and merchants, there is no reason to believe that change and variability were not also features of Stone Age life. Indeed, there may even have been a greater range of gender relationships in the past than there is at present (Paynter 1989:385); and it is possible that social complexity was greater in the Stone Age before hunter-gatherer societies became marginalized and fragmented (Schrire 1984b).

Meat Providers in the Stone Age of Southern Africa

Southern African Stone Age people seem to have hunted more large than small game during the Pleistocene because sites dated to this time period have high frequency percentages of bone from large, gregarious, mobile grazers. The hunters would thus have been tied to the seasonal migrations of plains game whose movements would have been controlled by the quality of the grazing (Deacon 1976:116). In contrast, many sites post-dating 10,000 BP, particularly in the Eastern Cape, are dominated by small, shy, nocturnal, territorial browsers that can be snared more effectively than hunted (Deacon 1984:256). In addition, the more recent sites have a wider range of prey than before, including birds and dangerous animals. Melkhoutboom and Boomplaas caves (Figure 4.1) are good examples of the change from grazing to browsing antelope: grazers such as hartebeest, wildebeest, and buffalo, and mixed feeders such as eland, were hunted extensively before 10,000 BP, but thereafter

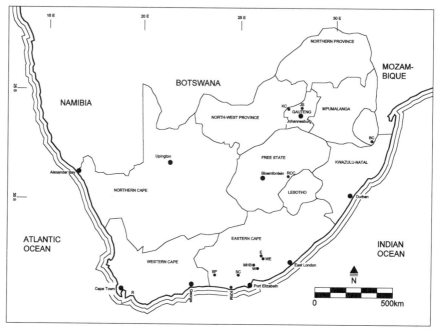

Figure 4.1. Southern African sites mentioned in the text. BC: Border Cave; BP: Boomplaas; E: Edgehill; JS: Jubilee Shelter; KC: Kruger Cave; KRM: Klasies River Mouth; MHB: Melkhoutboom; RCC: Rose Cottage Cave; W: Wilton; WE: Welgeluk.

proportions of large grazers declined in favor of small antelope such as grysbok, steenbok, and duiker (Deacon 1976; 1984).

It is generally assumed that big-game hunters who used a Middle Stone Age (MSA) technology (predating about 22,000 BP) used spears that were either stone-tipped or made of wood or bone. Triangular flakes and unifacially or bifacially retouched points are thought to have been hafted for use as spearheads. By about 22,000 BP all traces of MSA industries disappeared throughout southern Africa (Wadley 1993), and they were succeeded by Later Stone Age (LSA) assemblages, some of which were microlithic and bladelet-rich. Although no LSA tools look like spearheads, it is possible that the people of the bladelet-rich Robberg Industry hafted bladelets to form composite barbed spearheads (Mitchell 1988) and that spear hunting continued unabated. Between about 12,000 BP and 11,000 BP the microlithic Robberg Industry gave way to the macrolithic Oakhurst Industrial Complex, which appears to contain no stone tools suitable for use as either spearheads or arrowheads. However, sites from this period contain bone points similar to those used by both Ju/'hoansi and other southern African hunters as arrowheads and linkshafts. Regular arrow hunting may, therefore, date to this time period.

Although bone points are not common anywhere until after 10,000 BP, they were invented considerably earlier. A few bone points were found in the 38,000 BP levels of Border Cave (Beaumont 1978) (Figure 4.1) and in the 21,000 BP levels of Boomplaas Cave (Deacon 1984b:292), and a single enigmatic bone point was found in a Middle Stone Age context predating 60,000 BP in Klasies River Mouth (Singer and Wymer 1982) (Figure 4.1). Thus arrow hunting may have been known for tens of thousands of years, but it was not popular initially and probably did not alter the traditional pattern of spear hunting for large game. The change to hunting small browsers at approximately 10,000 BP cannot, therefore, be linked to the moment of the invention of the arrow. If technological invention influenced the change, then the invention may have been in the form of the modest snare-line trap because it seems possible that the small, territorial browsers were more often snared than hunted (Deacon 1976; Klein 1981). It is easier to trap shy, nocturnal, solitary antelope than to stalk them in wooded areas. It seems likely that people were using snares for hunting small browsers such as steenbok, grysbok, and gray duiker because snaring is most likely to have resulted in the catastrophic mortality rates (where prime-age adults were killed in about the same proportions as they occur in live herds) seen in faunal assemblages (Klein 1981:62). Klein thinks that Middle Stone Age people may also have used traps because the Middle Stone Age browser samples, though small, also have a catastrophic mortality profile. Thus both arrow hunting and snaring may have had their origin in the Middle Stone Age.

At Melkhoutboom the relative quantity of unworked bone fragments to stone artifacts is not constant throughout the sequence; more bone relative to stone is present in the later Pleistocene (Deacon 1976:110), and this trend is also apparent at other southern African sites. Therefore, the post-10,000 BP popularity of bow and arrow, and the targeting of small antelope, does not seem to have increased the amount of meat brought back to camp sites. The shift to hunting small browsers may, however, have been beneficial in other ways. Since the browsers live in fixed territories that do not change seasonally, they can be hunted or trapped anywhere at any time of year, in contrast to the migratory, grassland animals (Deacon 1984b:256). This may mean that smaller meat packages were obtained more reliably and regularly than when mobile herds were followed. Furthermore, when the hunters set traps close to home, they brought the game to them. The reverse is necessary for arrow or spear hunting. When hunters were freed from following game migrations, people could schedule their movements to take advantage of plant food seasonality. Deacon's (1976) work in eastern Cape sites suggests that, indeed, plant food staples rather than game movements dictated seasonal mobility after 10,000 BP. At Melkhoutboom the underground corm of the Watsonia appears to have been the plant staple, and Deacon (1976:105) suggests that the seasonal mobility of the Cape Folded Belt populations was closely tied to Watsonia ecology.

If gender relationships in the Late Stone Age bore any relationship to those of the Ju/'hoansi in the Kalahari, then it is possible that after 10,000 BP the new importance allocated to plant seasonality gave women a large measure of control over band mobility. Conversely, band mobility may have been tied to the migrations of large game during the Pleistocene, and this may have meant that women had less control than men over band mobility before 10,000 BP. Of course this assumption is based on the premise that only men were involved in the spear hunting of the large game, an assumption that may be entirely without foundation. Today, Basarwa women do not take part in spear hunts, though these modern spear hunts probably bear little resemblance to those of the Pleistocene. Today spears are made of metal and the hunts are often conducted with the aid of dogs or from horseback. Such accoutrement enable men to hunt alone or in small groups. No dogs are present in any Stone Age sites, nor did dogs appear in southern Africa before about 400 AD (Plug 1996, personal communication), thus people in the Pleistocene did not have access to metal, dogs, and horses. Spear hunting is thus likely to have relied on large group size for game drives. Pleistocene people may have conducted themselves rather like the Ju/'hoansi in the elephant hunt described by Lee, or perhaps like the Mbuti net hunters. Mbuti band size averages between 50 and 60 people, which allows efficient net hunting by 10 or 11 men carrying spears and nets and a similar number of women who drive the game (Ichikawa 1983). Mbuti cannot have dispersal camps with fewer than 20 adults because this is the minimum number needed to hunt effectively. If a male-only hunting party was employed for net hunting, a band size of well over 100 would have been a requirement. Presumably spear hunters not using nets would have needed even more personnel than the Mbuti, and it seems unlikely that nets would have been employed in the Pleistocene spear hunts of southern Africa. Although plant fiber cordage is present in several Late Stone Age sites (Deacon 1984b:292), no netting has been found in Pleistocene sites, even where organic preservation is good. Thus women are likely to have been employed in the spear hunt for at least part of the year because, judging by the size of southern African caves and shelters occupied during the Pleistocene, band size is unlikely to have been larger than modern Mbuti band size. The size of the cave and shelter sites with later Pleistocene deposit provides some indication of demography, because several of these sites could house up to 50 or 60 people; some of the sites, however, would not have accommodated more than about 30 people. It is therefore difficult to see how the people occupying these shelters could have organized drives and spear hunts for large game without using women's labor.

Participation in the hunt seems to ensure that women can claim rights over a portion of the hunted meat. If women were present at the hunt in the Pleistocene, they may have had a better share of meat than if they remained at home and waited for meat to be brought back to them. The principle that women present at the hunt get a better share of meat than those who wait at home can be illustrated by the Mbuti and Ju/'hoansi examples that I have already mentioned. Mbuti women who have participated in the hunt, and who have carried their husband's game back to camp, receive a forequarter of the animal in the first round of meat distribution

(Ichikawa 1983:69). In Ju/'hoansi society, however, where women do not take part in arrow hunting, it is only male hunters who receive meat in the first round of sharing. It seems, then, that the Mbuti woman's share symbolizes her partnership in the hunt. Hunter-gatherer women in the Pleistocene may have found themselves in a similar position to Mbuti women and they may therefore have had more of a share in large game meat than modern Ju/'hoansi women.

Food sharing that is equitable or otherwise can sometimes be detected through the stable carbon isotope composition of human bone collagen. Unfortunately, skeletal samples are not abundant enough in the Pleistocene to make a study of gender similarities or differences in diet. Holocene skeletons are, however, far more abundant, and Sealy's study of 74 Western Cape skeletons, most of which post-dated 3000 BP, shows unequal access to resources, based on gender (Sealy 1992; Sealy et al. 1992). The pre-3000 BP skeletons display few gender differences, but in the post-3000 BP sample the stable carbon isotope composition of the human bone collagen suggests that, while female skeletons were similar to those of their pre-3000 BP predecessors, on the whole male skeletons had more positive ^{13}C values. This implies that after 3000 BP men's diet was enriched with marine foods, for example, seal meat and fish. Sealy's study implies that women consumed less marine food than men but more terrestrial food (presumably plants but possibly terrestrial animals). After about 3000 BP, men seem to have eaten a considerable amount of food away from the home base, and sex-segregated work parties may have become the norm. Parkington (Chapter 2) suggests that the change in men's diet coincided with the establishment of "megamiddens" of marine shells between 3000 and 2000 BP. It may then be unwise to assume (as many archaeologists do—for examples see Barich, Chapter 6) that the gathering of shellfish was always women's work.

Of great interest is the chronological difference in the skeletal evidence; the gender similarity in the small pre-3000 BP sample suggests that gender relationships in the Western Cape may have changed only after about 3000 BP. This is an important observation, showing that archaeologists must not expect gender relationships to remain static through time, and that they should also anticipate regional differences in social behavior.

Social, including gender, relationships may also have been affected by other changes that took place at the beginning of the Holocene and during it. Demographic change is evident in the early Holocene (Wadley 1993). It is implied by a noticeable increase in the occupation of caves and rockshelters. By about 10,000 BP many rockshelters that can hold no more than 10 to 15 people were occupied, and thus a demographic shift to smaller bands of higher densities is inferred (Deacon 1976:163). By 3000 BP the groups seem even smaller and the density even higher because many more tiny shelters are occupied (Deacon 1984b:232–236, 322). A few large sites were, however, still occupied and these may have represented occasional aggregation camps. Large-scale aggregations may have taken place only a few times in a decade (Wadley 1987), and under such circumstances it may have been impossible to spear hunt in large groups as a regular means of obtaining meat. Arrow hunting, however, relies more on stealth and aim than on large group cooperation and may be effectively conducted by individuals or small groups. Thus the social and demographic changes after 10,000 years ago in southern Africa may have promoted the greater popularity of arrow hunting and snaring. Large frequencies of bone points in sites post-dating 10,000 years ago (Deacon 1984b) do indeed suggest that arrows were in regular and frequent use by this time.

In some ways the shift to individual or small group hunting with bow and arrow or snares involved a shift to individual or family-based "ownership" of meat products. On the one hand, this may have adversely affected women's access to game meat if, as among modern Ju/'hoansi, women were excluded from the hunt. On the other hand, the Agta, Tiwi, and Chipewyan examples suggest that women may have been hunting in their own right.

Individual "ownership" of meat products by either men or women after 10,000 years ago would have necessitated reorganization of the sharing rules that applied during the Pleistocene. In some of the post-10,000-year-old levels in Rose Cottage Cave, in the eastern Free State of South Africa, the spatial distribution around several hearths of animal bone from, for example, springbok and warthog suggests that the modern Basarwa practice of sharing large game with everyone in a camp may also have existed (Wadley in press b). Interestingly, the same type of widespread distribution may also apply to the bones of Procavia capensis, the small rock hyrax that, today, would not be shared in a Ju/'hoansi camp. At Kutse, however, small creatures may be shared by less successful Basarwa hunters who wish to maintain a sharing bond but have nothing else to contribute (Kent 1996b:151). As happens today, we may imagine that hunter-gatherer women in the Stone Age were also active trappers and collectors of small animals, so many of the faunal remains in the Stone Age sites may have been contributed by women. Consequently, the women probably butchered and shared these meat provisions with their immediate families and perhaps also with other band members.

Other important changes are apparent in the South African archaeological record between 4000 and 3000 BP. The changes include the appearance of broad-spectrum gathering and an increase in the frequencies of ornaments, elaborate burials, and portable and parietal art (Deacon 1984b) that often displays shamanistic imagery (Lewis-Williams 1984). The broad-spectrum gathering included increased plant food gathering in several areas, as well as the harvesting of quantities of small creatures such as crabs, toads, lizards, and freshwater shellfish. Marine crustaceans were collected from southern African coastal sites as far back as the MSA, but freshwater shellfish and other aquatic creatures appear in quantities only after about 4000 BP in Stone Age sites in the middle Orange River area, the Eastern Cape, the Northern Cape, eastern Free State, and Gauteng (Deacon 1984b).

In the Eastern Cape sites of Wilton, Scott's Cave, and Melkhoutboom, frequencies of freshwater mussels increased in the topmost deposits at about 2000 BP (Deacon

1976). In other Eastern Cape sites, Welgeluk, and Edgehill, freshwater mussels, fish, and tortoise increased much earlier, at about 4000 BP (S. Hall 1990:88–98).

At Jubilee Shelter, in Gauteng, shellfish became prolific after 3000 BP (Wadley 1987:117), and at Kruger Cave, also in Gauteng, extensive shellfish middens post-dated 1300 BP (Mason 1988).

Archaeologists' explanations for the appearance of gathered shellfish and aquatic creatures vary, though most discount the role of environmental change (Deacon 1976:52; S. Hall 1990). Parkington (1980:83) sees higher population density as necessitating a general trend toward broad-spectrum gathering. Deacon elaborates this idea, suggesting that fish and molluscs were a food supplement for hunter-gatherers inland and that their collection may have been stimulated by local adjustments in group territories and annual movements, as a result of the influx of pastoralists and Iron Age people and the consequent demographic changes (Deacon 1984b:265). The Welgeluk, Edgehill, and Jubilee Shelter evidence suggests, however, that the contact situation with pastoralists and farmers should not be emphasized, because the broad-spectrum gathering was under way before their arrival.

It is difficult to gauge whether the broad-spectrum gathering preceded or post-dated the population increase. From my own theoretical standpoint, I favor a social stimulus for such gathering. As I pointed out earlier, the broad-spectrum gathering is accompanied by a florescence of activities that are related to shamanistic practices. Among the Ju/'hoansi anyone may become a shaman, but experienced and aged shamans seem to have been particularly respected (Katz 1982). A desire for the longevity of valued shamans may have prompted the gathering of foods that would particularly benefit the aged. Shellfish would fulfill such a need. Shellfish are protein-rich and can be a supplement or substitute for meat; the soft shellfish "meat" is a particularly valuable source of protein for the aged (and the young) who might have difficulty chewing hard meat (Claassen 1991:279). On the one hand, then, the apparent population increase after 4000 BP may be linked to an increased life expectancy of the aged and the very young through a better diet than in previous times. On the other hand, the shellfish may have provided better diets for all age groups of the population: shellfish and fish caught in winter have high fat contents and this fat would have assisted with the metabolism of lean game meat. African game is particularly lean in the winter months, and protein from this meat cannot be metabolized in the absence of carbohydrate or fat (Speth and Spielmann 1983). As Gifford-Gonzalez points out in Chapter 7, a shortage of fat and carbohydrate may have limited hunter-gatherers' reproductive success. The consumption of freshwater mussels may, then, have improved women's diets with the result that there was a positive effect on hunter-gatherer birthrates.

Shellfish were probably collected in winter (S. Hall 1990). In the summer rainfall areas this would also be the dry time when most hunting and snaring were undertaken to prevent summer dew and rain from ruining the effectiveness of hunting equipment. Shellfishing would therefore compete with hunting and snaring time; in other words, it was being carried out when protein supplies were at their highest, not their lowest. Consequently it is unlikely that shellfish were regularly gathered by hunters, though they could have been gathered by snare-line operators whose time was less constrained. This means that shellfish could have been gathered by both men and women.

Among many hunter-gatherer groups the collection of shellfish usually forms part of the food package brought home by women (Murdock and Provost 1973:207), but we presently have no means of knowing the gender identity of the shellfish gatherers in the southern African Stone Age. When women who are normally plant-food gatherers begin collecting shellfish, we need to know whether tasks were reallocated or rescheduled, whether some form of specialization developed, or whether the women were simply working harder (Claassen 1991:277). If women were working harder, this could imply that they were supporting intensified male sociopolitical activities (Collier and Rosaldo 1981; Hastorf 1991:148) or that they were establishing some independence from the hunters on whom they depended for meat. If the gathering of shellfish was a form of resistance, then we must assume that some type of social change took place between 4000 and 3000 BP, and that this involved greater gender segregation and less meat sharing outside the group of hunters than was previously the case. This is a possible interpretation because, as I have already shown, skeletal evidence suggests that western Cape people were far more gender-segregated after than before about 3000 BP. Perhaps gender segregation also intensified in other parts of southern Africa in the last few thousand years.

In sites such as Rose Cottage Cave and Jubilee Shelter there are discrete activity areas for bead making, bone point manufacture, stone tool knapping, and plant food processing. Such areas may represent the type of gender-segregated work parties that are evident in Ju/'hoansi aggregation camps, but it is necessary to approach such interpretations with extreme caution. As Dobres (1996, personal communication) points out, it is unwise to make assumptions about gender attribution in the past, and I have already shown that gendered stereotypes of hunters and gatherers are inappropriate.

Dobres's circumspection is well founded, as the preliminary study of lithics at Rose Cottage Cave shows. A residue analysis of stone tools (Williamson 1996) has revealed that both blood and plant residues are frequently present on a single stone flake. This suggests that a sole person might be involved with both meat butchery and plant food processing. Further archaeological support for this type of behavior comes from the microwear analysis of stone segments from Jubilee Shelter in the Magaliesberg of Gauteng (Wadley and Binneman 1995). Segments have long been assumed to have been arrowheads, particularly because, in Egypt, segments were found mounted as part of projectile heads (Clark et al. 1974). The Jubilee Shelter segments contain only plant polish on their cutting edges, suggesting that while they may have been used as arrowheads on occasions, they were not exclusively used as such. Of course the presence of the plant polish does not imply that the tools were not used by men, but it does suggest that no secure gender attribution can be made.

We should not assume from these examples that women merely borrowed men's tools without ever making their own. Gero (1991) has convincingly argued that Stone Age women are unlikely to have waited passively for men to produce tools for them and that they are most likely to have produced their own flakes. In Rose Cottage Cave it is not possible to identify the gender of the stone knappers, yet the spatial evidence tends to support Gero's claim (Wadley in press a, in press b). Stone flakes have diffuse distribution across the excavation grid in many of the occupation levels, suggesting that flakes were used for many activities in many places. With such a distribution it seems most likely that both women and men were using the flakes. Not all archaeologists are equally optimistic about the possibility of recognizing gender in the spatial patterns of Late Stone Age sites (for example, Kent, Chapter 3), but Casey's conclusions (Chapter 5) are similar to my own. She notes that "basic tools" have wide spatial distribution in FKWMH, Ghana, and are likely to have been used by both men and women (Chapter 5).

Conclusion

In this brief paper I have shown that a diverse array of gender systems may have operated in the past. Of significance for archaeologists is the conclusion that hunter-gatherer gender relations were as open to change in the past as they are today. The well-worn labels "woman the plant food gatherer," "man the hunter," and "man the meat provider" are not appropriate for the Stone Age any more than they are appropriate for modern hunter-gatherers. Such gender stereotypes mask the subtleties of gender relations, render women almost invisible in the Stone Age, deny that they could ever have participated in the hunt, and imply that they played a timeless, unchanging role. The evidence presented here suggests that women's and men's roles may have changed in the past, and that, where inequalities existed between Stone Age men and women, these are unlikely to have been accepted passively. What is most important is to realize that Stone Age social and gender arrangements were not static and that ethnographically recorded examples of the male-oriented hunt, with their associated ritual and strict meat-sharing rules, should not be seen as an immutable model for the Stone Age.

Acknowledgments

I thank Bonny Williamson for the residue analysis of the Rose Cottage Cave tools and Kim Sales for drawing Figure 4.1. I am also most grateful to Sue Kent, Simon Hall, and Marcia-Anne Dobres for useful discussions. I am particularly grateful to Sue Kent for all the information she provided on the people of Kutse.

JOANNA CASEY ∎

Chapter Five

Just a Formality

The Presence of Fancy Projectile Points in a Basic Tool Assemblage

This paper looks at the lithic technology of the Kintampo Complex, a Ceramic Late Stone Age complex that existed in Ghana, West Africa, around 3,500 years ago. The Kintampo Complex is characterized by a lithic technology based primarily, but not exclusively, on the bipolar production of basic (that is, expedient or informal) tools. Basic tool assemblages become common throughout the world at the end of the Pleistocene and are coincident with sedentary lifestyles, broadened resource bases, and/or domestication. Several recent papers have sought to explain the increasing importance of basic toolkits with decreasing mobility (Gero 1991; Parry and Kelly 1987; Sassaman 1992; Torrence 1989). Gender has played a part in all of these explanations, by relating the change to a shift in male activities such as hunting (Parry and Kelly 1989; Torrence 1989; Sassaman 1992) or by highlighting the increased visibility of women's activities in sedentary communities (Gero 1991). Data from a series of Kintampo sites in northern Ghana shed new light on the issue by demonstrating that the production and use of basic tools was not the exclusive preserve of either men or women and that the high proportion of basic tools in post-Pleistocene archaeological sites indicates not so much a rise in basic tool production as a reduction in the production of highly formal tool types. Basic tools can perform virtually all the same functional duties as formal tools, so what needs to be explained is why people would devote time, labor, and resources to making elaborately worked tools that may not function any more efficiently than less ostentatious ones. With sedentism, relationships between groups of people change, and it is suggested here that the new combinations of basic and formal tools found in the sites of sedentary peoples may be expressing these new social relationships. Men and women have different opportunities for expression, and these, too, are reflected in the archaeological record.

Basic Tools and Archaeological Sites

My use of the term "basic" tools as an alternative to the terms "expedient," "unstandardized," or "informal" tools is an attempt to get away from the notion that formal, bifacially flaked tools are the only legitimate tool type, and that their presence in archaeological sites requires solely analysis, not explanation (Casey 1993). Unmodified pieces of stone have much sharper edges than formal, bifacially flaked stone tools, are much more quickly and easily produced, and can perform most of the functions of formal tools (Hayden 1977), yet their presence in archaeological sites most often goes unnoticed or unremarked, and seems to inspire a search for explanation rather than analysis (when they are mentioned at all). Any discussion of basic tools is usually couched in negative terms, as though these tools are the ugly stepsister of "normal" tools such as bifaces (Kleindienst 1992). In contrast, the study of bifaces and other formal tool types has been raised to an almost fetishistic level (Gero 1991; Hayden 1977) and as a consequence has masked other important issues that also may find expression in the archaeological record.

Highly formalized bifacial tools have long been associated with hunting and warfare, and therefore with male activities. An emphasis on analyzing formal tools in archaeological assemblages consequently ignores female behavior and renders women invisible in the archaeological record. Only recently have archaeologists started to consider women as agents of stone tool manufacture and use. A recent interest in basic tools has suddenly opened the discussion of lithic technology to include women, but often with the insidious suggestion that while men make precision instruments, women make (or use) expedient items out of substandard local materials or flakes scavenged from the debris left from the male makers of formal tools (Sassaman 1992). The implication is clearly that if women are ever agents of stone tool manufacture, they are merely passive (or untalented) agents.

Four recent papers have attempted to explain the increased significance of basic tools in early sedentary archaeological sites. Torrence (1989) suggests that the "devolution" of lithic assemblages associated with domestication came about owing to a reduction in the short-term risks associated with hunting. She suggests that hunting is a high-risk strategy that requires a reliable set of tools, but that domestication and resource management reduce these short-term risks, with the result that "expedient" tools were adequate for the job at hand. Parry and Kelly (1987) note that where lithic raw materials are plentiful, basic tool assemblages predominate. They suggest that formal tools that can be resharpened and reworked will be made when people have difficulty gaining access to good lithic raw material, either because they are highly mobile and are frequently out of range of the source, or because they have settled far from it and have to rely on long-distance trade or travel to obtain it. Makers of basic tools, by contrast, live near to sources of good lithic raw material, or travel there sufficiently often that material can be stockpiled and utilized expediently. Gero's (1991) data from highland Peru indicate that basic tools become more common as domestic contexts, and hence women's activities, become more visible in the archaeological record. Her data chart a change through time, from ceremonial contexts where formal tools are made from exotic raw materials, to domestic contexts where flake tools made from local materials predominate. Sassaman (1992) suggests that with increasing sedentism, men spent more time in the settlements making and repairing their tools. At the same time, a broad-spectrum economy increased women's need for tools that they could obtain by scavenging waste flakes from men's flint-knapping activities, as well as by using locally available raw materials.

All four of these models indicate that basic tools are adequate to the tasks that settled peoples perform. Parry and Kelly (1987) explicitly regard basic tools as being the most desirable tool form overall, while Sassaman (1992) and Torrence (1989) regard basic tools as being adequate for women and adequate for settled peoples, respectively.

But if basic tools are functionally adequate for most purposes, why does the manufacture of highly elaborated bifaces persist in assemblages that are otherwise devoid of formal tools? I believe that the answer has to do with relationships between settled groups of people and the mobility of male hunters, which should be clarified by analyzing the place of basic and formal tools in the economy of the Kintampo peoples in northern Ghana. First, I will demonstrate that the entire technology of the Kintampo peoples is oriented toward the production of basic tools, and that the production of bifaces is only a minor component of that technology. Next, I will demonstrate that basic tools are used preferentially by all members of the society. There appear to be very few situations where specialized chipped stone equipment is necessary, and these needs are easily met by the production of semiformal tools that are produced identically to the informal tool types. I will also discuss the place of hunting in the settled, subsistence agricultural regime, showing that the needs for wild animal protein do not diminish with sedentism, nor with the addition of minimal numbers of small livestock. Finally, I will speculate on why the production of formal tools persists, even though most practical needs are easily met with basic tools. Whereas the models chart a change through time, the data represent a point in time. However, the data are capable of demonstrating the place of basic and formal tool technologies in the context of a settled prehistoric complex.

The Kintampo Complex

Some 40 or 50 Kintampo sites are known from Ghana, primarily from the center of the country in the savanna and forest ecotone. Kintampo assemblages are characterized by pottery, groundstone tools, grinding stones, and evidence for permanent or semipermanent structures. They may also contain worked stone projectile points; geometric microliths; bored, grooved, and pitted stones; stone beads; stone arm bands; and chips of quartz and siliceous mudstone, usually reduced by bipolar percussion. In rare instances, bone harpoons have also been found. The most diagnostic artifact of the Kintampo Complex is the "Terra Cotta Cigar," a flattened, elliptical object made of stone or clay. They are often scored, sometimes bored and abraded, and virtually always broken, but no function has been determined for them. They do not appear to have ever been made by anyone other than the Kintampo people, to whom they were obviously very important because they are found in profusion at virtually every Kintampo site. The material culture of the Kintampo peoples points to a settled, horticultural lifeway, but little is known about their subsistence base. Organic remains have been found at only two Kintampo sites (Carter and Flight 1972; Davies 1980; Stahl 1985a,b), but only at one of these were they recovered systematically. Domestic sheep or goat have been confirmed at both of these sites, but the analysis of plant remains has thus far produced no evidence of cultigens. The most intensive treatment of the Kintampo subsistence base is at K6 Rockshelter (Stahl 1985a,b). Here a change through time from deep forest faunal species to commensal species and those that prefer open and cleared land seems to indicate a change to the environment and the scheduling of human activities due to stock raising and land clearing for cultivation. Radiocarbon dates have been determined for only seven Kintampo sites (Stahl 1985a,b; Kense 1992), and while they range from more than 4000 BP to less than 3000 BP, they tend to cluster between 3000 and 3500 BP.

The focus of this study is the Gambaga Escarpment in northern Ghana, the location of the most northerly Kintampo sites yet known. During surveys in 1987, five large Kintampo sites, plus numerous small, random scatters of quartz and mudstone that are undoubtedly attributable to the Kintampo Complex, were identified north of the villages of Gambaga and Nalerigu (Figure 5.1). Test excavations were undertaken in 1987, followed by full-scale excavations in 1988 and 1996. The material from 1987 and 1988 has been fully analyzed (Casey 1993) but the material from the 1996 excavations has not. The 1996 excavations concentrated on the Birimi Site (BM) to the northwest of Nalerigu, a site that had only barely been tested in 1988. This site is the largest and most intact of any Kintampo site yet known. It has the potential to more fully answer many of the questions that have been raised about Kintampo, in this paper and elsewhere. I will use some of the data from this site as corroborating evidence for the trends that are visible in the other Kintampo sites, though, unfortunately, full quantitative data are not yet available.

Basic Tool Manufacture and Use

Table 5.1 lists the total cultural material from the 1988 excavations. The vast majority of the lithic material was chips of siliceous mudstone and quartz, some of which had obvious evidence of use. The Gambaga Escarpment upon which the site is located marks the northern edge of the Voltaian Formation, a massive geological formation of bedded sandstones and mudstones. The mudstone found at the sites is a silicified variety that outcrops some 20 km away from Fulani Kuliga (Pavilish et al. 1989). No closer sources have yet been found. Quartz is found at the bottom of the escarpment. Because neither rock type is found anywhere near the sites, it can be assumed that every piece was brought there by human agency.

The method of lithic reduction of the Kintampo people is bipolar technology where a nucleus of raw material is rested on a firm surface and struck from above with

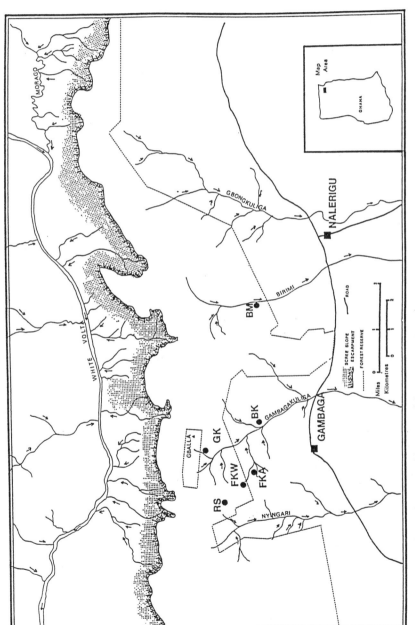

Figure 5.1. Map of the study area and location of the sites investigated.

an impactor. Although bipolar technology is known from the Lower Paleolithic at Olduvai Gorge (Leakey 1971) to the ethnographic present (Brandt et al. 1992; Hayden 1973; Strathern 1969; White 1968) and from all continents where evidence for human occupation has been found, it is still regarded with suspicion by many lithic analysts who view it as being an inferior technique that produces pieces with "undesirable attributes" (Patterson and Sollberger 1976:41). This, of course, assumes that the lithic analyst can know the "desires" of the prehistoric flintknapper. Ethnographic examples indicate that the objective of bipolar technology is to quickly reduce a chunk of rock into a variety of pieces, and then to pick out the ones with useful edges for immediate use (Masao 1982:265; McCalman and Grobelaar 1965:12; Sillitoe 1982:35), and this appears to be borne out in the archaeological record. Bipolar technology, and consequently the purposeful production of basic tools, is often overlooked in the archaeological record because many analysts accept only the presence of classic "bipolar flakes" that show crushing on both ends, and *Pièces Esquillées*, which are wedge-shaped, battered pieces often associated with bipolar assemblages, as evidence of bipolar reduction. These items can be byproducts of bipolar reduction, but they are not always produced, nor are they necessarily the objective of bipolar reduction (Casey 1993). A more profitable way of viewing bipolar technology, or any other technology oriented toward the production of basic tools, is to define it by the actual operation or activity, not by any conception of what the desired end product may have been (Haynes 1977:5). Assemblages that contain large amounts of amorphous shatter with little evidence for formal tool production are likely oriented toward the production of unmodified basic tools.

The vast majority of lithic material at virtually all Kintampo sites is quartz (over 75 percent) that comes from the bottom of the escarpment some 5 km away. At present, there is no reliable way of identifying use-wear on grainy quartz using the low-power approach—the only practical method of analyzing large quantities of lithic material (Flenniken 1981; Odell 1979; Odell and Odell-Vereecken 1980; Shea 1988; Sussman 1988a,b; Tomenchuk 1983, 1985). I restricted the identification and analysis of use-wear to the mudstone materials where it could be more easily and positively identified. It should also be noted that the only basic tools that can be identified are those where use has left some traces on the edge of the piece. Activities that use an edge repeatedly or involve resistant materials that chip, blunt, or leave striations on edges will be recognized while those used only once, or against soft materials, will not. This is a huge source of bias in the archaeological record because the number of identified basic tools is undoubtedly only a fraction of the number of unmodified pieces that were used throughout the lifetime of the site. The absence of formal tools to perform most cutting, piercing, incising, and scraping functions would seem to argue strongly for basic tool technology's being the primary technology of the people at these sites. A total of 286 pieces had been recognizably used, and many of these had more than one used edge.

Site	Mudstone Total	Mudstone Microliths	Mudstone Points	Mudstone Basic Tools	Quartz Total	Quartz Microliths	Quartz Ground	Sandstone Ground	Greenstone Ground	Ceramics Total	Grand Total	Percent
FKWMH	1681	78	2	145	8793	5	9	37	62	1267	11840	69.33
FKW 2	23	0	1	8	12	0	0	2	1	5	43	0.25
FKW 3	33	0	1	12	12	0	0	16	34	1	96	0.56
FKW 4	14	0	2	7	13	0	0	7	9	1	44	0.26
FKW 5	30	0	0	11	38	0	0	3	18	35	124	0.73
FKA 6	48	0	0	20	174	0	0	10	8	24	264	1.55
FKA 7	99	3	0	36	107	0	0	4	8	34	252	1.48
FKA 8-10	2	0	0	2	43	1	0	3	6	1	55	0.32
GK1-8	158	2	0	6	1402	10	0	6	9	4	1579	9.25
BM	98	0	0	27	136	0	0	4	3	43	267	1.56
RS	339	3	0	12	2141	26	0	1	0	33	2514	14.72
TOTAL	2508	86	6	286	12871	42	9	93	158	1448	17078	100

Table 5.1. Total cultural material of the Gambaga sites (1989) (raw counts).

Among the advantages of bipolar technology is that it can break up very small pieces of lithic raw material that could not be knapped freehand (Crabtree 1972; Flenniken 1981).

The presence of large numbers of broken quartz pebble fragments and the few large pieces of mudstone found at any of the sites seems to suggest strongly that bipolar basic tools were the only option available to the Kintampo peoples, perhaps because of a lack of sufficiently large-sized raw material; but the recent discovery of a Middle Stone Age component to the Birimi Site (Hawkins et al. 1997) seems to refute this. The Middle Stone Age material, though heavily patinated, is siliceous mudstone, probably from the same source as the Kintampo material. Today, mudstone is a commercial resource used to make gun flints and strike-a-lights (consisting of a piece of flint, a piece of steel, and a piece of flammable material), and the source to which we were directed is the only one in the area known to produce high-grade mudstone. Patinated Middle Stone Age pieces occur in profusion on the site in all stages of production, suggesting that the source of the raw material was close enough for the workers to have made regular trips there. In contrast to the Kintampo peoples, the Middle Stone Age people were selecting large pieces of mudstone to produce prepared cores, bifaces, and Levallois flakes and blades. At some Kintampo sites, the presence of random Middle Stone Age pieces indicates that the Kintampo peoples were mining the Middle Stone Age sites for raw material, and further reducing it to suit their own needs. The Kintampo people were clearly not making basic tools because of a raw material restriction.

Another possibility for the Kintampo peoples' reliance on basic tools is that they did not possess the technology or the need to make bifacially flaked stone tools. The presence of projectile point fragments at the sites indicates that this is likely not so. Kintampo projectiles are flaked and/or ground and they come in a variety of styles, from small, triangular ones with concave bases to long, delicately flaked and serrated ones with rounded bases (Figure 5.2). Theoretically, they could have been received in trade, or scavenged from Saharan sites whose points they strongly resemble (Davies 1966:30, 1980:216; Flight 1976:219), but the presence of broken preforms, points, and flaking debris in association at the Birimi Site clearly indicates that at least some of the Kintampo people possessed the knowledge for bifacial production, and manu-factured their own points rather than receiving them in trade from elsewhere.

Since virtually the entire technology is oriented toward the production of basic tools, there was no restriction on the size of raw materials, and the skills for producing formal tools were present and being used under special circumstances, these factors seem to indicate that the emphasis on basic tools was a choice for the Kintampo peoples and not something that they were forced into because of circumstances. The next question that needs to be addressed is, who were the users of the basic tools? Sassaman (1992) and Gero (1991) suggest that women primarily, but not exclusively, make and use basic tools, and that such use becomes evident in the archeological record either because women's needs and the ability to fulfill them have increased, or

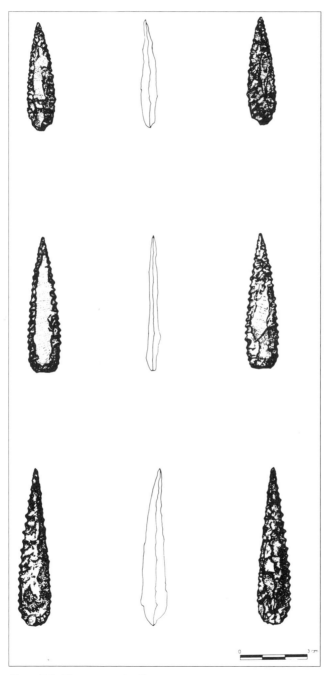

Figure 5.2. Kintampo projectiles.

because with sedentism and the identification of domestic contexts they have suddenly become visible in the archaeological record.

Discrete loci of human activity were evident at only one of the sites that have been analyzed. Fulani Kuliga West Main Hill (FKWMH) is a sandstone outcrop of approximately 70×20 m. This is a section of the site I have termed Fulani Kuliga West (FKW), which appears to have been a very large site that over the years became exposed and eroded—a biased sample of which is found in the deep, unstratified deposits downstream at FKA. FKWMH appears to have escaped the severe erosion by virtue of the fact that the outcrop on which it sits is level and solid, while around the outcrop the land has considerable gradient and consists of sandy silts. Evidence for the integrity of the site exists primarily in the presence of lithic materials of every size range—from large grinding stones to tiny stone chips.

Visible on the surface of FKWMH are concentrations of sandstone often accompanied by daga (chunks of burned clay with the impressions of sticks and poles in them). Such concentrations are not uncommon in Kintampo sites (Anquandah 1976; Davies 1967, 1980; Dombrowski 1976, 1980; Stahl 1985a) and are thought to represent the remains of structural features, the foundations of which have sometimes been recovered (Dombrowski 1976, 1980). The integrity of the structures at FKWMH have been lost, so their actual shape and size is not known. Apart from a few ceramic sherds that appear to be very recent, nothing at the site suggests that it was occupied by anyone other than Kintampo peoples. No materials for dating were obtained from the site, though the affiliation is clearly Kintampo on the basis of the artifacts.

A test unit excavated in FKWMH indicated that a maximum of 36 cm of deposit covered the outcrop, with the actual bedrock being entirely exposed in some parts. Cultural material was confined to the surface of the site, followed by some 20 cm of silty sand, and finally 16 cm of gravel before bedrock was encountered. Our strategy for investigating the site was to construct a grid of 555 m squares over it and then map and collect each of the squares. Figure 5.3 shows FKWMH with the superimposed collecting grid. The concentrations of stone and daga are clearly visible. Figures 5.4 through 5.8 show the distribution of different artifact categories across the site, supporting the suggestion that the concentrations are activity areas and allowing us to interpret the nature of the represented activities.

Figure 5.3 shows the distribution of cultural material at FKWMH. Material is relatively evenly distributed with peaks at Units 7, 15, and 18. Units 31 through 34 are distinguished by their extremely low frequencies of artifacts. Site patterning is much more obvious when specific categories of artifacts are shown. Figure 5.4 shows the distribution of siliceous mudstone that concentrates at the western end of the site with a notable peak in Unit 7. Figure 5.5 shows the distribution of basic tools. Here three peaks are evident—again at the western end in Unit 7 and its adjacent units, in Unit 18, and in Unit 23. Mudstone and basic tools are virtually nonexistent at the eastern edge of the site in Feature 4. Elsewhere (Casey 1993) I have mapped the distribution of nine shape categories of basic tool edges. While there is some low-level

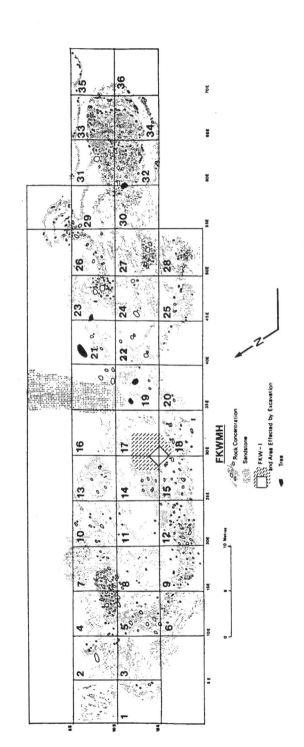

Figure 5.3. Fulani Kuliga West Main Hill with superimposed collecting grid.

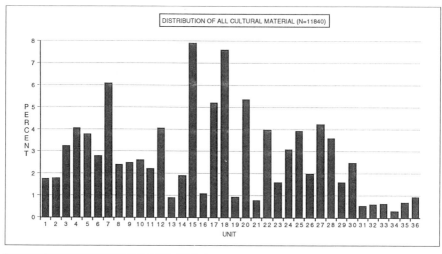

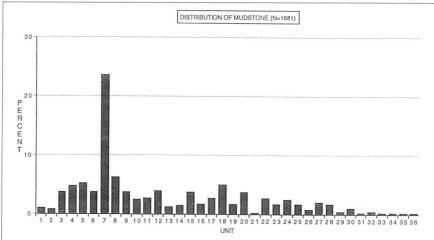

Figure 5.4 (top). Distribution of all cultural material.

Figure 5.5 (bottom). Distribution of mudstone.

correlation between activity areas and edge shapes, correlations are not completely clear, and it is not apparent whether the analytical categories I have used bear any meaning for the people who were actually making and using the tools.

The distribution of more formal tool types also sheds light on the activity areas of the site. Figure 5.7 shows the distribution of siliceous mudstone geometric microliths that are confined almost exclusively to Feature 1. An entirely different distribution is apparent for ceramics that are most common in Feature 2 (Figure 5.8).

Ethnographic evidence suggests that the material remaining behind on living surfaces does not necessarily give an accurate picture of the activities that were

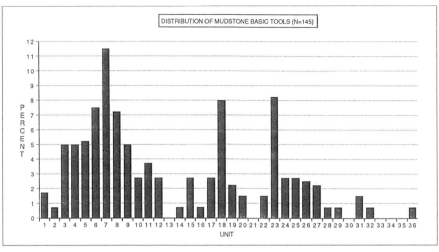

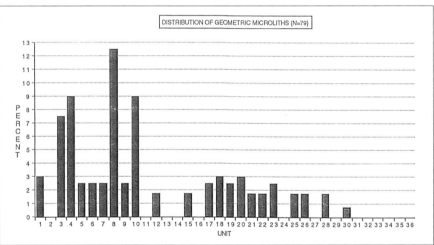

Figure 5.6 (top). Distribution of mudstone basic tools.

Figure 5.7 (bottom). Distribution of geometric microliths.

undertaken there (Binford 1973:242–243; Yellen 1977:97), and that there is great variation among different peoples in their propensity to create activity areas that may be recognized or accurately interpreted (see Kent 1984, 1987). As Kent points out (Chapter 3), gender-specific areas are rare in the sites of noncomplex peoples, and she cautions against making simplistic assumptions about gendered activity areas based on the presence of either lithic materials or pottery. She demonstrates that in domestic contexts, male and female activities often overlap, and that this can obscure any patterning of activity areas that may be expected to exist. I would also add that the movements of young children, who are often ungendered beings and therefore are

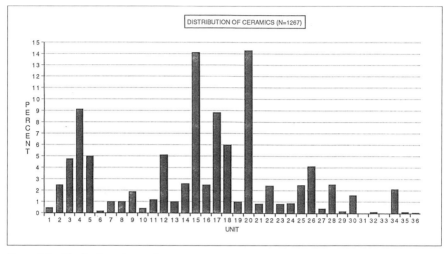

Figure 5.8. Distribution of ceramics.

often not subject to any gender restrictions or conventions that may exist, will move freely between the activity areas, often bringing the waste products from one activity area into another and consequently further obliterating the patterning. Furthermore, postdepositional processes of various sorts (trampling, bioturbation, slope wash) will undoubtedly ensure that materials in reasonably close proximity during the lifespan of the site have an excellent chance of becoming mixed at some point between the time of deposition and excavation. I would suggest that as long as production takes place within the domestic sphere, it is unrealistic to expect to find pristine areas of gendered activities—even less so in the absence of permanent architecture to delineate and protect the areas. We can, however, find areas where activities undertaken by either males or females predominate, and these areas clearly give us insight into the structure of the site.

Bearing this in mind, I feel that a case can be made for regarding as valid the evidence for activity areas at FKWMH.

The features at FKWMH can be interpreted as indicating loci of gendered activity. The high concentration of ceramics at Feature 2 is perhaps a locus of domestic activity where quantities of ceramics were necessary for temporary storage and food preparation. In ethnographic sources, it is predominantly women who are engaged in the preparation and serving of food (Hastorf 1991:134), hence it is likely that this area represents a locus of female activity.

It is most likely that the geometric microliths at FKWMH were associated with the production of composite tools for hunting. The association of geometric microliths with hunting requires some explanation because the function of such microliths is somewhat debatable. They are found in profusion in European Mesolithic sites, and in Africa they may appear as early as 40,000 BP, but they reach their peak in the Late

Stone Age all over the continent (Phillipson 1980:229). Wherever microliths have been found in contexts that have preserved evidence for their use, they have been hafted singly or in series as points or barbs for projectiles (Phillipson 1980:229) or set in handles for use as knives or other cutting implements (Soper 1965); they may have served many other purposes as well (Stahl 1989; McIntosh and McIntosh 1983:236). Although microliths are most often thought to be associated with hunting, the fact that their appearance coincides with an increase in technologies used to process plant foods may also be significant. There is no clear evidence that the microliths from FKWMH were used for the collection of plant foods. An absence of microliths with sickle sheen as an indicator of plant harvesting is not surprising, as the technology used today to harvest grasses in northern Ghana does not involve the use of sickles, scythes, or other specialized cutting implements. The large heads of domestic millet and sorghum are snapped off when dry, often over a blunt instrument, and the grasses that are collected on the stem for use in thatching and mat making are harvested by "capturing" a bunch of them in the hook of a metal instrument and snapping them off near the root with a quick jerk. In fact, only two microliths in the combined assemblages from all the Gambaga sites showed any evidence of use, and these were two *mèches de fôret* that had been used as drills. If Feature 1 at FKWMH can be interpreted as an area for the production of composite hunting tools, it is most likely the locus of male activity. Ethnographically, women often play an important role in the acquisition of animal protein (Wadley, Chapter 4), but they serve predominantly as trappers, as bearers, and in supporting roles as butchers, participants in drives, and supernatural support. With few exceptions (e.g., Estioko-Griffin and Griffin 1981), hunting that involved the use of projectiles is an activity that is undertaken by men (see also Hayden 1992b).

Significantly, basic tools are present at all activity areas that contain tools, and their amounts are roughly proportional to the amount of artifactual material deposited in each area. This would seem to indicate that basic tools are used equally by men and women. Mudstone flaking debris (which probably also contains unrecognized basic tools) is most common at Feature 1, which is where the vast majority of geometric microliths were located, and such debris would seem to indicate that much of it was the result of stone tool manufacture. But lithic debris, particularly quartz debris (and unrecognized basic tool debris), is also present in quantity throughout the site in areas where formal stone tool manufacture is not evident. This suggests that lithic reduction for the purpose of making basic tools carries on continuously all over the site as necessary, and is not the exclusive preserve of any specialist, whether a man or a woman.

The Hunting Hypothesis

Changes in hunting strategies have been cited as having contributed to the "devolution" of lithic technology at the end of the Pleistocene. Torrence (1989) suggests that with sedentism and domestication, the need to hunt wild animals for protein diminishes and toolkits no longer need to be so specialized in order to reduce the risks that are inherent in the hunting of large mammals. Neither sedentism nor domestication necessarily reduces the need for wild protein, though reduced mobility may force a change in the hunting focus and consequently in technology.

The presence of geometric microliths argues for the continued importance of hunting in the Kintampo sites along the Gambaga Escarpment. Unlike the highly formalized geometric microliths from North Africa (Tixier 1963), the geometric microliths from FKWMH can be described as semiformal at best. Whereas the North African geometrics are made on blades and result in highly standardized specimens, the Kintampo geometrics are made on wedge-shaped chips of stone that result in a variety of irregular shapes. I have made some attempt to classify these according to morphology (Casey 1994), but shape categories often overlap, and the Kintampo peoples seem to me to be little concerned with the difference between a trapezoid and a triangle. Functionally, the Kintampo geometrics seem to require at least one sharp edge, with the other edges blunted by steep bipolar crushing. They are recognizable as tools that have been formed for a purpose, but fortuitously shaped pieces appear to have also served that purpose equally well, receiving only minimal backing as necessary.

In both Europe and Africa the shift to the use of microliths has been under apparently contradictory circumstances. Over much of Africa this shift coincides with the expansion of forests at the end of the Pleistocene, and a concomitant shift in hunting focus from large, gregarious herd animals and the large projectiles that were used to hunt them, to small, solitary, forest-dwelling species (Phillipson 1980). Quite the opposite phenomenon has been noted in West Africa where geometric microliths are associated with savanna environments and apparently high animal biomass (Shaw 1978/79). In Europe, the appearance of geometric microliths has been interpreted as being a strategy for reducing risk in changing environments that have become either more homogeneous (Myers 1989) or more diverse (Jochim 1989). Projectiles fitted with microliths are undoubtedly equally capable of killing a large animal as a small one, but virtually all researchers stress the versatility of microlithic tools, indicating that microliths are easily made and composite tools easily repaired.

Evidence from central Ghana indicates that small, wild animal species account for the majority of faunal species in Kintampo sites along with low numbers of domestic sheep or goat (Carter and Flight 1972; Stahl 1985a,b). This combination of wild and domestic fauna is typical of many subsistence farming communities that rear domestic stock, because it is not practical for people who tend small herds of domestic animals to slaughter them regularly for consumption (Segobye, Chapter 12; Swift 1981; White 1986). Sheep and goats only produce one or two offspring a year, so regular consumption would quickly decimate the population. The addition of small stock to the prehistoric economy was probably more significant as an item that can be traded, that produces byproducts such as milk, that can consume the waste generated by the processing of plant foods, that can fertilize garden plots, and that may have forced changes in mobility; but it is unlikely that changes in diet brought about by the addition of ovicaprids had to do with a significant increase in animal protein, or in a reduced need to hunt it. It is likely, however, that with reduced mobility, the focus of hunting shifted away from long-distance trips into the bush and became concentrated closer to the settlements.

Finer Points

The Kintampo peoples lacked neither the technology nor the raw material for making formal tools. Nor did they lack the need to continue to hunt animals for meat. They therefore possessed many of the criteria necessary for the production of formal tools, yet they did not produce them. Basic tool technology was a choice that the Kintampo peoples made, and it appears that basic tools adequately served their purposes. The question should therefore change from "why don't people make formal tools" to "why do people make any formal tools at all if basic tools can perform virtually the same functions as formal tools but are easier to make?" The shift in mobility may be the key to this question, but not for the technological reasons suggested by Torrence, Sassaman, and Parry and Kelly.

Gero (1989:103) has suggested that a reduction in biface production at Huaricoto in Peru marks a change in the role of bifaces as transmitters of information. She suggests that other, more plastic media (such as clay) overshadowed bifaces as information-bearing objects that served to mark social relations. The ability of artifact forms to reflect social relationships has been discussed by numerous authors (Wobst 1977; Hodder 1982, 1993; Weissner 1983, 1993; Sackett 1973, 1977, 1982, 1985, 1989, 1993, to name but a few) with the conclusion that the information encoded in artifact "style" is complex, seems multidimensional, and may or may not be intentional.

I would like to suggest that the finely made Kintampo projectiles had a very important function in transmitting information, and that they appear in assemblages where less elaborate tools perform most tasks. I hypothesize this because they continue to send their messages to the same sources that are the intended recipients of the information encoded on tools in formal assemblages, though with less frequency than expected by mobile hunters.

Ease of mobility has often been cited as one reason why men and not women undertake most of the hunting in human societies. It has been demonstrated that there are few physical barriers to women's hunting or travel, yet overwhelmingly in the ethnographic record it is men who do the majority of both these things in most societies (Hayden 1992b). Men travel to hunt, but their tools may have a life and mobility independent of the men to whom they belong. Projectiles that miss their mark and cannot be retrieved, or that penetrate the prey but are lost as the animal escapes, or that break and are abandoned by their owners, are, in a sense, calling cards indicating the presence of a particular society or even a particular man. They are little packages of social information, and, just as the information on a calling card is accessible to anybody who understands the symbols printed on it, so too can someone understand the symbols encoded in the projectile. But who is the intended recipient of these communications?

Today in Gambaga, most hunting is performed on the farm, but there are many men who specialize in hunting animals beyond the reaches of the fields. People who go into the far bush, or hunt at night, risk coming into contact with supernatural beings, wild animals, and other humans whose territories abut the forests on the other side. Hunters are in danger from all these sources, and they do not go out to hunt without taking both magical and practical precautions that have material correlates in the hunter's regalia, equipment, and even the charms around his house. Hunting and trapping in the farms and fields is contrasted by a complete lack of supernatural assistance, and though a significant amount of animal protein—in many cases, the most significant amount in the diet—is gained from the more pedestrian hunting on the farm, it is not regarded as being a particularly noteworthy endeavor, and certainly not worthy of the elaborate preparations that a "real" hunter must make when he ventures beyond the limits of the village's fields.

It is likely that the contrast between the unremarkable basic tools or semiformal microliths and the exquisitely designed projectile points is the material expression of symbolic behavior for social or supernatural protection. Once people settle down in an area, they claim it as their own in a very real sense. The construction of permanent structures, the clearing of land, or the custodianship of communities of plants and animals establishes a particular physical environment as being the property of that group of people. Within this bounded area, life can be controlled and predicted, and all persons are known. Consequently, hunting and other extractive activities may be performed with regard only to the task at hand. Outside this controlled environment, life is wild and unpredictable. The act of settling and taming an area sets up a dichotomy between the domesticated and the wild, between culture and nature (Hodder 1990), and consequently, when one travels outside the safe boundaries of the living area, it becomes more important to prepare and protect oneself. One means of doing this is to encode tools with messages.

Mobile hunters and gatherers who roam the landscape litter it with evidence of their presence. The messages are subtle, even invisible, to our unaccustomed eyes, but the lost and broken projectiles, knives, and other tools are clear evidence of the presence of other groups of people, or even single individuals. These messages are not necessarily particularly elaborate. They may simply be marking the presence or the range of the person or group to whom they belong. Perhaps they claim territory beyond the immediate physical reach of the band or the individual. The recipients may be human beings who are real or imagined, or they may be supernatural sources. With sedentism, the need for people to send messages marking their presence to people or things outside the controlled environment becomes confined to particular circumstances.

The role of women as agents of external symbolic communication cannot be discounted, but evidence for their role is not as obvious as it is for men. The ethnographic record indicates that women regularly travel long distances in pursuit of resources, but there are four possible suggestions as to why they are not primary participants in long-distance messaging. First, women's tools may also have been symbolically encoded, but were made of organic materials that have not survived the archaeological record. Second, it may be that women's tools are lost and broken less frequently, and physically stray less far from the woman herself, reducing the need to encode them. Third, some of the tools that we do find, such as extravagantly flaked knives and scrapers, are likely to have been the property of women, and when the likelihood of their being broken or discarded in the field is high, they are also symbolically elaborated. Finally, it is possible that in the past, as now, women's activities simply received less recognition and were considered less worthy of social and spiritual elaboration.

At the same time that external messaging was being confined to fewer instances, symbolic communication within the group was also changing. Ceramics increase in importance, not only as functional objects, but also as carriers of information. Ceramics are usually associated with women, who are both the primary consumers of ceramic vessels while often being their producers as well. Whereas men appear to be the primary agents of symbolic communication directed toward the external world, women are likely to have been important agents of symbolic messaging within the new, larger, and more stable communities. During the Kintampo period we also see beads, bracelets, and other items of personal adornment, and more permanent structures. More attention appears to be have been spent in communication among people who live together, with less directed toward the outside world, and possibly the unknown.

Conclusion

This paper examines the question of why elaborately made lithic tools become a minor component of the assemblages of less mobile peoples. With sedentism comes increased attention to the immediate environment. In subsistence terms, this means intensification of technologies for procuring and processing local resources. Sedentism forms a positive feedback loop whereby the acts of accumulating waste, storing food, and clearing land attract additional foods in the form of voluntary plant species and commensal animals that can be easily harvested and trapped in those areas that have been domesticated and claimed by the acts of clearing and building. Thus, while cultural or environmental influences may promote a change in mobility, the act of settling and impacting the surrounding environment can reinforce and enhance this change. The shift from a mobile to a sedentary mode of existence brings a shift in focus from a large territory with its dispersed resources, flexible kin ties, and fluid relationships with people, resources, and the supernatural, to a small territory with fixed relationships with both people and resources, as well as a delineated and reasonably controlled living environment. With sedentism comes an increased attention to the elaboration and maintenance of social relationships within these domestic boundaries.

The need for travel outside the domesticated boundaries of village and field was probably greatly reduced with sedentism, as people had most resources at hand and had to spend more time within the boundaries to protect, collect, and process them. Women's work greatly increases with sedentism, because the resources that are reliable and can be enhanced and stored often require increased amounts of processing. Since it is women who worldwide are primarily responsible for transforming raw ingredients into food (Hastorf 1991), it is likely that the bulk of the additional work of processing, and perhaps even producing the tools (such as pottery) necessary for the task, fell to them. Both these factors—the decreased need to travel, and the increased demands on women's labor—may have resulted in lower mobility for women.

Men's mobility would also have been lessened for precisely the same reasons as women's would. But while the processing of foodstuffs is a daily occupation, the collection or cultivation of seasonal resources is a sporadic one requiring periods of intensive labor followed by periods of rest. Obviously, we cannot know who was producing or harvesting the resource that enabled the Kintampo peoples to settle in northern Ghana, but over much of Africa it is women who often do this (though not in Gambaga) while the men specialize in other occupations such as hunting, waging war, or growing cash crops (for example, see Goheen 1996). Regardless of whether men were intensively involved in farming or harvesting, or engaged in other occupations, it is likely that they had greater opportunity for travel than did women. It is also likely that they had more need. Certainly during Kintampo times somebody needed to make the journeys to fetch lithic raw materials and trade for ground-stone axes. Given the demands on women's time, it is likely that these travelers and traders were men. Women in large households can and do, of course, exchange household duties with other women in order to enable them to do other things, but often there seem to be greater restrictions on women, particularly on women during their childbearing years. Such restrictions are not necessarily related to women's being encumbered with small children, but do concern the control over women's childbearing potential, and particularly the issue of paternity. Obviously it is difficult to read this into the archaeological record.

What is relevant in the archaeological record, however, is the increased elaboration of domestic equipment such as pottery, which functions primarily locally and in the sphere of women's influence, while at the same time tools that are often elaborated in hunter-gatherer societies become less so in sedentary societies, with the exception of a single tool type. I have argued that the persistence in elaboration of this single lithic tool type has to do with hunting strategies that take hunters beyond the "safe" zones of villages and fields. Within the domestic area, the acquisition of resources is not accompanied by much elaboration or ceremony, though other aspects of material culture are (perhaps the serving of food?). But, given the dangers of crossing the boundary between the domestic and the wild, elaboration of the equipment needed to undertake the journey successfully is probably accompanied by ceremony.

The material from northern Ghana does not chart a change through time, but rather indicates the way in which materials are used at one point in time in a settled community. However, this example has the power to suggest reasons why the phenomenon of early settled peoples redirecting their symbolic energies away from the elaboration of lithic tools may have come about. Men and women were clearly producers and consumers of basic tool technology, but it is their differing opportunities for travel and contact outside the domesticated areas that shape their participation in symbolic messaging.

Acknowledgments

The Social Sciences and Humanities Research Council of Canada (SSHRCC) has been very generous in its support of this project. Fieldwork in 1987 and 1988 were carried out under the direction of Dr. F. J. Kense, and SSHRCC has supported my own work with a doctoral fellowship (1998–1990), postdoctoral fellowship (1994–1996), and research grant (1994–1997).

I would like to thank Sue Kent and Joan Gero for reading and making comments on earlier versions of this paper.

Chapter Six

Social Variability Among Holocene Saharan Groups

How to Recognize Gender

A Theoretical Premise

The difficulty in defining past events based on role differentiation in society is part of the more general difficulty, for the archaeologist, of characterizing human agency. Because of the influence of natural sciences, typology and stratigraphy were for a long period the main focus of archaeological studies. Only later did the discipline approach lifestyle reconstruction. Furthermore, such a reconstruction, put forward by the program of the new archaeology, was meant as the reconstruction of *processes* in which the actors remained in the background. Indeed, the adaptive and systemic explanations that dominated the scene from the 1960s to the 1980s neglected putting emphasis on the *individuals*.

Nevertheless, in North African archaeology the processual study of food production and of the state also involved the study of concrete, social organizational phenomena. Let us consider how human groups planned to use the environment, as an example. Moreover, the broad-spectrum exploitation of resources, the evidence of sedentism, wealth accumulation, and emergence of ranking linked with resource control and redistribution, represented more mature specifications about the social context. Although such reconstructions remained in the realm of adaptive interpretations of observed phenomena, they featured in detail the type of relationship that was supposedly instituted between the social group and territorial space. Further, they implicitly introduced elements of choice and decision by the actors in the reconstruction drawn from cultural material data. The problem of developing methods to properly recognize elements connected with human actions from data often very scant and fragmentary was overcome, at that time, by making reference to the sphere of living societies. Ethnoarchaeology showed how to derive materials from ethnographic societies that could serve as reliable models against which archaeological data could be measured.

Recently, having shifted the latest archaeological orientations from the reconstruction of processes to the inquiry of contexts, a renewed interest in social structure asserted itself. For this effort, more attention is also given to agents that are not directly observable but that work within the documentation, such as gendered identities. Being part of the social trend of postprocessual archaeology, gender studies delve into differentiations in the social participation of sexes. At the same time, as noted by Kent (Chapter 3) and Gifford-Gonzalez (Chapter 7), such studies reveal how a certain dominating mentality led to obscuring and mystifying certain problems and roles. If it is true that postprocessual literature, either contextual or structural, has placed emphasis on meanings as opposed to functions, the recognition of roles, in the sense of "meaning" attributed to the sexes, is certainly one of the most promising fields of study. Nevertheless, there has been a unanimous call for a more effective methodology to record the engendered relations (Dobres 1995b; see also Parkington, Chapter 2). Actually, until now, gender archaeology has been manifested primarily at the theoretical level. Only rarely has it faced the problem of active research (Claassen 1992a). The question of how to develop a theory capable of understanding and recognizing human agency in past events has been neglected. Consequently, also overlooked has been the problem of how to characterize the role taken by the various social components.

We think that in these conditions the traditional relationships among paleoethnology, ethnology, and anthropology must be further reinforced. However, using the ethnographic analogy in a simple form does not help much. We agree with Gifford-Gonzalez (Chapter 7) that there is a need for reinterpreting analogy as a way of systematically transferring knowledge from a familiar to an unfamiliar context warranted by the existence of causal relations (Barich 1988). Contextual studies of contemporary forager societies have allowed for new interpretations (e.g., Testart 1982), in some way contrasting with the traditional views linked to hunter-gatherers. Nevertheless, it is necessary to take it one step further: such interpretations are an example of the reference basis on which a more profound analysis, directed toward attributing meaning to human activity, can be developed.

A Case Study: Hunter-Gatherers of the Holocene in Central Sahara

The situation we present here has been taken from an archaeological context—the Saharan Holocene—whose abundant and varied documentation could easily be reread in light of previous considerations. As a matter of fact, it seems to be a promising sample to investigate from a gender perspective. We refer to a rather wide context, in time and space: approximately from 10,000 to 7000 BP in the central Saharan belt from Mauritania to Sudan, and from lower Tunisia to Niger (Figure 6.1). The continuous and uniform element is given by the form of adaptation. It is a complex of similar situations, all strongly based on exploiting aquatic resources, that were defined as "aqualithic" (Sutton 1977). In Mali, the lacustrine phase between 8500 and 6900 BP was recognized through stratigraphic sections in the ancient lakes

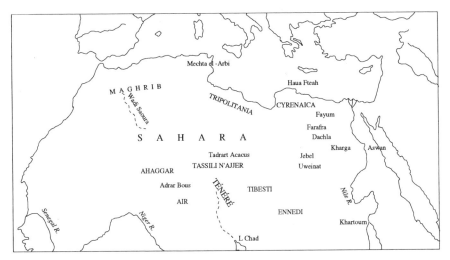

Figure 6.1. Map of North Africa and the Sahara.

bordering the Erg (Petit-Maire and Riser 1983). In Algeria, research in the Hoggar and in the Tassili regions has shown a long cultural sequence documented in the ancient sites of Amekni (Camps 1969) and Ti-n-Hanakaten (Aumassip 1984). Other human occupation centers, pertaining to the early and mid-Holocene, were recognized in Chad and Tibesti by French and German archaeologists (Courtin 1969; Gabriel 1977). Lately, the most recent research in Niger, Libya, and the Egyptian Sahara has placed the first human presence at the very beginning of the Holocene, after the resuming of the monsoon season.

In literature these similar adaptation phenomena are often referred to as the "Saharo-Sudanese Neolithic," according to the definition coined by G. Camps (1974, 1982), which set off a debate that is still going on today. Actually, these situations can be better defined as transitional contexts, in which prototypes appeared for the first time, that were later destined for domestication, through repetitive gathering and selection processes.[1] Until now these societies have been studied in a processual perspective, featuring the elements of change. Lately, attention has moved from consideration of cultural change to context—that is, to the consideration of horizontal, synchronic, interrelations in the cultural system. These reconstructions have been useful for specifying social functioning.

The Saharan region appears as a generalized ecosystem of fishing and hunting-gathering activities aimed at a broad-spectrum utilization of resources. Subsistence relies primarily on shellfish, fish, and small game, plus, overall, plant resources. Large game is a minor dietary component. For this reason, women could have played an important role in food procurement. Efforts to expand the exploitable base, using resources at a short distance from the home bases, brought about a change in settlement behavior. Ultimately, the limited nomadism was followed by

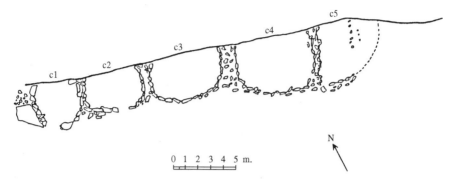

Figure 6.2. Plan of the Ti-n-Torha East settlement site in the Tadrart Acacus, Libya (modified after Barich 1974).

semiresidential arrangements. We can list Ti-n-Torha East in Libya (around 8500 BP: Barich 1974) and site E-75-6 at Nabta Playa in Egypt (around 8200 BP: Wendorf and Schild 1980) as examples of a real village-type organization showing stone-lined huts for family units (Figure 6.2). Similarly, the family household is the basic economic unit related to such structures.

The year was divided into two parts, the dry and rainy seasons. In summer, at the return of the rains, the community temporarily left the main settlement and dispersed into the hinterland. The Ti-n-Torha group's seasonal scheduling was primarily tied to crop maturation rhythms—those belonging to the millet group. During winter, the group migrated toward the bottom of the valley to collect and process plant food and to fish in the small permanent pool. They also hunted migratory birds. During summer, mostly ungulate hunting (barbary sheep, gazelle, hartebeest) was practiced on the plateau by task groups—probably adult males. Perhaps, in summer, tending the earliest proto-domestic items was also performed. The simultaneous appearance of large ceramic vessels and permanent dwellings allows us to affirm that in this way preliminary food storing was established, together with major sedentism, demographic growth, and role division between the sexes. Ethnographic observations indicate that women tended to be responsible for procuring wild and domestic plants (Ehrenberg 1989:84–85). The amount of wild gramineae species (Pennisetum, Brachiaria, Echinochloa, Urochloa, Setaria, Cenchrus, Panicum) found at Ti-n-Torha Two Caves (around 8500 BP) reveals the importance of wild plants in the diet (Barich 1992; Wasylikowa 1992). We can suppose, therefore, that in this context women, who probably also practiced both fishing and small land-mammal hunting, played a primary role in food procurement. The participation of women in acquiring food probably resulted in a gender equality that was not present in later societies. It should be remembered, in fact, that in environments subject to recurrent shortages, such as those under study, gathering, more than hunting, must have represented the principal form of sustenance. Furthermore—as suggested above—female involvement also in small mammal hunting has been hypothesized by various authors (Estioko-Griffin and Griffin 1981; see also Wadley, Chapter 4). It is interesting to note that this type of condition must have had a long tradition, since it had already existed in the Pleistocene.

Foragers or Collectors?

The examples under study, which come from the contextual reading of data from a multidisciplinary range, find strong relational analogies with the pattern suggested by Testart (1982) in his study of complex gatherers. With this definition, the author indicated the more sedentary foragers of the Northwest Coast and California Indians who, following Binford's typology, could also be defined as collectors (Binford 1980). The most distinctive element in respect to other hunter-gatherers (e.g., Bushmen/Basarwa) is the increased sedentism and seasonal food storage:

> The usual residence of hunter-gatherers practicing storage is a village or a permanent camp built around food reserves from which seasonal expeditions requiring a certain mobility, such as hunting, are launched. (Testart 1982:524)

The increased sedentism in relation to food storage had a notable effect on the birth spacing in the women of the Northwest Coast. Births, in fact, do not need to be spaced at intervals as among the mobile hunter-gatherers. Testart observed (1982:525) that, while the higher population density among hunter-gatherers had been explained, up to now, with an increased environmental productivity, this, in reality, must be put in relation to food storing and consequent semisedentary customs. Food storage could also be the basis for the rise of social inequality (Testart 1982:525). Conversely Kent (Chapter 3) very relevantly emphasizes the frequent "invisibility" of foragers and their being undifferentiated at the gender level, since their group organization is without stratification. It is necessary to note that among the Saharan hunter-gatherers, broad-spectrum exploitation of a limited environment was not able to create real surplus products nor, therefore, any form of ranking.

Pottery Making

Increased sedentism also produced an increased availability of goods. If we are looking at highly mobile groups, or groups living in transient camps, we find only very light equipment; while in base camps ornaments (necklace beads and pendants), amulets (animal bones, both pierced and decorated), and less portable implements are found. Among these we can also include grinding equipment (lower and upper grinding stones) and hoes, associated with the harvesting activities of the women who, most likely, were also their producers (compare Goodale 1971, for Tiwi women of Australia). Finally, with increased sedentism and availability of more goods, the production of a larger number of containers, either basketry or pottery, was encouraged.

As is well known, the Saharan epipaleolithic societies are among the most ancient pottery makers. The earliest examples were found in the central-western regions of

Libya and Niger (Tagalagal and Temet in Niger: 9330 ± 130 and 9550 ± 100 BP; Ti-n-Torha in Libya: 9080 ± 70), while toward the east, on the Nile, pottery appears later, generally in the 9th millennium BP contexts. A question still unanswered today is why the early groups were inclined to produce ceramics. More than a necessity for holding liquids, for which groups could also have used ostrich egg containers, it was perhaps the need to store solid goods, made available by the intensification of harvesting activities, that called for ceramic production. As Ehrenberg (1989:87) notes, it was probably the women, the most directly involved in harvesting activities, who felt the need to innovate. Even now, data known from modern societies attribute an important role to women in the development of ceramic technology. In Mali, pottery is produced primarily by women for each of the numerous groups (Bozo, Somono, Peul, Bambara, Songhai, Dogon) that today populate the inner Delta of Niger (Gallay et al. 1996:29–33). The scarcity of fragments in the earliest settlements of the 10th millennium BP tells us that up to that moment vessels had not been destined to a domestic use, but rather had been reserved for particular purposes. At Nabta, compared with the large amount of small pits for cooking in settlement E-75-6, which contained charcoals and plant remains, the amount of ceramic sherds is very low. Close has suggested that this production could imply some social and symbolic function (Close 1995:28–29). It can be added that in this and other analogous sites particular spatial concentrations that could be studied in the way indicated by Kent (Chapter 3) and Casey (Chapter 5) were not recorded.

In these ancient Saharan sites there is proof that, from the beginning of the occupation, the economic model also included cattle breeding. These sites allow us, therefore, to investigate the transition from a gathering economy, integrated with herd tending, to a pastoral-based economy, whether exclusive or predominant. In this way we might be able to clarify the fundamental transformation undergone by the female role during the passage from one type of organization to the other and, eventually, her probable loss of meaning. Understanding this transformation represents a rather important goal, whose success is tied to the possibility of adequately evaluating the established relationships within the group. In fact, while during the initial phase of pastoral organization women could have added herd tending to their other activities (Ehrenberg 1989), later on, with the increase of the herds, pastoralism became a male prerogative, reducing women to a marginal role.

The early cattle evidence is known in the early Holocene Libyan Sahara and, above all, in the Egyptian Western Desert (Kiseiba, Dachla, Wadi Bakt). Wendorf and colleagues (Wendorf et al. 1990) built a mobility model for the Nabta and Kiseiba groups that foresees cyclic movements between the basin's bottom in dry months and the plateaus in the rainy season. Such a model also features the role of task groups (males and/or females) that, periodically, on the return of the rains, left the base group to pasture the first herds (Wendorf et al. 1990). By the mid-Holocene the pastoral economy prevailed, and even increased in importance, becoming a dominant economic strategy in a phase of climatic deterioration. Many small hearth places started appearing on all the Saharan plains about that time, with a particular intensity around the oases. They are clear evidence of shepherds' rest-stops (Gabriel 1984, 1987). The social meaning achieved by pastoral organization during the 7th millennium BP is also documented by funerary tumuli discovered in the Sahara. The structures uncovered right in the Nabta Playa region (megalithic alignments, calendar circles, and so on) have a great importance because they are a sign of pastoral-based ranking (Wendorf and Schild 1995). Some ritual cattle burial findings show the ideological value attached to this same resource.

Up to this point we have considered the material remains of the culture, to which data from tombs can be added. These are very rare throughout the Saharan area and consist of isolated tombs, or groups of two or three, within the sites themselves. A notable exception is represented by the necropolises of Mali (Taoudenni basin), which, instead, group a noteworthy number of individuals (Dutour 1989). Rituals are elementary and grave goods are exceptional. Nevertheless, various tombs of children and women (such as the Uan Muhuggiag and Amekni examples: Mori and Ascenzi 1959; Camps 1969) highlighted a social consideration of both classes.

Making Inferences from Rock Art

These reconstructions, which widely use ethnographic comparison, were carried out according to the ecological-functional paradigm. But Saharan archaeology can rely on another formidable source of information, especially significant for our research since it is an expression of the symbolic world of society. As a matter of fact, an important contribution can come from the rock art field, provided that the study is focused on the artwork meanings through an analytical reading of them. This position can be traced back to Leroi-Gourhan (1968) and attributes meanings with reference to contexts and actions (Conkey 1989:152). By analytical procedure, nuclei of concepts specific to single prehistorical groups, as an expression of specific relationships established within the social group and with the outside world, could be identified. The degree to which our interpretations are valid could be measured against similar nuclei of thought—analogs—established through the analysis of ethnographic and oral sources. We can accept the association (Barich 1990; Sansoni 1994) of the multiresource environments that we have described up till now, with a rather significant corpus of paintings: the "round heads" art, so called for the way in which the human face is represented. Known in Tassili and Libya (with a few documented also in Tibesti), this is an extremely diversified art, which therefore corresponds well to a society that is just as diversified and changing. Obviously, direct reading can offer only a preliminary approach to these paintings, whose symbolic and ideological content could also have altered the relationships in reference to reality (Bednarick 1990/91; Hassan 1993; see also Parkington, Chapter 2). For example, the scarce characterization of the human figure can mean that there was a disinterest in the individuality of the portrayed

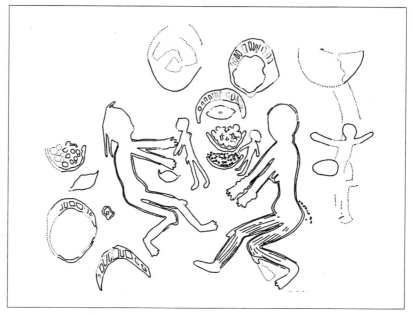

Figure 6.3. A family life scene from site Sefar XXI (Tassili n' Ajjer, Algeria). A man and a woman together with two children, surrounded by containers probably holding vegetables (round-head style; modified after Sansoni 1994, Fig. 82, p. 138).

person, who supposedly played a ceremonial and symbolic role in the scene (Sansoni 1994).

However, the copiousness of depicted scenes, on the whole, allows for reconstructing the surrounding environment: the rather luxuriant ambiance of the humid tropical savanna belt, which we learned about through excavations. Mufflons, gazelles, antelopes, and buffaloes were the most typical animal species. There are fish at Wadi Djerat, Tassili (Sansoni 1994: Fig. 25), and in the Acacus Mountains at Imha and In Taharin (Mori 1971:45–51) and also plants, even if they are few. As an example, one can quote a scene in the Tassili that represents a family ritual (Sefar XXI, Sansoni 1994: Fig. 82) (see Figure 6.3). From our point of view, it is interesting to note that in the artworks males and females performed distinct roles, and that the female figure (in contrast to the bubaline Maghrebian rock art, in which women are scarcely represented) occurs much more frequently. This fact could mean that the woman had gained higher value in the social organization (Sansoni 1994:208). This significance attributed to the female gender agrees with the organization that has been reconstructed and that emphasized the role carried out by women in gathering plants and manufacturing pottery.

The mastery of ceramic technology—transformation of material from an inanimate to an animate condition, from crude to cooked—eventually attributed a great status to

Figure 6.4. Worship scene from the Sefar LXI site. The female figures all in a row bear body paint designs inspired by the ceramic repertoire (round-head style; modified after Sansoni 1994, Fig. 82, p. 138).

women. The fact that women were so closely linked to ceramics, to pots, so much as to be identified with them, goes along with what appeared in the "round-head" art. It is not by chance that the female figures are sometimes richly decorated with motives typical of the ceramic repertoire (Figure 6.4). This testifies to the metaphorical meaning given to the woman, the main creator of the new vessels (see Aschwanden, quoted in Collett 1993:506–507).

The large diffusion of the Bovidian art (starting from about 6000 BP) corresponds to the emergence of pastoral ideology. The copiousness of cattle scenes indicates that herds were the most highly valued social good, perhaps right at the time when the effective contribution of cattle to the diet and economy could have been rather limited (Holl 1989:348).

As noted by Gifford-Gonzalez (Chapter 7), an "androcentric" mentality reinforced the thesis of the pastoral world's attributing a greater meaning to the male figure. Even the art would document this reversal of roles. Recently C. Dupuy has highlighted the underrepresentation of the female figure in the pastoral engravings (Dupuy 1995:205). Actually, as Ehrenberg showed (1989:102), when animal husbandry enters a mixed economy, the women's role depends on the scale of herds. When herding is the prevalent activity, men tend to be more involved in herding, leaving women a marginal role such as processing milk. Based on the documentation known in the Sahara, throughout the 8th millennium BP there was a mixed economy, in which the gathering tradition was still strong; therefore we can suppose that a division of gender roles also continued. Maybe women primarily carried out gathering, together with tending the first herds and milking, while men were more involved in hunting. However, Lyn Wadley (Chapter 4) warns that we must define the women's involvement in hunting better, and, as an example, she mentions the cooperative (man/woman) hunting among Mbuti. The Saharan model seems to have been progressively pushed to the east. Today it is reproduced by some Nilotic populations (see the Nuer, whose pastoral component, however, is much more relevant than in the Saharan example).

We are dealing with a crucial transformation, rather delicate for the balance of gender relations, which requires attentive study and making use of all possible information available. Even the study of the pottery inventory can indicate structural change. The decorative motifs of the early Holocene offer a wealth of themes that allow for individuating site-specific characteristics, both in syntax and techniques. We suppose that this phenomenon pertains to societies that are matrilocal and matrilinear, where the art of pottery is handed down directly from mother to daughter. On the other hand, the greater uniformity of mid-Holocene ceramic motifs could also be attributable both to women's circulating within wider circuits following the patrilocal custom, prevalent among pastoral societies, and to the consequent style's intermingling.

Conclusion

In the study of Saharan societies, ethnographic observation has encouraged contextual analysis, which, in turn, contributed to the specification of the social pattern. The early Holocene societies (from 10,000 to 6000 BP), in which gathering activities prevailed, gave an important significance to women for their contribution in food procurement. This position the women held probably was changed in the mid-Holocene as the organization also changed and the pastoral economy predominated. Essentially, these contexts can be a useful domain for investigating the progressive structuring of roles. It is necessary, however, to develop methods to reach a more sophisticated level of meaning, avoiding dangerous simplifications. Ethnology shows how to derive information about spatial arrangements, which can be useful for recognizing a differential access and utilization of resources, from the contextual study of settlements. Definitely, this is a new perspective even for whoever applies very systematic recording methods. Finally, rock art interpretation, if directed toward understanding the profound message expressed by the scenes the art bears, could also contribute to our better recognizing the true division of roles based on gender.

Note

1. According to the orientation of European studies, such communities could be defined as "Mesolithic." Nevertheless, for Africa it seems preferable to avoid definitions based on the dynamics of temperate regions.

DIANE GIFFORD-GONZALEZ ■

Chapter Seven

Gender and Early Pastoralists in East Africa

Introduction

African pastoralists' preoccupation with the sexual, social, and productive attributes of livestock is mirrored metaphorically in the same spheres of human life (Galaty 1982; Llewelyn-Davies 1979; Meeker 1989; Saitoti 1986; Saitoti and Beckwith 1980; Spencer 1965, 1988). The self-identity of young man and name-ox or, as Deng (1972) has put it, "personality ox," among many Nilotic-speakers (Evans-Pritchard 1940; Gulliver 1955; Klima 1970; Thomas 1965) and some Cushitic speakers (Almagor 1978) is the best-known version of such blurring of the line between animals and human actors, or, more properly, the merging of the social and productive identities of each. This is not a universal trait of pastoral societies; other herding groups in Eurasia and the Americas stress neither age-grading nor identification of person and animal to such a degree. Yet this is apparently an old trait of African pastoral systems; Saharan rock art probably testifies to the gender of both humans and domestic animals. Holl (1995) has pointed to the likely testimony of some paintings to age-based transitions that male and female actors made in negotiating their lives in that milieu. The sexual attributes of livestock (and wild animals) are clearly depicted in well-preserved paintings, and the sex of human actors can usually be readily inferred from their depictions. In cases where actual physical attributes of sex are not emphasized, it appears that cultural means of denoting gender (and age?), such as hairdo, body ornamentation, and personal gear are employed (Holl 1995). Thus, in their design choices and execution, early testimonials to African pastoralist existence bear witness to the importance of representing sex and gender systems of both humans and animals. The intertwined aspects of gender, person, and society among African pastoral peoples are pervasive, but what can we realistically hope to recover of the social or ideological contexts in which prehistoric pastoralists lived? And how? This chapter explores these questions using East African data.

Two points are generally agreed on by researchers currently studying the development of food production in East Africa. First, paleontological and archaeological evidence points to the introduction of all major domestic species into East African ecosystems, be they domestic food animals (cattle, sheep, goats, and, later, dromedaries) or domestic plants (millets, sorghum, varieties of legume). Second, though a diversity of opinion exists over the nature of early food-producing economies in Kenya and Tanzania, investigators agree that the evidence points to a relatively greater commitment to pastoral livestock than to farming in the location and layout of encampments, and in the biological remains and associated artifacts. It is therefore appropriate to focus on how to investigate archaeologically the social relations, including the role of gender, of people with strong commitments to pastoral livestock.

The term *gender* as used here does not mean "women." It refers to socially defined, differentiated roles, based usually but not always on the discernible sex of individuals. The study of gender in eastern Africa should address roles of both male and female actors in prehistoric, stock-owning societies. We who have spent time with modern agropastoralists and pastoralists in the region have had it forcefully impressed on us by members of those societies that age and gender are fundamental organizing principles that structure individuals' experience of life and their roles as producers and consumers.[1]

This chapter lays groundwork for such research by resituating some known archaeological evidence within a more socially and gender-conscious context. It begins with a theoretical passage now well traveled in other geographic contexts but novel in Africa (see also Kent, Chapter 1; Wadley, Chapter 4; Stahl and Cruz, Chapter 11; Segobye, Chapter 12; Hall, Chapter 13): whether and how archaeological study of gender is possible. The extant literature on past and present East African pastoralists is shown—as has done the literature in other venues—to already feature gender, in the form of unconscious, androcentric perspectives on human action. Such methodological androcentrism impedes intelligent exegesis of archaeological sites, because it hinders collection of data on the full range of human activities that create them. I argue that gender cannot be investigated systematically without a wider reorientation of research toward a socially focused archaeology and without specifying those approaches best suited to the prehistoric East African archaeological cases dealt with here.

Framing a more balanced approach to gender in studying prehistoric East African pastoralists is especially challenging, because ethnographically documented pastoralists and agropastoralists in the region themselves often stress the centrality of male actors in kinship, public discourse, ritual, and aesthetics. Moreover, this material presents another kind of challenge, that of the prudent use of ethnographic analogy. In contrast to cases discussed by many other authors in this volume, the East African "Pastoral Neolithic" is beyond the reach of ethnographically based "direct historic approach." It is therefore useful to consider how ethnographic and other actualistic information can be used in such cases (see also Kent, Chapter 3).

The second part of the chapter turns to an example of a more socially focused approach to interpreting archaeological materials, specifically the widespread phenomenon of Nderit ceramics in what is now Kenya and Tanzania. My approach demonstrates the mobilization of "uniformitarian" assumptions within a socially directed inquiry advocated in the first half of the paper, as well as the virtual inevitability of raising questions about gender within such a framework.

Issues in the Archaeology of East African Pastoralists

This section takes up issues that exist in the background of any more socially inclined interpretation of archaeological sites, including those incorporating gender. It begins with a review of the ways that extant archaeological and ethnographic accounts of East African pastoralists are implicitly gendered. It then develops an argument for making the goals of archaeological inferences and reconstruction more social, specifying the types of "social archaeology" that seem most appropriate to the societies under study. Finally, it offers a brief review of the appropriate use of ethnographic and other actualistically derived analogies in defining archaeological problems and construction narratives based on archaeological data.

Most Archaeological Accounts Are Implicitly Gendered

Gender has been a topic in anglophone archaeology for about a decade and a half, rather later than the topic emerged in other social sciences and humanities. Wylie (1991) has discussed the reasons for this late emergence in some detail, as did Conkey and Spector (1984) and Gero (1985). A central point of these analyses is that, though it has often been asserted that "you can't dig up gender," traditional archaeological approaches both to first-order behavioral interpretations of artifacts and sites and to development of higher-order historical narratives are themselves implicitly or explicitly gendered. Male agency is assumed for nearly any significant technological breakthrough or directional change in social organization (Watson and Kennedy 1991). Berns (1993) has made the case that European analyses of West African "high art" ceramic artifacts implicitly assume that these were products of men, despite overwhelming historic and ethnographic evidence of long and widespread ceramic manufacture by women of the region. Wright (1991) has made similar observations regarding ceramic production in southwest Asia, as has Handsman (1991) regarding exegesis of prehistoric figurines from Lepenski Vir. Gero (1985, 1991) and Kehoe (1990) have noted that fabrication and use of stone tools, especially more labor-intensive types, is normally ascribed to male hunters or food producers rather than to women. Jarvenpa and Brumbach (1995) note that, when mentioned at all, women's toolkits are assumed to be less technologically complex than men's. They cite recent theorization by Hayden (1992b) as a case in point. One may add Binford's earlier (1987b) argument that Acheulian handaxes are products of wider-foraging, butchering males, whereas females account for contemporaneous scatters of nondescript flake tools. Jarvenpa and Brumbach (1995) go on to describe as counterexamples the labor-intensive, high-curation tools in historic and modern

Chipewyan women's hide-working kits, also documented by Spector (1982, 1991) for Plains Indian women.

As in other regions of the world, archaeological research in East Africa has often set analytic categories and findings into implicitly gendered research designs and narratives. In the East African case, hunters, pastoral stock owners, or ironworkers are assumed to be the active agents creating the form and extent of the archaeological record, and these occupational roles are assumed to be filled by males. Few archaeological analyses of the Pastoral Neolithic or preceding phases of East African prehistory have focused on such social interactions as exchange and political relations, but those few that do interpret these too as male domains. None consider the role of women in creating the media with which and in which these interactions might have taken place, despite some obvious—if theoretically arguable—linkages between archaeological evidence linked to production, exchange, and social display (for example, ostrich eggshell beads, gourds, milling stones, ceramics) and spheres of female activity in East African ethnographic cases. The same cannot be said of elision of modern gender roles with specific classes of archaeological data imputed to men—wild animal bones signifying decision making by male hunters, domestic animal bones likewise standing for male herders and their actions. I stress that I am not advocating such simplistic uses of "ethnographic analogy" as a way to incorporate "women's roles" into archaeological analyses—quite the contrary (see below). The example is simply intended to indicate that selective mobilization of analogy is part of the implicitly gendered way archaeological interpretation is done.[2]

The only archaeological analysis of early pastoral evidence that has offered a more explicitly gendered (and more social) reading of the early pastoral archaeological record in the region is Robertshaw's (1989, 1990) scenario for "big man" lineages and monopolistic trade networks among makers of Elmenteitan lithics and ceramics in the Mara-Loita region of Kenya. I would interpret Robertshaw's project less as a deliberate exercise in gendering the archaeological evidence than as one that proceeds from assuming male agency in any economically important activity.

Androcentrism in Pastoralist Ethnographies: Implications for Archaeologists

It is small wonder, however, that most archaeologists' models of pastoral society accept women as noninstrumental, and women's work as marginally important to production, trade, and social life. Most older and many more recent anthropological accounts of pastoralism are largely androcentric in both focus and tone—what is reported is what men do, and what men do is what is important. That men wield overt economic and political power and that they dominate public discourse in most African pastoral societies has apparently blinded (male?) ethnographers to women's roles, areas of autonomy, and subtler exercises of power. It may indeed be difficult for male ethnographers to work closely with female informants among peoples practicing strong social partitioning of men and women. But in East African pastoral encampments women are everywhere, milking, preparing milk products, tending adult livestock, nurturing their children and young livestock, butchering and cooking animals, preparing other kinds of foodstuffs, carrying water and firewood, making and cleaning houses, singing, arguing, importuning, and otherwise participating in a rich web of socially contextualized work and experience. Lacunae in traditional ethnographies on roles of women—and of children—thus reflect a literal turning away from the daily business of the pastoral encampment.

For archaeologists, the prevailing androcentrism of most ethnographic literature on pastoralists is not just a peripheral problem of gender politics, to be taken or left according to one's own personal inclinations. It especially ill serves those of us who study the remains of everyday life, whether in residential sites or in special-purpose locales. If we lack actualistic evidence on details of house construction (how much time and labor per structure type), food preparation (energetic trade-offs of different methods of cooking and processing), water and wood gathering (how much is required by specific technologies of cooking), cleaning and refuse disposal of a settlement (efficiencies versus symbolic action)—all because these tasks are in the hands of women and children and thus have been discounted—what can serve as our referential sets for working with archaeological materials? To the extent to which our own cultural mind-sets keep us from documenting important categories of behavior that produce archaeological traces, we are deprived of important classes of data about archaeological materials (Gifford-Gonzalez 1993). This is not a matter of "paying attention to women," because we are well-advised not to associate certain tasks and roles *a priori* with either gender, or to adults over children. Rather, we must not refrain from investigating important areas of resource use and site formation simply because they are in the hands of persons whom our culture—or even the culture under study—depreciates.

Exceptions to androcentric norms of description are found in the work of human ecologists and development economists. These include McCabes and Dyson-Hudson's (1982) and Wienpahl's (1984) research on livestock management and household production in Turkana homesteads, Arhem's (1985) close study of Maasai divisions of labor and output among households in the Serengeti Conservation area, and Homewood and Rogers' (1991) ecologically and regionally contextualized study of Maasai subsistence strategies in the same area. Like archaeologists, these researchers must study the overall situation of humans within a regional context, linking details of household social relations and economy to socioeconomic systems and regional ecology. Such an approach leads to ample documentation of pastoral and agropastoral women's actions and manipulation—if not outright ownership—of major resources. As well, economic historians and anthropologists such as Kjekshus (1977) and Hakansson (1994) also have documented women's roles in local and regional agropastoral and pastoral economic systems (see below). Recent academic literature and cinema from more feminist perspectives have also enhanced understandings of gender relations in East African pastoral systems (Hodder 1986; Llewelyn-Davies 1979; Moore 1982; Williams 1987).

What may we glean from such research that is relevant to archaeological cases? Historically, East African pastoral women actively participated in production and distribution systems, as well as in actual exchange negotiations. Confined neither to house nor to homestead, they sometimes traveled impressive distances solely in the company of other women, carrying goods and conducting trade. Kjekshus (1977), citing early Arab and European travelers' accounts in what is now Tanzania, notes that Maasai women regularly traveled scores of kilometers to preordained, nonurban market locales for trade, even during times of intertribal warfare or raiding. Similar patterns of interethnic trade by women are summarized by Hakansson (1994) for Gusii and Luo in the 19th century. Late 20th-century pastoral women's minibus expeditions to trade in East African metropoles thus have precolonial antecedents.

Detailed economic analyses indicate that females commonly held rights both to allocate harvested and stored plant foods and to the products of flocks and herds under their care. Despite male ownership of productive agrarian land and livestock, women's on-the-ground control was the basis for their manipulation of household economics and negotiation of social success within patrilineal, patrilocal societies. For example, Hakansson (1994) has noted that Gusii men wishing to mobilize cattle for bridewealth and other status-enhancing activities, or grains with which to brew beer and stage feasts for visitors, had to negotiate with wives for grain and labor, and even were forced to bargain for the "loan" of cattle they had previously committed to a specific wife's sons. Thus, far from being a simplistic patriarchal world in which men controlled land, livestock, and women, historic Gusii society comprised a complex set of competing entitlements and obligations, in which persons of different ages and genders attempted to negotiate their most advantageous possible life courses.

The foregoing discussion of the gendered nature of mainstream archaeological interpretation—and some counterexamples that emphasize women—might appear to be an argument for filling in the present androcentric "half-truth" of archaeological interpretation with a gynecocentric exegesis of the missing half. It is not. In Conkey and Spector's (1984) terms, such a "just add women and stir" remedy for redressing androcentrism merely follows and reifies the culturally specific gender categories implicit in the Western archaeological tradition. Insistence on *a priori*, "boys-do-this, girls-do-that" perspectives blind us to the potential social variability with which we may be confronted archaeologically.

Studying Gender Archaeologically Requires a Social Approach

The archaeological study of gender will be productive only if a broader shift is made toward more socially focused analytic approaches. Gender is one of a number of socially constructed categories that place individuals and groups within larger sets of economic and political relationships and guide the allocation of rights and obligations within a society (see Conkey and Spector 1984). A socially focused approach requires that we abandon anglophone archaeologists' traditional inclination to view archaeological evidence as products either of individual effort or of poorly delimited, yet unitary, "groups." Traditional archaeological perspectives may testify more to our own cultural construal of work as individualistic and autonomous within a largely undifferentiated societal unit, than to any quality inherent in the archaeological evidence itself. What kind of "social archaeology" is useful for exegeses of sites created by unranked, unstratified, food-producing or foraging groups? The "chiefdoms–civilizations" social archaeology (Earle 1987; Renfrew 1984; Renfrew and Cherry 1986; Sanders and Price 1968) does not, from my point of view, readily integrate with the empirical evidence of smaller-scale social groupings nor with the more fluid social arrangements such as presumably characterized pastoral and forager societies in prehistoric East Africa.

East African archaeology has shared with other regional traditions the tendency to view hunter-gatherers as fundamentally ecologically driven. Moreover, ethnographers and historians have until recently assumed that East African farmers and pastoralists were subsistence-oriented producers who, if involved in exchange at all, passively responded to the stimuli of trade initiated from the Indian Ocean Coast (Kjekshus 1977; Koponen 1988). Both assumptions have come into question more recently, and evidence is mounting that at least some East African food producers regularly planned to produce surpluses for intergroup trade as part of their normal social and economic regimes, with the aim of acquiring prestige goods (Hakansson 1994).

Recent work on the archaeology of "complex hunter-gatherers" elsewhere in the world (Price and Brown 1985; Price and Feinman 1995) indicates that socially directed theory and method can be developed and applied to such groups. I believe approaches that start with a fundamentally economic analysis of social relations among individuals and small groups in the procurement, production, and distribution of resources and commodities (Bender 1985; Hayden 1992a; Marquardt 1985) are most useful. With a focus on resource acquisition, production, and distribution in the context of social relations, one can accommodate consideration—if not immediate discernment—of gender (see also Stahl and Cruz, Chapter 11; Segobye, Chapter 12; Hall, Chapter 13). Such an approach does not necessarily negate or dismiss ecological models but rather includes them in a more complex model of human social and economic behaviors (Hayden 1992a; Jones 1996). With their varied emphases on the "structures of everyday life," these approaches allow us to link information on present-day groups and the material remnants of the quotidian activities of ancient peoples.

Archaeological Uses of Ethnographic Data: The Case for Caution

Although I have done ethnoarchaeological research among modern pastoralists and agropastoralists in East Africa, I do not believe it prudent to equate pastoralists then with pastoralists now in a facile way. The most obvious difference between the prehistoric period and recent times is the colonial—and now, postcolonial—contexts in which historic and ethnographic documentation has taken place. Most of us are aware of how and why apparently "essential features" of modern pastoralist socioeconomic status, ethnicity, and territoriality may stem from developments in their very recent histories (Chang and Koster 1994; Chang 1967; Denbow 1984; Denbow and Wilmsen 1986; Galaty 1991; Galaty 1977; O'Brien 1977; Schrire 1984b; Yellen 1990b). Of even greater concern to archaeologists is the possibility that the situation of the earliest pastoral colonists of East Africa may well have been very different from that of pastoralists in the *precolonial* 2nd millennium of the Christian era. The latter point will be developed in the last section of this paper, but it raises the question of how to use analogies with modern pastoral groups in doing archaeological analysis. One must choose one's parallel cases based on an understanding of the nature of analogical reasoning, avoiding, for example, the notion that all pastoralists live (and lived) in segmentary patrilineages, that a modal pastoralist personality type exists, that all of them conceptualize and handle cattle, camels, small stock, and wild animals the same way, or that all mobilize labor and reduce economic risk similarly.

In an earlier paper (Gifford-Gonzalez 1991), I discussed problems and potentials of analogical reasoning in historical sciences such as archaeology in some detail. Here I note two points relevant to using contemporary studies in archaeological research. First, most archaeological reasoning, including that based on "uniformitarian" assumptions and on the "direct historic" approach, is analogical (Wylie 1982, 1985). Archaeological epistemology, hypothesis formation and selection, as well as methods of inference, are normally and unavoidably analogical (Binford 1981; Gifford 1981; Gifford-Gonzalez 1991; Gould and Watson 1982; Smith 1977; Wylie 1982, 1985). Even the logical sorting of alternatives before explicit articulation of hypotheses or models occurs within a matrix of analogical comparisons and judgments that Wylie (1989) has called "suppressed analogy" (see also Salmon 1982).

Second, criticisms of misused ethnographic analogy (Ascher 1961; Binford 1967, 1987a; Freeman 1968; Gould 1978, 1980; Gould and Watson 1982) in fact object to the failings of formal analogies, in contrast to relational ones. Formal analogies extend to the less-known case-associated traits of the known case, based solely on points of resemblance in form between the two. This is the very problem critics of the abuse of ethnographic analogy identify as the error of unjustifiably imputing aspects of a living society to an ancient one. In the case of gender studies, the grossest such errors might include assuming men were never gatherers, women were always potters, and so forth. Of more concern, perhaps, are the potential pitfalls of the "direct historic" approach, which deploys an elaborate system of formal analogies (for example, assuming that protohistoric Sotho gender arrangements were like those of ethnographic Sotho in all respects). Stahl and Cruz (Chapter 11) and Hall (Chapter 13) work through this issue discerningly, as have Lewis-Williams and Dowson (1988) in their discussion of the relevance of San ritual and rock painting to European paleolithic art. More strongly warranted analogical inferences depend on relational analogies, where properties are ascribed to the less-understood partner in an analogical pair based on knowledge of the functional or causal relationships of those qualities in the better-known member of the pair (Copi 1982; Hesse 1966). For example, paleontologists routinely impute an ontogenetic history to a fossil bone, based on its resemblances to modern bones for which such histories are universal causal and functional conditions.

How does the foregoing relate to using research findings on modern pastoralists (or others) to investigate gender or other social aspects of ancient pastoralist society? If we recognize that analogies are more warranted if based on systematic or causal relations, we must employ ethnographic evidence to move us beyond facile gender and cultural stereotyping, to locate those enduring and universal facts of pastoral life to which all groups and households engaged in the keeping of herds and flocks must respond. From the multiplicity of modern cases, one can discern underlying factors with which any group relying on cattle, sheep, goats, donkeys, or camels must cope. These include the climatic patterns characterizing the areas inhabited, basic biological requirements and behaviors of the species managed, and other synecological interactions particular to the region, all of which require strategic, socially coordinated responses from pastoralists. By arguing from first principles established by these factors, we may develop a framework for thinking about the parameters and challenges of early pastoral life. In turn, this can lead to better definition of research problems and relevant types of archaeological evidence. The second part of this chapter considers the specifics of the East African case, focusing on gender in modern groups and three planes of analysis that follow logically from the foregoing and contribute to an understanding of gender in the archaeological record: (1) risks and risk reduction in pastoral systems, (2) regional ecology and epizootiology, and (3) functional artifact analysis.

Background on Early Pastoralism in East Africa

Details of the sequence of food-producing economies in eastern Africa are not yet widely published, and this section attempts to summarize the current state of knowledge.

Unlike many other regions where food production either developed or was introduced, research in East Africa has been sporadic, largely done on the individual initiative of foreign researchers from several different national traditions of archaeology, and uncoordinated through central planning or voluntary, consensual research design. Indigenous scientists have been hampered by the paucity of resources devoted to archaeological field research and by their administrative obligations to museums, universities, and antiquity services. These factors account for some, but not all, of the rather skimpy nature of archaeological data points, advanced materials analyses, and contingent nature of interpretations.

Environmental and Human History

Analysis of pollen cores and limnological analyses of lakes of the Kenyan Central Rift and adjacent highland lakes of Kenya, together with more limited studies of the

Lake Turkana basin, have produced enough information to outline climatic and vegetational history of the region. Table 7.1 summarizes a dynamic pattern of climate and vegetation change in the terminal Pleistocene and Holocene, to which humans would have had to adjust. Lake Turkana, the area with the earliest evidence of domestic animals in the region, underwent dynamic variations in level from terminal Pleistocene through Holocene (Butzer 1971), and during the early Holocene moist phase, it was an outlet lake joined to the Nile drainage system. As in more northern parts of Africa, this moist phase seems to have seen development of a lacustrine-focused economy that included introduced domestic animals and ceramics in its later phases (Table 7.1). The mid-Holocene arid phase may have prompted emigration from the Lake Turkana basin toward pastures farther south. As they moved south, immigrants would have encountered hunter-gatherer populations also adjusting not only to differences in the locations and relative proportions of biotic communities but also to a shift in rainfall from a unimodal to a bimodal pattern in south-central Kenya (Marshall 1990).

Ambrose (1984a,b) has modeled a dynamic vegetational sequence for the steep-sided Central Rift of Kenya (Figure 7.1 and Table 7.1), asserting that these both called for reorganization in indigenous foragers' land use and influenced the timing of domestic bovines' and caprines' introduction into south-central Kenya. Only after 3000 BP would optimal habitats have opened up for savanna-adapted ungulate species, including domestic cattle, sheep and goats. Less is known of vegetational history of the more southern Athi-Kapiti, Loita, and Serengeti plains. We may expect that wet phases would have led to expansion of woodlands from adjacent uplands into savanna habitats, while during times of increased aridity, savannas would have expanded into wooded zones and arid steppe into former grasslands, with concomitant reorganizations in animal communities. Marean (1990, 1992b; see also Marean and Gifford-Gonzalez 1991) has documented presence of arid-adapted large animal taxa in terminal Pleistocene deposits at Lukenya Hill, on the Athi Plains south of Nairobi, reflecting the late Pleistocene dry phase.

Archaeological Evidence and Chronology

It seems likely that pastoral colonization of what is now the savanna region of Kenya and northern Tanzania was inhibited by climatic and ecological factors until sometime around the late 4th and early 3rd millennium BP. At that point, one can discern at least three (possibly more) coeval flaked-stone industries and three ceramic traditions associated with remains of early domestic animals in Kenya and Tanzania. All ceramic traditions are associated with ground stone palettes, rubbing stones, and so-called stone bowls. The last were interpreted by Leakey and Leakey (1950) as mortars and some possibly as indirect heat cooking vessels, and again as grinding equipment by Robertshaw and Collett (1983a).

The Elmenteitan and the Eburran (L. S. B. Leakey's [1931, 1935] "Kenya Capsian") lithic industries are typically Later Stone Age, blade-based and incorporating geometrics. The Eburran is local to the Central Rift of Kenya, enduring from around

YRS BP	CLIMATE & VEGETATION	LAKE TURKANA	SOUTH AND CENTRAL KENYA	SOUTHERN KENYA NORTHERN TANZANIA	EAST LAKE VICTORIA SOUTHWESTERN KENYA	YRS BP
1,000	Similar to modern regime	Immigration and coalescence of modern ethnic groups	Pastoral Iron Age w/ Lanet ceramics from 1300 BP Iron Age w/ Kwale ceramics from 1800 BP Pastoral	Iron Age w/ Kwale ceramics from 1800 Iron Age: w/ Lelesu ceramics 1800 BP Pastoral	Iron Age: w/ Roulette ceramics Iron Age: w/ Lelesu ceramics 1800 BP	1,000
2,000	Similar to modern regime, establishment of modern vegetation. Onset of seasonally bimodal rainfall.[1]	Mosaic of pastoralist and hunter--gatherer occupation of northern Kenya. Continued use of Later Stone Age lithics by some regional populations into first millennium BP	Neolithic w/ Akira pottery ~2000 BP; w/ Narosura pottery ~2800 BP. "Nondescript PN" w/ ceramics Elmenteitan 2500-1300 BP[2] Eburran Phase 5 w/ domesticates Njoro River Cave Elmenteitan crematory 3100 BP[4]	Neolithic w/ Akira pottery ~2000 BP; w/ Narosura pottery ~2800 BP; some with domestic fauna. Some "PN" w/ ceramics, show continuities of local lithic traditions	Iron Age: w/ Urewe ceramics ~2200 BP Elmenteitan lithics and ceramics throughout inland region ~2500-1300 BP[3]	2,000
3,000	Moister trend begins.					3,000
4,000	Much drier than present: Kenyan Central Rift lakes very low by 5500 BP, then	Nderit and Ileret ceramics 4400 BP: caprines, lake fauna, pillar sites, exotic materials	Eburran Phase 5:[5] associated w/ caprines, Nderit ware at Enkapune ya Muto[6]	Local Later Stone Age industries, associated with low frequencies of Nderit pottery	Kansyore ceramics, quartz-based Later Stone Age in lacustrine sites, with wild terrestrial	4,000
5,000	subsequently dry up until ~3000 BP[7]	Lake-focused Later Stone Age	HIATUS[8]	Localized Later Stone Age	vertebrates and lake invertebrate fauna to ~4700 BP[9]	5,000
6,000	Gradual, irregular drying phase, with lowering of	"bone harpoon" sites with lacustrine and terrestrial	Eburran Phase 4	lithic industries associated with wild fauna,	Kansyore	6,000
7,000	lake levels. Very moist, heavy and lower-altitude forest cover and high stands of lakes in Kenyan	fauna ?8000 ~4000	Eburran Phase 3,4	some associated with Kansyore pottery[10]	ceramics with quartz-based Later Stone Age lithics, arguable dates	7,000
8,000	Central Rift, Lake Naivasha overflows south, Lakes Elmenteita, Nakuru fuse, Lake Turkana		Eburran Phase 3	Evidence for erosional	to 8000 BP	8,000
9,000	at very high stand.[11]	Later Stone Age	Eburran Phase 2	disconformity in Later Stone Age	HIATUS	9,000
10,000	Onset of very wet phase of arguable length, to 7000 BP, [or 5600 BP]. Rainfall to 35% higher than modern. Highland forest line to 1000 m[12]	Later Stone Age	Eburran Phase 1, 2	sites on or adjoining the Serengeti [e.g. Nasera] 7000 - 17,000 BP[10]	HIATUS	10,000
11,000	Dry phase[13]	Later Stone Age		HIATUS?	HIATUS	11,000
12,000	Brief wet phase, Kenya Central Rift lakes, Lake Turkana overflow.[14]	Later Stone Age	Eburran Phase 1	HIATUS?	HIATUS	12,000
12,500 to 17,000	Hyperarid phase, Central Rift lakes very low, Lake Victoria dries?[15]	HIATUS?	Later Stone Age	HIATUS?	HIATUS	12,500 to 17,000
17,000 to 21,000	Dry, cool phase, forests retreat to refugia, steppe expands, regional lake levels low.[16]	Later Stone Age	Later Stone Age	Later Stone Age	Later Stone Age	17,000 to 21,000

Table 7.1. Archaeological and climatic sequence in East Africa, from around 20,000 BP, with references appended. All dates approximate.

Table references appear at end of chapter.

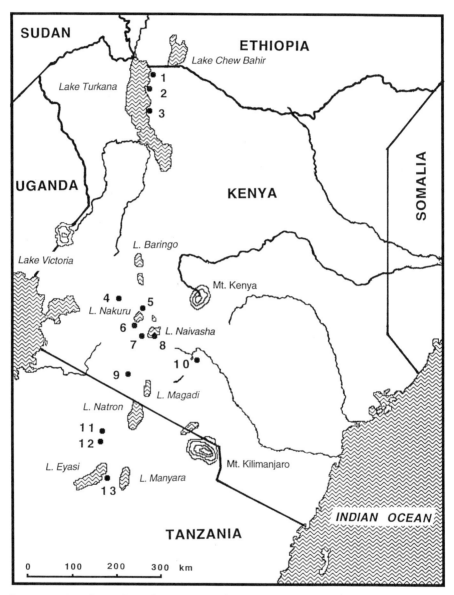

Figure 7.1. Map of East Africa, showing sites and regions mentioned in the text. Key to numbered sites: 1 = FWJJ5; 2 = GAJ14; 3 = Jaragole; 4 = Njoro River Cave; 5 = Hyrax Hill; 6 = Prolonged Drift; 7 = Enkapune ya Muto; 8 = Crescent Island Causeway; 9 = Narosura; 10 = Lukenya Hill; 11 = Olduvai; 12 = Nasera; 13 = Mumba Cave.

12,000 to about 3000 BP (Ambrose et al. 1980). The third lithic grouping is in fact a more heterogeneous assortment of microlithic Later Stone Age assemblages united under the heading "Savanna Pastoral Neolithic" (Ambrose 1984b; Bower 1991; Bower and Nelson 1978; Bower et al. 1977). This term may mean different things to different researchers. I suggest that the heterogeneity within this grouping, its general similarities with East African Later Stone Age industries, and, in well-studied cases, its specific continuities with earlier, local core-reduction and tool-making practices (see Mehlman 1989), suggest that it may not be a new imported technology, but rather an array of diverse and in some cases autochthonous technologies.

Reliable radiocarbon dates for Elmenteitan and Savanna Pastoral Neolithic sites are few, but the earliest coincide relatively closely with the onset of modern climatic conditions (Collett and Robertshaw 1983b; Merrick and Monaghan 1984). In south-central Kenya, the three lithic industries overlap in time, and two have adjacent, often mutually exclusive geographic ranges. Thus, there is reasonable archaeological evidence for the coexistence of groups with distinctive artifact-making practices in the 3rd millennium BP.

In contrast, different ceramic traditions cross boundaries between some lithic industries, suggesting a complex social situation. Of the ceramic traditions, the Nderit predates the others and appears to have spread southward from the Lake Turkana basin to the Serengeti (Bower 1991; Marshall in press). Nderit pottery is normally associated with Savanna Pastoral Neolithic lithics but is encountered with what Ambrose (1984b, 1990) characterizes as Eburran 5 lithics at Enkapune ya Muto Rock Shelter and Hyrax Hill Neolithic Village sites near Lake Nakuru (Figure 7.1). Later sites containing Savanna Pastoral Neolithic lithics yield another, ceramic tradition, including Narosura/Akira pottery. According to Ambrose (1984b) these ceramics are also associated with Eburran Phase 5 lithics at the Crescent Island Causeway Site, Lake Naivasha (Figure 7.1). Elmenteitan (formerly Remnant) ceramics are usually associated with Elmenteitan lithics but have sometimes been recovered from Eburran Phase 5 deposits (Ambrose 1984b) and were among the ceramics diagnosed at Prolonged Drift, considered a Savanna Pastoral Neolithic site on the basis of lithics (Robertshaw and Collett 1983a).

Subsistence diversity is reflected in these assemblages, but again not always neatly along "cultural" lines. Savanna Pastoral Neolithic and larger Elmenteitan sites contain predominantly domestic animal remains and lie in locales favored by modern pastoralists. Bone isotope research (Ambrose and DeNiro 1986) suggests that Savanna Pastoral Neolithic makers relied more on animal products than did makers of Elmenteitan artifacts. Robertshaw and Collett (1983a) note that numerous Savanna Pastoral Neolithic and Elmenteitan sites could have supported rainfall-dependent farming and that groundstone axes or adzes and stone bowls may have been agricultural implements. Sites with late Eburran lithics contain domestic animals. At Enkapune ya Muto Rock Shelter, the Eburran 5 level has domestic caprines (and Nderit/Ileret ceramics) in a level dating 4900–3000 ^{14}C years BP (Ambrose 1990; Marean 1992a), the earliest uncontested dates for domestic stock in the Central Rift.

At the risk of glossing over problematic aspects of as yet sketchy evidence, I offer a summary of what these data suggest. As the climate and biotic communities of southern-central Kenya approached conditions similar to those of today, successive immigrations of food-producing groups took place, the earliest of which involved makers of Nderit ceramics. Indigenous foragers would have had to respond to these incursions in some way, and evidence is accumulating of incorporation of domestic animals and of various ceramic wares into sites with local lithic traditions.

By mid- to late 3rd millennium BP, the upper Mara River drainage of southwestern Kenya saw replacement of Savanna Pastoral Neolithic lithics and associated ceramics by a third tradition, the Elmenteitan, which overlays Narosura ceramics in some occurrences (Robertshaw 1990). The two groups then occupied adjacent, mutually exclusive ranges for several hundred years, both using domestic cattle, sheep, and goats, but maintaining distinctive lithic and ceramic manufacturing techniques over time. The makers of Elmenteitan artifacts, perhaps more committed to cultivation, occupied woodland-grassland ecotones and open grasslands of the Mau Escarpment and Loita–Mara plains, while makers of Narosura/Akira ceramics occupied the grasslands of the Central Rift and plains south into Tanzania and were heavily committed to livestock rearing (Ambrose 1982a).

Nderit Sites: Frontier Ecology and Social Relations

The widespread phenomenon of Nderit ceramics presents an opportunity to explore a social approach to East African archaeological materials. Nderit pottery, Louis Leakey's (1931, 1935) "Gumban A," plus so-called Ileret Ware from east Lake Turkana, includes vessel forms ranging from very large bowls to smaller vessels, all of which are typified by internal scoring of the bowls, application of multiple, broad panels of incised or comb-stamped impressions over most of the outer surface of the vessels, and incised or milled rims. The earliest examples of this tradition are in the northeastern Lake Turkana basin, with dates between 4500 and 4000 ^{14}C years BP (Barthelme 1985), associated with remains of domestic livestock, fish, and other aquatic vertebrates in apparently residential encampments. At least five nonresidential funerary sites in the Lake Turkana basin, as yet neither well dated nor well published, have yielded Nderit-style ceramics (Koch 1994). Based on commonalities of artifacts, architecture, and handling of the dead, Koch (1994) defines the Jaragole Mortuary Tradition and the Jaragole Ossuary Tradition by Nelson (1993). The sites comprise implanted stone pillars up to 2 meters long, funerary mounds containing apparently deliberately fragmented human remains (interpreted by Koch and Nelson as secondary burials), fragments of many large and often exquisitely wrought Nderit-style ceramics, zoomorphic ceramic figurines (of both wild and domestic animals, the only such known from East Africa), marine shells and lithics from distant sources

(Nelson 1993). Nelson (1993) reports that fragments of at least 650 large ceramic bowls were recovered from the Jaragole Pillar Site. Bones of aquatic and terrestrial vertebrates have been excavated, but no taxonomic identifications have yet been published.

Nderit-style ceramics in south-central Kenya and northern Tanzania are not associated with such elaborate funerary practices, nor have ceramic figurines been recovered from any sites. At GvJm44, one of many sites clustered around Lukenya Hill, south of Nairobi on the Athi Plains, Nderit ceramics are associated with stone bowls and domestic animals (Figure 7.1). Nelson (1993; 1992 : personal communication) has noted that decoration on Nderit sherds around Lukenya seems more cursorily applied than it is on sherds in the Central Rift area, much less the Lake Turkana examples. Nderit sherds are associated with a predominantly nondomestic animal food base in some sites, as at Ambrose's Enkapune ya Muto rockshelter in the Mau Escarpment (Marean 1992a). On the Serengeti, Mehlman (1989:458) reports rare Nderit-style sherds, confirmed by Bower and Wandibba, in association with a local and long-lived lithic industrial tradition at Nasera Rock, north of Olduvai Gorge. Nderit ceramics are also found associated with an exclusively wild fauna at the Gol Kopjes site, also on the Serengeti (Bower 1988, 1991; Bower and Chadderdon 1986). Overlying levels at the same site continue in the association of wild migratory and resident fauna with the later, Akira ceramic tradition.

How best to interpret sites with predominantly or exclusively wild fauna and Nderit ceramics? Two alternative explanations have been advanced in the literature. The first interprets these as camps of hunter-gatherers who obtained the pots through exchange with food- (and ceramic-) producing neighbors, a case strengthened by independent lines of evidence suggesting continuities with earlier, preceramic local traditions (e.g., Eburran Phase 5, Mehlman's Nasera data).[3] Others believe the sites are best understood as evidence of immigrating groups practicing a flexible mix of herding, foraging, and farming (Bower 1986, 1991).[4] In the absence of other information, either scenario would seem tenable, and both have been previously proposed for some combination of ceramics and wild fauna in the East African Neolithic.

I propose a third alternative here, that Nderit pottery makers were present at the camps of local foraging peoples, reflecting networks of alliance and exchange during the early pastoral colonization of Kenya and northern Tanzania, in which gender may have figured prominently. This suggestion is necessarily speculative, inasmuch as I have not engaged in field research from this point of view, and relevant excavated collections are half a world away. There is no *a priori* reason why one of these explanations should be privileged over any other, and it will ultimately require assessing the relevant evidence on a site-by-site basis. However, exploring why the last option may be viable for the period when Nderit ceramics spread into East Africa is an example of a more socially focused approach. The next section develops an argument from first principles drawn from contemporary pastoralist studies and epizootiology.

Pastoralist Ecology, Economy, and the Archaeological Record

Researches on modern pastoralists emphasize the constant and pressing need for herding labor within such systems (Ingold 1980) and the relation of this to pastoral social systems. Because successful stock owners are by definition perpetually short of labor, pastoralists are open to recruiting new members by any and all means, and "definitions of identity tend to be inclusive rather than exclusive" (Waller 1985:349). Historically documented pastoralists expanding into East African savannas did not act as hermetically sealed, "tribal" units, emphasizing their differences with newly encountered groups, but rather engaged in flexible and intense, if often ambivalent, relations with neighbors (Galaty 1991; Sobania 1991; Turton 1991). Alliances were common, mediated by intermarriage, in some cases by wholesale transfers of larger social groups from one linguistic and "ethnic" entity to another, and by rituals.

Demands of prospering herds and flocks for herding personnel may be a universal aspect of pastoral systems, but other social relations, particularly those between food producers and peoples who, if not exclusively foragers, gather and hunt many wild foods, may be much more dependent on historic context. Among the most influential recent writings on such relations have been those of Bailey (1988; Bailey and DeVore 1989) on the asymmetrical social and economic relations of Efe foragers with their Lese food-producing neighbors in Zaire. Bailey argues that male Efe hunters are at great disadvantage in finding spouses, because Efe families favor marrying daughters into Lese households as a form of risk reduction and "upward mobility." This reduces the number of potential spouses for Efe men and heightens competition among them for mates. Cronk (1991) documented a similar process of "hypergyny" among the Mukogodo of northern Kenya, who recently shifted from a foraging-dominated life to pastoral subsistence very similar to that of their neighbors the Samburu. Samburu men "marry down" to Mukogodo women, providing their parents with livestock, now preferred to traditional hunters' bride service, and thus forcing Mukogodo men to accumulate livestock to stay competitive for wives.[5] Blackburn (1996) documents a similar pattern of asymmetrical out-marriage among Okiek of the Mau Escarpment in Kenya. Social and economic asymmetries between contemporary pastoralists and hunter-gatherers today are so pervasive that they may gradually drive one social system, if not the people themselves, to extinction.

It is tempting to extend this model to prehistoric cases in which communication between food producers and foragers is evident. Speth (1990) cited hypergyny as a force driving social and subsistence change among hunter-gatherers on the American plains who entered into close exchange relations with Pueblo food producers in protohistoric times. Taking a somewhat different tack, Robertshaw (1989) uses ethnographic data and Ingold's (1980) theories on the ideological correlates of pastoral production to develop a scenario for status and power asymmetries between hunting peoples and pastoralists, assuming again that presently observable power relations pertained in prehistory as well.

However, archaeologists should use such contemporary models with caution. Ethnographically documented interactions have taken place in the colonial and postcolonial context, when food producers emphasized their bounded, "tribal" identity rather than inclusiveness, to vindicate land claims (see Waller 1985; Sobania 1991). Today's observed asymmetries may have obtained in precolonial times, but they should not be assumed *a priori*, without arguments about why this should be the case. The earliest food producers with domestic stock faced a different social and ecological milieu than do recent herding peoples, and this may well have placed them in a different relation to indigenous foragers than is typical of historically documented cases.

Risks and Risk Reduction on the East African Neolithic Frontier

Contemporary pastoralists recognize that climatic fluctuations typical of the grasslands they inhabit, as well as unpredictable but recurrent epizootics, put them at constant risk of herd decimation (Dahl and Hjort 1976; Dyson-Hudson and Dyson-Hudson 1970, 1980; Homewood and Rogers 1991; Ingold 1980). To buffer the impacts of largely unavoidable disasters, herders employ various risk-reduction strategies. These include: dispersing stock holdings widely through loans to other herders; parceling out animals of one male stock owner to multiple wives and their offspring in far-flung locales; developing exchange relations with farming peoples, often supported or mediated by marriage; farming and, last and ideologically least, gathering and hunting.

For the earliest pastoral peoples moving into what is now Kenya and Tanzania, some such strategies were less likely options. Stock loans, bond friendships based on livestock exchange, and far-flung marriages require a certain density of pastoralists in the landscape to be reliable insurance in times of herd disasters. At least for the span of time over which we see Nderit pottery as a widespread phenomenon, it is not evident that such densities existed. Instead, prudent pastoral stock owners may well have depended both on a highly flexible subsistence strategy of their own, as suggested by Robertshaw and Collett (1983b; see also Galaty 1991) and on establishing close and relatively peerlike relationships with indigenous hunter-gatherers.

For pastoralists entering the Central Rift and regions to the south, new disease challenges to their livestock would have made the chancy world of pastoral production even more dangerous. Possibly novel animal diseases include trypanosomiasis (sleeping sickness), spread by tsetse fly in brushy habitats, and the tick-borne East Coast fever (ECF) and ungulate-borne malignant catarrhal fever (MCF). Present-day African pastoralists avoid sleeping sickness by keeping their cattle away from brushy zones. However, herders have proactively modified tsetse distributions by burning underbrush and moving goats and cattle into riparian habitats during drier months, the time of lowest infection risk (Lamprey and Waller 1990; Stenning 1958).

The third novel disease threat to livestock may have been both less manageable and avoidable, even once recognized: wildebeest-derived malignant catarrhal fever (WD-MCF), a herpes virus close to 100 percent fatal in infected cattle, is transmitted by wildebeest calves a few days to less than three months old (Mushi and Rurangirwa

1981). Wildebeest have not been documented in or to the north of the Lake Turkana basin (Dorst and Dandelot 1970; Gautier 1981; Van Neer and Uerpmann 1989). They did, however, definitely inhabit the Central Rift as far north as Lake Baringo in the 3rd millennium BP; their bones are sometimes found in sites bearing domestic stock (Gifford et al. 1980; Gifford-Gonzalez and Kimengich 1984; Hivernel 1983). Thus, their presence in newly entered areas would have presented potentially disastrous circumstances to herders.

Social Dimensions of Early Forager–Food Producer Interactions

Heightened disease vulnerabilities, combined with lower stock densities for herd-replacement through pastoral alliances, may have made ties to local hunting and gathering peoples a considerably more important risk-reduction strategy for pastoralists than has been recently observed during the first entry of stock-owning groups into East Africa. Local foraging groups could offer labor during good years for livestock and local knowledge of exploitable wild foods during bad. Hunter-gatherers reciprocally would have gained pastoral products and perhaps cultivated cereals, valuable inputs to seasonally fat- and carbohydrate-poor diets (Speth and Spielmann 1983). The Kenyan forest environment has been shown to be poor in edible plant resources, limiting foragers' ability to obtain carbohydrates in that zone, though some other East African savanna-woodlands are more productive of dry season foods (Vincent 1985a,b). Introduced domestic African grains, typically harvested in summer after planting with the spring rains, would have been available at precisely the point in hunter-gatherers' yearly cycles at which nutritional stress reached its highest levels.

Ceramic technology itself, as I believe is evident from the "Nderit" sites, would have been a major medium of interaction. Recent zooarchaeological discussions have converged in concluding that substantial nutritional gains, especially in extraction of fat, can be realized by boiling in comparison to roasting or baking (Gifford 1993; Lupo 1995; O'Connell et al. 1988). Archaeological sequences in East Africa testify to the appearance of ceramic vessels with or without domestic stock. Where some domestic animals appear at the same time as ceramics, as at Enkapune ya Muto, ceramics need not reflect a wholesale shift to a food-producing way of life, but rather a technological enhancement of the existing foraging pattern (Marean 1992a; see also Parkington, Chapter 2, and Wadley, Chapter 4). Historically documented groups that rely heavily on wild foods, such as the Okiek and the Hadza, traditionally made their own ceramic vessels; others obtained their pots through exchange—but all use them.

With much of the spectrum of insurance against herd decimation seen in contemporary situations unavailable to early pastoralists, more equitable, reciprocal exchange relationships may have obtained between them and indigenous foragers than are observable today. Spouses may have moved in both directions. The concept of hypergyny is thoroughly gendered, and we may prudently refrain for the moment from assigning either relative status or gender to the "spouses" in the prehistoric Nderit case. To do so requires that we advance logical arguments about why we might suppose, for example, women were potters, or men were stone workers. If the genders of people who may have moved between groups cannot currently be discerned, we can at least conceive of circumstances in which pastoralists had much less of an upper hand in marriage transactions than they might today. A similar point has been made by Habicht-Mauche (1991) regarding the Plains–Pueblo Indian interactions in the protohistoric period of which Speth wrote.

Nonetheless, one wonders, did certain aspects of food producers' ways of life—not their emplacement in an essentialized category of "pastoralist," but concrete, socially manipulable features of society and technology—accord new colonists advantages when dealing with indigenous groups? If so, might these practices, and the social statuses they produced, induce foragers to shift toward intensive production of wild or domestic commodities for trade with such groups? For example, modern Okiek of the Mau Forest of Kenya "mine" the forest for honey and wild animal pelts, not only for themselves but also as their most valuable item of exchange with food producers (Blackburn 1982, 1996; Kratz 1986). Okiek honey is often made into a mead wine essential to Maa-speakers' rituals, which also require wild animal skins. Intensified grain production, often the option of poorer agropastoralists, might provide foragers with social leverage via an important item of exchange, a luxury food for pastoralist feasts and rituals, especially when brewed into beer (Hayden 1992a). Nderit-making pastoralists entering a riskier, less known, and less productively stable environment than the Lake Turkana basin in its wet phase heyday may have paradoxically been more motivated to emphasize feasting and give-aways during times of relative herd affluence to solidify ties with local foraging groups against the bad times.

Archaeological Expectations

What archaeological evidence exists to assess these possibilities? Space does not permit a comprehensive enumeration, but a few lines of inquiry can be suggested. First, do sites with local continuities in lithic traditions incorporate new technologies in ways that might reflect specialized production? If Ambrose has correctly identified Eburran 5 lithics at the Crescent Island Causeway Site at Lake Naivasha, it may be such a case. The site lies next to a constant source of nonalkaline water, in excellent soil for cultivating sorghum (Robertshaw and Collett 1983a), and has yielded very high concentrations of "stone bowls," interpreted by most as seed processing equipment (C. M. Nelson 1992: personal communication; John Bower 1993: personal communication).

Ceramic analyses should be especially informative in these terms. If the use of Nderit ceramics signified membership in exchange networks, rather than in a specific cultural-economic "ethnic" group, paste composition of vessels could indicate whether pots were moving between groups, or whether potters were doing so. Habicht-Mauche's (1987, 1991) demonstration that persons in "bison hunters" camps on the western plains of Texas made cookpots virtually indistinguishable from those of the Rio Grande Pueblos from local Plains clay sources is an example of this type of research. Kiriama's (1984) petrographic analysis of Nderit ceramics and that of Langdon and Robertshaw (1985) of Elmenteitan ceramics suggest localized pottery production. Systematic analysis of other East African Neolithic ceramics will be relevant to assessing spatially extensive patterns of social alliance and exchange. We already know obsidian was traveling over great distances during this period (Merrick and Brown 1984; Robertshaw 1988).

Closer technological and stylistic analysis of ceramics can also elucidate the place of pottery production in social display. For example, one explanation of the rather "sloppy" decoration on the Lukenya Hill Nderit pottery noted earlier is that these were made by foragers attempting to signify their membership in the social network in which such pots circulated. Yet another explanation for the less intensive and carefully applied decoration of Lukenya Nderit pots is that their makers may have been food producers who were simply not participating in display of "valued-added" wares as intensely as others making and using the ceramics, perhaps because of their location or resource base.

Future analysis of dietary status and life history in light of determinable sex within the Neolithic skeletal sample, and closer examination of funerary handling of individuals, should shed further light on early East African food producers' society and aspects of gender. This project is complicated by lack of cemeteries and a rather small skeletal sample (Schepartz 1988), but some interesting possibilities exist. For example, stone vessels apparently had great significance in the social and ritual lives of Nderit and other early food producers, because these appear in burials associated with Nderit, Narosura, and Elmenteitan lithics or ceramics. The Njoro River Cave crematory presents an interesting if unique case. The cave yielded at least 47 males, 20 females, plus 11 individuals too poorly preserved to make a sex determination (Leakey and Leakey 1950). Lavish funerary furniture includes decorated gourds, necklaces of semiprecious stones and sedge beads, worn in some cases by putatively female individuals, and an intricately carved wooden vessel about 15 cm high with proportions of a drinking vessel. Equally interesting is the virtually identical number of three separate types of grinding-related equipment—stone bowls (78), lower grindstones (77), and pestle-rubbing stones (78)—and their equivalence to the number of individuals estimated to be represented in the excavated sample (78). While bodily ornamentation seemed to vary with gender and age (Leakey and Leakey 1950:26–37), deposit of grinding equipment and persons in equal numbers reflects a different system of signification in which gender differentiation was not apparently so marked (see also Robertshaw and Collett 1983a). These examples illustrate the potential of conceptualizing artifacts in a social context.

Conclusion

Given its speculative nature, I do not purport the foregoing Nderit example as the only possible reading of that data; rather, it suggests how a more socially oriented approach to the East African archaeological materials might develop. I will end with two observations. First, including gender in archaeological research need not entail loss of methodological rigor. Considering socially coordinated production, distribution, and consumption (and gender as a factor in them) in fact demands that we dispense with sloppy thinking about relations of ecology, technology, and production (Bender 1979), and with implicit, ethnocentric or androcentric epistemologies of archaeological objects and sites. Far from sanctioning scientifically weak archaeological interpretations, adding a consideration of gender to archaeological exegeses can unite various strands of archaeological theory into an undoubtedly challenging but nonetheless well-grounded enterprise.

Second, as we move toward archaeological study of human social relations, we move to another, more complex level of inference, in which no single body of theory or method that has served us well at earlier levels may suffice (see Gifford-Gonzalez 1991). Well-worn paths to inference available to us at less complex levels won't get us where we want to go, nor do they necessarily even indicate promising directions to take. We must innovate on what we know, while remaining committed to archaeology as an evidence-based and -monitored practice. Archaeologists in Europe and the Americas have gone some way in this project already, and we may learn about how to conduct such research from their work. Interesting examples juxtapose multiple lines of evidence and multiple bodies of relevant theory and method, resituating plausible lower-level inferences within more complex arguments, generating new expectations, and testing them with archaeological evidence. This work requires a discerning use of actualistic knowledge, plus a critical assessment of our own working concepts of "the social." It should not abandon the concreteness of empirical archaeological evidence, nor the rigor of a systematic, self-testing methodology. Jones' ecologically grounded (1996) study of prehistoric food procurement systems along the central coast of California is such a rigorous approach to assessing the role of gender, as are the chapters in this volume by Parkington, Stahl and Cruz, and Hall. This kind of work demands a more sustained and intense collaboration than has hitherto typified research on the later span of East African prehistory.

Africa seems to have always presented humans with great challenges. We who study her past can choose whether we will engage with the challenge of knowing more of the distinctive lives of African men, women, and children who lived before us.

Acknowledgments

Writings of and informal conversations with John Bower, Fiona Marshall, Bernard Mbae, Michael Mehlman, and Charles Nelson, many of whom have shared as-yet unpublished information with me, have helped me greatly. As well, I have profited from reading the excellent research of Stanley Ambrose, Curtis Marean, and Peter Robertshaw. My analyses of East

African faunas were undertaken with the permission of the Kenyan and Tanzanian governments and the support of the National Museums of Kenya. Susan Kent, Arek Marciniak, and Michael Mehlman offered very helpful comments on earlier drafts. I alone am responsible for the errors of fact and judgment herein.

Notes

1. For example, after my initial interviews with the local head of Kenyan Police and the state-sponsored Administrative Chief about my planned ethnoarchaeological fieldwork, I first physically entered the large Dassanetch settlement at Ileret in far northern Kenya. An assertive female adolescent immediately strode up to me and demanded in Swahili, "Are you a girl or a woman?" It was obvious that which option I specified would determine my status among the scores of onlooking women, whose interest in me was quite different from that of the Administrative Chief, who had treated me not only as a foreign white under the protection of a powerful (white Kenyan male) player in the informal politics of the area, but also as an honorary male.

2. Let me stress that this structure of research is neither the product of conscious "bias against women" nor restricted to male researchers. I believe most of my own ethnoarchaeological and archaeological research in East African prehistory has been as androcentric as anyone else's, and that we all have participated in theoretical systems that downplay the social context of human action.

3. Mehlman (1989) suggests a very similar scenario for incorporation of Kansyore tradition ceramics, without domestic animals, into local forager groups circulating around both Nasera Rock and Mumba Cave.

4. Collett and Robertshaw (1983a) have proposed that sites containing Elmenteitan ceramics and wild fauna, such as Prolonged Drift (Gifford et al. 1980), are the products of "pastoralists in recovery" from disastrous losses of their livestock.

5. As well, Wilmsen (1989; Wilmsen and Denbow 1991) has argued that San speakers of the Kalahari have been in close and asymmetrical relations with neighboring food-producing groups, and with imperialist European powers beyond, for at least a century, which relations have determined their participation in or dropping out of food production as a subsistence base.

Notes from Table 7.1

1. Hills 1978; Marshall 1990.

2. Ambrose 1980; Bower 1991; Langdon and Robertshaw 1985; Leakey 1931; Leakey and Leakey 1950; Marshall 1986; Merrick and Monaghan 1984; Nelson 1980; Robertshaw 1988, 1989, 1990; Wandibba 1980.

3. Ibid.

4. Leakey and Leakey 1950; Merrick and Monaghan 1984.

5. Ambrose 1984a,b for all Eburran citations.

6. Marean 1992.

7. Richardson 1972; Richardson and Richardson 1972.

8. Ambrose 1984a,b; Ambrose et al. 1980.

9. Robertshaw et al. 1983; Robertshaw 1991.

10. Mehlman 1989.

11. Butzer 1971; Butzer et al. 1972; Hamilton 1982.

12. Butzer et al. 1972; Coetzee 1987; Hastenrath and Kutzbach 1983.

13. Butzer et al. 1972; Hamilton 1982; Isaac et al. 1972.

14. Butzer 1971; Butzer et al. 1972; Hamilton 1982

15. Butzer et al. 1972; Hamilton 1982; Isaac et al. 1972; Johnson et al. 1996; Livingstone 1975, 1980; Richardson 1972; Richardson and Richardson 1972.

16. Butzer et al. 1972; Hamilton 1982; Isaac et al. 1972; Livingstone 1975, 1980; Richardson and Richardson 1972.

PETER SCHMIDT ■

Chapter Eight

Reading Gender in the Ancient Iron Technology of Africa

An archaeology that seeks to recuperate gender relations and their structuring ideologies is *ipso facto* an excursion into interpretation. When we attribute social beliefs
and behavior to the material record, then we engage in inferential means of constructing the past—an interpretive process. To understand how ideologies about gender
relations arise out of economic relationships and come to structure modes of production, we must also insist on a scientific approach to underpin and substantiate any
linkages between ideology and its material expressions (Schmidt and Patterson 1995;
Wylie 1987, 1995).

In this paper I want to examine whether ideas about gender relations—especially
ideas that proscribe specific productive and ritual roles during iron smelting in African cultures—can be uncovered in the archaeological record. If archaeology provides
us with a window into the past that allows us to understand better how ideologies of
gender structured production, then we can further advance knowledge about how and
under what circumstances such ideas developed and how they came to change
through time with altering social and economic relations. This is an approach that
depends on a historical method, looking for change and assuming dynamism while
simultaneously accommodating continuity. Like Hall's treatment of Sotho/Tswana
gender relations over several centuries in southern Africa (Chapter 13) and Stahl and
Cruz's study of changing relations of production by women potters among the Banda
of Ghana (Chapter 11), I believe that gender-structured relations of production are
best privileged and understood when seen over time in changing economic and social
contexts.

One methodological challenge that we face in trying to work within a historical
framework is one that Stahl and Cruz capture: to avoid the trap "to treat ethnographic scripts of gendered activity as isomorphic with the past" (Stahl and Cruz,
Chapter 11). The way to avoid such projections into the past is to use a comparative
method (Stahl 1993; Schmidt 1997a; Stahl and Cruz, Chapter 11) that measures the
"degree of fit" of ethnographic cases and their material manifestations with archaeological materials that resemble the ethnographic materials. This results in strong

inference, but inference that has the capacity to uncover, confront, and explain exceptions and contradictions arising out of historical change.

My approach here is to first examine historical and ethnographic examples of African iron smelting, focusing on examples where material symbols are tightly linked to gender attributes in a technology that is socially constructed as human reproduction (Herbert 1993; Childs and Killick 1993; Schmidt 1996a; MacLean, Chapter 9). Human reproduction is a powerful symbolic armature that is often richly elaborated in African iron smelting cultures through ritual performance, during which material objects come to signify other symbolic meanings that amplify the core meanings, as well as sometimes depart from the core paradigm.

As will be seen, there are demonstrable continuities through time in rituals and symbolism linked to iron production in Africa, sometimes reaching back for more than two millennia (Schmidt 1997a; Schmidt and Mapunda 1997). While these cases help us to understand the power of some of the symbolic paradigms over time, it was only when these cases were reexamined with questions of gender relations and their possible changes over time that exceptions to and variations on these continuities came more clearly into focus—demanding that we must explain why they occur. To accomplish this I first examine the variation of meaning of gendered ritual items—usually found in ritual pits in iron smelting furnaces—in a number of related African cultures. A review of a select number of examples provides different social, economic, and ritual contexts for physical items that signify different meanings. Several of these examples are from research that I have conducted in Africa. The rest are drawn from the research of anthropologists and archaeologists working elsewhere on the continent.

The first goal is to understand how gender relations were expressed in the technological domain of African iron smelting and whether it is possible to read these gendered-informed materials in the archaeological record through time. This pragmatic goal needs to be grounded in a reflexive reconsideration of the paradigms that have governed inquiries into gender and iron technology. Over the last decade there has been an accelerated examination of the cosmological and symbolic systems that structure iron smelting technology in Africa. Herbert (1993) has provided us with an extensive exegesis of gender and iron smelting. She unwraps many of the finer nuances that inform a paradigm of human reproduction in African iron smelting, a reproductive paradigm that provides an ideological platform from which various productive systems elaborate and innovate. Herbert provides a helpful analysis of how other beliefs such as appeasement of ancestral spirits also play an important role in iron smelting ritual, bringing out clearly that there is not just one domain of beliefs, but rather an enormous matrix that incorporates ideas of fertility translated into gynecomorphic characteristics of the furnace, the placement of special offerings to insure fertility, protection against malevolent forces, and taboos against certain sexual activities and states.

Herbert's exegesis and my work among the Barongo iron smelters of Tanzania (Schmidt 1996b) have provided a richer understanding of how myth, ritual, and performance converge to structure gender relations in the organization of work, the division of labor, the transmission of mystical knowledge, the performance of rituals, the application (or nonapplication) of proscriptive taboos, and the participation of various age groups in the practice of iron smelting. All of these gender-informed categories affect how iron smelting technology and its attendant activities—particularly ritual—become a playing field for gender relations. The paradigm under which such ritual control takes place is represented as a reproductive process in which the iron smelting furnace takes on the metonymic form of a fecund bride replete with the reproductive organs required to give birth to a fetus. The constellation of other symbols is now familiar: bellows are testicles, the blow pipes are phalluses, the slag is afterbirth, and so on. An integral part of this paradigm as anthropologists have constructed it—mostly from male voices—is the domination of the male smelters over most aspects of the metaphorical female reproductive process. Representations of this inversion are amplified by principles of proscriptive exclusion—taboos—that prevent females from participation in the processes of reproduction. Thus, female reproduction under the aegis of the iron smelting paradigm is a male activity that advances males economically and enhances their power and prestige in their communities. The ritual mystifications that surround iron smelting, it has been further argued, may also have a material basis, for they mask a technical process and thus protect the economically priceless secrets of the lineage from the female interlopers from other patrilines.

The reproductive paradigm in African iron smelting is not without its anomalies and contradictions—the women who in fact mine and process iron ore, the women who participate in sacred rituals, and the women who participate in actual smelting. But these examples are seen as ambiguous exceptions, as anomalies that create dissonance for arriving at a normative, universal process. In archaeology, however, we have learned that it is the anomaly, the piece of evidence that does not fit the model or analog, that begs to be explained and therefore holds the key to understanding change and reveals deeper systems of meaning.

I want to reexamine the normative reproductive paradigm in African iron smelting to see if its common representations of gendered roles can withstand critical scrutiny. There are several compelling reasons to examine entrenched assumptions about the ideology of gender in iron smelting. First, the corpus of information about gendered roles has been derived in good part from male iron smelters. Often oral testimony has not been accompanied by in-field observations that might disclose contradictions to male representations. Second, as noted above, important insights can be gained from a closer-grained examination of several case studies that provide important information on the role of females in iron smelting ritual and in crossover roles played by males in iron smelting. These examples illustrate that gender is a fluid concept in some iron smelting cultures—highly situational, plural, being simultaneously male and female. These examples also show, I suggest, that the paradigmatic representations that dominate our thinking are incomplete representations of the reproductive process, and thus these examples unlock a new dimension of meaning that challenges and remakes the dominant paradigm. Such paradigmatic revision is a necessary first step before we can begin to question how gender can be read in the archaeological record of iron technology. If our comprehension of gender in iron smelting is incomplete or based on false premises, then any attempts to infer gender in the archaeological record are inevitably flawed and misleading.

There are two primary and interrelated ideas associated with rituals that transform iron smelting from a technological activity into a profoundly human and cultural activity: ideas of fertility and notions of protection against evil or malevolent forces, including unhappy ancestors. A "fertile" furnace will produce large amounts of iron and therefore contribute to the reproduction of society—based as it is on agricultural productivity dependent on iron tools. Similarly, the interdiction of malevolent forces—be they unhappy ancestral spirits or witchcraft—is critical to the success of the technology. Without this power the smelters fail to reproduce. Ritual applications for both reasons, then, lead to a similar result, and hence it is no surprise that most African iron smelting cultures for which we have well-informed knowledge practice both forms of ritual during iron smelting. But this summary of variation does not lead us to knowledge about *how* and *why* these beliefs have come to be tied together under the aegis of the reproductive paradigm. Thus my primary task here is to trace the configurations of meanings through time and to see to what extent they are tied to changing gender relations in the productive economies of Bantu-speaking peoples over the last several millennia.

A starting point in this exercise is the work of Schoenbrun (1993a), a historical linguist who in his linguistic reconstructions of Eastern (ca. 1000 BC) and Great Lakes Bantu has argued that women dominated in the most economic domain, namely, that women were in charge of all agricultural activities.[1] By 500 BC, however, iron technology was gaining economic prominence among the same societies. If males controlled iron technology, then we might expect to see this new field of economic activity, with its new divisions of labor and gender competition, socially constructed with metaphors that make explicit gender identities and differences. I want to use this hypothesis—of initially strong male symbols that mark a new male-dominated economic domain—to see if we can determine the significance of some of the later changes seen in gendered symbolism of African iron technology.

Another methodological issue here is how we can discriminate among the various ideological signatures that occur in the archaeology of African iron production. It is important that very clear lines of association be drawn between beliefs and the specific objects that are used in ritual applications. A ritual bundle that goes into the base of a smelting furnace, for example, usually does not have an exclusive purpose, such as protection against witchcraft. In fact such ritual bundles usually have multiple meanings that are derived from a variety of domains—perhaps human fertility, with protection against witchcraft at the same time.

Anthropologists and archaeologists have long been aware that iron smelting rituals often result in special offerings being placed in various places in the furnace, usually under the foundation or on the floor or in a pit or a pot buried beneath the floor (Cline 1937; Van Noten 1983; Schmidt and Childs 1985; Van Grunderbeek 1992; Herbert 1993; Childs and Killick 1993; Schmidt and Mapunda 1997; Schmidt 1997a; also see MacLean, Chapter 9). The archaeological and ethnological examples from the central and eastern part of the continent for burial of ritual items in the furnace pit are too numerous to detail, but many iron smelting cultures placed important ritual items under the foundation of the furnace; the Fipa (Barndon 1992, 1996) and Chewa (Van der Merwe and Avery 1987) are examples. Some cultures also dug a special pit in the furnace base to accommodate these sacred objects: the Babungo of Cameroon (Fowler 1990, Herbert 1993), the Barongo of Tanzania (Schmidt 1996b), and smelters in Gitwenge, Burundi (Celis and Nzikobanyanka 1976) are examples of this practice.

Gender and Iron Smelting Ritual in Contemporary Cultures

The Pangwa

The Kinga, Bena, and Pangwa northeast of Lake Nyasa in southern Tanzania once practiced iron smelting technologies that have much in common (see Figure 8.1 for the location of ethnic groups and archaeological cultures). The taboos and symbolism of the Pangwa furnace have been documented by Stirnimann (1976), but only by using informant testimony. The Pangwa practice taboos similar to other Bantu-speaking iron producers, such as sexual abstinence by the smelters, the prohibition of menstruating women, and the exclusion of persons "hot" from recent sexual activity. Menstruating women are prohibited from touching charcoal and iron ore, but they can assist in its transportation in baskets, so long as its handling is done by a "clean" worker. The front of the furnace had breasts just below the rim, and the front opening (*umlomo*) was where the medicine pot, with its complex concoction of symbolic semen, was inserted and where the bloom or "baby" was also delivered (Stirnimann 1976).

Of interest in the Pangwa process is the use of a medicine pot inside the furnace. Collett (1985, 1993; also see MacLean, Chapter 9) has argued persuasively that pots are vessels that metaphorically mimic the reproductive female attributes of the iron smelting furnace, a function that is amplified when the pot is situated inside the iron smelting furnace. The perforated cover on the pot allowed the ritual ingredients to escape into the furnace. A plethora of sexual symbols were included among the ritual objects, among them: four juicy, 30 cm long phallic creepers; leaves and a root that produce white liquids symbolic of semen; a plant with red flowers symbolic of menstrual blood; and red sand, a symbol of dried blood. Most important in this suite of symbols is that the entire female reproductive cycle is incorporated in

HAYA
BARONGO
PANGWA
FIPA/LUNGU
MOANDA, GABON
GRASSFIELDS AND NDOP PLAIN, CAMEROON

Figure 8.1. A map of the ethnic groups and archaeological cultures discussed in the text.

the ritual ingredients: menstruation, impregnation, gestation, birth, permanent separation of the child, and a return to fertility. Although symbols for semen tend to predominate, nonetheless this historic example unifies both male and female symbols rather than presenting a dichotomized symbolic field identified strictly with one gender.

Most of the magical objects put in the ritual pot are meant to ensure the fertility of the furnace. It is not clear from the ethnographic descriptions whether the pot is buried in the base of the furnace or sits on the floor. Another description of iron smelting in the same region suggests that the medicine pot was buried in a hole located in the base of the furnace (Schmidt and Mapunda 1997). This being the case, then the pot and the lid would endure subsequent smelting in the furnace. Thus the Pangwa case provides an example of concrete material evidence for a fertility ritual that would be preserved archaeologically. Furnace pots and lids pertaining to fertility issues would leave behind definitive archaeological signatures. The most important historical observations that arise from the southern Tanzanian evidence are these:

that this region experienced significant disturbances during the 19th century Nguni incursions from the south, perhaps leading to multiethnic configurations in smelting behavior, and that the incorporation of objects symbolic of the complete female reproductive cycle suggests that women may have been incorporated during the recent past into the ritual process—parallel to their partial incorporation into the productive process.

The Fipa and Lungu

Archaeological and historical inquiries about iron smelting in Ufipa (southwestern Tanzania), with an emphasis on the histories of technologies in the region, have opened important new insights into the meaning of various ritual paraphernalia as well as the antiquity of various ritual practices (Mapunda 1995; Schmidt 1997a; Schmidt and Mapunda 1997). Mapunda has found that there were several different technologies that preceded the tall shaft furnace operated by natural draft among the Fipa. In his study of the history of technological behavior in the region, he gathered information pertinent to understanding other ritual practices. At one site he found pots on the surface that were set upside down in the presence of a termitary. He was told that these pots were used in exorcism rituals and that, once exorcised, a malicious spirit would be captured in the pot and contained there (Mapunda 1995).

Another important part of Mapunda's study was his discovery that still-standing, large *malungu* (*lilungu* singular) furnaces were in active use, not for iron production, but as sacred vessels for contemporary rituals. On one occasion he came across several ritual gourds placed in three different furnaces, one gourd with a white foam bubbling out of it. An interview with a nearby resident revealed that this medicinal vessel was meant either for treating infertility or for protection against "evil intentions" (Mapunda 1995:193). It is significant that a larger vessel—a smelting furnace closely identified with fertility—after six decades of inactivity as a smelting furnace is linked to treatment of infertility. Both the Fipa and the Lungu (another ethnic group living along Lake Tanganyika) believe that the magical herbs (*vizimba*) buried in the furnace floor are eternally powerful, as well as all the materials that have been influenced by the *vizimba*. Consistent with the powerful continuity of the reproduction paradigm among Fipa today is the local practice of recycling slag for amulets, and its widespread use among healers as the catalyzing ingredient in medicinal potions used to cure infertility. Healing of infertility either entails the use of these objects inside the furnace, which both the healer and patient enter naked through the birthing or mother door, or the healing occurs outside the furnace with sacrificial items (including the head of a rooster) placed inside the furnace. The salience of the Fipa and Lungu observations is that fertility symbolism associated with iron smelting furnaces is not separated into dichotomized fields, suggesting that gender separations are less defined in this culture area over the last century or so. Clearly, common ritual and technological practice were in vogue, further suggesting a diminution of competition and an opening of the process to women, at least at a ritual level.

The Barongo

The Barongo iron smelters are extraordinary ritual and technological bricoleurs, living to the southwest of Victoria Nyanza in Tanzania. The Barongo belief system is well documented and explicitly tied to rituals and their applications to iron smelting, thus providing both a solid empirical study (Rosemond 1943; Schmidt 1996b) and an ethnographic model of significant reliability. As technological and ritual bricoleurs, the Barongo afford many insights into ritual and technological life. These inseparable worlds lead us deeper into an understanding of how ideology in technological life creates a material and gendered text that, with adequate context, should be readable.

The head smelter and chief ritual specialist among the Barongo takes great care in selecting an acceptable, low termitary for the smelting pit (Schmidt 1996b). The *kitindi* or smelting house is then constructed over the site. When this task is completed, the smelters turn to the preparation of the smelting pit (*nyombe*) over which the furnace is constructed. The pit location is staked and a circle drawn to demarcate the excavation, which then leads to a pit with a cone-shaped floor sloping at 45 degrees to a small medicinal pit in the bottom. Eleven pieces of bark, tubers, wood, and leaves are then carefully packed into the pit by the chief ritual specialist. One of these objects is used to cure infertility and another has a bright red sap in its bark, symbolic of menstrual blood (Schmidt 1996b). The inclusion of menstrual symbolism in this and yet another ritual context among the Barongo significantly expands our knowledge about a ritual cycle—also seen among the Pangwa—in which the entire female reproductive process is ritually acted out as part of the reproductive paradigm (Schmidt 1996b). This marks a considerable departure from an imperfectly explicated iron smelting symbolism in which menstruation has been taken to mean the opposite of fertility: a state of sterility (Herbert 1993; Muhly and Schmidt 1988). We see in this example the strong emergence during historic and later prehistoric times of unified, pluralistic symbols of fertility and reproduction, in which gender separations are erased.

After all the interstitial gaps among the ritual items were filled with earth, the head smelter and his ritual specialist removed their clothing, sat astride the pit, back to back, and moved 180 degrees counterclockwise, pushing the earth into the pit with their genitalia and buttocks, an activity that has also been associated with contempt for "bad things" among the Bazinza (Bjerke 1981) (Figure 8.2). After the bottom was smoothed to fit the pit contour, the head smelter sprinkled two protective medicinal powders called *rukago* across the pit in several directions. The head smelter later explained that one medicine was to bring a "heavy child" and the other was used to interdict those with malicious intent (Schmidt 1996b).

Thus the pushing of the earth into the furnace is both an act of contempt for evil influences and a symbolic intercourse and fertilization of the furnace "womb." In the Barongo ritual cycle it is the second potent stage that transforms the furnace into a fecund bride. The human coupling with the furnace is metonymic in effect—a

Figure 8.2. A Barongo master smelter with his chief ritual advisor pushing earth into a Barongo furnace pit after the medicines had been buried in the bottom. The impregnation ceremony also seals the pit against evil or malicious spirits.

transformational process that is further reinforced by the placement of symbolic menstrual blood into the ritual pit (Schmidt 1996a,b). When the Barongo incorporate items specifically associated with females—fertility medicine used to treat female fertility problems and a species of wood symbolic of menstruation—the furnace becomes a container of reproductive materials, not simply a receptacle for the male gender (for example, objects symbolic of sperm).

This first ritual cycle, which captures the full reproductive female cycle, is followed by a second ritual cycle that repeats the process as well as directly incorporates a prominent woman—at the height of her reproductive powers—into the ritual, thus starkly contradicting normative paradigmatic proscriptions against the participation of women. A half hour after the furnace was lit, the wife of the head smelter entered the smelting house. She was joined by one of the smelters, who, like the woman, wore on his head a protective charm (*kizingo*) made of cowry shells. Together both spat beer three times on the furnace as they stood between different *tuyeres* (blow pipes). The beer was then passed to two other senior smelters, who spat it on the furnace at their *tuyere* stations. After this ritual, the head smelter and his assistant opened the artery of a goat at the same ritual station; with its arterial blood spurting across the slag charge on top of the furnace and splattering on the furnace walls and bellows, the goat was taken around the furnace counterclockwise. Beer in this culture is symbolically identified with fertility; the ritual mimics a local nuptial rite in which bride and groom spit beer or milk on each other. In this instance the fecund "bride" is the furnace, while each smelter is a "groom." The integration of a smelter's wife into fertility rites applied to the iron smelting furnace is also known among the Chokwe of Angola (Martins 1966; Herbert 1993), as is an offering of beer. A menstruation taboo apparently is also not applied among the Chokwe.

The Barongo integration of menstruation into the symbolic reproductive cycle is consistent with other beliefs associated with female reproduction. The varied Barongo rituals form a suite of interrelated meanings that unify all stages of the reproductive process. The woman's menstrual state was of no consequence, but her reproductive capacity was essential in a ritual in which she substituted, as the bride, for the furnace. Each woman involved was in the flower of her reproductive life.

The role of blood sacrifice in the Barongo smelter is distinctive in its attention to the full saturation of the slags stacked on the top of the furnace. Given what we already know about the representation of menstruation and periodicity of reproduction in the Barongo reproductive symbol system, this ritual deserves further attention. The Barongo industrial goal is to induce slag to flow through the furnace, and in this ritual context—given what we already understand of metonymic menstrual characteristics of the furnace—it appears that the sacrificial blood is regarded as a purifying agent that cleanses the womb and prepares it for reproduction. The Barongo rites contain two reproductive cycles, the first captured in menstrual cleansing and impregnation during the pit ritual, the second captured in menstrual cleansing during the sacrifice and the later impregnation of the furnace (when the smelt is underway) by the injection of fertility objects into the phallic *tuyere* to make it stronger in the reproductive process. The ritual structure is indeed a homology for reproduction, a model much more complete than the contradictory opposition of sterility. The Barongo dialectical resolution of this previously baffling contradiction compels us to set aside the Western orthodoxy that blood sacrifice is not associated with menstruation (for example, Herbert 1993:86). As a system of thought that does not construct menstruation as polluting, there are no associated taboos that address the prohibition of menstruating females.

Barongo rituals place gender-specific objects in the bottom of the furnace (Figure 8.3). Conditions of reduction that prevail in iron smelting should make it possible to recover and read such gendered meanings in the archaeological record—assuming that the species of the sticks of wood can be identified successfully. There is also reason to expect that such devices will remain undisturbed in old furnaces, as the power of the ritual devices used by the Barongo extend the useful life of the smelting pit. The potency of the medicines goes on without interruption. If the furnace is abandoned, then these ritual devices remain in the ground. In 1984 I witnessed a six-year-old ritual bundle removed from its ritual pit as a unified, solid mass of partially charred sticks and adhering earth (Figure 8.4)—suggesting that these materials would have been sufficiently preserved to provide an unequivocal archaeological signature of the Barongo ideology and its ritual incorporation of the complete female reproductive cycle.

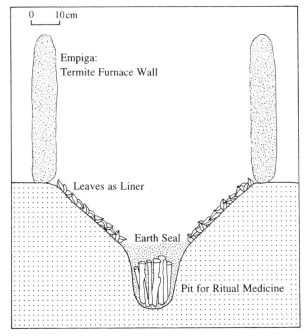

Figure 8.3. Profile of a Barongo furnace pit made by Barongo smelters at Bwanga, Biharamulo District, showing the location of the medicinal devices in the bottom of the furnace.

The Haya

Another pertinent example I want to use is from Buhaya, immediately to the west of Lake Victoria in Tanzania. Haya ritual practices during iron smelting capture, are, in some ways, a ritual style that helps set the stage for assessing continuities and changes in gender-marked rituals in Buhaya as well as other regions of Africa. After several years of direct observation of Haya iron smelting and a corresponding absence of ritual applied to the smelting furnace proper, I learned from the testimony offered by an aged smelter that after the furnace base was constructed he dug a pit in the bottom of the furnace; an old woman then brought sticks and a white liquid called *empuri*, made of kaolin and water. Beyond childbearing years and infertile, the woman wetted the sticks with the *empuri* and presented them to the head smelter, who then inserted them in the small pit and covered them with soil (Schmidt 1997a). The medicine was meant to interdict witchcraft, ameliorate any bad effects from violation of the taboo against sexual activity, fend off those who might bring bad luck, and infuse the furnace with fertile properties. *Empuri* is widely known as a cure for infertility. The placement of this semenlike liquid in the ritual hole is, like the Barongo example, an active fertilization of the furnace. Of interest here for our discussion is that the *empuri* ritual incorporates a cross-gender role—the old woman

Figure 8.4. A medicinal bundle being removed from a Barongo furnace in 1984, after five years of exposure to termites and the elements.

of postmenopausal or infertile status who is like a man (Herbert 1993:231), warning us that the presence of archaeological signatures such as kaolin in furnace pits must not be taken to mean a male gender-marked ritual process. In the case of the Haya, this cautionary tale is mitigated by the historical information that overcomes a simplistic equation between kaolin and male ritual activity. While kaolin may well symbolize semen, the ritual agents for its placement may in fact be females transformed into ritual males.[2]

The Archaeology of Gender and Iron Smelting Furnaces

The previous discussion leads naturally to the question of how these historic and ethnographic examples throw light on the antiquity and evolution of reproductive symbolism, whether symbolic items used to ward off witchcraft or symbolic items used to appease ancestors in iron smelting. My purpose in this section is to tease out what the development of these different systems of meaning has to do with changing gender relations in this ritualized sphere of economic production, how these reflect changing socioeconomic relations, and in what archaeological contexts we might expect to find expressions of gender-marked ritual processes or behavior in iron smelting.

When smelting rituals focused on harmful forces, especially witchcraft and unhappy ancestral spirits, then rituals incorporated herbal, bark, and tuber devices that compose the local healing repertoire. Such objects were often sticks put into bundles with the other objects, inserted into the furnace pit, and sealed. Among these objects may have been one or more items that also pertained to fertility, or to female reproductive functions such as menstruation. Such bundles of sticks tended to be multifaceted belief bundles, but they also incorporated key gender-related objects. Important for our purposes here is that such objects signify the incorporation of females into other parts of a ritual process that represented the full cycle of reproduction, from preparation of the womb (menstruation) and fertilization to gestation and parturition. A ritual cycle that embraced women is a significant departure from our conventional understanding of the reproductive paradigm—one that separates women, stigmatizes them as polluting and sterile, and excludes them from economic rewards derived from the technology. The only way to sort out specific meanings within these bundles is to build much more complex models from ethnoarchaeological studies, wherein the species of plants and trees symbolically associated with medicines for female fertility and menstruation are specifically examined for cross-cultural regularities.

When pots were used as ritual devices in furnaces, they seem inevitably to have been associated with fertility rituals, at least insofar as the use of whole pots is concerned. Because of the mostly ephemeral quality of ritual objects placed in the pots, fertility pots might be predicted to present an archaeological signature limited to the pot itself. However, the lessons of ritual bricolage inform us that partial pots were also used in ancient Ufipa in southwest Tanzania as inverted caps on the bundle of magical sticks—some of which are undoubtedly related to female reproduction—thus mixing reproductive symbolism with a symbolism of exorcism.

Mapunda (1995) brings into focus in Ufipa some of the deep-time traditions that inform the archaeology of that culture area to the southeast of Lake Tanganyika. Mapunda examined characteristics of the *malungu* or high-shaft furnace on the Fipa plateau in order to understand the relationship between that better-known tradition and those traditions he was documenting to the west along Lake Tanganyika. His excavations of one lilungu furnace on the plateau and several along the escarpment and shoreline throw important light on the ritual process during the last century and the early part of this century: He found that under the floor of a *lilungu* furnace (dated to 1932–1934) on the plateau at Kalundi there were rectangular strips of wood, now charred, laid in the special pit excavated in the furnace floor. Measuring 18–20 cm by 5–10 cm and about 0.5 cm thick, these *vizimba* were intended to expel evil spirits as well as "catalyze" the smelting process (Mapunda 1995:204). They are also deeply identified with the fertility of the furnace, and as long as their integrity remains secure, they continue to ensure the potency of the furnace for years afterward.

Further evidence of ritual treatment of *malungu* furnaces was obtained by Mapunda along the lake shore at Kirando where only one tall furnace was located

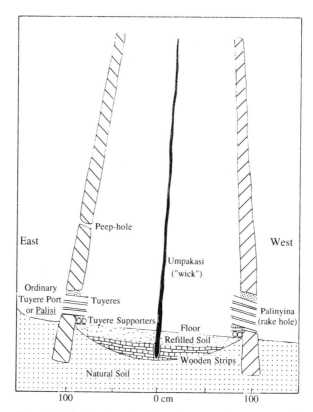

Figure 8.5. Profile view of a *lilungu* furnace, a 3 to 4 meter tall natural draft furnace used by the Fipa of SW Tanzania.

(site HvIk-39). There, too, Mapunda excavated three tiers of charred wood identified as *vizimba* in the furnace pit of a 19th century experimental furnace built by plateau immigrants—showing a significant consistency in ritual (Figure 8.5). Another important observation for the archaeology of the region is that today artifacts are found scattered on the furnace floors, artifacts that mark the *later* use of the furnaces as places were infertility is cured. Are these fertility rituals intended to cure women or do they pertain to men? At this point we need further ethnographic information on this matter, but it is apparent that the postsmelting Fipa practices offer an opportunity to link later artifact distributions in furnaces with specific gendered ritual. Also important to archaeology in this region is the widespread absence of iron slag on smelting sites of antiquity. This results from the purposeful collection of iron slag from ancient sites and its subsequent use both as ritual devices and as medicinal powders (after grinding) to cure infertility in women. Thus, we see on the landscape a skewed distribution of archaeological remains that is caused by gendered beliefs related to medicinal cures for infertility.

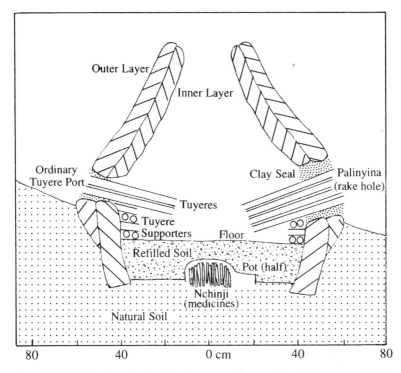

Figure 8.6. Profile view of a *katukutu* furnace with a central pot lying over *nchinji* medicines.

As we have seen earlier, Mapunda (1995) found that inverted pots among the Fipa are related to exorcism of evil spirits and are usually found associated with termite mounds—the same context in which iron smelting furnaces are constructed. This association with local belief seems to be a powerful indication that in this region similar meanings may be attached to pots in furnaces. Along the plains next to Lake Tanganyika and on the eastern escarpment, Mapunda found many sites with 1 meter high shaft furnaces (katukutu) using a natural draft. Mapunda's documentation of this technology provides a remarkable record of prehistoric ritual activity, perhaps unparalleled in African archaeology. Radiocarbon datings of these furnaces show that most are 350 to 450 years old, or approximately the 15th to 17th centuries (Mapunda 1995). In nine katukutu furnaces excavated, Mapunda found that eight had a pot at the center and that six of these pots shielded what is locally referred to as *nchinji*—vertical sticks sharpened and driven into the ground (Figure 8.6) (Mapunda 1995). The pots had been broken in half, most of them along their vertical axis, with one half used to cover the *nchinji* and yet others with the base covering the *nchinji*. *Nchinji* have meanings analogous to the vizimba used by the later Fipa smelters of the plateau—mostly directed to the interdiction of witchcraft and as protection against the malicious intentions of spirits as well as living people.

Mapunda feels that local explanations of *vizimba* also apply to *nchinji*. If this explanation holds, then it means that fertility signifiers would likely have been mixed into the bundle of ritual meanings, but without explicit gender signifiers. With these technological and ritual parallels drawn between the two technologies, we understand better that the ideologies informing Fipa iron smelting early this century are similar to those of 300 to 400 years ago. But more important for our argument here is that gender markers during this earlier period of iron smelting in Ufipa seems to have faded, being overwhelmed by concern for witchcraft. This was a period in Ufipa during which new ethnic groups were coming into the region, undoubtedly creating competitive intergroup tensions in which concern for economic domination and access to critical resources prevailed over economic divisions based on gender. I believe that the changes seen in Ufipa illustrate a period when gender-to-gender economic competition became secondary to competition—seen archaeologically as an explosion of witchcraft concerns—between unrelated social groups over control of essential resources used in iron production.

The archaeological evidence from the Kagera region, where the Haya live, also suggests that it is possible to discern ideological characteristics of features found on the floors of ancient furnaces that may be gender-related. The KM2 site near Kemondo Bay contained many Early Iron Age smelting furnaces, many of which had small pit features located in their floors. Of the 12 features that were certain furnaces at KM2, six contained pit features in their floors (Schmidt and Childs 1985:73). None of these small pits showed any signs of inclusions, such as charcoal, kaolin, or other preserved materials. In 67 percent of the cases, these pits were found in furnaces with abrupt vertical walls; the others were in furnaces with bowl-shaped bottoms. There was no apparent pattern through time. In view of the ethnographic models discussed, how might we interpret the evidence at the KM2 site?

It seems compelling, in light of other evidence discussed in the ethnographic record, to suggest that these pits are the remnants of a prehistoric ideological system. But why do some furnaces lack the ritual pit? During historic times Haya iron smelters also varied in their applications of ritual. Sometimes ritual varied according to new social and environmental circumstances. Witchcraft became a more dominant concern, for example, during the early 20th century when Kiziba smelters went to exploit the forests of Kianja kingdom, then foreign and hostile territory (Schmidt 1997a).

At the KM3 site, just 1.5 km south of KM2 near Kemondo Bay, we gain another important glimpse into Early Iron Age ritual practices. Of the seven furnace pits excavated at KM3, only one showed clear evidence of a ritual pit in its floor. Furnace no. 8 was a shallow bowl furnace dated to the 1st century AD and contained a small pit in its floor that was sealed with a small sandstone block (Schmidt 1983; Schmidt and Childs 1985). Within the small pit there was a 6 cm tall phalliclike piece of

Figure 8.7. A close-up view of the piece of bloom (once concealed beneath a sandstone block) in the ritual pit of furnace no. 8, KM3.

prehistoric iron bloom (Figure 8.7). This bloom has no relationship to the techno-logical operation of the furnace. Its function appears to have been linked to rituals performed prior to smelting in that particular pit, the oldest at the KM3 site. The use of this piece of unworked metal in a ritual pit evokes comparison to other iron smelting rituals meant to ensure the production of an excellent, hardy, or high-quality product that mimics the attributes of the ritual device.

The reason for the absence of ritual pits in other KM3 smelting furnaces is not clear.[3] We now understand that these ideologies, despite their continuities, vary widely in consistency of application. Is it possible that the use of one powerful ritual application at a smelting site was sufficient for the other furnaces through time? This bears exploring. It seems more likely, though, that we may be missing other ritual applications in the other furnace pits. For example, in furnace no. 3 at KM3 there was a dense layer of charcoal on the furnace floor, in which charred logs were laid in parallel—much like Furnace no. 9, which had similar configurations. Botanical analy-sis of charred woods in furnace no. 9 indicates that the species of wood appearing as a concentration of charred logs in the center of the furnace floor is the same as a tree commonly used in the Great Lakes region to ensure fertility or cure infertility in women. The specificity of this medicinal item and its relationship to women, rather than reproductive objects or substances related to men, seems to suggest a gender orientation more closely identified with women. While these ritual objects at the

KM3 site attest to a plurality of gender identifications, they occur in separate furnaces and thus differ from the more unified plurality that is seen in the Barongo furnaces of this century.[4]

Further variation in Early Iron Age ritual practices is seen at the Rugomora Mahe site in Katuruka, and at the RM2 site immediately to its south. Of the pit features linked to Early Iron Age smelting at the Rugomora Mahe site, three have clear but distinctly larger pits in the floor of the furnace, approximately 20–25 cm in diameter and 15 cm deep (Schmidt 1978). Another Early Iron Age iron smelting pit at the RM2 site had similar characteristics. There were no distinctive inclusions that indicated the specific ritual intention of these pits, but such variation from the KM2 cases and the one distinctive KM3 example seems to suggest strongly that ritual treatments differed in the region, perhaps according to social group rather than any variation through time. The sizes of the ritual pits at these sites resemble those of the Barongo and many other groups that place large bundles of protective medicines in the pits.

Perhaps the most convincing evidence for an ideology of fertility and reproduction in an ancient furnace in East or Central Africa is seen in the archaeology of the same industrial complex in the Great Lakes region, at Kabuye in Rwanda. At the Kabuye II site, Van Noten excavated an Early Iron Age furnace dating to the 6th century AD (Van Noten 1983: Plate 15). Below the floor of the furnace he excavated a sealed and elegantly decorated globular pot (Figure 8.8). The fact that the pot was upright, sealed, and in the base of an iron smelting furnace suggests that this ritual device was related to fertility concerns—an interpretation that is repetitively affirmed by the ethnographic cases that are similarly structured. Moreover, as earlier suggested, the pot as a female-gender signifier strongly suggests that by 600 AD a significant shift had occurred—a diminution of the strong male symbols seen in the earliest period discussed below. There have been many other furnaces excavated in both Rwanda and Burundi without such devices implanted in their bases. Does that mean that the Kabuye II example is idiosyncratic, or is there an alternative hypothesis that might help to explain the variation in the archaeological record of the highland region? At this juncture the negative evidence may point to a period of lessening concern with such symbolic statements in the practice of iron smelting. Alternatively, it may point to an archaeological failure to observe other, less obvious, and perhaps more ephemeral ritual expressions, such as the charcoal identified at the KM3 site in Buhaya.

Among those of us engaged in the study of ancient iron working in Africa, there is a growing confidence that deep-time traditions and systems of meaning are manifest in the archaeological evidence that we encounter in iron production centers. The most convincing evidence for such deep-time systems of meaning has been discovered in Gabon. In southeastern Gabon I excavated several sites in Moanda, an important Early Iron Age center for iron production (Schmidt et al. 1985; Digombe et al. 1988). A very deep (174 cm) furnace pit was excavated over several seasons at the Moanda II

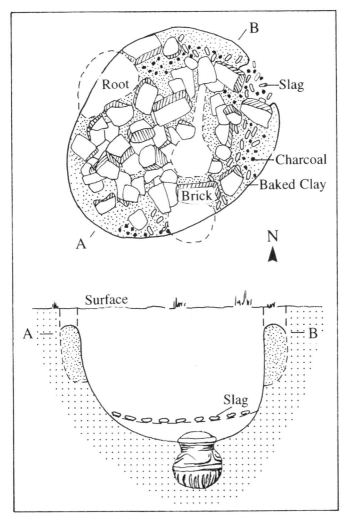

Figure 8.8. An Early Iron Age pot burial beneath a furnace pit at Kabuye II, Rwanda. This furnace was excavated by Van Noten and dated to the 6th century AD—pointing to great continuity in ritual practices. After Van Noten 1983.

site. The walls of a tall (3–4 meter) shaft furnace, using a natural draft without slag tapping, had collapsed into the furnace pit. On clearing most of the wall fragments an upright *tuyere* (a clay blow pipe used to convey the air blast) filled was found on the floor of the furnace pit (Figure 8.9). Inspection of the tuyere contents showed that it was filled with kaolin, a white clay widely symbolic of purity and fertility (Figure 8.10). The symbolic qualities of kaolin among the Haya iron smelters immediately come to

Figure 8.9. The wall of the tall shaft furnace had collapsed into the furnace pit. On the floor of the pit at –174 cm was an upright *tuyere*—the round object seen in the center.

mind: they used a kaolin slurry, symbolic of semen, in their *empuri* ritual to infuse their furnaces with male fertility. The presence of kaolin in an upright *tuyere*—an explicit and widely acknowledged phallic symbol among iron smelters in Africa—is an unequivocal representation of fertility. The Moanda *tuyere* can be accepted as an enduring and powerful symbol of ritual reproduction in African iron smelting at a time when iron working was first taking hold on the continent and when older gender-related roles were being renegotiated. These deep-time systems of meaning have continued among iron working groups, cross-culturally, for more than two millennia.

As we have already learned, the iron smelters of the Early Iron Age displayed a range of ritual experiment as rich and varied as their later counterparts. Archaeologists, however, have yet to develop the skills to recognize the significance of different ritual expressions and to appreciate how these mark changing social and gender relations. There are several reasons to suggest that this can be done. First, many of the materials included in the ritual packages can leave traces in the archaeological record, either in an unaltered or minimally altered form—as in the case of pots, rocks, and kaolin—or in charred form—as in the case of vegetal or bone materials. Second, Africa is still rich in oral traditions pertaining to iron production. This is because in many parts the production of iron continued until the beginning of this century, and some former iron workers, who can offer firsthand information regarding the meaning of the materials applied for ritual purposes, are still alive. Third, the fact that iron production survived

Figure 8.10. The upright *tuyere* on the furnace floor, filled with kaolin, is widely associated with fertility and purification rituals.

for a long time (over two millennia) has left a rich archaeological record in Africa. It is therefore possible to trace social and economic correlates of changing symbolic expressions, including those that are gendered, through space and time.

We have seen from the review of ethnographic cases that this ideological system continued to meet multiple needs by accommodating local ideologies of healing and spirit appeasement while at the same time retaining ideologies of reproduction—a process that allowed for a wide degree of creative freedom. Because other beliefs came to be incorporated with those pertaining to reproduction—a paradigm wrapped up in gender issues—I now want to conclude by suggesting how these different belief systems represent changing gender relations over the last several thousand years.

Finding and Defining Gender in the Archaeological Record: Some Trends over Time

Following the working hypothesis stated earlier in this paper, iron smelting marked a significant cleavage during the first millennium BC in economic activities linked to different genders—agriculture being female, and iron smelting being male. The archaeological record in the period immediately following 500 BC captures an era when these significant economic reorientations were taking place, when economic and gender roles were being renegotiated, when males were becoming dominant in their own economic domain, and when identities were being renegotiated as well. It was also a period during which there was a significant movement of Bantu peoples back toward western Africa with iron technology as part of their economic repertoire (Schoenbrun 1990), suggesting that the Gabonese evidence is closely related to the same cultural and technological traditions from eastern Africa.

I see the iron smelting furnaces of SE Gabon, dating to the 3rd and 4th centuries BC, as physical manifestations of this era of change and renegotiation of gender roles. The strong symbolic statements of the early Gabonese furnaces—the phallic, upright *tuyeres* filled with symbolic sperm (kaolin)—are symbolic male affirmations of control and identity, as males marked out their domination over this part of the economy— juxtaposed with female control over the other primary productive sphere, agriculture. Once male dominance had been established and amplified by control over a symbolic female domain, we find that later male gender expressions became less obvious through time. A millennium later, signifiers such as pots and medicinal devices—associated with females—had crept into the symbolic repertoire. Although less explicit than the forceful male symbol from Gabon, these symbols nonetheless drew on themes of fertility in the first half of the 1st millennium AD when male identity with iron smelting had been established and gender roles more clearly defined in economic production.

The archaeological signatures for this period are the more "subdued" phallic symbols such as observed at the KM3 site at the turn of the millennium, and the increasing use of more female fertility symbols such as the "fertility" pots at the Kabuye site in Rwanda (600 AD) and fertility medicines on the bottom of furnaces at the KM3 site in Buhaya (300 to 400 AD used to cure female infertility. As MacLean notes in Chapter 9, Collett (1985, 1993) and Herbert (1993) have convincingly shown that the pot is a sign for female activities of transformation arising out of cooking. This element of plurality appears to parallel similar processes seen in South America, in the latter prehistory of Amazonia. There, as populations became denser, cleared more land, and grew more dependent on agricultural production in the last millennium AD, figurines with phallic attributes also incorporated female attributes (breasts), and male figurines sported female hairstyles (Roosevelt 1997). In the Buhaya archaeological record in Africa we may well be observing similar processes related to a more settled way of life with larger populations (Schmidt 1997b), significant modification of the once-forested landscape, and more consolidated male control over the productive economy. We also see through time a lower archaeological visibility of medicinal objects placed in furnace pits. This may reflect lessening tensions in gender divisions in the productive domain, or it may simply be a commentary on our failure to recognize pertinent archaeological signatures.

As gender roles are more clearly defined through time, I see that a growing concern among the peoples we study was competition between social groups and between ethnic groups over access to iron smelting and its specialized knowledge.

The growth of chiefship and political centralization in the 2nd millennium AD was closely tied to control over iron production (Dewey and Childs 1996). With the linkage of wealth and power established, competition accelerated to gain access to this mode of production. One way this was played out was through magical attacks on iron smelters by rival groups seeking the secrets of the industry. Some of the exclusionary taboos that prevented female access (and thus access of their own patrilines) to iron smelting may date to this era of increased intergroup competition. It appears that iron smelters developed a repertoire of magical responses to neutralize both unhappy ancestors as well as the devices of sorcerers and witches arrayed against them. We read this process in the archaeological record of the 2nd millennium, best documented by the bundles of magical sticks used by ancient smelters near Lake Tanganyika between the 14th and 17th centuries (and maintained by many cultures up to this century).

Gendered symbols also appear to have changed during the late 2nd millennium, from being wrapped together with symbolic medicinal devices that addressed ancestral and witchcraft (intergroup competition) concerns to an open incorporation of females in rituals and in production. During the 19th and 20th centuries an even greater complexity arose in gender relations in iron smelting, expressed in specific ritual material objects that leave distinct archaeological fingerprints. I see these later trends as being related to the breakdown of exclusive lineage and ethnic control over iron production. In central Tanzania during the late 19th century, for example, successive wars and the slave trade disrupted traditional patterns of production, out of which arose the multiethnic Barongo iron smelters. This history parallels the history of the southern highlands, where the Nguni incursions among the Pangwa and Kinga disrupted traditional modes of production. I believe that multiethnic participation in iron smelting, as among the Barongo, seems simultaneously to have opened ritual performance to women, breaking down the ritual taboos that earlier excluded them.

This is a record of decreasing gender divisions, incorporating not only women but also many social and ethnic groups into iron smelting. In this sense it is also a record of less competition between groups and between men and women over the social relations of production, rather than a process of balance between industrial economy and domestic economy, as MacLean argues in Chapter 9. This change is marked by a multigendered ritual that is manifested materially by specific devices that symbolically incorporate menstruation and thus represent the full cycle of female reproduction. These archaeological signatures, then, mark the last of several significant changes in social relations of production in which gender played a central organizing role over the two and a half millennia of African iron smelting.

Notes

1. Schoenbrun (1993) initially speculated that Eastern Bantu societies were matrilineal but has since dropped this idea because of the difficulty of inferring gender relations from social structure.

2. The examples used may seem to suggest that this ideological system was confined to East and Central Africa. This would be a misleading implication, for there are well-documented indications that similar beliefs, translated into material manifestations, occurred among the Fang in Gabon (Tessmann 1913), among the Babungo smelters of the Ndop Plain in Cameroon (Fowler 1990), and among the We and Isu smelters of the Grassfields in Cameroon (Rowlands and Warnier 1993), as well as other areas of West Africa (see Schmidt and Mapunda 1997).

In his study of Babungo smelting and smithing, Ian Fowler makes several observations that pertain to the question of continuity of belief in this region, especially the life-giving force of Nywi he sees as closely associated with a pot of leaf medicines buried in the floor of the furnace. The medicines activate the force in the extraction of life and fertility from the earth and its transformation into bloom (Fowler 1990). The pot as container of these transformational forces is linked to fertility and reproduction.

3. For a complete description of the sizes, shapes, contents, and dates of each of the furnaces, see Schmidt and Childs 1985.

4. We must keep in mind that the ritual practices of Fipa smelters—wherein layers of sticks are used on the furnace floor—may be related to the Early Iron Age phenomenon seen at KM3.

Chapter Nine

Gendered Technologies and Gendered Activities in the Interlacustrine Early Iron Age

"Men and Women Do Things Differently"?

The sexual division of labor provides one of the most promising mediums through which to explore gender in past societies (see also Stahl and Cruz, Chapter 11). Anthropology has shown us that there is commonly a clear distinction between those technologies and activities that are regarded as "male" and those that are regarded as "female" (e.g., D'Andrade 1974; Murdock and Provost 1973), and there exists the possibility of identifying similar distinctions in the archaeological record. The sexual division of labor has been described as "the original and most basic form of economic specialization" (Murdock and Provost 1973:203), and there has been a general tendency to see an inherent distinction between female "domestic" tasks and male "industry." Studies of chimpanzee populations in the Tai forest, Ivory Coast, have shown a clear difference in tool use between the sexes and the beginnings of sexual specialization of activities amongst primates (Boesch-Achermann and Boesch 1994). Recently, however, feminist scholars have begun to question the long-held belief in a simple, direct relationship between gender and gendered activities, as well as challenge the idea that biological and social differences between men and women lead naturally to a sexual division of labor (Moore 1991:408–409). Instead, they suggest that there is a more complex, fluid relationship between gender and technology and, importantly, that gender must be understood as a set of historical relations.

Technological phenomena, though often divorced by archaeologists from their social framework, are nevertheless full social phenomena (Lemonnier 1989:156), and past activities can thus only be fully understood when all aspects, including the question of gender, are considered. In this paper, the technologies and activities that first appear in the archaeological record of the Interlacustrine Region (the area of the east-central African Great Lakes, comprising Uganda, western Kenya, the eastern border of Zaire, Rwanda, Burundi, and northwestern Tanzania) in Early Iron Age Urewe communities will be examined as social phenomena. It is probable that these technologies and activities were gendered, and the changing relationship between male and female sections of the community that may have resulted from, or be reflected by, these technological innovations will be explored. In the discussion of this particular case study, the wider issues of the sexual division of labor will be reexamined; to what extent were activities divided "naturally" into domestic female tasks and industrial male tasks and to what degree is it possible to see more complex cultural constructions of gender?

Seeing the Early Iron Age Community

Technological distinctions have commonly been used as convenient chronological labels by archaeologists. In the prehistory of the Interlacustrine Region (see Figure 9.1), the terms Late Stone Age and Early Iron Age have been applied to two distinct and, to a certain degree, successive communities that were active in the region during the 1st millennium BC. The inadequacy of these basic terms has been increasingly recognized, echoing the continent-wide debate for a reappraisal of chronological terminology, yet the fundamental impact that we perceive technologies to have on our lives is indicated by the continued use of these terms. In the Interlacustrine Region, however, the adoption of metals was only one of a series of technological and economic changes that can be recognized from the archaeological record at this date, the beginning of ceramic manufacture and use and the adoption of farming practices being the most prominent.

While these changes have been the subject of some debate (e.g., Robertshaw 1994; Van Neer 1995), the Early Iron Age communities of the Interlacustrine Region have remained largely anonymous. Viewed as packages of subsistence strategies and technical achievements, the question of social identity has only very recently become a subject of archaeological discussion (MacLean 1996b).

The relative paucity of archaeological evidence from this period may have encouraged much of this past neglect. While concentrations of smelting activity have resulted in excavation and detailed discussion of early iron technology (e.g., Schmidt 1980; Van Grunderbeek et al. 1983), no Early Iron Age settlement has yet been examined. Indeed, only three possible Early Iron Age house structures have been recorded: in Zaire (Van Noten 1979:69), Tanzania (Schmidt and Childs 1985), and Uganda (MacLean 1996d). At present, therefore, we only have evidence for some technologies and activities, yet, as has been stated, technological phenomena must be recognized as full social phenomena. In this paper I will attempt, through an examination of these archaeological data and of ethnographic data from the region, to build a picture of social change in the 1st millennium BC from a discussion of the social aspects of these new technologies and activities.

Figure 9.1. The Interlacustrine Region.

The Archaeological Evidence for
Interlacustrine Communities in the 1st Millennium BC

In 1993 and 1994 an archaeological survey was conducted in the district of Rakai, which lies in southwestern Uganda between the shores of Lake Victoria and the Tanzanian border (see Figure 9.1). The aim of this fieldwork was to establish comparative activity and settlement patterns for Late Stone Age and Early Iron Age communities (see MacLean 1996a,c,d), and thus to provide a more controlled picture of activity in the region than was available from various previous excavations. The evidence obtained from the Rakai surveys supplemented the available archaeological data, and enabled a basic understanding of 1st millennium BC activity in the region to be reached (MacLean 1996a).

At the beginning of this period bands of foragers using a microlithic technology inhabited much of this area. These foragers did not use ceramics and are represented today by scatters of quartz implements and debris. Evidence from Rakai supported the claim that these aceramic Late Stone Age communities were, to some degree, nomadic, and they appear to have moved throughout much of the region, settling temporarily in both rockshelters and open sites (frequently located on hilltops). Work in Karagwe, northwestern Tanzania, has suggested that, in this area at least, movement may have been seasonal as groups followed the migrations of animal herds (Reid and Njau 1994).

At a handful of sites located along the shores of Lake Victoria and its larger rivers, evidence of contemporary, culturally distinct groups, termed Kansyore, has been found. These groups were also using a microlithic toolkit but in addition were manufacturing and using poor-quality pottery. The tendency for Kansyore sites to be located at more turbulent stretches of water, faunal evidence from some sites, and the decoration of pottery using fish bones and shells suggests that these were specialized fishing communities. While they may also have been seasonally mobile, it is possible that they were more permanently settled than the inland forager groups.

In the middle of the 1st millennium BC we see the appearance of very different communities throughout the region. These groups were manufacturing and using a good quality ceramic, Urewe ware, and had replaced the lithic toolkit with iron. Extensive smelting debris has been recorded in certain locations, most notably in northwestern Tanzania, southern Rwanda, and central Burundi (Schmidt and Childs 1985; Van Noten and Raymaekers 1988; Van Grunderbeek et al. 1983; Schmidt, Chapter 8), but appears to be absent in other areas, such as Rakai. Analysis of the available regional pattern of Urewe material (ceramic scatters and ironworking debris) suggests that centers of population existed that may have been controlling the production and distribution of iron (MacLean 1996a). The Urewe communities were, to some degree, food producing. They cleared and settled the more fertile hillsides and gentle lower slopes, and, though no convincing archaeobotanical or palynological evidence yet exists, it appears likely that they were experimenting with a range of crops, including sorghum, finger millet, and possibly bananas (MacLean 1996a; P. de Maret 1996: personal communication). By the 1st millennium AD, there is evidence for domestic cattle and goats or sheep in the west of the region (Van Neer 1995), and it is possible that the first farming communities also had some livestock.

The Early Iron Age Urewe communities thus represent a period of considerable technological and economic change in the region, a period in which new activities were adopted and incorporated into the social framework. Those activities for which we have direct archaeological evidence, and those that we can convincingly assume from more indirect data, are detailed below.

Early Iron Age Activities—Indicated by Direct Evidence

Ceramic production   Fragments of Urewe pottery are, at present, the prime indicator of past Early Iron Age communities. Although ceramics were manufactured by the Late Stone Age Kansyore communities before the appearance of Early Iron Age Urewe ware, Kansyore settlement appears to have been limited, both geographically and in numbers of communities, and across most of the region Late Stone Age communities did not manufacture ceramics. Thus, away from the few Kansyore communities settled around Lake Victoria and its rivers, ceramic manufacture first appears in the Early Iron Age communities. Urewe ware is clearly unrelated to the Kansyore pottery in form, decorative style, or technology. Urewe ceramics generally take the shape of necked vessels or shallow bowls, being characterized by a thickened, everted, beveled rim and the occasional presence of a dimple in the pot base. Decoration is commonly confined to a band on the rim or shoulder, and consists of incised patterns, including bands of cross-hatching, zigzag, parallel lines, and pendant loops or triangles. The fabric is of good quality, being well made and well fired, and tends to be rather thin—occasionally no more than 3 mm (Soper 1969:150). Both the interior and exterior surface can be highly burnished with either a black graphite or a red ochre finish.

Iron production   There is substantial evidence for Early Iron Age iron production, primarily, at present, from northwestern Tanzania, southern Rwanda and central Burundi. This evidence consists of furnace bases, fragments of furnace superstructure, *tuyeres* (blow pipes), and slag. Attempts have been made to reconstruct these early furnace structures (Schmidt and Avery 1978; Van Grunderbeek et al. 1983), and it appears, from excavated evidence, that they were of a non-slag-tapping low shaft type. A particularly interesting feature of these early furnaces is the use of molded "bricks" in the construction of the walls (Van Noten 1979), and these have been recorded at sites in Rwanda (Raymaekers and Van Noten 1986) and Tanzania (Schmidt and Childs 1985). Some bricks were decorated, most commonly with parallel grooving, but also with more curvilinear motifs and circular impressions.

Early Iron Age Activities—Indicated by Indirect Evidence

Land clearance   The Rakai surveys identified distinct settlement patterns for the Late Stone Age and Early Iron Age communities. The aceramic Late Stone Age sites were found to be generally restricted to locations such as the tops of steep hills, upper slopes, and ridgetops—areas with skeletal, shallow soils. The Urewe sites, in contrast, were located on the most fertile local soils, along gentle slopes and the tops of gentle, flat-topped ridges. This suggested a shift in settlement and a corresponding shift in environmental exploitation, a movement that may be expected to have resulted in some degree of environmental change.

Fortunately, palynological and paleolimnological evidence gives some indication of the environment of Rakai at this period (see Schoenbrun 1990 for a discussion), and we are able to look for evidence of this change. Rakai appears to have been more forested than at present, with semideciduous and swamp forest covering much of the area, and papyrus swamps following valley bottoms and the lakeshore. Throughout the region, soil complexes, or catenas, are found, and in Rakai these tend to result in vegetation catenas (Langdale-Brown et al. 1964:35). In the 1st millennium BC it is probable that, while the swampy valley bottoms were filled with papyrus, hill slopes were forested, and the skeletal, shallow soils of the summits supported a sparser form of vegetation. Movement from these summits down to the hill slopes, as indicated by the Rakai survey, would suggest a movement into the more forested areas and thus some degree of land clearance. This is supported by the palynological evidence, which Schoenbrun (1990) has interpreted as indicating human-related deforestation beginning in the middle of the millennium. Therefore, using the archaeological evidence from Rakai for changing settlement patterns and the paleoecological evidence for environmental charge, it is possible to see the beginnings of significant land clearance by Early Iron Age communities.

Agricultural production   The settlement patterns identified in Rakai also suggest a change in subsistence base. The location of aceramic Late Stone Age sites in relatively inaccessible locations and on the poorer soils does not seem to suggest agricultural production. Rather, the hilltops and ridgetops they preferred would have provided greater visibility and defense, and would have been covered with thinner vegetation, factors that would have been more desirable for foraging groups. In contrast, the Early Iron Age communities, as we have seen, were clearing the wooded slopes and settling on the most fertile soils, that is, on the best agricultural land. Therefore, the archaeological evidence from Rakai suggests that the Early Iron Age communities were the first to begin agricultural production in this area. Unfortunately, supporting botanical or palynological evidence is lacking at present. Finger millet and sorghum were tentatively identified in the pollen record of Kabuye, Rwanda (Van Grunderbeek et al. 1983:42), yet the amounts recorded were very small and there was a lack of conviction in their identification. Nevertheless, it would appear that we can describe the Early Iron Age communities as agricultural producers.

Ceramic use—pot cooking?   With the beginning of ceramic manufacture we must also consider the question of ceramic use. Pots could have been used for a variety of general tasks: water collection, water storage, food storage, food preparation, and so on. Ethnography indicates that pots have also been used in more specialized ways, in salt production, for burials, and during magical rituals, for example. However, I feel that there is one area—cooking—in which the introduction of ceramic vessels would have had a particular impact. Pot cooking enables a dramatically different method of heating and cooking foodstuffs. Without ceramic vessels that, containing mixtures of liquids and foodstuffs, can withstand prolonged heating on a cooking hearth, foods must be roasted or smoked over a fire or baked on a hot, flat "griddle"—"dry" methods of cooking. The development of ceramic vessels enables the heating of liquids and thus allows the development of "wet" methods of cooking: boiling, steaming, frying, and the like. It has been suggested that animal stomachs could have been used for heating liquids prior to the discovery of ceramics (Tannahill 1988:15–16), yet their availability and function would have been comparatively limited. It is with ceramics that true versatility begins.

The uses to which Urewe pottery was put are not yet known, as concerns have largely been with Urewe ware as a diagnostic artifact and its relation to other ware types. There has been no examination of pot form, of evidence for heat treatment or residues. However, I will suggest that it is probable that Early Iron Age communities began using ceramics for the heat treatment of foods, and thus we can see the beginnings of pot cooking technology in these communities.

From the archaeological evidence, supplemented by paleoecological data, we have been able to identify four new activities/technologies that were adopted and developed by the Early Iron Age communities of the Interlacustrine Region: ceramic production, iron production, land clearance, and agricultural production. It has also been suggested that a fifth technology, pot cooking, was developed at this time, though this is as yet unsupported by ceramic analysis. These activities have all been recorded as being practiced by groups within the Interlacustrine Region, either today or within the recent past, and within these communities each of the activities has been gendered. Having recognized patterns of labor division by sex in the present, can we begin to extend these patterns back over two thousand years—that is, do certain technologies automatically become "male" or "female"? Can we identify them as "domestic" or "industrial," as has been done traditionally, or are we able to suggest more complex and fluid relationships between activities and gender? The potential gendering of the Early Iron Age interlacustrine technologies/activities cannot be explained simply through an examination of recent ethnographic data, but rather it needs to be examined as an earlier stage in an historical process. Thus, each technology or activity must be examined using a combination of ethnographic and archaeological data if some degree of understanding is to be gained.

Gendered Technologies

Of the five technologies/activities identified, two—iron production and pot cooking—are associated with a single sex, not only in all groups within the area today, but throughout sub-Saharan Africa. The remaining three activities, though gendered, may be determined as either male or female. Thus the more strictly gendered technologies, iron production and pot cooking, are considered first.

Iron production Iron production technology is strictly gendered, not only in the Interlacustrine Region, but throughout Africa; smelters and smiths, without exception, are and, in the recorded past, have been male. Indeed, in a great many societies around the world the working of iron has been a solely male occupation (Murdock and Provost 1973:207). How do we explain this? It is not a condition inherent in the technology, because women are capable of both smelting and smithing, despite the strenuous nature of the work, and African women have been recorded as significantly contributing to the labor of preparation for a smelt (Herbert 1993:27–28). The few exceptional references to women assisting during a smelt or with forging (e.g., Wright 1985:162) indicate that women are capable of this work, and there is nothing in iron production technology that excludes them, yet in societies throughout Africa they have been excluded. This strict genderization of iron production is not a result of the technical requirements of the technology; rather, it is a cultural reaction to that technology, and a remarkably consistent one.

In many cultures the correspondence of iron smelting to the processes of gestation and parturition has been integrated into conceptions of the iron production process. Eliade (1962) has demonstrated that the understanding of ores as embryonic metals is a common one, found in a surprising number and variety of societies. Hidden in the "womb" of the earth, ores are believed to develop naturally into pure metals over many centuries; extracted by the miner, they are matured and birthed with unnatural haste through the medium of the furnace/womb. The perception of the smelting process as a symbolic form of intercourse and procreation is found throughout Africa, and has been documented for the great majority of societies in eastern and southern Africa. It is suggested here that this may be a common conceptualization of the smelting process, resulting from the very nature of iron production technology and its perceived inherent resemblance to the human reproductive process. Within such conceptualizations iron technology itself can be seen to be essentially gendered, for through the function of both the earth and the furnace as womb it closely reflects the role of the mother. It is not, therefore, so surprising that the role of the father may be played by the ironworker, and that the ironworker is culturally male.

It is thus suggested that the genderization of iron technology should be seen as an expected cultural response to a common conceptualization of the process. However, no matter how common a practice in the ethnographic record, it would not be convincing simply to project these beliefs back over two thousand years to the early iron-using communities of the Interlacustrine Region. We need to examine both the ethnographic and archaeological record for clues to past perceptions of the iron production process. As we have seen, the conception of iron technology as a form of procreation has been documented for most eastern and southern African groups. This is interesting, as archaeological evidence suggests that iron technology originally spread from the Interlacustrine Region throughout eastern Africa and down to southern Africa (Miller and van der Merwe 1994). If elements of early interlacustrine conceptualizations are to be discerned, it is in common themes from these areas in which they may appear. We can indeed discern common themes, and yet the great diversity of ritual behaviors that has been recorded and the very different ways in which similar beliefs are manifest may, perhaps, be interpreted as a potential indica-

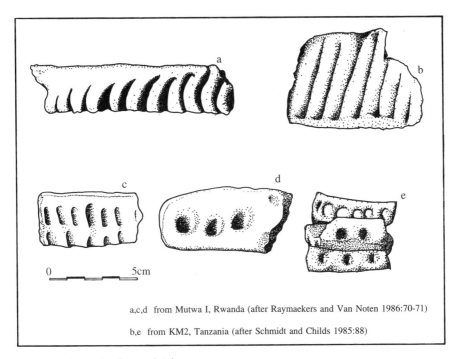

a,c,d from Mutwa I, Rwanda (after Raymaekers and Van Noten 1986:70-71)

b,e from KM2, Tanzania (after Schmidt and Childs 1985:88)

Figure 9.2. Decorative furnace bricks.

tion of the time depth of these beliefs. It is not improbable to suggest that origins of this common conceptualization may lie in the developments of the Early Iron Age.

There is, in addition, some archaeological evidence for the antiquity of these beliefs. Two decorated prehistoric furnaces have been recorded at the multiperiod site of Ziwa, in eastern Zimbabwe. The later furnace, now approximately dated to the 17th century AD, was decorated with a clay figure of a woman "in the act of giving birth" (Bernhard 1962:236). The earlier furnace unfortunately remains undated, though Early Iron Age smelting debris was recorded at the site and also bore the remains of a clay figure in a similar posture. The connection of these explicit images with the perception of iron production as procreation would appear to be straightforward.

Returning to the Interlacustrine Region, while there are no explicit images such as those of Ziwa, we do have some evidence for certain aspects of early smelting ritual. Small pots and holes have been found hidden at the base of furnaces in Rwanda and Tanzania (Van Noten 1979:65–67; Schmidt and Childs 1985:74–75, 81), and these have been interpreted as symbolic features, possibly containers for smelting "medicine," a practice common in recent times (Schmidt, Chapter 8). In addition, we have the decorated furnace "bricks" (Figure 9.2).

A functional purpose has been suggested for the designs impressed into these bricks; it has been proposed that they resulted naturally from the construction tech-

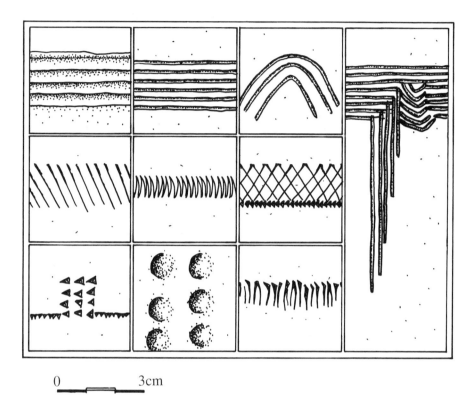

0 _____ 3cm

Figure 9.3. Decorative motifs used on Urewe ceramics.

nique, coil building, and were useful in creating a better surface on which to apply a plaster lining (Raymaekers and Van Noten 1986:81–82). However, the considerable number of undecorated bricks indicates that these impressions were not considered functionally necessary. In addition, decoration was applied to Rwandan bricks manufactured before the construction of the furnace, and to both Rwandan and Tanzanian bricks after the construction of the furnace (MacLean 1996a:252–253), which would suggest that they did not result from the construction technique. Ethnographic evidence has shown that symbolic decoration is frequently an important ritual element of furnace structure, and it is suggested that the motifs used on the Early Iron Age bricks had a symbolic purpose.

Collett (1985:130) has proposed a connection between the motifs found on furnace bricks and those used to decorate Urewe pottery (Figure 9.3), and a detailed analysis of the stylistic attributes of these two forms of decoration has supported his claim (MacLean 1996a:253–255). Similarities can be seen in the area to which decoration was confined (horizontal bands), in the use of repeated parallel impressed/incised lines and punctates, and in the location of decoration (such as around the rim). The archaeological evidence thus indicates some conceptual connection between iron smelting furnaces and Urewe pots in these Early Iron Age communities. Returning to the ethnographic data, a way of understanding that connection can be suggested.

In many eastern and southern African groups the linked processes of iron smelting and procreation are only two elements in a wider cosmological system of heat-mediated transformation; the third element is that of pot cooking (Collett 1985:119–22; 1993:504–507). These three processes represent the transformation of *natural products*, stone/ore, blood and semen, plants and animals, into *cultural products*, iron, a child, cooked food, and are linked through their fundamental nature of irreversibility and by the use of heat as a primary force in the effecting of the transformation. The cooking pot is seen as analogous to both the furnace and the womb or body of a fertile woman. It can, therefore, be suggested that the symbolic association between furnaces and pots in the Early Iron Age communities of the Interlacustrine Region could indicate that this cosmological system may have had its roots in this period, and that the conceptual triad of transformations is represented in the archaeological evidence.

It is possible, therefore, to support the claim for a gendered iron technology at this early date. The perception of smelting as an act of symbolic procreation can be seen to be not only a common general reaction to the nature of the technology, but also a specific cultural reaction of certain African groups that may be traced back to the Urewe communities of the Interlacustrine Region. We can indeed suggest that the earliest iron technology was gendered and that the first ironworkers were male.

Pot cooking   The cooking of food in interlacustrine societies is generally a female activity and, though there are exceptions—men may roast meat at local bars for example—the cooking of daily family meals is a strictly female task. Traditional pot cooking is a strictly female technology. When considering iron technology it was suggested that women were excluded, so why should we not continue this approach with pot cooking? Cooking technology is often largely ignored by archaeologists (Brumfiel 1992), being relegated to the realms of the simple, domestic, and female. Yet to produce a successful range of cooked food requires a similar degree of knowledge and skill to any technology, be it iron production or ceramic manufacture. The control of a family or community's food supply is a very important control, and one that has been manipulated in very many societies. This manipulation may be blunt (the withholding of meals), or it may be more subtle (the cooking of food that results in mild ill health) (e.g., diarrhea or constipation, Kureishi 1990:208) or the pollution of meals (Thomas Ellis 1982:104–105), and is a very important source of female power. As with iron technology, men are certainly capable of pot cooking, and there is nothing inherent in the technology that excludes them—yet they too are excluded.

Can it be assumed that cooking technology is inherently female and that pot cooking was a female technology in the Early Iron Age interlacustrine communities? Woman's role as domestic cook would appear to be so widespread and so universally accepted that, without any evidence to the contrary, it will be suggested that this was indeed the case. This is one area in which biology may be allowed a fundamental role, as the breast-feeding of a child may extend into the feeding of the family and as women's initial control of food supply may be maintained and extended.

As we have seen, the innovation of pot cooking was a radical one, allowing significant culinary developments. Indeed, it can be argued that, for certain food-stuffs, boiling rather than roasting or baking is nutritionally advantageous, resulting in an improved diet (Gifford-Gonzalez, Chapter 7). I suggest that these innovations were female. The archaeological evidence for the cosmological connection of pot cooking and iron production in the Urewe communities was discussed above. Iron production was seen as a new male technology, and I propose that pot cooking was its female equivalent, equally complex, equally powerful, and linked conceptually in a developing belief system. These two new and corresponding technologies have important implications, which will be discussed below.

Ceramic production   Ceramic production has also been a gendered technology in recent interlacustrine groups, yet there is no clear restriction to a single sex. While potters have often been seen as the female equivalent of the male smith (in many groups pots are made by the wives of ironworkers), in the Interlacustrine Region we also find groups in which ceramic production is a male technology (e.g., see Grace 1996). The situation is more complex, and the ethnographic data cannot thus be used to suggest a simple gendering of this technology in the past.

It has often been assumed that in most, if not all, societies the first potters were women (see Wright 1991 for a criticism), early ceramic production being perceived as a "domestic," and therefore female, technology. Yet there is no clear evidence to suggest that this was always, or often, the case. Certainly, in the Interlacustrine Region we have very few archaeological clues as to the identity of the manufacturers of Urewe ware. Studies of the clays used for Urewe ceramics indicate that, in Rwanda and Burundi, pots were made on a local scale for primarily local use (Van Grunder-beek 1988), and in Tanzania clay selection was being practiced, with the best clays being reserved for furnace rather than ceramic manufacture (Childs 1988). Ceramic production was, therefore, a small-scale, "domestic" activity, but we cannot, on this evidence alone, also claim it was a female technology. The only remaining social evidence that can be gained from these recovered pot sherds are the motifs used in their decoration. However, these motifs have been interpreted as relating to the function of the ceramics—as vessels associated with cooked food—not to the production process. They provide information about the user, not the manufacturer, of the pot.

The ethnographic data from the region indicates that, though ceramic production will be gendered, it may be perceived as either a male or a female technology. Unfortunately, there are no obvious archaeological clues to the identity of the manufacturers of Urewe ware and we cannot, therefore, begin to determine the manner in which Early Iron Age ceramic technology may have been gendered.

Land clearance and agricultural production   Land clearance and agricultural production are, to a certain degree, related activities, and so will be considered together.

In Rakai today, the initial clearance of land is a male responsibility, while the planting and maintenance of most food crops is generally a female one; plants intended for other purposes, such as beer making or barkcloth, are largely grown by men. The first clearance of land would appear to establish a male interest in the food produced, which would otherwise be wholly controlled by the women of the community. This pattern is a common one throughout the region.

Both these activities were identified indirectly, using a combination of archaeological and paleoecological evidence, and this lack of archaeological data does not allow much discussion of the possible division of labor in the past. There is, however, the evidence of historical linguistics. Schoenbrun (1990, 1996) has considered in detail the history of agriculture in the Interlacustrine Region using linguistic, ecological, and archaeological data, and he has suggested that Early Iron Age gender roles can be identified. A very similar situation to that which exists today has been proposed, with women possessing both agroecological knowledge and seed stocks and thus controlling agricultural production. Schoenbrun associates deforestation and clearance with new territorial conceptions of land, seeing men as both fortifying and diversifying their positions as power brokers in land use. Schoenbrun's arguments do, therefore, provide some support for the proposition that this basic sexual division of control and production began in the interlacustrine Early Iron Age communities. While it cannot be definitely concluded that initial land clearance was considered a male activity and agricultural production a female one, this is, nevertheless, suggested.

Changing Gender Relations in the Interlacustrine Early Iron Age

In the Interlacustrine Region today most activities and technologies are gendered to some degree. The patterns of sexual division are both basic and complex, allowing the establishment of distinct male and female identities at the individual level and the cohesive functioning of the community as a whole. In this paper we have identified the functioning of five new technologies/activities in the archaeological record of the Early Iron Age communities that inhabited the region, and we have examined this archaeological information, using both ethnographic and paleoecological data, for evidence of past gendering. In conclusion, it has been suggested that, during this period, iron technology and land clearance were considered "male" activities, while agricultural production and pot cooking were considered "female" activities, though no conclusions can yet be drawn concerning ceramic production.

The interlacustrine Early Iron Age was a period of great technological change, and the appropriation of certain activities by different sections of the population must have resulted in parallel social change. Iron production, often a relatively secretive process, appears to have been associated with very public displays of control: the attempted control of female fertility by the male smelter, as revealed in smelting cosmologies, and the economic control of production indicated by the restriction of smelting debris to certain areas. It was a new source of male power, perhaps offering unprecedented opportunities for restriction and authority. I would suggest that the use of ceramic vessels for cooking was, in some respects, the female equivalent of iron production. It was a technology from which men could be excluded, and it too offered new opportunities for control of important resources—cooked food and the health of the community. The cosmological linking of these two technologies by groups throughout eastern and southern Africa suggests not only their common perception as equivalent processes, but also their similar and vital impact on systems of perception.

A similar connection can be seen between the two remaining gendered activities, land clearance and agricultural production, which would again appear to form a male/female complement. Women, through their control of new agricultural resources, would have been in a relatively powerful position, not only producing important basic foodstuffs for the community, but also controlling the processing of those foodstuffs. Through initial land clearance, a male interest in this food source would have been established, and, as Schoenbrun (1990, 1996) suggested, new conceptions of territoriality may result from these developments. Again we are seeing a pattern of distinct and balanced male and female control.

What insight does this particular example of past division of labor provide into how and why different activities become associated with different sexes? It certainly cannot be concluded that all these tasks were naturally divided into those that were domestic and female and those that were male and industrial, yet there are certain areas in which we can suggest biological sex will be a primary factor—for example, the preparation of domestic meals by women. Perhaps one mistake that has been made in the past is the failure to identify strongly female technologies as technologies—to see them as simple rather than complex. It is also a mistake to assume that women may be controlled through these technologies rather than in control.

Interestingly, the relationship between sex and genderization appeared particularly explicit in the past, and present, functioning of iron technology. It is proposed here that certain technologies may have a potential to be perceived as inherently gendered, through their perceived correspondence on some level to human sexual differences, particularly to the process of reproduction. Iron technology provides a strong example of such inherent potential, with similar perceptions being recorded in many very different societies. It is, therefore, suggested that sex may actually be a very influential factor in the sexual division of labor, not only, as traditionally assumed, in the very basic division of labor resulting from the female role as childbearer, but also in the perception of technologies as being possessed of sexual characteristics.

Finally, the pattern of labor division that, it is proposed, developed in the Interlacustrine Region suggests a further important factor, that of balance. Male and female sections of the community established distinct, but complementary, areas of control. Anthropologists and archaeologists have traditionally been guilty of placing their own values on the activities of others, of concentrating on what they perceive to be important (supposedly male industrial activities), and ignoring what they consider to be commonplace (female domestic activities). In recent years scholars have sought to overturn these male biases, yet in so doing have sometimes been equally guilty, simply shifting from a male central focus to a female one. Perhaps the interlacustrine evidence indicates that we need to see societies as essentially balanced, that male and female activities and spheres of control are different yet equivalent, and that the development of a new and potentially powerful gendered technology will often produce a balancing reaction.

Chapter Ten

Engendered Spaces and Bodily Practices in the Iron Age of Southern Africa

"The house and body are intimately linked. The house is an extension of the person; like an extra skin, carapace or second layer of clothes, it serves as much to reveal and display as it does to hide and protect."

—Carsten and Hugh-Jones 1995:2

Introduction

Recent developments in social theory, anthropology and archaeology have all high-lighted the importance of the body as a mediating element in the constitution and reproduction of society. In particular, it has been noted that bodily practices, whether these are part of the routine performance of everyday life or are of a more specific goal-oriented nature, provide the principal vehicle through which elements of the material world acquire meaning. Since different individuals, differently situated within society have variable spatial and temporal rhythms of activity, and thus different bodily practices, their actions can give rise to a multiplicity of meanings for identical artifacts, spaces, or elements of the built environment.

This multivocality of material culture poses a number of interpretative chal-lenges, since no single view of the meanings of things and their relationships with social categories and individual identities can ever be sufficient (Hodder 1989). There are various reasons for this, of which three are of particular importance to the task of developing gender-sensitive interpretations of material culture patterning. In the first place, it is entirely conceivable that members of different social categories, such as the gender groupings "men" and "women," will perceive the world and act on it from quite different standpoints. Among the Marakwet of Kenya, for example, Moore has shown that whereas men regard women as highly individualistic and relatively pow-erless, women present themselves as both powerful in a number of domains and socially cohesive (1986). The source of this power, however, is different from that of Marakwet men. Whereas the former draw their power from institutionalized sources of jural and economic authority, the power of Marakwet women lies in and through their bodies. This is partly as a result of their practical autonomy over household production and space, but, more especially, because of their sexuality, which Marakwet women recognize as something that men desire but can never appropriate (Moore 1986:171–188). Yet, as Moore explains, though Marakwet women have a different perspective on the world from that held by Marakwet men, women's presentations of themselves are inevitably contingent on male representations of their position and value. As such, their alternative model of social reality remains structurally subordinate to that held and generated by men and, as a result, is in some sense hidden (Moore 1986:184–188). The interpretative challenge, therefore, is to find ways of making such latent meanings visible, rather than simply accepting that the dominant representations of social reality are an accurate reflection of gender and other relations within society.

A second problem that needs to be addressed when attempting a gendered reading of material culture arises from the variation that exists *within* any particular social category, especially as this can be as significant as the variation that exists *between* opposing categories. For example, in many societies, and not just so-called traditional ones, younger men and women often have lower status, less practical power and jural authority, and even less individual autonomy over their actions, than their elders (see also Parkington, Chapter 2). This can have a number of consequences for the partitioning of space, the use of artifacts, and the meanings and symbolic associations that arise from these. For instance, in her discussion of wife–wife relations in the organization of rice farming among the Mende of Sierra Leone, Leach notes that the senior wife of the household has a more active role in household decision making and the organization of farm labor than her junior cowives. Partly as a consequence of this, senior wives are much more closely associated with upland farm plots, whereas junior wives are more usually associated with household space (Leach 1992:84). Both domains could be said to be "female spaces," but clearly the origins of their gender association and their relative status as the domains of women are *not* identical. By the same token, the "meanings" of these different spaces will not be exactly the same for senior and junior wives alike. Gender identities, in other words, far from being fixed categories associated with unique sets of behavior and associated symbolism, are instead situationally and contextually contingent, and members of the same gender "category" may well relate to a particular place or set of objects in quite different ways (Strathern 1987; Moore 1994). Interpretative approaches that treat all members of the same social category as being equivalent in all respects not only obscure these types of subtleties but may even misconstrue the social significance of particular material representations.

A third challenge, which follows from this, lies in the fact that gender identities, perhaps more than most other types of social identity, are by no means fixed and immutable during an individual's lifespan. This is because gender identities are derived from the individual body, and since bodies age, these identities may also be subject to change. The social institution of initiation is an obvious illustration of this. Since, in most societies that place an emphasis on initiation as a means of conferring an engendered identity on individuals, prior to initiation, boys and girls are generally treated alike and in some sense as "sexless" or "androgynous" (see, for example, Ashton 1952:35–37, on Basuto attitudes and practices). Equally, restrictions on behavior and access to certain spatial domains that may apply to fully adult women and men are often relaxed in the case of elderly members of society. In such instances, as is the case among contemporary Tswana communities, men and women become once more almost "androgynous" (Segobye 1997: personal communication).

An individual's "gender identity," therefore, may go through a number of trans-formations during her or his lifespan, and, as a consequence, at any particular time a specific place or assemblage of artifacts may have multiple gender associations, depending on the age, status, and other kinds of nongender identities of the individuals who inhabit or make use of them (see also Kent, Chapter 3, with respect to differences between higher and lower status women in Sotho-Tswana societies). Similarly, the gender associations of a place or artifact can also change over its own lifespan, in either a systematic or nonsystematic manner. A good example of the former is the manner in which the gender associations of particular houses within Dogon villages change in response to the developmental cycle of the domestic group, which in this case is the extended lineage (Lane 1994).

Clearly, as the foregoing discussion suggests, understanding the role of gender differences in the structuring of the archaeological record requires more than a simple matching of spaces and objects to either men or women, or both. In particular, there is a need to move beyond the use of single, unifying, representational models of society, so as to accommodate alternative readings of the material evidence. More specifically, attempts to infer gender relationships from the patterning of material culture should not simply assume that the dominant forms of representation are necessarily an accurate reflection of the social realities that existed in the past. Equally, it needs to be accepted that even within the same gender category, individuals may have different perspectives as to what it means to belong to that gender category and, furthermore, that these understandings are also liable to change as individuals age and assume alternative identities.

To illustrate these points, I now turn to a discussion of the organization of space within Iron Age (ca. AD 350–1850) settlements in southern Africa. I begin with a discussion of current approaches to their interpretation, particularly in terms of the ethnohistorically derived Central Cattle Pattern model (Huffman 1982, 1986), and highlight some of the weaknesses of these approaches in the light of the remarks above (see also Kent, Chapter 3, and Segobye, Chapter 12, for additional discussion of this topic). Next, I outline an alternative approach to reading the evidence, which seeks to illustrate how women may have held different perceptions and under-standings of space from those of men, as a consequence of the differences in their bodily practices. By way of conclusion, I also endeavor to place these different inter-pretations of space in some form of diachronic perspective, and examine how even minor changes in the layout of houses and settlements generated new meanings for space and social and personal identities, which in turn precipitated further transformations of bodily practices.

Representational Models of Gender in the Iron Age of Southern Africa

For many years, models of the organization of southern African Iron Age societies have incorporated notions of gender as an important structuring principle. This is in marked contrast to most other regional and/or period-specific approaches to archaeological interpretation that have been developed for the material traditions of the African continent. The two most dominant models concern, respectively, the organization of settlement space (Huffman 1982, 1984a,b, 1986, 1996b,c) and the form and decoration of iron smelting furnaces (Childs 1991; Collett 1993). Both sets of models rely heavily on ethnographic observations and oral traditions concerning recent southern African communities and cultural practices, on the grounds that the latter are directly descended from prehistoric populations of the region. This type of use of ethnographic data to interpret the archaeological remains of groups ancestral to present-day communities is thus a variant of the "direct historical approach" first developed by Steward (1942; see also Huffman 1996c:6).

Utilizing this approach, Huffman has identified two broad types of settlement layout, which he infers reflect rather different systems of political organization, gender and power relations, worldviews, and symbolic structures. Huffman terms these the Central Cattle Pattern (often abbreviated to CCP) and the Zimbabwe Pattern. These have different spatial and temporal distributions, but neither appears to have been restricted to any particular ethnic group.

The Zimbabwe Pattern has a fairly restricted geographical distribution, being found only in the areas of present-day Zimbabwe, eastern Botswana, western Mozambique, and the Northern Province of South Africa. Moreover, the Zimbabwe Pattern has no exact present-day equivalent and instead appears to have been associated exclusively with the elite centers of Zimbabwe traditional polities, from their origins at K2 and Mapungubwe in the 11th century AD, to their ultimate demise in the early 19th century with the collapse of the Rozwi and Monomutapa empires. Many elements of the Zimbabwe Pattern, however, are preserved in recent Venda and Shona cultural beliefs and practices (Huffman 1986, 1996c).

The Central Cattle Pattern, by comparison, appears to have had much wider spatial and longer temporal distributions, which included the commoner settlements belonging to the Zimbabwe tradition facies. For more recent periods, the Central Cattle Pattern is associated, principally, with Sotho-Tswana and Nguni speakers (e.g., Kuper 1980, 1982). However, elements of the structural system have been documented among other Eastern Bantu language speakers elsewhere in southern Africa. These include Bakgalagadi of central and western Botswana (Kuper 1970), Bakalanga of eastern Botswana and western Zimbabwe (van Waarden 1989), and the various Shona-speaking communities of southwestern and central Zimbabwe.

The core component of the Central Cattle Pattern type of settlement layout, as the term suggests, is the location of cattle byres at the center of the settlement, or settlement subsection such as a ward. The reasons for this, as discussed above, have to do with the central importance of cattle within these societies as both economic and symbolic resources. In particular, cattle provided the main element of bridewealth exchanges; were more highly valued socially and economically than other kinds of livestock and also agricultural produce; and featured prominently in various rites of passage and annual rituals of social renewal. Conventionally, cattle were managed by males, though there were no absolute restrictions on this, and adult women as well as children could also own cattle (e.g., Schapera 1938:215–221) .

Combined with these cultural evaluations of cattle, the central location of the cattle byre had a determinant effect on the location of other elements of the settlement. Thus, those elements and practices that were linked conceptually with cattle were located either in or adjacent to the byre, whereas those that were conceptual opposites were located away from the cattle byres. Houses, for instance, being more closely associated with female activities, were typically arranged in an arc or circle around the cattle byre. The court, being a male domain, on the other hand, was generally situated immediately adjacent to the byre. Similarly, adult male burials were more commonly placed within the cattle byre, whereas adult females and uninitiated children tended to be buried in the compound, and stillborn babies and infants beneath the house floor.

There were exceptions to this spatial organization of burials, and these highlight the operation of other structuring principles, namely those of age seniority and status. Thus, for example, female members of high-status elites, including juveniles as well as adults, were sometimes buried within the settlement cattle byre rather than beneath the floor of their house or compound, as among Bapedi (Mönnig 1967). Adult female burials, and also child burials, have been found within the remains of cattle byres at a number of Iron Age sites in the region, which date to between the 6th and 11th centuries AD, suggesting that this practice is of some antiquity (see Whitelaw 1993). Age seniority and status also influenced the location of individual houses relative to one another. Typically, the house of the senior wife, or compound of the senior male, was located directly opposite the entrance to the settlement. This position was also generally up slope from the entrance, and in many ethnic groups was situated on the western side, thereby creating an association between the concepts senior, up, and west, and their opposites: junior, down, and east (see Figures 10.1a and 10.1b).

In view of the historical and cultural connections between the various Later Iron Age populations and contemporary Sotho-Tswana and Nguni peoples, many archaeologists have argued that the similarities in settlement layouts on Later Iron Age sites can be taken as evidence for the existence of symbolic and ideological continuities over the last five hundred to a thousand years (e.g., Huffman 1982; Evers 1984; Taylor 1984; Loubser 1985; Pistorius 1992). More recently, the Central Cattle Pattern model

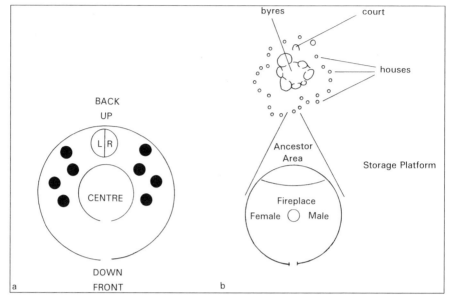

Figure 10.1. Spatial characateristics of the Central Cattle Pattern.
(a) Key spatial dimensions (after Huffman 1982); (b) Idealised village layout and house plan (after Huffman 1989).

has also been employed to interpret the organization of space in Early Iron Age sites, including those occupied over 1,500 years ago by some of the earliest agropastoral communities to settle in the region (e.g., Huffman 1990, 1993; Whitelaw 1993, 1994, 1994/95). This is despite the fact that there are acknowledged disjunctions between other aspects of the Early Iron Age and Later Iron Age material traditions and settlement systems, such as differences in ceramic styles (e.g., Huffman 1989) and settlement locations (e.g., van Schalkwyk 1994/95).

Whereas the use of the Central Cattle Pattern model has greatly enhanced our understanding of southern African Iron Age societies in general, a number of concerns have been leveled at its more recent application to interpret the very earliest agropastoral settlements in the region. It has been noted, for instance, that whereas elements of the Central Cattle Pattern model are present in many Early Iron Age settlements, others appear to have been organized differently. These include the 7th to 8th century AD site of Ntsitsana in northern Transkei (Prins and Granger 1993:170), and the late 10th to early 11th century AD site of Pitse in southern Botswana (Campbell et al. 1996:10) (see Figure 10.2 for the location of these sites and others mentioned in the text). In addition, it has been noted that even where livestock byres appear to have been centrally located and encircled by residential structures, other aspects of the evidence from Early Iron Age settlements point to the existence of practices that diverge from those predicted by the ethnographic model of settlement organization (see also Segobye, Chapter 12).

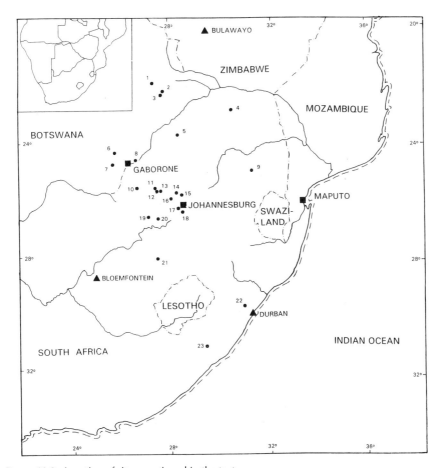

Figure 10.2. Location of sites mentioned in the text.

Thus, for instance, there are several examples of centrally located pits on Early Iron Age settlements that appear to have been used for rubbish disposal, possibly of a ritual nature, rather than as grain-storage bins (Whitelaw 1993:75–76; Maggs 1994/95:176; Lane 1994/95:59). Even though some of this evidence may be the result of secondary reuse of storage pits, Whitelaw has shown that at least some pits seem to have had rubbish disposal as their primary function. He has also noted that many pits have a characteristic filling that includes a number of "bottomless pots." Whitelaw has tentatively interpreted these as part of the debris associated with "girls' puberty or initiation rituals," arguing that the deliberate, but careful, breaking of the vessels could have been perceived as a form of "symbolic defloration" (1993: 76). More recently, he has tentatively suggested that intrasite variations in the spatial location of such pits may have been correlated with their relative position within the local political hierarchy, such that on "low-status sites they were in the centre, while on high-status sites they were in the residential area" (Whitelaw 1994/95:47).

By contrast, pits are generally absent from Later Iron Age and historic Sotho-Tswana and Nguni settlements, having been replaced by various forms of granary and grain-storage bins, as well as surface middens. There is little evidence to indicate the use of either for the disposal of objects associated with initiation or puberty rituals, though aspects of these ceremonies were conducted in and around the central areas of the chiefly settlements (e.g., Schapera 1938; Hammond-Tooke 1981), rather than in the residential areas as may have been the case during the Early Iron Age. As argued below, this difference has a number of implications for our understanding of processes of embodiment in the Early Iron Age and their possible relationships to the spatial and social organization of these societies.

Other disjunctions have also been noted between Early Iron Age settlement evidence and the ethnographic data on which the Central Cattle Pattern is based. Maggs, for instance, has argued that a number of Early Iron Age sites in Natal contain evidence for iron smelting, and not just forging, within their central areas (Maggs 1994/95:176; see also Vogel 1984 for potentially similar evidence from southern Zambia). This would have been in marked contrast to later practices, when iron smelting was either undertaken well away from the settlements or in physically and ritually secluded areas.

Huffman has recently responded to some of these criticisms (1996b,c), as well as to more general ones concerning problems associated with the use of ethnographic and ethnohistoric data to interpret Early Iron Age settlements (e.g., Segobye 1993; Stahl 1993; Lane 1994/95). In particular, he has stressed that the Central Cattle Pattern is an idealized model "that characterizes settlement organization at the level of cultural norms" (1996c:11). As such, "it is not designed to investigate daily behaviour and dynamics" (1996c:7) but emphasizes instead "the underlying principles that give structure to society" (1996c:6).

It is not immediately clear, however, whether this implies that the Central Cattle Pattern is unable to explain evidence for internal variation in elements of Iron Age settlement organization, or that such variation as has been detected is of no consequence to the analytical role of the Central Cattle Pattern model. Since Huffman, as yet, has not discussed in detail his understanding of the significance of the reported variation, this point remains unresolved. However, his insistence that the Central Cattle Pattern is an "idealized" model lays it open to a criticism common to *all* similar representational approaches. This is because meaning does not reside in the material world but must be invoked through practice—that is, an engagement by individuals, in and through their bodies, with physical objects and other individuals (Bourdieu 1977; Moore 1986, 1994). Thus, for the reasons outlined above, while certain representational significances of physical space and objects may achieve dominance, and so provide an "idealized, normative model of socio-spatial relations," the existence of such a model does not explain either its genesis or its continuity through time.

Writing the Past

One of the more notable features about recent discussions of the Central Cattle Pattern, whether in support of the model or as qualifiers, has been the virtual neglect of a consideration of the houses on such sites. Instead, most attention has been directed toward examination of the central zones, the areas *without houses*. In particular, work has concentrated on how to correctly distinguish between cattle from small-stock byres through phytolith and phosphate analysis (e.g., Huffman 1990; Whitelaw 1993); forging from smelting debris (e.g., Huffman 1993; Prins and Granger 1993); grain-storage pits from "ritual" or "rubbish" pits (e.g., Maggs 1994/95; Whitelaw 1994/95); and the degree of empirical correlation between the range of features found in these central areas and those predicted by the ethnographically derived model (e.g., Lane 1994/95).

The major exception to this is Huffman's reanalysis of Mason's (1981, 1986) initial interpretation of various types of stone-and-clay features at Broederstroom as the remains of beehive-shaped houses, and his suggestion that they represent, instead, the remains of collapsed grainbins (Huffman 1990; 1993:222). Yet, even in this case, the ultimate objective is not to clarify the status of those structures that were houses, but rather to support an argument about the characteristics of a "central area." This interpretative neglect of Early Iron Age houses even extends to current publication strategies, such that physical descriptions of house remains are generally fairly abbreviated, and that detailed house plans, with a few notable exceptions (e.g., van Waarden 1992; Pearson 1995; Campbell et al. 1996) are generally absent from excavation reports. Instead, the house remains located on these sites are reduced to mere symbols on generalized site plans (e.g., Huffman 1990:5; 1993:221, Figs. 2 and 4; Prins and Granger 1993:156, Fig. 2; Whitelaw 1994:47–53, Figs. 30–33).

In short, houses, the acknowledged primary "female" domain, seem to have been written out of the interpretative agenda. It is interesting to note, therefore, that quite different strategies have been adopted to the publication of empirical data on Iron Age houses by archaeologists whose work has been less directed by the Central Cattle Pattern model (e.g., Maggs 1976; Mason 1986; Pearson 1995). As in other forms of practice, in the writing of archaeology, in the inscription of collective memories, position is everything.

Engendered Spaces and the World Reversed[1]

If we take the term "without" to refer to position rather than lack, a somewhat different understanding of Iron Age settlement space can be generated. Since, in terms of the Central Cattle Pattern model and much of the evidence, the cattle byres, communal grain-storage facilities and forging debris are, in a sense, *within* houses, encircled and enclosed by residential areas. Viewed from this perspective, houses provide, at one and the same time, both a protective barrier between the settlement and the outside world and the settlement element that is in most immediate contact with the outside world. In other words, in this particular "order of things," houses, because of their position, are ambiguous spaces, liminal zones that lie betwixt and between opposing worlds.

That this was so in historically documented Sotho-Tswana and Nguni societies is evident from the dual meanings of the vernacular words for "house" and their etymologies. In Setswana, for example, the word *ntlo* can mean a physical structure, a dwelling, and the social group of uterine kin—a wife and her children—who are its principal inhabitants.[2] As Comaroff and Comaroff have observed, such uterine houses formed the "atoms" of the Tswana social system, their "uniqueness and indivisibility" being marked by, among other things, "the only term in the kinship lexicon for a discrete, impermeable group of agnatic peers . . . *setsalo* (from *tsala*; 'womb'[3]), a singular noun which implied the merged social identity of those born of one mother" (Comaroff and Comaroff 1991:133).

As the Comaroffs observe, there were other lexical and behavioral clues to the centrality of the house within 19th century Tswana economies, sociopolitics, and cosmologies. Under the system of levirate, for instance, a man who married his brother's widow was said to do so in order to "enter his house." Sororatic arrangements had the similar purpose of ensuring that the uterine house did not die, and "a woman who gave birth on behalf of a barren (or deceased) sister or cousin was known as *seantlo*, the personification of a *ntlo*" (Comaroff and Comaroff 1991:133). Houses, though built collectively, were "referred to as a rule by the name of the wife occupying them" (Schapera 1938:228), and their boundaries and those of the compound (*lolwapa*) were frequently protected symbolically with various forms of medicines and charms. *In extremis*, the backyard (*segotlo*) of the ruler's mother's "house" could be used as a place of sanctuary by any member of the *morafe* (polity) fleeing from a punishment handed down by the ruler's court (*kgotla*) (Comaroff and Comaroff 1991: 134–135).

As the builders and principal occupants of these houses, women's bodies were, at one and the same time, the source of both practical and symbolic sustenance. Houses were the primary units of production and consumption, the agricultural produce from each woman's field being used to feed her *ntlo*. Each house was also the focus of the reproduction of the respective agnatic units that made up the wider polity. Just as the actions of women's bodies within houses invested these spaces with meaning, so houses could also stand as metaphors for women's bodies, and, by extension, also the "body politic." Jean Comaroff has noted, for instance, the anthropomorphic symbolism attached to the Tswana house (1985),[4] and in particular the resemblance of the formal layout of at least some to the female reproductive anatomy, such as the Batlhaping house illustrated by the explorer Burchell in the early 19th century (Comaroff and Comaroff 1991:133) (see Figure 10.3a). In this regard, it is interesting to note that rather similarly shaped two- and three-celled houses occurred at the 18th-century site of Olifantspoort 20/71 (Mason 1986:380; see also Hall, Chapter 13, Fig. 13.3) (Figure

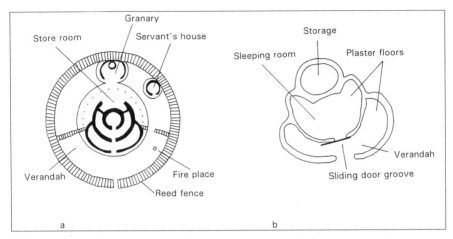

Figure 10.3. Precolonial Tswana house plans with gynecomorphic forms.
(a) 19th-century Batlhaping house (after Burchell 1953); (b) 18th-century house from Olifantspoort 20/71 (after Mason 1986).

10.3b), situated several hundred kilometers away to the northeast in an area more closely associated with Bakwena ancestry.

Many other taboos and practices associated with the house also reinforced the conceptual links between sex, childbirth, houses, and women's bodies. For instance, in Setswana the phrase *go tsena mo ntlong*, literally "to go into the house," is used to describe the process whereby women go into confinement within their mother's or mother-in-law's house[5] during the final stages of pregnancy and remain there until about three months after the birth of the child (Segobye 1997: personal communication). The doorway of the house in which the expectant mother (*motsetsi*) was confined was also symbolically sealed by placing a log across it, from which point onward the woman's husband (among other potentially polluting individuals) was not allowed to enter the house (Mogapi 1990). The process of smearing cow dung (which in Sotho-Tswana cosmologies was generally regarded as a cooling agent) on house floors was also said to make women "hot," just as sexual intercourse and pregnancy made them "hot," and so came to symbolize conception (Larsson 1990:82–83). In view of this, it is perhaps significant that on the first day after the end of confinement, the floor of the house in which the woman had stayed was usually replastered with cow dung (Mogapi 1990), thereby implying the renewal of conjugal relations.

This gynecomorphic symbolism, however, can also be extended tentatively to the layout of settlements as a whole, at least for more recent periods. As the published site plans indicate, a great many Moloko tradition settlements of the more recent Later Iron Age that are found distributed across the Highveld areas of Northern Province, North West Province, and Gauging (all formerly part of Transvaal) in South Africa, and adjacent parts of southeastern Botswana, exhibit a broadly similar form of successive concentric rings of walling, houses, alleyways, and livestock enclosures.

Typically, the outer ring consists of a continuous, stone-built enclosure wall, often with scalloped embayments, that generally contains a primary entranceway often flanked by low walls to form a funnel-like passageway. Additional openings can also occur, and the exact number can vary considerably. Normally, however, these are not as prominently marked as the primary entrance. House remains, sometimes associated with granary bases, rear and front courtyards, and even grain-threshing floors, occur immediately inside the outer enclosure wall in a concentric ring. Usually, an intervening band of "unenclosed space" or "linear movement zone," indicated by a general absence of walling and other structures, separates the ring of domestic structures from a central cluster or clusters of livestock enclosures, possible courts, and, in some regions, forging niches.[6]

Examples of sites exhibiting these broad characteristics include the stone-walled sites of Molokwane (Pistorius 1992), Boschoek (Huffman 1986), Klipriviersberg 5/65 (Walton 1956; Mason 1986), Potchefstroom (Walton 1956) Olifantspoort 20/71 (Mason 1986), Platberg 32/71 (Mason 1986), Klingbeil (Evers 1984), and Doornspruit (Dreyer 1995), all variously dated to between the 17th and mid-19th century AD. As Figure 10.4 shows, the precise form of these settlements varied considerably. However, viewed as a whole, all of them exhibit a general resemblance to the human womb, or, more broadly, the internal organs of the female body. Thus, for instance, the zone of houses could be likened to the uterus wall; the primary, funnel-shaped entrances to the vagina; the internal passageways to fallopian tubes; and the livestock corrals to the ovary.

This characterization of late Tswana settlement layout as resembling the internal female reproductive organs may seem highly speculative. Certainly, no explicit exegesis on these lines appears in the ethnographic or historical documentary sources, unlike that for some other societies (e.g., Dogon—M. Griaule 1949; G. Griaule 1955; Batammaliba—Blier 1987; and Barasana—Hugh-Jones 1979). Moreover, the models of human anatomy and theories of conception held by Sotho-Tswana speakers have only been partially documented. There are, however, some suggestive indicators that help support such a reading of this particular settlement form, over and above the general gynecomorphic symbolism associated with individual houses discussed above.

Specifically, though theories of conception held by different Tswana speakers may have varied, it appears to have been generally believed that children were produced by a mixture of the blood inside the woman's womb (i.e., her menstrual blood), and a man's semen (which was also likened to blood, and sometimes known by the name *madi amasweu*, "white blood") (Schapera 1978:166–168; Comaroff 1985).[7] Also, for a child to be conceived, intercourse had to take place between the man and woman several times (see Schapera 1978:167). The rejection of semen, either because the woman's womb was "too narrow" or because "it had not closed" after intercourse, was perceived as one of the major causes of barrenness (Schapera 1978:173–174). Menstrual blood, though regarded, at least by Bakgatla, as the source of the child's own blood (the father's semen providing the flesh), was also regarded more generally as a

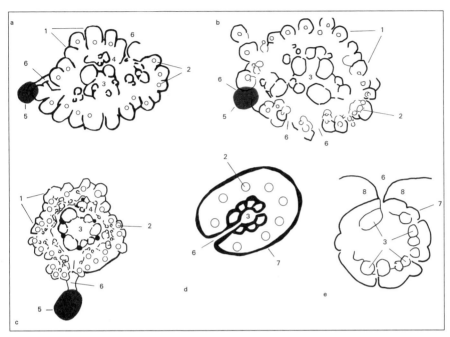

Figure 10.4. Later Iron Age stone-walled enclosures.
(a) Molokwane (after Pistorius 1992); (b) Platberg 32/71 (after Mason 1986); (c) Boschoek (after Huffman 1986); (d) Klingbeil 2530 AB 3 (after Mason 1967); (e) Doornspruit (after Jones 1935).

source of pollution. Among some Tswana speakers, it was considered that sexual relations between a man and a woman during her menses could lead to "the man's urethra becoming 'blocked' because of the 'hot' blood of the woman" (Booyens 1985:138).

These theories of human anatomy and conception, therefore, seem to share a number of common themes, including regulated entrance, the mixing of complementary opposites (hot, red, menstrual blood; cool, white, semen), and closure (or its lack). Given that cattle, through their association with men, were conceptually linked with both "semen" and the concept of "coolness" (Kuper 1982), it is perhaps not too far-fetched to suggest that their regular entrance into the settlement each night and the associated closing of gateways could be conceived as analogous to sexual intercourse and the practices followed after confinement. The more general notion of women as containers or vessels would also help to underline this bodily analogy, especially in view of the association between women and clay, through their tasks as potters (see Hall, Chapter 13) and house builders. Indeed, when viewed from the perspective of raw materials, the outer settlement arc of clay houses could have evoked, at least potentially, a number of conceptual linkages among settlement layout, pottery vessels, and women's bodies.[8]

Changing Places

Whether 19th century and earlier Tswana communities conceptualized the layout of their settlements in precisely these terms is difficult to verify. However, it is interesting to note that a number of changes appear to have taken place during the course of the Iron Age in southern Africa, in terms of both the internal arrangement of houses and the use of enclosure walls. When considered from the perspective of a gynecomorphic model, as opposed to that of the Central Cattle Pattern, taken together these developments suggest that there were a number of significant changes to the meaning of settlement space from the Early Iron Age to the Later Iron Age, and that these may have been related to changing gender relations.

For example, though the evidence is not always abundantly clear, in general, Early Iron Age settlements appear to have lacked outer boundary walls, and in many cases also lacked the kinds of courtyard walls used to enclose domestic space during later periods. This could be simply a result of differential preservation, arising from the use of organic materials such as reeds and thornbushes during the Early Iron Age, as opposed to stone and daga in the Later Iron Age. Certainly, traces of courtyard fences made from reeds have been noted at a number of Early Iron Age settlements, including Magagarape in southern Botswana (Campbell et al. 1996). Also, toward the end of the Early Iron Age, more houses have evidence of the presence of external courtyard walls that typically enclose an area with traces of food preparation and water storage activities. Such sites include Pitse in southern Botswana, occupied between ca. AD 961 and 1021 (van Waarden 1992; Campbell et al. 1996).

The manner in which Early Iron Age and later settlements grew and developed during the period of their occupancy also appears to have differed. Specifically, sites with evidence of several phases of occupation belonging to the initial period of Early Iron Age settlement, such as Broederstroom, Kwagandaganda, and Magagarape, all exhibit a distinctly linear pattern of expansion, such that the location of the core of the settlement seems to have shifted on several occasions (see Figure 10.5).[9] The overall impression gained from these site plans is one of settlement flux and periodic relocation of houses, cattle byres, pits, and other facilities as new members were incorporated into the community. This contrasts markedly with the pattern exhibited by terminal Later Iron Age sites, which, by and large, seem to have grown by the *accretion* of new wards around a primary core (e.g., Olifantspoort 20/71, see Hall, Chapter 13, Fig. 13.3).

The evidence for the intervening periods is less clear cut, however. On the one hand, many of the later Early Iron Age Toutswe tradition sites in Botswana, including Toutswemogala, Bosutswe, and Kgaswe, occupied between the 7th and 13th centuries AD, appear to have had a central settlement core from their initial establishment that persisted until their final abandonment (Denbow 1983, 1986). On the other hand, at some slightly later sites, such as Modipe Hill in Botswana (Pearson 1995) and OXF1 in Free State, South Africa (Maggs 1976), it is difficult to identify a distinctive core that might have been associated with the senior, founding kin group

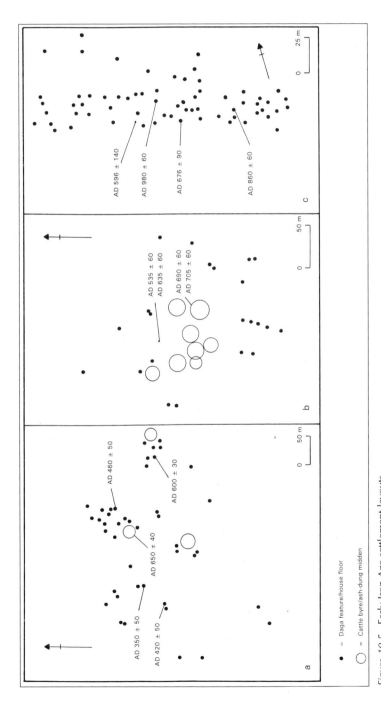

Figure 10.5. Early Iron Age settlement layouts.
(a) Broederstroom (after Mason 1981); (b) Kwagandaganda (after Whitelaw 1994/95); (c) Magagarape (after Campbell et al. 1996).

(Figure 10.6). At both these sites, however, there are obvious signs, as exhibited by the use of stone-walling, of the beginnings of "enclosure" and the creation of more permanent boundaries.

The precise sequence and timing of changes to the manner in which settlements grew, therefore, could have varied quite considerably. Nevertheless, the more fluid mode of settlement expansion during the initial Early Iron Age, as compared with the more accretional developmental sequence during the terminal Later Iron Age, suggests a rather different approach to the constitution of "houses" as a type of social institution. Thus, in the later periods, there is a very clear emphasis on boundedness and the control of access to both the settlement itself and the individual houses it contains. The use of stone-walling during this period, while undoubtedly fulfilling a defensive role as well, would have helped to reinforce these notions, particularly if, as seems probable, the wall were built by men.[10] This emphasis on boundedness would have had practical consequences for the movement of human bodies in and through settlement space, thereby generating a specific set of incorporeal practices. As discussed above, these inhabited spaces also acquired distinctive symbolic significances that centered on an ideology in which women's bodies were represented as the nexus of both settlement fusion and fission.

During the initial Early Iron Age, on the other hand, settlements seem to have been more open and "permeable," suggesting that there was less concern with kinship identity, and, by implication, less concern with the boundedness of houses as coresidential, property-owning, unilineal descent groups. Also, there appears to have been less fixity to the space of settlement itself, such that the limits of the settled area tended to shift over time. Both these factors could be an indication that membership of a settlement, and rights of access to its resources during the Early Iron Age, may have been calculated rather differently than in the terminal Later Iron Age.

The fact that there are also apparent differences between Early Iron Age and terminal Later Iron Age initiation practices lends support to this view. Specifically, the ethnohistoric data indicate that the greater proportion of Sotho-Tswana initiation ceremonies took place away from residential areas, and in seclusion. It was in these initiation schools that previously androgynous members of the community were transformed into either "men" or "women," a process that often entailed some form of bodily mutilation accentuating the physical differences between male and female bodies (e.g., Hammond-Tooke 1981; Schapera 1978). These newly formed adult bodies were later reintegrated into the body *politic* in public ceremonies normally held in the central space of the principal settlement.

The evidence for initiation ceremonies during the Early Iron Age is more circumspect, but nevertheless some differences are apparent. For instance, pits and ashy middens containing deliberately broken pots, clay figurines, and other debris possibly associated with initiation or puberty ceremonies often occur in *residential* areas, though they can also occur in or around cattle byres (Loubser 1993; Whitelaw 1993, 1994/95). Human incisors, which appear to have been deliberately extracted, have

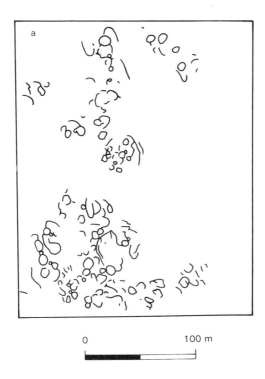

0   100 m

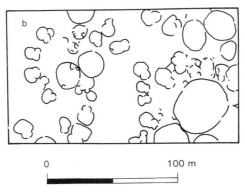

0   100 m

Figure 10.6. Later Iron Age settlement layouts.
(a) Modipe (after Pearson 1995); (b) OXF1 (after Maggs
1976).

also been found in the cattle byres at a number of sites, including Broderstroom, Klein Africa, Diamont, and Mount Ziwa (Huffman 1990). Whitelaw has interpreted this evidence as "consistent with the practice in many modern Bantu-speaking communities of marking initiates in some physical way on their transition to adulthood" (1994/95:44). However, since identical dental alterations occur on *both* male and female bodies (as at Kwagandaganda [Whitelaw 1993]), the practice is unlikely to have been associated with the definition of engendered bodies in a way that was analogous to male circumcision or the lengthening of the labia in later Sotho-Tswana populations. Instead, the practice of dental alteration during the Early Iron Age may have been a form of incorporating foreigners, or more simply nonkin, into society. This action was further publicly legitimized by the disposal of the teeth in the very core of the settlement. Certainly, given the somewhat precarious nature of the initial expansion of agropastoralism into the region, there are likely to have been many occasions when the need to bring new members into the community, possibly from neighboring foraging groups, would have been strategically advantageous and perhaps even necessary. The application of DNA testing on skeletal material from these sites could be one way of verifying this hypothesis.

Turning to the houses themselves, there is further evidence that their internal layout, and hence, possibly the symbolism of space, in the Early Iron Age was different from that in the Later Iron Age. As discussed above, there has been a tendency among archaeologists working on Early Iron Age sites to ignore the details of internal house space, and consequently published information is rare. The limited number of large area excavations, with three-dimensional recording of individual artifact locations, also imposes other interpretative constraints (see Kent, Chapter 3; also Lane 1994/95:60). The major exception comes from Mason's extensive work in the south-central Transvaal (1986) and some recent excavations in Botswana (e.g., van Waarden 1992; Pearson 1995). The Central Cattle Pattern model predicts that houses should have both a central fireplace and a storage platform at the rear. There should also be evidence for a left–right female–male division of space, as one stands facing into the interior of the house from the door (see Figure 10.1). By contrast, the excavated houses at Magagarape, Strauss, and Broederstroom, some of the earliest Early Iron Age sites in the region, lack evidence for any kind of storage platform. Hearth locations are also variable. Both of the excavated houses at Strauss 22/88, occupied during the mid-6th century, contained centrally located firebowls. At Broderstroom, most are located somewhat off-center and to the rear of the house, whereas at Magagarape, none of the houses appear to have had hearths (Mason 1986; Campbell et al. 1996). The excavated house from Pitse, occupied toward the end of the first millennium, had three internal hearths, with the main cooking hearth located to the left of the door. Another difference between Pitse and some of the very earliest Early Iron Age houses is the addition of an external verandah, used to enclose a distinct food-preparation zone (Figure 10.7a–c). House inventories from both Pitse and Broederstroom, nevertheless, suggest that throughout the Early Iron Age, a variety

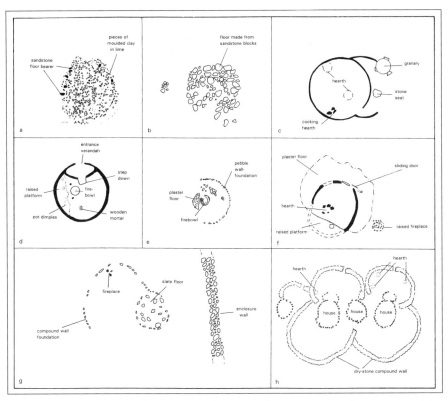

Figure 10.7. Iron Age house plans. (a) Broederstroom (after Mason 1986); (b) Magagarape (after Campbell et al. 1996); (c) Pitse (after Campbell et al. 1996); (d) Olifantspoort 29/72 (after Mason 1986); (e) Olifantspoort 2/72 (after Mason 1986); (f) Olifantspoort (20/71 (after Mason 1986); (g) Kaditshwene 13/66 (after Mason 1986); (h) OXF1 (after Maggs 1976).

of activities with possible gender associations were performed inside houses. These appear to have included food preparation, cooking, tool and ornament manufacture and/or repair, as well as storage.

Several mid- to late 2nd millennium AD sites excavated by Mason all contained houses.[11] These exhibit further variation. Of particular significance are the well-preserved house floors found at the 16th century site of Olifantspoort 29/72.[12] Like the Early Iron Age houses, these show evidence of a range of internal household activities (see Hall, Chapter 13, for details). Unlike the Early Iron Age houses, however, several, though not all, of the excavated houses contain raised platforms. These could have been located to one side of the door, as suggested by Mason (1986: 239) (see Figure 10.7d), or at the rear, as suggested by Hall (Chapter 13), which would be more in line with the Central Cattle Pattern model. These conflicting interpretations arise because of the lack of unambiguous evidence regarding the precise location of doorways in these structures. Other 16th to mid-18th century

Later Iron Age houses also contain evidence for the presence of a storage platform, or the demarcation of a such an area by means of a molded clay ridge, such as at the Roberts Farm 41/85 site (Mason 1986:279). The recently excavated house floors at Modipe Hill in southern Botswana, on the other hand, contained no traces of this type of internal division (Pearson 1995).

The internal layout of houses at late 18th and early 19th century settlements appears to have been different again. At sites such as Olifantspoort 20/71 and 21/71, for example, most houses seem to have had a storage platform at the rear, and were associated with at least a front *lolwapa*, and in some cases also one to the rear (Mason 1986:380 ff., 540).[13] However, in the majority of cases, hearths were located outside the house, in the *lolwapa* (see Figure 10.7f), the main exception being Mason's Type I Class at Olifantspoort 20/71, which he interpreted as functionally specific "cooking huts." The use of external hearths seems to have become more common through time and has been recorded at a number of other terminal Later Iron Age settlements, including Molokwane (Pistorius 1992); it was also noted by Burchell when he visited Batlhaping settlements in the early 19th century (Burchell 1953). This spatial segregation of cooking and food-preparation activities from sleeping areas may also have been linked to changing meanings of the "house," and specifically from the kind of concept that invoked notions of mutual cooperation between the sexes to a domain more exclusively linked to sexual reproduction and the demographic replacement of agnatic kin.

Without more detailed plans of the distribution of artifacts within and around these houses, it would be premature to suggest that there were, or that there were not, distinct male and female zones within these houses (see also Kent, Chapter 3, for further discussion of the analytical problems associated with this type of exercise). However, the available evidence *does* indicate considerable variation with respect to the internal organization of house space through the Iron Age. Regardless of whether these features were more closely associated with women than men, or vice versa, we can at least infer that the position of "bodies" and their relationship to these features was not constant over the course of two millennia, as the Central Cattle Pattern model would imply. More careful recording and publishing of spatial data could help reveal further the meaning of these different bodily orientations.

Conclusion

In recent decades, a single interpretative model of the spatial organization of Iron Age settlements in parts of Zimbabwe, Botswana, and South Africa has become widely accepted. Known as the Central Cattle Pattern model, this has focused attention away from purely economic and/or ecological concerns, toward a consideration of the ideological basis and symbolic practices of these societies. In this regard, the application of the Central Cattle Pattern model has been a welcome development. Like other representational models, however, it has failed to consider adequately the potential for alternative readings of the spatial organization of the material world, and the role such alternative readings play in the constitution and reconstitution of society. In particular, as illustrated in this chapter, by focusing on the apparent centrality of cattle and other male-associated elements, a number of significant changes to the form, structure, and potential symbolism of those parts conventionally associated with women have been overlooked.

By contrast, it has been argued here that the organization of settlement space and the symbolism of different elements needs to be read from a variety of different positions, and most especially that of women. Adopting such an interpretative strategy has suggested a number of differences between the symbolic structures and ideologies of Early Iron Age and Later Iron Age communities in southern Africa. In particular, it is evident that the *position* of houses changed, even though their *spatial location* relative to cattle byres, ash middens, and forging debris may have remained broadly similar. To understand this difference between "position" and "spatial location," it is important to start by populating houses and other elements of Iron Age settlements with bodies—bodies that moved through space and looked out upon space, and that through their routine activities invested space with meanings that may have simultaneously revealed and concealed the nature of social relations within the settlement.

This chapter has also traced some of the variations through time and across space in the layout of Iron Age settlements and houses. In terms of settlement space, it has been suggested that Early Iron Age villages tend to exhibit more permeable and shifting characteristics when compared with Later Iron Age settlements, which tend to be more fixed and bounded spatial units. These changes, it was suggested, may well relate to the changing status of women within Iron Age societies, associated with an increased concern with controlling female sexuality and reproduction. One consequence of this appears to have been the development in the Later Iron Age of a more overt gynecomorphic spatial symbolism. The steady compartmentalization of settlement space into a series of physically bounded units during the Later Iron Age would also have altered the spatio-temporal rhythm of routine practices of both men and women—which, it is suggested, would have recursively reinforced the changing ideological attitudes toward women.

The changing internal layout of houses during the Iron Age also encouraged new forms of routine practices, by which the moral ideologies of the community were incorporated within individual bodies. Whereas in the Early Iron Age, internal house space appears to have been largely undifferentiated, during the early part of the Later Iron Age new elements were introduced into houses, such as internal storage platforms and external courtyard walls. Cooking hearths were also gradually separated from other household activities, either by removing them from the house altogether, or by placing them in a separate structure, as at Olifantspoort 20/71. This spatial differentiation of tasks persisted into the historic era. Increasingly, separate houses were constructed for different household activities, such as cooking, sleeping, and storage. In addition, the internal position of storage platforms may have changed from the side to the back of the house, which would have altered the body's relation to it, and so, potentially, the symbolic reading of internal space.

The combined effects of these changes, it is suggested, steadily transformed space into a contested domain, in which men and women negotiated for position, such that control over house space may have become a source of practical power and authority within society. In addition, by moving women away from the male core of the settlement, a new contradiction was created, in that the "female house" became at one and the same time a protective "boundary" that excluded others, and most especially male affines, and a permeable "skin" that linked the settlement, through matrilateral ties with the outside world.

Certainly, the initial farming populations to establish themselves in the region, whether as a result of migration or local adoption of a new economic strategy, may have had little cause to restrict membership, at least until such time as the viability of an agropastoral lifestyle had been proven. The extensive evidence for contact between these early farming communities and the indigenous foraging groups (e.g., Wadley 1996) lends some support to this view. In contrast, during the later period, land would have been in scarcer supply as a result of population expansion and *mfecane* displacement (see for example, Cobbing 1988; Hamilton 1995), thereby creating conditions under which the control of access by right of residence to settlement resources, including symbolic capital, would have been of greater concern. Under these conditions, far greater premium would have been placed on the role of descent as a means of reckoning an individual's right of abode. In turn, this could have prompted increased symbolic elaboration of female sexuality, and the need for its control, as well as a simultaneous devaluation of the other contributions made by women to the production and reproduction of the domestic group.

Whether such changes resulted in increased gender oppression and subordination of women, as has often been suggested by anthropologists and historians of 19th and 20th century southern African societies (see Hall, Chapter 13), is more debatable.[14] As Hall's work shows, with the adoption of maize as the staple crop, women, through their control of agricultural production, would have had considerable practical power within the household, even though their social power may have diminished. Also, female members of individual households, along with their male counterparts, would have had their own vested interests in ensuring the reproduction of the domestic group. Equally, as the introductory discussion showed, a woman's power—whether social, economic, or practical—is unlikely to have been static throughout her life and instead would have changed with age and from context to context.

It is probably inappropriate, therefore, to construe past gender relations in terms of fixed contrasts between members of two homogeneous and inimically opposed social categories. Rather, following Strathern's insights (1987), archaeologists need to develop interpretative frameworks that treat gender relations more as situational constructs than as fixed categories, and in ways that allow for as much consideration of the variations within social categories as between them. To do so, however, requires archaeologists to pay greater attention to the subtle differences between similar architectural and artifactual forms than has been the case with previous attempts to understand the organization and meanings of settlement space. This chapter has sought to do this by refocusing the analytical attention away from the central cattle enclosures and other allegedly male domains, and onto the houses that frequently encircled these areas. In so doing, alternative perspectives on the possible meanings of settlement space during the Early and Later Iron Age of southern Africa have been generated. There is, however, a need to go beyond these, to address the significance of the variations between individual settlements and houses, and to posit how these may have been related to differences in the wealth, age, status, or economic strategies of the people whose lives we purport to study.

Acknowledgments

I would like to thank Andrew Reid, Alinah Segobye, and Susan Kent for their constructive comments on an earlier draft of this paper. I am grateful, also, to both Alinah Segobye and Maitseo Bolaane for explaining aspects of traditional Tswana customs concerning pregnancy and childbirth, and for assisting with sources and translation of Setswana phrases. I remain solely responsible, however, for any errors in the text.

Notes

1. This concept of "a world reversed" is drawn from Bourdieu's analysis of the contrasting meanings and understandings of the spatial organization of the Kabyle house that arise from the different bodily positioning of men and women (1977:90–92). For parallel applications of this concept, see Moore (1986:171–183), Blier (1987:149–156), Jacobson-Widding (1991:31–32), Udvardy (1991), and, most especially in this context, Kuper's comments regarding the inversion by Zulu diviners of the layout of their homesteads (1980:18).

2. "Each wife in a polygamous household has her own establishment or 'house' (*ntlo, lolwapa*). By this is meant the social group comprising the wife herself, her children, and any other people directly attached to her. Each house is distinct from and independent of the rest, and has its own property in the form of cattle, fields, and household utensils, which are inherited within that house" (Schapera 1938:15). Interestingly, in the light of Leach's (1992) observations about the negotiated nature of wife–wife spatial relations among Mende, and Kuper's (1980) model of Sotho-Tswana and Nguni settlement layout, Schapera continues, the "dwelling-enclosures of the various wives are as a rule built on to one another, but are not arranged in any

specified order. The husband sometimes ranges them according to the ranking of the wives; *he may, however, also place them as he likes* [1938, emphasis added]. In other words, the ranking of uterine houses was mutable" (see also Comaroff and Comaroff 1981).

3. Note, however, that in some dictionaries *tsala* is given as the term for a "womb in an animal," whereas *popelo* or *sebopelo* are said to be the terms for a human womb (e.g., Matumo 1993:425, 644). The verb *go tsala*, however, means to beget or bring forth, and the term for "birth or childbearing" is *tsalo* (Matumo 1993:425, 644).

4. Various aspects of the traditional Zulu house were also symbolically linked with different body parts. In particular, the door was equated with a woman's vagina, and the *ufindo* framework with the lower spine (Berglund 1976:115–117). More generally, the house was perceived as comparable to a woman's womb. As one of Berglund's informants commented, "It is like a woman in that it has little ones inside it. . . . The woman has a stomach (i.e. the womb). A home has a hut" (Berglund 1976:168).

5. Typically, a woman would give birth to her first child at her mother's house, and all subsequent children at her mother-in-law's (Bolaane 1997: personal communication).

6. As typological studies by Mason (1968), Maggs (1976), Jones (1978), and others have highlighted, there is enormous variation in Late Iron Age stone-walled settlement forms. The basic form described here more or less corresponds with Mason's Type 3 and Maggs's Type Z and Type N forms. As Mason (1972), Maggs (1976), Jones (1978), and Collett (1982) have noted, these different ruin types have different geographical and topographical distributions, which could be associated with differences in function and/or season of occupation. Other differences, however, may have a more cultural basis, especially in relation to the emergence of different Sotho-Tswana ethnicities during the 17th and 18th centuries.

7. Judging from Schapera's work among Bakgatla in Botswana (1978), no single term was used for either semen or menstrual blood.

8. Jean Comaroff's exposition of the contrasting space–time maps of the 19th century Tswana town that can be generated if one takes the settlement center (i.e., male domain) or periphery (i.e., female domain) to be "the core" (*kaha ntle*) indicates that as well as "containing," women, through both their spatial position on the fringes of the settlement and their status as affines, also helped *link* the settlement with the outside world. This contrasts sharply with the inwardly focused model of space–time generated from the perspective of male concerns, and especially those of agnatic kin (Comaroff 1985:54–60).

9. It should be noted, however, that Whitelaw, the excavator of Kwagandaganda, considered that "with the exception of small shifts, the layout [of the site] was 'fixed' for the duration of the occupation" (1994/95:42). His Figure 5 in the same paper (1994/95:43), however, does indicate that the area of the cattle byres moved somewhat to the southeast between the earlier and later phases of occupation. Judging from the radiocarbon dates obtained from selected features, a general southeasterly

or easterly movement also appears to have occurred at both Broderstroom and Magagarape (see Figure 10.5, this chapter).

10. The invention and introduction of sliding house doors in the 19th century may have been equally related to intensifying concerns about bodily practices, rather than simply for defensive purposes (see Maggs 1993). Note, also, that the door slide was an explicit female symbol (see Hall, Chapter 13).

11. As Hall (Chapter 13) notes, there is a general lack of evidence from the area concerning the internal organization of houses for the period ca. AD 1000–1450.

12. Mason suggests that this site was occupied as early as the mid 13th century, on the basis of a single radiocarbon date of AD 1240 ± 120 from "Hut A." However, another charcoal sample from the same context yielded the later date of AD 1510 ± 90, while charcoal from "Hut S" yielded the date AD 1600 ± 90 (Mason 1986:230). The earlier date, therefore, could be attributable to "old wood," such as from timbers used for constructing "Hut A," or, more probably, from firewood.

13. This tradition of demarcating front and back *malapa* is also evident in the layout of settlement further to the south, as for instance at the site of OXF1 near Ventersburg in the Free State, which was probably occupied during the 17th century AD. Although most compounds at this site had external hearths, frequently situated to the right of the compound entrance, they also occurred inside some houses (Maggs 1976).

14. This is not to suggest, however, that historians and anthropologists are wrong to argue that the changes in the social position and rights of women during the 19th and early 20th centuries were brought about, to a considerable extent, by the imposition of Victorian concepts of the roles of women onto precolonial, southern African communities (see Schmidt 1992, for a useful discussion and case study).

ANN STAHL AND MARIA DAS DORES CRUZ ■

Chapter Eleven

Men and Women in a Market Economy

Gender and Craft Production in West Central Ghana ca. 1775–1995

The rhythms of daily life in rural Banda-Ahenkro—seat of the Banda paramount chieftaincy—are clearly orchestrated along lines of gender and age. Women rise early to kindle wood fires and cook the morning porridge; young girls sway beneath head-pans brimming with water on their way home from the boreholes; children move between home and the diesel-powered corn mills carrying loads of corn and corn flour; men move from compound to compound greeting neighbors and relatives, perhaps stopping by the paramount chief's compound to greet the chief and discuss community affairs. As sunshine floods the village, men head to farm, to clear, to plant or harvest, depending on the season. Women too may begin their day by traveling to farm, spending the morning weeding, cultivating, and collecting firewood. They return to the village burdened with head-loads of firewood or foodstuffs in time to begin preparing the evening meal. Women who remain in the village spend their day processing foodstuffs: cleaning calabash seeds, winnowing cowpeas, pounding corn if they are unable to afford the services of corn mill, or sorting and tying tobacco leaves in preparation for drying. Many children over the age of six spend their mornings in local primary schools, though only a handful of the boys continue on to secondary schools. Girls over the age of about nine are busy with household chores and tending small children. Thus, men, women, and children appear to play scripted roles in the daily drama of household production and reproduction.

Archaeological analyses of gender and production often assume an isomorphism between such ethnographic scripts and archaeological patterns of household production and reproduction (see Parkington, Chapter 2, and Gifford-Gonzalez, Chapter 7). Yet historical anthropological studies demonstrate that productive relations may have changed considerably as societies were incorporated into a market economy (Etienne 1977; Kriger 1993: note 6). Roberts's (1984) study of 19th-century textile production among the Maraka of Mali provides an example. Drawing on archival and oral historical sources, Roberts made a case for how increased market demand for indigo cloth altered gender-property relations among Maraka men and women, despite the fact that the technology and allocation of men's and women's tasks remained the same. Before the 19th century, production of indigo cloth took place within the household, drawing on the labor and property of husbands and wives. Husbands cultivated cotton, while wives grew indigo. Women cleaned, carded, and spun raw cotton, while weaving was a male domain. Cloth was consumed primarily within the household. As demand for dyed cloth increased among Islamic elites, indigo acquired a market value. Husbands began to use slaves to cultivate indigo to be sold at market, and deployed slaves in an expanded weaving enterprise. Despite their intensified involvement in spinning and dyeing, wives no longer controlled the source of dye, nor the finished product. The social relations of production were transformed again when Maraka slaves left their masters early in the colonial period and established themselves as independent craftspeople, undermining the control of elite males over production of indigo cloth. The textile industry experienced further changes as cheap (and less durable) imported cloth undermined, though did not altogether stop, local cloth production in this area (Roberts 1984:247; see also Etienne 1977; Kriger 1993).

Roberts's case study has important implications for how archaeologists approach the study of gender in the past. When we emphasize household divisions in terms of gender-specific tasks, attention is diverted from how the labor process shapes the reciprocity of gendered tasks and property relations that, Roberts (1984:248) argued, changed with increased involvement in a market economy. The implication for those of us interested in modeling gender in the more distant past is that we must be attentive to how gender relations in recent societies—the source of our analogical models—were shaped by involvement in a market economy (Costin 1996:117). Inattention to this may lead us to assume a false isomorphism between contemporary and past gender relations. We can overcome this problem in two ways: first, rather than using analogical models as illustrative devices, we can adopt instead a comparative approach that is attentive to how archaeological evidence may diverge from ethnographic expectations (Stahl 1993; see Hall, Chapter 13); and second, we can study the effects of a market economy on gendered production and consumption, which requires a focus on historically recent societies. We know that the effects of this involvement were uneven. While local handicrafts disappeared in some areas, they persisted elsewhere, but often in altered form.[1] The challenge is to examine how production and consumption intersect with gender from a processual, historical perspective. Not only will this help us to sort out patterns that might be unique to societies involved in a market economy, it can also help us understand gender relations as dynamic processes.

Our case study works toward the second of these goals and is set in the rural Banda area of west central Ghana, today more than 70 km distant from the nearest major market centers (Wenchi, Techiman, Bole, and Bonduku; Figure 11.1). In this paper we examine how an ethnographic model of men's and women's roles in the contemporary market economy compares to past patterns of gendered production. Using a direct historical approach (Stahl 1994a), we draw on archival, oral historical,

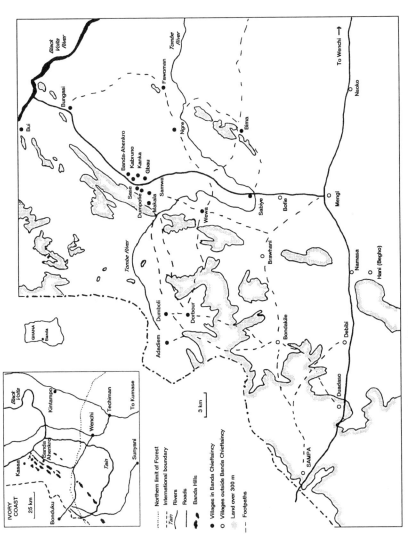

Figure 11.1. Towns and villages mentioned in the text.

and archaeological insights to examine how craft production changed in response to historically documented shifts in the regional and subcontinental political economy from the late 18th century to the present. This period witnessed dramatic shifts in subcontinental trade relations as the Atlantic trade eclipsed earlier trans-Saharan networks. Political dislocation and warfare disrupted the regional economy, especially at the close of the 19th century. Drawing on oral historical sources, we explore how gendered patterns of production may have been impacted by warfare and other political economic factors. Archaeological data are used to investigate changes in craft production, especially potting and weaving. Final sections explore the implications of assuming isomorphism in gendered patterns of production.

Contemporary Craft Production and the Market Economy

The Banda area lies immediately south of the Black Volta River and is centered on a range of razor-backed hills that rise dramatically out of the surrounding, low-rolling landscape. These hills, composed of resistant metamorphic rock, trend north-east-southwest and present a barrier to east-west movement for a distance of about 50 km south of the Black Volta. The area is connected to the network of paved roads by an untarred track that dead-ends at the Black Volta River. To the south it intersects with a gravel road that connects the market centers of Wenchi and Sampa (Figure 11.1). Occasional trucks travel to the area to transport foodstuffs to market or bring kerosene for sale. Locally produced foodstuffs (tomatoes, onions, ground-nuts, and fish) and crafts (such as pots) dominate the local markets, and people must travel to market centers like Wenchi, 75 km distant, or Techiman, another 35 kilometers beyond Wenchi, to purchase cloth, clothing, and household equipment.

Despite its remote character today, Banda is thoroughly integrated into a market economy. The agricultural sector in villages east of the hills is geared to production beyond subsistence needs.[2] The primary cash crops are yams, calabash (gourds), and more recently (since the mid-1980s) tobacco. Cassava (manioc) has become increasingly important over the last 20 years as both a staple subsistence item and a cash crop. Surplus beans, groundnuts, and condiments may be sent to market centers if planted in large quantities; however, they are more often sold in small portions at the weekly village markets. Cash is a prerequisite for household reproduction. Money is required for a variety of needs—to purchase seed stocks when the previous year's stores run short; to hire seasonal agricultural labor (for example, to prepare yam mounds); to purchase commodities like cooking oil, sugar, Maggi cubes or soap, as well as condiments when household gardens run short; to purchase fish or meat; to buy kerosene or perhaps batteries; to have corn ground at the mill; to clothe family members; to pay school fees; to purchase the tools necessary for household reproduction (such as cook-ware and agricultural tools); and to buy materials, and perhaps to hire skilled labor, to build a house. Petty transactions in the local market are conducted primarily in cash, though pottery is sometimes exchanged through barter. Social payments too are monetized, with funeral obligations met with cash (see also Arhin 1995:98). In sum, as is the case throughout much of Africa today, it is ". . . impossible to be a social adult without the capacity to mobilize sums of money that are quite substantial relative to people's incomes" (Guyer 1995:24). Some of these needs can be met without cash, as they are in difficult times (Dei 1988; Posnansky 1980, 1984; Stahl 1994b). Houses can be built using locally available materials (earthen walls and thatch roofs); however, people increasingly prefer "sandcrete" blocks, aluminum roofing sheets, and carpentered windows and doors. Corn can be pounded in wooden mortars rather than ground at the mill. And local oils (such as shea nut butter) can be substituted for bottled, manufactured varieties. Yet these manufactured goods, once luxuries, are today perceived as necessities (Arhin 1976/77:459–460).

As elsewhere in West Africa, money provides the sole means for acquiring cloth in Banda today. Cloth provides an important means by which individuals create and maintain status. Today, the prestige cloths in Banda are strip-woven *kente* cloths and manufactured wax prints. *Kente*, produced primarily by Akan weavers to the south using imported thread, is worn almost exclusively on ceremonial occasions. Wax prints are today manufactured in Ghana and Côte d'Ivoire; however, the most durable and expensive wax prints are imported ("Dutch" wax prints). They have virtually replaced locally made cloth (see Maier 1995:95).

Travelers in the 18th and 19th centuries moving throughout West Africa repeatedly commented on the quality of cloth produced throughout the subcontinent. Local cloth was woven on narrow looms. The strips were sewn together to create large cloths that might be tailored into garments (see Idiens 1980). Indigo-dyed cloth became an especially valued exchange commodity (Roberts 1984; and see Johnson [1980] on cloth strip currencies). Yet most cloth was apparently produced for household consumption (Etienne 1977). Although cloth played an important role in the European trade from an early period, European cloth was less durable than local cloth (Steiner 1985). As late as 1889, Freeman noted the lack of European cloth in the large Bonduku market. Although he observed "a few European articles for sale, fish-hooks and small fragments of looking-glass being the goods most in request . . . I did not see any European cotton goods exposed for sale, which is not a matter for surprise seeing that the native cotton cloths are greatly superior to those made in Europe, and are sold at very moderate prices" (Freeman 1967 [1898]:179). Contrary to the expectation of prestige goods models that stress the importance of exotic origins, locally made cloth was, and in many cases continues to be, the prestige dress of choice (Crossland 1989:52; Etienne 1977:56; Okeke 1980:113; Picton 1980:82, 84; Roberts 1984). Today, however, locally produced cloth is seen as more expensive than manufactured textiles.

Cloth production across a broad sweep of sub-Saharan West Africa drew on the reciprocal labor of men and women—often, but not exclusively, husbands and wives (e.g., Etienne 1977; Roberts 1984). Although responsibility for cultivation varied, women typically carded and spun cotton, while weaving was most often the province of men (see Kriger 1993; Okeke 1980:113; Picton 1980). Both Etienne (1977) and Roberts (1984) describe the role that cloth production played in creating mutual obligations between husbands and wives, signified by the importance of cloth in gift-giving. In Banda, a prospective husband was expected to give his bride a special cloth (*nyankacha*) composed of 12 strips of white woven cloth. The bridegroom and his friends gathered on the first day of the marriage rites to sew together strips of cloth provided by the bridegroom's mother's sisters. With the decline of local cloth production over the last 30 to 40 years, husbands are now expected to present their brides with gifts of manufactured cloth (i.e., wax prints). During the severe economic crisis of the early 1980s, young men in Banda were forced to postpone marriage because they were unable to afford the high cost of imported cloth, most of which was smuggled into the country.[3] Cloth was also a means by which the bride's mother displayed her wealth. Those who could afford to undertook a procession to the husband's house, bearing household goods and cloth to be presented to the bride. The number and quality of pieces of cloth was linked to the mother's wealth, and it might be years after the *bijam* (wedding) rites that a mother could afford to "send the daughter to the husband's house." Cruz interviewed women who "never went to the husband's house," implying that they never were able to afford the gifts of cloth and household goods. Thus gifts of cloth were, and are, central to the construction of social relations, with the crucial difference that the source of cloth has shifted from an item of household production to an item obtained through the market economy.

Local spinning and weaving declined within the last two generations. In 1931, a touring District Commissioner (Russell 1931a,b) noted that weaving was common around Banda-Ahenkro and Adadiem (a village on the west side of the Banda hills; Figure 11.1). Documentary sources suggest that cotton was grown only sporadically on the eastern side of the Banda hills, and then only for household consumption. Raw cotton was, however, abundant in the markets at Sampa and Bonduku (Chief Commissioner 1926; Russell 1931b:4, 6). The tools required for producing thread and cloth were simple, and their acquisition was easy; thus, according to oral sources, virtually every woman was a spinner, and every man a weaver. As elsewhere, cloth was produced primarily for the household, though women recounted to Cruz that they occasionally sold their thread to dyers and weavers who produced for the market. While dyeing appears to have been a specialized activity of Muslim men on the western side of the hills, some elders in villages on the east side of the hills recall that dyeing was a household activity (Stahl, interview at Bui, 6/25/89). Middle-aged and old women still have spinning equipment in their houses today and display with pride their spinning skills. Spindle whorls are still made in the area today, as a specialized product of Muslim men in the village of Kokua near the border with Côte d'Ivoire (Crossland 1989:52, 78–79, Fig. 23). Peddlers purchase the whorls at the Kokua market, reselling them at surrounding markets (Crossland 1989:79). Interviewees in villages throughout the Banda area reported that they most often obtained their spindle whorls from Kokua, though one old man in Makala reported that local women occasionally made their own (Stahl, interview at Makala, 6/30/89). While it is clear that growing involvement in the market economy removed textile production from the household, the effects on male–female property relations are less clear. Cash became the medium through which cloth was accessed, but Banda women may have been less dependent on men to access cash than in other case studies (e.g., Etienne 1977; Roberts 1984). Today some Banda women engage in cash crop production independent of their husbands (see below). Pottery production too provided a means by which women could access money and goods.

The potting craft was eroded, though not eliminated, as the Banda area became increasingly enmeshed in a market economy. Today metal and plastic vessels offer alternatives to locally produced earthenware pots. Yet pottery continues to be made and used in the area, and provides a means by which women in villages on the western side of the Banda hills access cash today. Although local potting has diminished in the face of competition from metal vessels—first imported, and more recently made in Ghana (at Tema)—pottery is still produced in three villages on the west side of the Banda hills (Adadiem, Bondakile, and Dorbour). Women in Bondakile produce on a large scale and supply a number of surrounding markets (Crossland 1989:51–82). Potters in Adadiem specialized in the production of large vessels, such as those used for water storage, but demand for their product has dropped off considerably as people increasingly use metal or plastic basins and drums. In Dorbour, where Cruz undertook a three-month study of contemporary potting (Cruz 1996, n.d.) women produce a variety of vessel forms, though on a smaller scale than at Bondakile. Potting is complementary to farming, and its proceeds provide women with a supplementary cash income. In fact, the pressures of monetization seem to be the primary motivation for women taking up potting today; more young women in Dorbour are learning potting than previously, and several older women who formerly spun cotton as their primary craft activity are today learning potting. In one case, a young widow recently began to perfect potting skills she learned as a child in order to provide for herself and her children. Other women who lack potting skills acquire unfired pots from potters, which they subsequently fire and sell for a small profit.

Potters in Dorbour obtain their clay near the Palati River where several clay pits have been dug. They dig their own clay, often with the help of children or their male relatives. Women may not enter the pit while menstruating. Men may dig clay to sell to potters who are unable to do it themselves. By contrast, women in Adadiem are not allowed into the clay pit. The source of clay here was opened relatively recently (in the last 10 to 15 years) and is reportedly inferior to their previous source, now exhausted. Women in Adadiem told Cruz that the clay in the old source disappeared when women were forced to begin digging the clay as men increasingly migrated to cocoa-farming areas of the south. Women in Bondakile are also dependent on male relatives to dig the clay (Crossland 1989:55). Although the case is less marked in Dorbour, potters in all three villages rely on the labor of relations, most often men, to acquire raw materials for potting. The stories told by Adadiem potters suggest that this is a point of contention between men and women—male out-migration limited women's access to their male relative's labor, diminishing women's ability to generate a product that was their property.[4] While cash generated by male labor on southern cocoa farms may have flowed into the household, women had more direct control over cash and goods acquired through potting.

While the labor of men and children is crucial in acquiring raw materials, pots are made exclusively by women, who may be helped by a daughter who is learning the art. Women fashion pots in their household courtyards, working on six to eight pots at once over the course of three days. Although a potter may make a wide variety of pot types, she works on one type at a time. The product is homogeneous in size and decorative treatment. In Dorbour, pots are made by modeling, pulling the clay upward using a rounded piece of calabash or a metal lid as a turntable. The potter fashions the rim and pot body on the first day; once these are dry, the pot is turned upside down and the base added on the second day, sometimes using a wooden paddle to shape the added clay. On the third day, after the base is dry, the interior is scraped to thin the vessel walls, and the body decorated using a corncob. The rim and shoulder areas are burnished with a pebble (see Crossland 1989:56–59; Frank 1993:387–390).

Firing is a collective activity, for it involves a rapid succession of activities that must be completed while the pots are hot. Yet each woman's pots are kept separate during the firing process. Pots are piled on a bed of small pieces of wood; additional branches or bark from larger trees are placed vertically on the sides of the pile. The entire firing process takes an hour to an hour and a half, depending on the size of the pile and the number of vessels; however, the firing itself takes only 30 to 40 minutes. Once the fire has died down, the pots are removed and may be blackened with dry groundnut shells or grass and dipped in a solution of pounded bark and water. The solution gives a shiny finish to the vessels and reduces their porosity. Only water storage vessels, which rely on the porosity of the pot to cool the water, remain unfinished (see Cruz n.d. for a more detailed account of contemporary potting; also Crossland 1989; Frank 1993).

The range of contemporary pot forms has been affected by competition with manufactured alternatives. Demand for large storage vessels and cooking pots that were a mainstay of Adadiem potters has been eroded by the growing availability of more durable metal and plastic forms. Potters in Dorbour make primarily small cooking and water storage pots, still valued for use on farms where people do not want to leave more expensive metal substitutes untended. Small ceramic pots are also used in most households for boiling herbs and barks used as medicine. Competition with manufactured alternatives has eliminated the production of some forms altogether (as in large men's and small women's eating bowls).

Potters have responded to declining market demand through innovations in style and marketing strategies. New forms have been added to the ceramic repertoire (for example, bowls with interior striations used for grinding vegetables, modeled after an Akan vessel form; see Crossland 1989:72–73). Younger potters in Dorbour experiment with new decorative treatments with an eye to increasing consumer appeal. Cruz's data also suggest innovations in marketing. Women on both sides of the Banda hills recall that women formerly traveled to the potting centers to acquire ceramic vessels. Formerly, parties of young women were sent to the potting villages by the mother of the bride to acquire the complement of pots that a mother supplied for her newlywed daughter. Other times women bought pots in excess of their own needs. They sold the surplus pots in villages and markets on the east side of the hills as well at more distant market centers (such as Wenchi and Techiman). With declining demand over the past several decades, potters themselves began to transport their wares to villages on the east side of hills or to the large market at Bonduku in Côte d'Ivoire. Potters from Dorbour or their female relatives head-load the pots a distance of roughly 20 km on footpaths through the hills to eastern villages where they sell their wares at small weekly markets at Banda-Ahenkro and Sase, and by traveling door-to-door. They stay with members of their extended family until they have sold their entire load.

Often times, attempts to model production in the past (whether concerned with issues of gender or not) treat the type of ethnographic baseline outlined above as a relatively direct model for past production (e.g., Crossland and Posnansky 1978). The result is a "mapping on" (Wylie 1985:94; 1988) of ethnographic detail to archaeological contexts, which limits our ability to examine change over time. Here, we use our ethnographic baseline as a comparative model (Stahl 1993:250–252) to identify patterns of similarity and difference between production and consumption, past and present. This enables us to understand how local craft production was affected by changes in the broader political economic context, which we briefly describe in the next section.

Political Economy of the 19th and 20th Centuries

The Banda area has a long history of involvement in a broader regional and subcontinental political economy. The area immediately north of the forest was home to a series of important transit markets from the 13th century (Arhin 1979:1–17) where goods from the north (salt, cloth, copper alloys, and slaves) were exchanged for forest products (kola nut, gold, and slaves). One of the earliest entrepôts was Begho, located ca. 35 km south of Banda-Ahenkro near the contemporary village of Hani. Forest gold and kola were funneled through Begho to the termini of the trans-Saharan trade (Posnansky 1987; Wilks 1982a,b). Begho, with its links to the Mediterranean economy, was eclipsed by the growing Atlantic economy and concomitant development of states in forested regions to the south from the 18th century. Asante, the most powerful of these, expanded its control over most of present-day Ghana during the first half of the 18th century (Wilks 1975; 1993). Banda was forcibly incorporated into the Asante confederacy in the dry season of 1773/74 (Yarak 1979) and remained under Asante hegemony until the British invaded Kumase in 1896.

As an inner province of Asante (see Stahl 1991), Banda was required to supply soldiers to serve in Asante wars. Oral historical and archival sources chronicle the frequency of war, especially during the second half of the 19th century, a time when British interests were becoming increasingly entrenched along the Gold Coast. The oral traditions of Banda and surrounding peoples are replete with references to warfare (Table 11.1). Episodes of warfare, though perhaps periodic and exaggerated by oral accounts (Ameyaw 1965), must have disrupted the daily routines of household production and reproduction, including craft production. Casualties were often heavy, leaving households with inadequate resources for household reproduction (Stahl n.d.). Some families augmented their numbers by purchasing captives, who were subsequently adopted (Stahl and Anane 1989:28). The accounts of wars associated with Banda's incorporation (1773/74) into Asante are particularly vivid (Ameyaw 1965). Banda won an initial encounter, but Asante forces regrouped and attacked again, two miles south of present-day Banda-Ahenkro. When it became apparent that defeat was inevitable, old men, women, and children fled into the mountains and took refuge in the caves above Banda-Ahenkro. Banda forces retreated into the mountains, positioning themselves on the crest of one of the hills, while the Asante occupied the towns below. Food was in short supply, and famine ensued in the hideout, ultimately forcing Banda peoples to surrender. During later conflicts, Banda peoples reportedly abandoned the area altogether. Banda traditions (Ameyaw 1965:7–8) describe sojourns in Bona to the northwest, Gyaman to the west, and Longoro/Nkoranza to the east/northeast at different points during the 19th century (Table 11.1). Scenarios of village abandonment are corroborated by observations of the first British representatives in the area. Lonsdale (1883) observed ruined villages all along the road from Wenchi to beyond Menji on his march to Bonduku, a time when Banda peoples reportedly had abandoned the area because of hostilities with Gyaman.

Asante's northern provinces were an object of British territorial ambitions in the closing decades of the 19th century. Banda officials signed a treaty with the British in 1894 (Ferguson 1894) as part of a wider effort to encircle Asante with groups loyal to the British, at the same time staving off competition from rival European powers (see Arhin 1974). When the British emissary first contacted Banda peoples, they were living in refuge at the village of Lawra or Bue (Bui), along the Black Volta River, in the aftermath of hostilities with Nkoranza (Table 11.1). Banda peoples were also under pressure from the mounted troops of the Imam Samori. Armed with guns, Samori's forces forged an empire through wars of conquest (1861–1898) that included areas from northern Sierra Leone to northern Ghana (Holden 1970; Muhammed 1977). Forced eastward under growing pressure from the French, Samori became a factor in Gold Coast politics during the 1890s, when he shifted his base of operations to Bonduku, capital of Gyaman. His forces pursued a scorched earth policy in western Gonja (immediately north of Banda; Figure 11.1), burning villages, confiscating crops, and enslaving captives (Haight 1981; Northcott 1899: 16). Samori's

Table 11.1. Conflicts Involving Banda.

Conflict with:	Date; Banda Ruler	Comments	Source
Asante	1733	Reindorf reported that Asante attacked Banda in retaliation for the murder of Asante traders in Banda	Arhin 1987:53
Nkoranza	Sielongo	Nkoranza people under Baffo Pim defeated Banda, and took Sielongo to Kumase to pay homage to Asantehene Osei Tutu	Bravmann 1972:160; Ameyaw 1965:2–3
Asante	1773–1774; Sakyi	Asante invaded Banda, establishing its hegemony over Banda peoples	Ameyaw 1965:3–5; Yarak 1979
Bole	Habaa	Nafana invaded Bole in a day-long skirmish, taking many captives who were sold into slavery	Ameyaw 1965:6; see also Fell 1913
Gonja	before 1802	Forces from Gbuipe (Ghofan) and Daboya (Ghobagho) razed Banda capital; prompted retaliation by Asantehene Osei Bonsu (1800–1823)	Goody 1965:11
Fante	c. 1806; Wulodwo	Asantehene Osei Bonsu (1800–1823) "asked for the assistance" of Banda in the war against Fante; family histories recount significant loss of personnel; Fell (1913) was told that only 7 out of 700 warriors survived	Ameyaw 1965:6; Stahl and Anane 1989; Fell 1913
Gyaman	1818–1819 Wulodwo	Asantehene Osei Bonsu (1800–1823) "sent for assistance" of Banda to quell rebellion in Gyaman (1818–19); Banda accused of cowardice and, fearing Asante reprisal, fled to Bona	Ameyaw 1965:7–8
		March 1820 the Bandahene was in Kumase to collect his share of the spoils of the successful Gyaman campaign	Dupuis 1966 [1824]:76–83
Bona	Wulodwo and Dabla	War broke out between Bona and Banda people when Banda tried to establish its authority over the town; with help of Gyaman, Banda people took refuge on lands outside Bona	Ameyaw 1965:8; see also Lonsdale 1882
Gyaman	Sahkyame (Wurosa)	Banda people (now back on their lands) attacked by Gyaman in retaliation for the murder of a Gyaman official; Banda dispossessed of their land, settled among Mo at Longoro	Ameyaw 1965:8
	Feb. 1882?	These are probably the hostilities referenced by Lonsdale 1882	Wilks 1975:294
Mo	Sahkyame (Wurosa)	Banda attacked by Mo forces at Gyama (Jamma, north of the Volta?); Banda driven off Mo lands	Ameyaw 1965:10
Nkoranza	1892–1893 Sahkyame (Wurosa)	Asante seek allegiance of Banda in war against Nkoranza, who were asserting their independence after signing a treaty with the British; Nkoranza defeated, but later attacked Banda, forcing Banda people to flee. (Some sought refuge at Akomadan; others settled on the southern bank of the Black Volta at Bue [Bui].)	Ameyaw 1965:10; Lewin 1978:11

troops reportedly stayed north of the Volta River, leaving Banda peoples at Lawra in peace. Nonetheless, Banda supplied foodstuffs to Samori, and a large number of Banda people on the north side of the river were taken captive (Fell 1913). Only after Samori was driven from the area by British-led troops did Banda people resettle their old villages.

The British were slow to establish an administrative presence in areas north of Asante. Although Asante's northern provinces were considered part of the colonial realm from 1897, effective administration did not begin for almost 20 years. Colonial officials were concerned with increasing the flow of raw materials to the metropoles (such as industrial oils, cocoa, and cotton) and the consumption of finished industrial products in the colonies (see Constantine 1984). Monetization of the local economy was a prerequisite to successful penetration of the market economy and was encouraged by leveling taxes in new currencies (Guyer 1995; Hopkins 1970). Officials also endeavored to extract labor from northern areas of the colonies to work the mineral and timber reserves that were generally concentrated in the south (e.g., Bassett 1995; Grier 1981). Yet the effects of these regional efforts varied. The limited documentary evidence suggests that Banda was not subject to sustained efforts to impose cash crop production (see neighboring regions of Côte d'Ivoire, Bassett 1995; see also Isaacman and Roberts 1995:9), nor to the same labor extraction techniques as areas to the north (see Grier 1981). District officials toured the area only sporadically.[5] Nevertheless Banda farmers were expected to send foodstuffs to the market at Kintampo, then the District Headquarters, though they did not always comply (Roy 1902). And the chieftaincy was required to provide carriers to serve district officials in numbers ranging from 42 to 80 per month. The Banda chief complained to the District officer in 1901 that his "men were away a month at the time carrying for the government, that the farms suffered in consequence of their absence, and that they themselves returned very thin and pulled down, unable to do a day's work for a considerable time afterwards, and when they were fairly fit and recovered they were sent off again" (Walker 1901). A 1926 report (Chief Commissioner 1926) noted that Banda had fulfilled its obligations in supplying food to colonial troops garrisoned in the area and was being called on to supply 250 carriers to accompany the troops when they decamped. The Chief Commissioner instructed the District Commissioner "not to make any fuss" should the Banda chief refuse to comply: "simply inform him that if the carriers are not forthcoming the troops cannot go, and he must carry on with the provision of food. The odds are that there will be more carriers than required" (Chief Commissioner 1926). Although the demands seem to have been sporadic, they surely impacted the availability of labor and agricultural surplus. Finally, some Banda men migrated south to work the cocoa farms around Sunyani, with consequences for household labor allocation.

Throughout the period in question Banda was linked to the Atlantic economy, its political economic life dominated first by Asante, and later by the British. Ultimately, products introduced through the Atlantic trade undermined local craft production.

While potting and cloth production survived well into the 20th century, we turn now to considering how production strategies may have been altered by broader political economic circumstances, paying special attention to the issue of how periods of warfare and dislocation, as well as pressures of monetization, may have affected craft production.

The Archaeological Data Set

Gold Coast colonial officials showed special concern for the problem of "sanitation." This encompassed a variety of practices, from refuse disposal, the disposition of human waste, and burial practices to "village planning" (and see Comaroff and Comaroff 1992:40–42 on the "body work" of colonial production). Village planning schemes involved relocation to nearby sites where villages could be laid out on a grid pattern (Gold Coast Colony 1910:14; 1918:20; Stahl 1994a). Local district commissioners were very successful at convincing Banda villagers to rebuild their villages (Stahl n.d.), resulting in a series of archaeological sites abandoned around 1920. We have conducted three seasons of archaeological investigations at one such site— Makala Kataa. Locals report that the site was abandoned when a British official, locally known as the "breaker of walls," convinced Makala peoples that their houses were built too close to one another and represented a fire hazard (Stahl 1994a). When Stahl first began working in the area, several older residents of Makala recalled living on the site as small children. This village was probably established after 1896 when the British pushed Samori's troops to the north and represents an occupation of roughly two decades. We refer to this area of the village as Makala Phase 1, or late Makala. An earlier village occupation occurred to the southwest, which we call Makala Phase 2, or early Makala. Based on dateable imports and thermoluminescence dates, this village was occupied during the late 18th and early 19th centuries.

During the course of three field seasons we have tested both occupation and midden contexts in both areas of the site. At early Makala, we have excavated 156 m^2 with a volume of 132 m^3. We excavated a comparable area at late Makala (155 m^2), but with a considerably smaller volume (90 m^3) given the shallow nature of the deposits in this area. We isolated architectural features in both areas, and these, combined with the character of midden deposits and material culture, suggest differences in length of occupation, and therefore the "permanence" of settlement, as well as in processes of site abandonment. The evidence for these differences will be detailed elsewhere; however, we briefly outline them here since they have important implications for the nature of production and consumption.

The early 19th-century occupation at early Makala has an air of permanence about it—the houses were substantial, probably coursed earthen-walled structures (McIntosh 1976), with individual structures joined in compounds. We have evidence for refurbishing and rebuilding in the form of superimposed floors and layers of slurry comparable to the plaster used to finish floors and porches today. The height of the midden and the density of refuse suggests a sizable occupation for a considerable period (on the order of decades). Yet evidence suggests that early Makala was abandoned rapidly. A kitchen area associated with one of the residential mounds at early Makala is especially revealing in this regard. Here we found a number of whole ceramic vessels left behind in useable condition, along with numerous grindstones and hearthstones. These are objects that would be salvaged in most cases (as illustrated by one of our workmen taking the hearthstones home to be used by his wife at the end of the field season!). When viewed in light of the oral histories that stress the frequency of warfare in the area, a scenario of rapid abandonment is plausible (see Cameron and Tomka [1993] on the signatures of abandonment).

Late Makala differs in several ways. The early 20th-century houses at Late Makala have a less permanent quality about them. There is less overburden on floors, suggesting that walls may have been constructed from less durable wattle and daub. Patterned post holes at the base of our units are consistent with this insight. Further, the mounds appear to represent isolated structures, not joined in compounds. Contemporary Banda peoples build this type of structure today on farms—in contrast to coursed earth structures, pole and daga buildings can be raised rapidly and require less material, though they are less permanent. This is consistent with the historic scenario that late Makala was founded after British forces eliminated the threat of Samori (that is, after 1896); this followed a decade of considerable dislocation, with Banda people moving about, seeking refuge in several places (Table 11.1). On their return to Makala, people may have constructed shelters relatively rapidly, intending to build more permanent structures in the event that peaceful conditions prevailed. Thus, the visit by the "breaker of walls" may have offered a convenient opportunity for rebuilding (Stahl n.d.). The evidence of abandonment differs as well. There was little in the way of useable material culture left at late Makala, consistent with people relocating a short distance from the site, allowing them to salvage useful items as needed (e.g., Lightfoot 1993; Tomka 1993).

How was production affected by periods of political economic upheaval that find expression in both the oral historical and archaeological records? By comparing material remains from these two temporally controlled contexts with our contemporary baseline, we are able to gain insight into changing patterns of ceramic production and consumption, which provide us a springboard for examining the implications for gender and the labor process.

Changing Patterns of Ceramic Production and Consumption

The early and late ceramic assemblages at Makala Kataa show considerable overlap in vessel form and decorative treatment; however, preliminary stylistic analysis documented increased homogeneity in decorative treatment through time (Stahl 1994a:197–199). This seemed to signal changes in production during the course of the 19th century. Large, abandoned clay pits on the eastern side of the hills attest

Table 11.2. Source of Neutron Activation Samples.

Samples	Clay	Ethnographic	Ahenkro Midden	Makala Phase 1	Makala Phase 2
No form	20	15	—	—	—
Small bowl	—	—	3	12	10
Large bowl	—	—	3	13	10
Small jar	—	—	3	13	10
Large jar	—	—	3	13	10
TOTAL	20	15	12	51	40

more widespread production in the past, and the Makala data suggested that potting may have become more geographically restricted during the course of the 19th century. Neutron activation analysis (see Arnold et al. 1991; Blackman et al. 1989, 1993), which provides insights into the geochemical signatures of clays and their sources, has helped sort this pattern out more clearly. Cruz analyzed 160 samples that included clay samples from functioning and abandoned clay pits, both east and west of the hills; contemporary ceramics from Dorbour, Adadiem, and Bondakile; archaeological ceramics from the early and late occupations at Makala Kataa; and archaeological ceramics from historic middens (1930–1960s) in Banda-Ahenkro, excavated by Andrew Black, a doctoral candidate at the State University of New York, Binghamton. Only rims were submitted for analysis, and the sample of archaeological ceramics was stratified by vessel form—large bowls, small bowls, large jars, and small jars (Table 11.2).

Neutron activation analysis differentiated three groups among analyzed clays and ceramics based on geochemical signatures (Cruz 1996). Clay samples collected from abandoned pits on the east side of the hills (Bui, Bungasi, and Sabiye) fell into one group (East side group). Clay samples and modern pots from Dorbour and Adadiem clustered into what Cruz has called the West side group. Bondakile clay and pottery formed a distinctive group. These clusters provided a baseline against which to compare the archaeological ceramics.

With the exception of two bowls, all vessels (n = 37) from early Makala (Phase 2) belonged to the West side or Bondakile groups, both on the west side of the Banda hills (Table 11.3). Chemical signatures suggest that bowls came disproportionately from Bondakile (n = 14), while the West side group yielded mostly jars (n = 20). By contrast, vessels from late Makala (Phase 1) were concentrated primarily in the East side group (n = 35), with the exception of large jars (n = 4) and large bowls (n = 4), which were associated with the West side group. No vessels in this sample originated in Bondakile. The small sample from historic middens at Ahenkro was divided between the East (n = 5) and West (n = 4) side groups. Thus, neutron activation analysis suggests changes in where villagers on the east side of the hills obtained their

Table 11.3. Results of Neutron Activation Analysis. Source of vessels by provenience and vessel type.

Provenience	Vessel Type	West Side Group	East Side Group	Bondakile	Other
Makala Phase 2	Small bowls	2	1	6	1
(early 19th century)	Large bowls	1	1	8	—
	Small jars	10	—	—	—
	Large jars	10	—	—	—
Makala Phase 1	Small bowls	2	7	—	3
(late 19th/early	Large bowls	4	9	—	—
20th century)	Small jars	—	10	—	3
	Large jars	4	9	—	—
Ahenkro Middens	Small bowls	—	3	—	—
(1930s–1960s)	Large bowls	1	—	2	—
	Small Jars	2	1	—	1
	Large Jars	2	1	—	—

ceramics, and perhaps by extension, changes in sites of production (for details see Cruz [1996, n.d.]).

The significance of these results is brought into focus when viewed against the political economic context sketched above. The early occupation at Makala Kataa dates to a the period after Asante had asserted its authority over Banda. The character of the archaeological deposits suggests a relatively long-lived occupation. The neutron activation data demonstrates that women in this period obtained their pots almost exclusively from producers on the western side of the Banda hills, suggesting first, geographically restricted production; second, production by women in villages west of the hills at levels beyond household needs; and third, a degree of regional stability. During periods of warfare, oral sources suggest that travel and market activity were restricted, especially travel through the sparsely inhabited hills. But the period of relative quiescence represented by early Makala appears to have ended abruptly, and historical sources point to warfare as a likely cause. While it is not possible to pinpoint precisely the length of hiatus between the early and late occupations, the neutron activation data suggest a change in where women acquired pottery. Now pots came primarily, though not exclusively, from sources east of the Banda hills. The size of the abandoned clay pits near Bui and Sabiye suggest production on a considerable scale. This does not mean that potters on the west side of the hills ceased production; they may well have continued to supply surrounding villages. However, only very specialized forms (large bowls and jars) found their way across the Banda hills. Women on the east side of the hills focused on production of smaller forms.[6]

In sum, we see a shift from a geographically restricted (that is, early Makala) to a more dispersed (late Makala and historic Ahenkro) pattern of production through the course of the 19th and 20th centuries.[7] The challenge is to identify why this shift occurred. One contributing factor may have been the unstable political economic conditions that prevailed at the end of the 19th century. Banda was involved in several wars from the mid-19th century, forcing Banda people to flee the area (Table 11.1). This quite obviously disrupted existing regional networks of craft production and trade. With the reoccupation of the former villages after British pacification (late Makala) the threat of warfare diminished, but for a people who had faced the threat of slave-raiding from Samori's troops and had experienced repeated episodes of warfare, women may have been disinclined to travel to moderately distant potting centers to obtain household necessities. Another possibility is that Banda women acquired new skills during their sojourns in other areas. Alternatively, oral histories suggest a significant influx of captives and refugees into Banda during the second half of the 19th century (Stahl 1991, in press), who may have included potters who took up their art in their new homes (see also Frank 1993).

Whatever the scenario, monetization and an expanding market economy probably played a role in women's decisions to· take up potting in villages on the eastern side of the hills, and just as likely played a role in its rapid decline in the second half of the 20th century as earthenware vessels came under increasing competition from metal forms. By the early 20th century, people were increasingly enmeshed in a market economy, as suggested by the plethora of petty trade goods including glass, imported beads, and pipes at late Makala (Stahl 1994a). We might anticipate altered productive strategies as men and women struggled to gain access to the currencies required to purchase these luxuries that ultimately came to be defined as necessities (Arhin 1976/77). By the mid-20th century, potters on the west side of the hills were again marketing their wares to consumers on the east of the hills, as illustrated by the Ahenkro midden data. Ultimately, women on the east side of the hills gave up potting altogether, while those on the west side persisted in their craft. If we take clues from Cruz's ethnographic data, women in the western villages altered not just their production strategies, but also their marketing strategies, to ensure a broader market for their products. This was a crucial change, for it shifted the burden of transporting pots (a not inconsiderable one) from the consumer to the producer. When women in villages east of the hills gave up potting, they gave up one means of accessing cash or goods obtained through barter. In some cases this may have increased women's dependence on their husbands and male relations to access the cash required to purchase clothing and household goods (see Etienne 1977; Roberts 1984), though some Banda women responded by taking up cash crop production (see below).

Our archaeological data are less robust when it comes to textile production. The only material trace we have of the apparently ubiquitous cloth industry is spindle whorls. We recovered these in small quantities from both early (n = 9) and late Makala (n = 9). Because spindle whorls are obviously curated, we might anticipate that they would occur in small quantities in archaeological context; however, their limited numbers makes it unlikely that market production of cloth was undertaken at either locale. An intriguing contrast is provided by our excavations at the earlier site of Kuulo Kataa (AD 1300–1650), which is contemporary with the site of Begho (35 km to the south) where Posnansky (1976:48) reported finding a "fairly large number of spindle whorls" from all levels in each locality. By contrast, excavations at Kuulo Kataa (covering an area of roughly 90 m^2) have yielded a single fragmentary spindle whorl from the upper 10 cm of deposit. While negative evidence is problematic, it raises the issue of whether ethnographic models that stress the role of domestic spinning and weaving in establishing and maintaining household relations have great time depth. Cotton cloth may have been a prestige item restricted to a small segment of the population during this earlier period (that is, before the 18th century), with other textiles (such as bark cloth) being more widespread. Rather than an item of household production, cotton cloth may have been produced by specialists in market centers like Begho.

A final category of craft that disappears altogether from the archaeological record at the end of the 19th-century is locally made smoking pipes. Local pipes are short, fat-stemmed affairs that were smoked by placing a reed into the end of the pipe stem. These pipes were ubiquitous at early Makala (n = 173). Stylistically they are quite variable; however, many had "quatrefoil" bases or stems common on 19th-century pipes in Ghana (see Stahl 1992:126–128 for a summary of Ghana pipe styles). Many were finely crafted—highly burnished, finely incised, with well-executed, highly individualized decorative treatment. While we await the results of neutron activation analysis on a sample of pipes, for now we are unsure of where they were made. By the later occupation, local pipes virtually disappeared and were replaced by imported European ball clay pipes. Whereas we recovered only three fragments of imported pipes from early Makala (all from surface or near surface contexts), there were 128 fragments of imported pipes from late Makala, and only 5 local pipe fragments. Here is a clear sign of involvement in the market economy, with equally clear effects on a local craft. This is a dramatic example of an object that shifts from a site of local to foreign production. Any suggestion as to whether pipes were produced by men and/or women is pure speculation, though the fact that spindle whorls are today produced by Muslim men suggests that men may have been involved.

Reflections on Gendered Production Through Time

As archaeologists work to engender a more distant past, there is a temptation to treat ethnographic scripts of gendered activity as isomorphic with the past. Some believe there is safety in numbers—if we can document similar patterns of gendered production in many societies (the criterion of ubiquity; Stahl 1993:249), then we can be relatively certain that similar patterns pertained in the past (e.g., Hayden's comparative ethnography, 1992a:34–37). But normative ethnographic accounts of what men and women do in the present overlook at least two important factors: individuality and history. While it is clear that growing involvement in a market economy and pressures of monetization forced Banda men and women to alter their productive strategies, individual choices differed (and see Kriger 1993). Thus, while some women in villages west of the hills chose to pursue potting as a strategy for generating cash, others became involved in cash-crop production. Cash-cropping is often perceived as a man's domain; however, there are no proscriptions against Banda women establishing farms, and indeed, some Banda women have become successful cash-crop farmers. For example, beginning in the mid-1980s, the Pioneer Tobacco Company began to encourage large-scale production of tobacco by supplying would-be tobacco farmers with seedlings and the supplies needed to build drying barns. Men were heavily invested in yams and calabash as cash crops and were reluctant to switch to tobacco. Women were first to take up the Pioneer scheme; when it became clear after one or two harvests that there was money to be made, men became involved in large numbers. Still, in 1995, the farmer with the largest harvest was a woman.[8] Nonetheless, women were dependent on the labor of others—often men and children—and accessing this labor was likely a source of tension as suggested by the stories of Adadiem potters. But not all women engaged in potting or cash-crop production, and thus they became dependent on their husbands and male relations to access clothing and tools of domestic production (such as cooking utensils). In sum, individual strategies varied.

History matters too, as does the broader regional political economic context within which household production and reproduction takes place. As Wolf (1982) argued, involvement in the world economy transformed the societies that anthropologists study, sometimes in patterned ways. The implication is that contemporary patterns may be the result of relatively recent historical periods, limiting the applicability of a comparative ethnographic approach to the study of a distant past. The ethnographic model of potting in Banda tells only part of the story. The archaeological data makes clear that potting—in contrast to textile manufacture—was geared to production beyond the needs of the household during the first half of the 19th century. Women (some of them, anyway) in villages west of the hills produced pots in excess of their household needs, which were consumed by women in villages east of the hills. Yet this pattern broke down late in the 19th century—and potting became more geographically dispersed. Now women in villages on the east side of the hills obtained only specialized forms from the western potting villages, other forms were now produced on the east side of the hills. This "choice" may have been made out of exigency—insecurities created by warfare and slave-raiding may have made regional trade a risky business, forcing women to adopt alternative strategies. In the long run, potters east of the hills gave up their craft, perhaps because their products were inferior, and in the face of declining demand, they could no longer compete with potters from western villages, who were now taking upon themselves the burden of transporting the pots. Changes in the sites of cloth and pipe production were more dramatic, shifting outside the local area altogether and fueling in part the need to generate cash.

As we have tried to demonstrate here, the observation that women make pots can be broken down into more interesting questions, such as under what circumstances do women choose to invest their labor in the manufacture of pots? And why were women content to rely on extra-household labor to produce a crucial tool of household production (pots), while production of textiles appears to have been a household activity? And why did potting persist while textile production declined? We suspect that the answers have something to do with the different roles of material culture in the social world (Stahl n.d.)—textiles were invested with more than the simple function of clothing bodies. They were, and are, important in creating and maintaining social relations (and therefore in social reproduction), as well as in creating and maintaining prestige, while pots in this case seem not to have been so invested (see Hall, Chapter 11; on clothing see Hendrickson 1996; see Costin 1996 for a case where control of textile production shifted to the state).

The value of the ethnographic model in this study is as a comparative model against which to assess patterns of similarity and difference in historic and archaeological sources. The dissimilarities highlight for us how the past may have differed from the present, and in turn cast present circumstances in greater relief—this exercise in thinking about the gendered nature of craft production in the *past* has made us think in new ways about production in the *present*, spurring us to ask new questions that our present data are sometimes unable to address. While one of us (Stahl) was initially skeptical about the value of adopting a gender focus, this has proved to be a rewarding avenue of inquiry because of the way it has humanized our understanding of the political economy. We come away with more questions than we can answer, but more engaged in the study than ever.

Acknowledgments

The Banda Research Project has been supported by numerous agencies and individuals. Archaeological investigations at Makala Kataa were funded by the Wenner-Gren Foundation for Anthropological Research (1989; G-5133); the National Geographic Society (1990; Grant #4313-90); and the National Science Foundation (1994; SBR-9410726). Historical and ethnographic research was supported by grants from the British Academy (1986) and the National Science Foundation (1994–1995; SBR-9410726). The Neutron Activation Analysis was supported by National Science Foundation funds through the Archaeometry Laboratory at the University of Missouri Research Reactor and Sigma Xi funds awarded to Maria das Dores Cruz. Hector Neff, Michael Glascock, and the staff of the Research Reactor gave critical help in the NAA analysis of Banda ceramics. Author Cruz further acknowledges the support of the Fulbright-IIE/Luso-American Cultural Commission and the Louise Woods Memorial Scholarship Fund.

The research was licensed by the Ghana Museums and Monuments Board, and we thank the Acting Director, Dr. I. Debrah, for his long-standing support and assistance. We are grateful to the staff of the Ghana National Museum and the Department of Archaeology, University of Ghana, Legon, for their kind assistance. Special thanks to Professor J. Anquandah, former Head of Department at Legon and now Dean of Social Sciences. Our work would not be possible without the support and patience of the Banda Traditional Council, including the paramount chief, Tolee Kofi Dwuru III, and his elders, Tolee Kojo Donkor and the women and elders of Dorbour, and the Banda people. Special thanks to the families in whose midst we have lived—first James Anane and his wife, Adjua, and more recently Sampson Attah and his wife, Afiriye.

Conversations with colleagues and students have influenced our thoughts on gender and political economy. Susan Pollock encouraged author Stahl to take gender seriously, and gender studies conducted by Binghamton students, notably Jennifer Astone and Catherine Dolan, demonstrated the value of a gender approach to her. We thank Susan Kent for the invitation to contribute. Susan Kent, Diane Gifford-Gonzalez, and Susan Pollock gave helpful feedback on earlier drafts. As always, thanks to Peter Stahl and members of the Banda Research Project for valuable input along the way.

Notes

1. For examples in textile production see Bassett 1995; Maier 1995; Roberts 1992; on metallurgy see David and Robertson 1996; Goucher and Herbert 1996; Rowlands 1989; Schmidt 1996a,b; Warnier and Fowler 1979.

2. Involvement in the cash crop sector varies somewhat, with villages along the Banda-Menji road more obviously involved in producing crops for market. Nonetheless, trucks travel to even the remote villages to buy surplus yams and calabash during peak harvest periods.

3. Smuggling was a common activity in border areas like Banda. Wax prints were purchased in Côte d'Ivoire and head-loaded into Ghana on foot paths. The sparsely inhabited Banda hills were ideally suited for this clandestine trade.

4. See Moore and Vaughan (1994), who examine the contesting claims of men and women with regard to agricultural labor in northern Zambia.

5. In 1931, Russell reported that seven or eight years had elapsed since the last tour of inspection of some Banda villages (Russell 1931b).

6. It may be that clays on the east side of the hills were unsuitable for production of large vessels, for the underlying geology east and west of the hills differs (Bates 1962; Kitson 1924:40–41; Gay 1956:2–5). This remains speculative without further

testing of clays. However, Cruz's informants stressed the importance of expertise in producing large vessels.

7. It is interesting to speculate on whether this corresponded with a shift in the nature of production. In the case of early Makala, villages west of the hills were clearly producing beyond the needs of their households. As production became more dispersed, and women east of the hills became involved in potting during the occupation of late Makala, were more women involved in potting (now for household consumption)? Or were the pots coming from eastern villages produced by a small number of specialists producing well beyond their household needs?

8. We have few details on the role of Banda women in cash crop production, a topic that will be the focus of future research.

ALINAH SEGOBYE ■

Chapter Twelve

Daughters of Cattle

*The Significance of Herding in the Growth of
Complex Societies in Southern Africa
Between the 10th and 15th Centuries AD*

This study examines the role of herding, especially cattle, in the growth of complex societies in southern Africa from the 10th century AD. Interpretations of the significance of cattle in the economies of Mapungubwe, Toutswe, and Great Zimbabwe as regional centers in the prehistoric economies of the southern African region have often concluded that cattle were an important resource in the emergence of ranking or hierarchical structures within these farming societies. In addition, since cattle have long been associated with male power, it is implied in the literature that women were subordinated both to male authority and to their role as reproductive labor, valued (or devalued) within the formal and informal exchange systems of resources, including cattle. This idea of the subordination of women rests on the interpretation of women's contribution to the economy as based primarily on their treatment as social capital. In other words, women were significant as daughters and mothers who could reproduce and bear male children as heirs to wealth and authority.

Introduction

Interest in the sociocultural organization of southern African societies within archaeology was generated by a wide body of literature on the form and structure of settlements in 19th century AD and contemporary southern African societies (Livingstone 1858; Schapera 1935; Kuper 1980). Early missionary writers observed the layout of settlements and the significance of these settlement patterns within society. They noted that not only did settlements serve as places to live, they were in fact spatial expressions of networks of social, economic, and political relations within these societies. In the Sotho-Tswana communities where missionaries like Moffat and Livingstone worked, these early recorders noted that the layout of a village and its associated settlement places was very much influenced by the king or chief and his royal court. Similar observations were made by writers working within Shona-speaking and Nguni societies living nearby (see Walton 1956). This cross-cultural consistency in the use of space and architecture, when considered along with the linguistic and other cultural indicators of related origins, enabled historians, cultural anthropologists, and archaeologists to make comparative studies of settlement systems and their meaning and to draw from these studies models of social and spatial organization (Huffman 1986).

Within the context of the settlement systems and culture systems of these southern African societies, the main determinants and indicators of wealth and status in society were patrilineal descent in relation to the royal clan, as well as access to and control of such resources as land, water, and food. However, the most important commodities—particularly in the 19th century AD, when an early European presence was being established in the region—were cattle and trade goods in the form of metals and animal products. The economic significance of cattle in these early societies has been documented extensively (Hall 1987; Smith 1992). Cattle were more than sources of wealth, however; they also served social and political functions that were expressed in other ways as well, including the material realm (use of space). The significance of cattle in southern African economies can be traced to the introduction of livestock into the region by early farming societies from the beginning of the 1st millennium AD. It would appear that by AD 200, cattle and other stock were present in southern Africa as far as the Cape (Walker 1994). Herding was adopted by Khoi communities, resulting in the rise of Khoi pastoralism in the region (Smith 1992). By the 7th century AD, most of the early farming societies in areas that are now known as Zimbabwe, Botswana, and South Africa had incorporated cattle herding into their economies. Their settlements were mainly nucleated small villages with subsistence-based production. Transformations in the nature of herding economies in the region appear to have started toward the end of the 1st millennium AD. This was also the period when long-distance trade goods began appearing in the material culture of the interior (Denbow 1986; Hall 1987). Most archaeologists studying societies forming in southern African concur that significant transformations in regional economies started around the 10th century AD (Denbow 1986; Hall 1987; Huffman 1978, 1982).

Southern African Societies from the 10th Century AD: Increased Socioeconomic and Spatial Complexity

The economies of the societies in the Limpopo-Shashe basin and the eastern Botswana hardveld were principally mixed farming economies. Cultivation of food crops, consisting of cereals, legumes, and other vegetables, was carried out alongside the activity of herding livestock, comprising cattle, sheep, goats, and chickens. The domestic dog was probably kept both for hunting and protection of the domestic residences. Most of these villages were situated on open plains, with considerations of water and access to pasture probably playing an important part in choice of area

(Denbow 1983; Segobye 1994). Although subsistence production was based mainly on domestic labor, it is likely that clientship relations existed between those who had more resources and those who had little or none. Further, ranking within the societies was probably made on the basis of age, patrilineage, and gender. It is likely that political leadership was ranked on the basis of kinship relations to the royal clan or clans. All these factors must have influenced the structuring of the economies of these societies, and particularly the area of production. This chapter focuses on the significance of labor resources, power, and social organization in the development of these societies from simple mixed farming economies to more complex ones with multiple activities carried out by different members of society and differential access to resources. Other studies have focused on how these changes affected the relations between the hunting and gathering societies that were founded by the incoming farming societies (Denbow 1984; Denbow and Wilmsen 1986). These studies have argued, variously, that the dominant nature of the farming economies over the foraging ones resulted in the relegation of foraging communities to lower ranks within society. The absence of formalized political leadership systems within foraging communities and mobile or semipermanent settlement further contributed to the low ranking of these societies within the broader scope of regional settlement systems. This study, however, examines the settlement systems of farming societies as the physical expressions of networks of social and economic relations that had direct bearing on political authority. Emphasis is further placed on the organization of labor within the production sphere, particularly the role played by cattle in terms of production. This chapter will examine the literature advancing the model that cattle were the dominant resource in these early complex societies and more or less determined the power relations within society, particularly relations of production and reproduction. It has been argued that the settlement systems of places such as Mapungubwe and Great Zimbabwe reflected this division, which one can call gendered division of labor, production, and space. The chapter will argue that while, broadly speaking, this may be true, models that have been proposed to date have focused too much on the role of cattle and by and large have ignored the significance of other activities and activity areas where women could (and probably did) exercise considerable power.

Following research at the Toutswemogala site and other related sites, a model of settlement and social organization was proposed by Denbow that ranked the Toutswe type settlements by size, location, and depth of midden deposits (Denbow 1982, 1983; Lepionka 1977). In brief, the model argues that between the 7th and 13th centuries AD an incipient state system developed in east-central Botswana. This comprised several culturally related but independent polities located in an area approximately 100 by 150 km. The main distinguishing element of these polities was the differential size of settlements and their associated middens, representing kraal (cattle byres) that were also differentiated by location. The largest and most important settlements were placed on prominent hilltops and numbered fewer than five. Denbow saw these settlements as the capitals of these polities and therefore designated them as Class 1 settlements (Denbow 1982). In the intermediate level were more numerous but smaller settlements, also located on hilltops. These, however, had less sizable middens and were placed on smaller hills and kopjes. These settlements, numbering about 15 and thus designated as Class 2 settlements, were located at a distance from the large settlements and obviously played an important role as intermediate settlements with the third class of settlements. This third category, Class 3, comprised small settlements that were mostly, if not exclusively, located on low-lying ground and contained relatively small kraal middens. These clustered around the Class 1 and Class 2 settlements and were thought to be residences for commoners and dedicated mainly to agricultural produce (Denbow 1983; van Waarden 1987). In brief, this model suggests that the early farming societies of eastern Botswana were structured on the basis of ownership of cattle that gave their owners both economic and political power. Owners were further able to exercise control over the use of space for settlement and other activities, such as agriculture. This model has also been used to explain the process of settlement change and resource use at Mapungubwe in the northern Transvaal (Voigt 1983; Hall 1987).

More recent research in eastern Botswana (Segobye 1994; Kiyaga-Mulindwa and Widgren 1983) has documented many more settlements in the Toutswe settlement area. Broadly speaking, in terms of distribution and settlement patterning, they more or less conformed to the pattern observed by Denbow. Variations, however, were noted in the internal arrangement of activity areas at both the intersite and intrasite levels. In addition, the distribution of material culture in these sites suggested that there were probably more fluid relations between the different types of settlements than had been proposed by Denbow's model. One important observation was that while in general these polities may have ceased to be regionally important after the 13th century AD (Denbow 1986; Voigt 1983; Hall 1987), they were not abandoned completely and in fact continued to be occupied until the 17th century AD (Segobye 1994; Kiyaga-Mulindwa 1992). It has been suggested that the main reason for their abandonment around the 13th century AD may have been environmental, brought about by increased aridity resulting in poor pasture for the large herds the people maintained (Denbow 1986; Voigt 1986). Given that crops are generally more sensitive to moisture conditions, it is likely that agriculture productivity would have declined more sharply than herding, if indeed there was a regional decrease in rainfall patterns. This in itself offers an interesting scenario for modeling changing relations of production during this period. If these climatic oscillations prevailed over the period of the peak of these early state systems, they would have had implications on the relationships of those involved in production, particularly those between male and female producers and ways in which they defined their domains. It is argued that rather than remaining unchanged over this seven-century period, gender relations— like other relations in the production-reproduction arena—must have undergone changes, some of which can be inferred from clues in the archaeological record. These changing relations have, however, been subsumed and, to an extent, ignored by models that projected the process of socioeconomic and political change as having been dictated by ruling patriarchs in these early state systems.

Inferring Significance from Women's Roles in Herding Societies

Archaeologists reading the settlement history of southern Africa have often worked on the assumption that, dating from the earliest expressions of mixed farming societies in the region, cattle have always been the most important resources within these societies. It is argued that while this may be true, the argument, like that of the "man the hunter" thesis in Stone Age research, underscores the importance of cultivation and foraging as food procurement strategies. In fact, dietary patterns of some of these prehistoric groups suggest that meat resources from cattle (as opposed to small stock and wild animals) constituted a smaller proportion of the overall food intake. This implies that other sources of protein were consumed. These food sources were most probably derived from agriculture and gathered vegetal foods. Both these activities, which were labor consuming, were undertaken by women. Therefore, in terms of relations of production and the domain of daily subsistence activities, women played a significant role in these early societies.

The main influence on the reading of the significance of cattle in the sociospatial organization of the early farming societies has been the rich ethnography of southern Bantu-speaking peoples, including Shona, Nguni, and Sotho-Tswana groups (Huffman 1986; Huffman and Hanisch 1987; see Hall 1984). Most early anthropological studies of 19th century AD Nguni and Sotho-Tswana societies made observations concerning the internal arrangement of these societies' residential places and other related activities areas (Schapera 1935, 1952; Walton 1956; Kuper 1980). Basically, scholars had noted the consistency in the use of concentric shapes and circles in the arrangement of homesteads, wards, ward clusters, and villages. In other words, from the smallest unit to the largest, circular forms were chosen. The significance of these was mainly as an expression of social (kinship) relationships within and between the different members of the society. As a result, the layout of the settlement was often a direct reflection of the kinship relations between different peoples. Because these societies were patrilineal, these relations were also expressed in terms of the ranking in order of descent between different male heads.

Interpretations of the social meaning of the use of space and the gender roles within these societies were also drawn from structuralist theory that postulated discrete dichotomies between male and female roles and other spheres of social relations. Within the context of the prehistory of early farming societies, assumptions about continuity in the settlement and culture history of the region's farming societies also strengthened the premise for modeling the social use of space in these societies (Huffman 1986). As a result, the tendency has been for studies to infer broad spatial and temporal continuities in relations of production, specifically gender relations within communities having mixed farming economies whose settlement systems were thought to conform to the model proposed by Huffman, namely the Bantu Cattle Pattern (also known as the Central Cattle Pattern) (Huffman 1986; Huffman and Hanisch 1987).

Discussion

This paper does not attempt to present an alternative model to explain socio-cultural behavior in these prehistory societies. Instead, it highlights the observation that some of the assumptions previously held to be absolute may need further research—particularly in light of both new research in the region and gender perspectives within archaeology. This chapter comes to the conclusion that postulating the process of complex social formation as an intrinsically male-directed process ignores the potential contribution women made to this process and, more specifically, the diversity in forms of social organization and social relations over time and through space. Relegating women and their activities to the level of secondary factors in the process of social and economic complexity in some ways assumes that women were passive commodities, to be traded, distributed, and stored in a process of wealth- and power-seeking by male heads. The idea that women were valuable only insofar as they were able to reproduce surplus labor and to bear daughters (who could, in turn, be married off for creating social or political alliances) oversimplifies relations between different members of society who in their daily interactions probably had to negotiate power and social identity in more ingenious ways.

In the Mogkware hills, where research was undertaken between 1988 and 1996, sites identified as Toutswe tradition settlements were found in different locations, including hilltops, slopes, and valleys. Although these settlements conformed to the pattern Denbow identified in the other sites in the hardveld area, it was noted that some sites had a greater diversity of activity areas, including pottery-making and metal-working places. In addition, some sites were located farther from areas with fertile soils suitable for agriculture and access to water resources. In light of these observations, it was concluded that the relations of production and access to resources in the area must have also included communal or shared access, because of the factors of location of settlements and resources in their immediate vicinity. In addition, the problem of recurring drought conditions and aridity made the entire production process risky. This could have had one of two contrasting effects. First, political leaders (male) could have increased their control over their diminishing resources and made more elaborate rituals concerning the use of these resources, thereby increasing their power. Second, communities could have been drawn together more, with less differentiation on the basis of ethnicity, gender, or other ranks. More-fluid rules of incorporation into different social categories and ethnic groups could have been preferred as a means for facilitating access to scarce food resources. This seems to have been the pattern that 19th century AD communities opted for, following the Mfecane wars. However, as mentioned above, it is harder to generate such a model without adequate information about the range of activities or directions of trade within and between the communities that occupied this region from the 10th century to around the 17th century AD.

Conclusion

This chapter has tried to identify the areas of input that can be made from a gendered reading of the prehistory of southern African farming societies prior to the arrival of known ethnic groups. Two main points are made. First, because research has not focused specifically on this issue in the past, current models have tended to assume that the process of socioculture change was more or less solely directed by male activities—primarily herding. Second, it has been assumed that a certain degree of continuity existed in the occupation history of the region that was reflected in similarities in settlement systems over an extensive area. As a result, the role of women in the societies has been subsumed under the dominant model of male-directed herding economies that were further enriched by long-distance trade after the 13th century AD when the Great Zimbabwe empire reached its peak. What this chapter calls for is a reexamination of this broad model, to take into account the changes within individual societies or polities where women's contribution to production could have led to power relations' being constituted differently among the different social groups. One area worth consideration is the reexamination of the role of craft production, including pottery and cultivation, in sustaining the wealth base of a homestead or village. Although the data may not be immediately obvious in the current archaeological literature nor serve as tools to investigate these issues, different approaches need to be considered, rather than science's simply resting in the comfortable assumption that one general model explains such a process over a long period of time and throughout such a diverse area.

SIMON HALL ■

Chapter Thirteen

A Consideration of Gender Relations in the Late Iron Age "Sotho" Sequence of the Western Highveld, South Africa

Introduction

From the early 1980s, Iron Age archaeologists in South Africa have been somewhat captive to a structuralist model for the interpretation of settlement space. This trend grew out of Adam Kuper's book *Wives for Cattle* (1982), in which an analysis of bridewealth and marriage patterns for Southern Bantu-speakers isolated several binary oppositions that categorized people in space at several different scales. With this synthesis Iron Age archaeologists could infuse spatial organization with the determining logic of social and cosmological structure (for examples of this approach see Huffman 1982; Evers 1984; Pistorius 1992).

It is hardly surprising that gendered space figures prominently in the model, which became known as the Central Cattle Pattern (or the CCP). Consequently, one opposition orientates gender in space through a left/right distinction, while a center/surround opposition underpins prime male political and economic power, bounded by the domestic domain of women and children. Men accumulate and control cattle and exchange them as bridewealth with other men for wives and their productive and reproductive labor. As the medium through which all social, legal, political, and ritual transactions flow, cattle, their corrals, and the male court are located centrally in the homestead. This explicit power is juxtaposed with the outer residential circle of houses, in which women are more spatially constrained.

However, as has been repeatedly stated in the literature and throughout this volume, these models reify structure and impose an uncritical durability on meaning that compresses time and muffles the contextual detail of social relations. In their rather mechanical application, structuralist models distance people from social action, which becomes a set of rules within which people inflexibly live. While the Central Cattle Pattern is unquestionably gendered, it is as though men and women occupied two separate worlds, where, in an immutable framework of categories, people do not interact or contest power through the manipulation of their symbolic framework in historically distinctive ways.

The prime objective of this paper is to approach gender relations as a dynamic that is under perpetual negotiation, whereby "structures produce not rules but dispositions, and underlie not determinacy but strategy" (Miller 1995:103). Some control over economic and political conditions are obviously critical in order to discuss changes in gender relations as strategic dispositions within specific historical contexts. This is attempted through a closer examination of the Sotho/Tswana[1] sequence in the western Highveld of South Africa from about AD 1400 (Figure 13.1). In contrast to static and ahistoric ethnographic models of Tswana society, there were relatively major political and economic shifts in this sequence that are recognized through significant changes in settlement organization and other categories of material culture. A central theme in correlating these material changes with gender interaction stems from widespread African beliefs in the socially negative force of pollution. These beliefs highlight dangers, usually to men, that result from improper sexual or social contact. As a result, there is always a concern to regulate social categories and the contexts in which interactions between them occur, particularly where women, through their sexual ambiguity, pose a threat to social and economic process. Anxieties about the maintenance of social order are materially expressed through the construction of boundaries that are symbolically displayed and patrolled. This paper attempts to recognize the physical and symbolic boundaries that regulated interaction between men and women and, in turn, see these as analogies for a wider social order (Douglas 1995:3).

The primary archaeological residue examined in this context is the "house"[2] (Lane, Chapter 10). Among Tswana-speakers, the house is the dominant setting for the physical and symbolic mediation of day-to-day encounters between men and women. As Comaroff (1985:54) states, the house "invisibly tunes the minds and bodies of those who people them to their inner logic." A second item of material culture used in this discussion is the ubiquitous artifact of Iron Age archaeology—the pot. It is surprising that while space became symbolic and gendered, albeit within a structuralist framework, Iron Age ceramic analysis continued to focus on mapping out large-scale relationships in time and space. Abstract ceramic classifications focused on migrations, streams, and traditions within the Early Iron Age and the nature of the Early Iron Age/Late Iron Age break (Phillipson 1977; Evers 1983; Mason 1983; Maggs 1984; Huffman 1989). At this scale of analysis the focus on large, regional linguistic and ethnic correlations completely submerges the more immediate social, economic, and ritual contexts of ceramic production, use, and discard. In this case, women, as both producers and significant users and manipulators of the most ubiquitous artifact in Late Iron Age archaeology, become essentially invisible. In contrast, it is instructive to note how the male transformation of iron ore and its accompanying symbolism has received much more attention in the literature. "Smiths constitute an ongoing obsession of social anthropology while potters appear only in

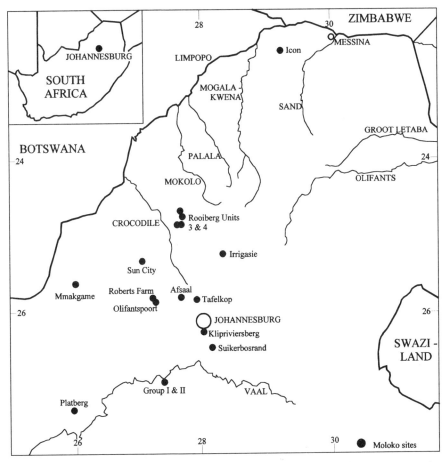

Figure 13.1. Map showing the area under discussion and the location of some Late Iron Age (Tswana) sites.

footnotes" (Barley 1984:93 from Herbert 1993). As a homology for the human body and the medium in which food is transformed and served, pots provide a rich means of symbolic communication that is socially exploited as they are moved parallel to, and across, boundaries. Consequently, I examine more sociological approaches that examine the role of pottery as an active ingredient in the construction of social categories and social interaction (Braithwaite 1982; Welbourn 1984; David et al. 1988).

With this background in place, the paper proceeds in two parts. The first describes, contextualizes, and interprets spatial change and the associated gender relations, predominantly at the level of individual households, while the second adds and articulates pottery to this. In sum, I suggest that from AD 1700, Tswana spatial and symbolic order was tuned more to defining a gender hierarchy, whereas, in the early Tswana period, discernible material and symbolic boundaries suggest gender symmetry.

The Spatial Expression of Boundaries

Ethnographers of the Southern Bantu draw sharp distinctions between the dispersed, exogamous households of Nguni-speakers and the endogamous towns of Sotho, and in particular, Tswana-speakers (Sansom 1974). From the ethnographic perspective, the large aggregated ward clusters (towns) that typify Tswana settlement patterns have been reified as an enduring cultural preference, as well as an adaptation to the relatively arid terrain over which Tswana-speakers have been historically settled. This comprises the inland plateau region to the north, south, and west of present-day Johannesburg, as well as eastern Botswana (Figure 13.1).

However, the pattern of town living as a defining characteristic of Tswana life breaks down under archaeological scrutiny. This shows that Sotho-speakers can be archaeologically identified from about AD 1400 on the Highveld, but that their initial villages were small and dispersed. The historically noted attribute of large ward clusters is a recent innovation, dating from the 18th century (Huffman 1986; Hall 1995). Clearly, the shift from dispersed homesteads to large aggregated ward clusters indicates considerable dynamism in political, economic, and social organization. These changes are most visible in the areas west of present-day Johannesburg, and it is in this area that attention is focused.

Here, the precolonial Tswana sequence can be subdivided into three phases, using either changes to settlement size and the presence or absence of stone walls to demarcate internal space, or the boundary between a homestead and the bush beyond. The start of the first phase is identified through a significant break in ceramic style from the preceding Eiland phase of the Early Iron Age. Evers (1983) correctly identifies an abrupt break between the final 11th- to 13th-century phase of the Early Iron Age and the following Sotho/Tswana sequence (Evers 1981). Radiocarbon dates from Icon and other sites show that early Sotho-speakers first appeared between AD 1300 and 1400 south of the Limpopo River, and farther to the southwest from about AD 1500 (Figure 13.1). Southern Tanzania is a possible point of Sotho origins (Huffman 1989, 1996c).

The first phase is poorly recorded, even though archaeological visibility is high. Mason has excavated several sites at Olifantspoort and elsewhere in the Magaliesberg, and at Rooiberg (Mason 1986: Fig. 1). Other data has been collected by Hanisch (1979), Hall (1981), and Boeyens (1997), among others. An understanding of settlement organization is limited to the location of hut floors and to detail on these floors. Villages are small, with maximum dimensions of about 100 m squared, and comprise loose circles of huts around a central cattle corral (Figure 13.2). The suggestion is that these were relatively short, single-component occupations (Hanisch 1979; Mason 1986).

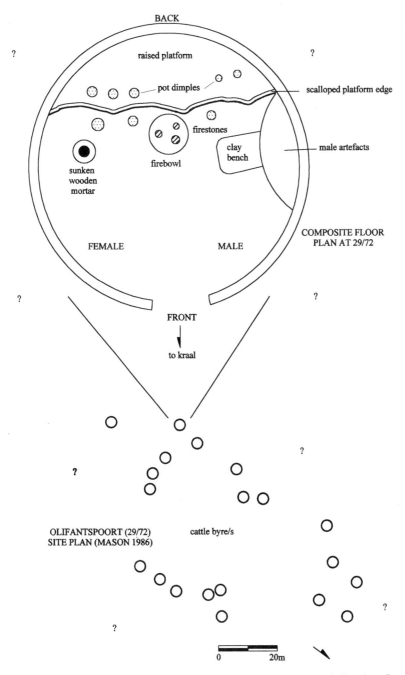

Figure 13.2. Site plan of a first-phase homestead and a composite plan of a first-phase floor.

Apart from the position of individual huts there is little other spatial evidence. There are no indications that individual households were separated by walls from their neighbors, nor is there any indication if or how homestead perimeters were marked off from the surrounding bush. Cattle must have been penned within pole or brush fences. Poor preservation limits clarity on midden location, though there is some suggestion from Irrigasie that a single homestead had several separate middens and that these may have been located behind huts (Lathey 1995). At Rooiberg small stone circles are interpreted by Mason (1986) as grain bin bases. These are located either right next to hut floors, or to the side and front of huts. Overall, the evidence indicates that first phase homesteads were uniformly small and dispersed, and probably part of small-scale chiefdoms with a political hierarchy of two levels, and certainly no more than three (see Huffman 1986).

The lack of spatial detail around huts is in sharp contrast to the wealth of detail preserved on the hut floors (Figure 13.2). This is particularly so for Mason's excavations of first-phase sites in the Olifantspoort area, particularly site 29/72 (Mason 1986:241 ff.), and Boeyens's excavations further west at Rietfontein (Boeyens 1997). The large amounts of collapsed pole-impressed wall daga lying on these floors indicates cone on cylinder structures.

Although there are no visible doorways onto the floors, these can be established through the positions of the raised platforms that were built over approximately one-third of the floor surface (Figure 13.2). This raised platform, or apse, expresses a southern Bantu organizational principle based on a front/back, public/private, and secular/sacred opposition (Kuper 1982). The apse defines the ritually charged and private rear of the hut that is often associated with ancestors, and the entrance to the hut is positioned in opposition to it. The apse can be used to store male and female goods, such as ancestral spears or private storage vessels (for Nguni-speakers, see Raum 1973:157). The apse, and the sharp curb at its front, marks a boundary between private/sacred and public/secular.

Other features associated with the apse or immediately in front embellish this theme, particularly in relation to the transformation of food. Pot dimples occur on the apse immediately back from the curb edge, as well as below the curb to the front. As vessels that store, transfer, and transform the raw ingredients and carry the cooked, it is appropriate that pottery straddles this zone. All floors at Olifantspoort preserved upward of seven pots, which include storage jars and a high number of serving bowls. A significant characteristic of these vessels is their elaborate decoration, an issue that is taken up in more detail below.

Equally important is the position immediately in front of the apse of a sunken wooden mortar that occurs on the left side (as viewed from the front) and a fire bowl and associated cooking stones, usually three, in the center. On several floors this arrangement is associated with a slab "table" (Mason 1986:243). The mortars comprise a shallow 0.25 m diameter dish, which slopes down to the rim of a 0.15 m diameter wooden mortar, which is sunk a further 0.15 m below the level of the floor and wedged in place with stones. The mortars are made from *Acacia* sp., a hard wood that is entirely appropriate for grinding down sorghum and millet (Mandy Esterhuysen: personal communication). At Rooiberg, first-phase floors also preserve fire bowls and permanently fixed lower grindstones (Mason 1986: 299). The presence of carbonized sorghum and bone, including a number of cattle molars, with pots and a fire bowl emphasizes food preparation and consumption inside the hut.

The position of the mortar on the left and, on two floors, a bench on the right introduces another categorization of space that alludes specifically to a gendered division of labor. A return to Southern Bantu ethnography indicates that a left/right distinction often allocates position to women and men respectively (Kuper 1982). The repeated pattern on these first-phase floors of left-side mortars and a link with cereal processing and women is too strong to ignore. Furthermore, the recessed nature of the mortar and the kneeling or bent posture implicated in its use contrasts with the raised clay seats built on the right-hand side that draw attention to male space where a formally seated posture emphasizes a more vertical orientation. This juxta-position of posture is similar to the example Lane draws on from Guyers's study of the Beti in Cameroon (Chapter 10). On some floors, a distinct space either behind the seats or on the right side on floors without seats preserves a range of debris, including iron artifacts.

It is through comparison with the spatial and material patterns recovered from AD 1700 third-phase Tswana ward clusters that the material described for the first-phase floors becomes significant. Without preempting this comparison, I point out at this stage that first-phase floors preserve configurations of features and material that express concerns about classification and the mediation of categories across boundaries. The close association between cereal mortars, fire bowls, male space, and pottery with the sacred back is entirely appropriate. Among the Tswana (Comaroff 1985), the preparation and cooking of food is a final step in the transformation of rank nature that must be subject to ritual sanction lest the potentially polluting essence of "without" and "beyond" disturb the order of "within." Women, who undertake most of the agricultural work, are the main medium through which pollution can be transferred. Furthermore, there is the well-documented notion that sexual pollution by women can contaminate food and endanger men. Among the Bemba, for example, menstruating women do not cook, and a Lele man can lose his virility if he eats food prepared by his wife who has neglected her postintercourse cleansing (Douglas 1995:152, 156).

These ethnographic examples are meant to illustrate some general notions about gendered labor, pollution, and the safe transformation of food that is facilitated through the close juxtaposition of boundaries on the first-phase floors. Whatever the exact meaning of these mediations, I strongly emphasize their compact nature within the compressed space of the hut interior. This last point is important in relation to the comparison with the third-phase floors given below, because, though boundaries as oppositions have been emphasized, their immediate spatial proximity on these

first-phase floors suggests a close knit symmetry in the integration of social categories. There is little evidence for spatial differentiation outside the huts, but on the
basis of the "house" as a microcosm of the larger system, I suggest that gendered loci
interface directly, without any physical or architectural intervention. Consequently, as
discussed below, there is a greater role for the mediation of boundaries through
mobile symbols, particularly pottery.

The second phase in the sequence starts between the early to mid-17th century.
The distinction is based on the appearance of archaeologically more resolved spatial
markers in the form of low stone walls. These define homestead boundaries, central
cattle byres, and stone wall rays at right angles to boundary walls, which must have
physically separated some individual households within homesteads (Taylor
1979:11). Sites are, however, still small. It is during this phase that Sotho-speakers
expand into the southern grasslands of the Free State south of the Vaal River (Maggs
1976: Fig. 1). At a crude level, this expansion and possible population increase may
be attributed to the onset of a warmer and wetter pulse between AD 1500 and 1675
(Tyson and Lindesay 1992; Huffman 1996).

The question of why site boundaries and corrals were more permanently and
visibly marked with stone at this time has not been adequately addressed. Environmental explanations focused on grassland occupation and a lack of wood are simplistic, because this stone wall phase also occurs in well-wooded regions. More likely is
that stone walls elaborate a landscape of increasing permanence and spatial claim, and
fissioning communities have to intensify the negotiation of place as spatial proximity
shrinks between homesteads. Equally, the physicality of walls solidify and embellish
boundaries that must correlate with changing emphases in social relationships.
Boundary walls elaborate a distinction between inside/outside, culture/nature, and
order/chaos; and the parallel internal definition of central byres and domestic margin
must, in part, inscribe the processes by which the outside is socially harnessed and
transformed.

It is in the third phase on the western Highveld, starting in the early part of the
18th century, that the spatial complexity that starts to develop in the second phase is
fully realized. Major settlement expansion takes place, whereby some chiefdoms come
to reside in a single place through the aggregation of homesteads into large ward
clusters. In the early part of the 19th century European travelers visited some of these
large Tswana towns. For example, Campbell (1822, I:181) estimated between 10,000
and 12,000 people residing in one BaRolong town, and higher estimates were made
for the BaHurutshe capital of Kaditshwene (Figure 13.1). In this phase it appears
that homestead fusion, rather than fission, becomes the norm. Figure 13.3 illustrates
site 20/71, which is a relatively small BaKwena third-phase settlement in the Olifantspoort area of the western Magaliesberg. This completely excavated site (Mason
1986; see also Pistorius 1992) provides a comparison with the first phase. Needless
to say, Tswana ethnography is directly relevant to this phase.

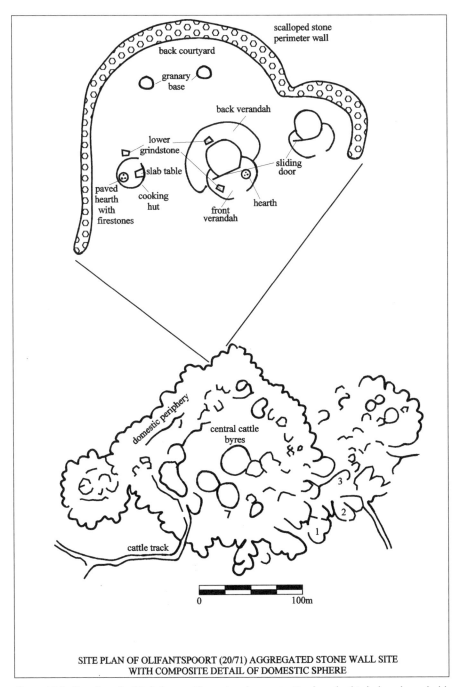

SITE PLAN OF OLIFANTSPOORT (20/71) AGGREGATED STONE WALL SITE
WITH COMPOSITE DETAIL OF DOMESTIC SPHERE

Figure 13.3. Site plan of a third-phase settlement and a composite plan of a third-phase household.

In contrast to first-phase sites, there is considerably more spatial detail in the third phase (Figure 13.3). Extensive stone walling demarcates the characteristically scalloped town perimeter, in which each individual scallop defines the back wall of a household's back courtyard. Large central cattle byres, cattle tracks, and some walls between the central byres and household circle make up the rest of the stone walling.

Within an individual household, space is divided between a hut with front and back verandahs under the eaves of an extended cone. The hut door always faces inward toward the town center. There is a front courtyard, which may be separated from the center by either a stone wall or pole fence (see Hammond-Tooke 1993:10) and a back courtyard behind the hut. To one side of the hut is a small separate stone enclosure, which may have been roofed. In some cases there may be lateral walls extending from the hut to the points of the boundary scallop that separates the front and back courtyard.

Compared to the compact arrangement of mortar, fire bowl, apse, and seat on first-phase floors, the Olifantspoort 20/71 floors are mostly featureless. Most huts have no apse and no internal fire bowl; none have clay seats. The density of other material on the floors is low and there is little evidence for food preparation within the hut. These activities have been segmented and allocated to discrete spatial loci. Grain bin bases indicate that cereal is stored in the back courtyard behind the hut. This is the private space of the household, and in particular, the domain of women. Lower grindstones are found permanently wedged in place under the eaves of the back verandah. The small separate enclosure to the side of the hut was clearly used for cooking. These enclosures preserve elaborate mosaic hearths and firestones, slab "tables," lower and upper grindstones and pots. The front verandah often has a hearth built at the junction of the verandah and hut wall. While some pottery is found on hut floors, many vessels are associated with the front and back verandahs and the cooking hut. Some bowls were set into plaster on the front verandah.

This summary of household space at a third-phase 18th century Tswana town indicates a greater degree of spatial detail compared to a first-phase households. The first-phase floors are multipurpose spaces for sleeping, for cereal storage, for the preparation and cooking of food, and for consuming this food. On the first-phase floors there was little physical separation of gendered activity. Following Kent's (1990a) general principle of increased spatial segmentation with greater sociopolitical complexity, the third-phase households exhibit more functionally discrete spaces that are conceptually and physically separated. Food storage, preparation, and cooking has been fragmented and "bounded" in dedicated spaces, and the main hut seems to be restricted for sleeping. The private/back, secular/front distinction has been elaborated in the back courtyard and verandah and front courtyard and verandah. The back courtyard is the last space before one encounters the bush beyond the homestead and it is appropriately female space, where cereal is stored and ground down. The cooking hut is further to the front, and the consumption of food, especially if guests were visiting, would take place in the front courtyard. It is in this space where men and women, and the products of their labor, meet. Cereal, the product of female labor, moves from the homestead margin of the back courtyard to the front, in contrast to domesticated meat, the concern of men, which would move to the front courtyard from the homestead center.

The discussion suggests that men and women were more spatially proximate in the first phase, in contrast to the third phase, where gendered work becomes spatially fragmented into physically defined, activity-specific loci. At the scale of the whole homestead, the implication is that the domestic margin increasingly segments to accommodate female labor and, at the same time, spatially isolates this activity from men when they are in the household. This is an example of a general principle that is summarized by Guyer (1991:261), namely that "female and low-status workers tend to engage in higher-frequency tasks carried out within narrow spatial confines, a pattern that male and high-status workers try to avoid." These spatial distinctions underpin a gendered division of labor that becomes more rigidly defined and separate between the first and third phases. I suggest that in the third phase the spatial configuration underpin hierarchy and control, in contrast to the symmetry in the first phase. Syntheses of Tswana oral records animate this archaeology in terms of a specific set of historical circumstance that highlight male anxieties over female labor and the security of the agricultural base. This historical background is only briefly described, and a full discussion can be found in Huffman (1986), Hall (1995), Manson (1995), and Parsons (1995).

The third-phase settlement attributes of large aggregations and a tendency for settlements to be located on broken and higher ground, indicates that defense was one determining factor (Huffman 1986; Hall 1995). Oral records indicate that the 18th and early 19th centuries were a period of increasing military competition between Tswana chiefdoms that eventually led to extensive destruction from the 1820s (see Hamilton 1995 for a wide range of views on this *Difaqane/Mfecane* period). Several causal factors contributed to these Tswana wars in which the Hurutshe senior chiefdom increasingly lost power to the BaKwena and Pedi in the east, the Tshidi-Rolong to the west, and the Ngwaketse to the northwest (Manson 1995:354). Some factors are interrelated and others independently coincident.

One cause of aggression focused on land and grazing. Higher rainfall through the 18th century resulted in consistently good food supplies and, consequently, demographic increase and pressure. With limited space to expand, competition over critical agropastoral resources steadily rose. The introduction of maize from the east coast at some time during the 18th century also added to agricultural production, which had significant demographic repercussions over the whole summer rainfall area where maize was viable (Marks 1967). Cattle raiding figured prominently in these wars and, as suggested by Manson (1995) and Parsons (1995), underpinned the concern of men to create wealth in cattle in order to accumulate wives through bridewealth and so maintain or increase a pool of female labor. Oral traditions suggest that at times women were forcefully obtained as an additional aspect of cattle raiding

(Manson 1995). Lastly, there was also intense competition over trade in skins, fur, feathers, metal, and ivory, and access to the routes along which these goods were passed. In the late 18th century this was exacerbated by the growing market demands from the encroaching colonial frontiers from the east coast and the Cape to the south (Manson 1995).

Overall, these factors intensified competitive entrepreneurship between rival Tswana chiefs. Fusion into large aggregated towns was a necessary outcome of historical circumstance, while greater political centralization also controlled the natural tendency for individual homesteads to fission. Although indications are that consistently good agricultural surpluses were produced through the 18th century, droughts at the end of this period and early in the 19th century (Hall 1976) undermined agriculture and contributed further to military tension, aggregation, and, above all, the need to regulate and control agriculture (Huffman 1996:59). It is within this historical context that the spatial segmentation within the third-phase settlements and individual households takes on meaning. The spatial elaboration of the domestic domain suggests more complexity in the management, control, and organization of female labor that relates to the larger-scale political and economic structures that were dependent on it.

That this structural complexity related to male control and male anxiety over the agricultural base can be elaborated through other aspects of Tswana social organization evident in early traveler records and Tswana ethnography. For example, men controlled the ritual that sanctioned female labor and the agricultural cycle. Field allocation, land preparation, planting, harvest, and first fruits were all stages in the cycle that could only proceed through the ritual sanction of the chief and household heads (Sansom 1974:147). Above all, the chiefs' ultimate control lay in rain-making (Schapera 1971). Furthermore, seasonal taboos ritually outlawed women from digging pot clay, making pots, or cutting thatch during the agricultural cycle (Schapera 1971:93). This seasonal restriction on potting underpins a fear of drought generated by the pollution of heat and its effect on agricultural fertility through the fired transformation of clay. While the ethnography does indicate that women had some control over agricultural produce, this power could not be formally accrued because of the relatively immediate consumption of food, in contrast to the male accumulation of cattle (Kinsman 1983). Female agricultural production, therefore, was under the ultimate control of men. In the circumstances of the late 18th century, ideologies of economic value were ritually underwritten and "powerfully legitimized structures of domination and inequality" (Comaroff 1985:67).

The segmentation of domestic space through physical and architectural boundaries increasingly isolated women during the third phase. At the center of this domain lay the hut, an explicit metaphor for the female body that symbolizes the centrality of biological and agricultural fertility for social continuity. This metaphor is explicitly rendered by the Tswana phrase *go tsena mo tlung* ("enter the house"), which refers to sexual relations within marriage (Comaroff 1985:56) (Lane, Chapter 10). However, the division of labor over the construction of the hut and the symbolic elaboration around the doorway allude to unity. Men work with wood and in the vertical by constructing the frame of the hut (Vogel 1983), and they must have also constructed the wooden sliding doors at Olifantspoort. The symbolic inference is that men control fertility through their construction of the frame, and particularly through their construction of the door. However, these doors, without exception, slide open to the left, female side, in and along a recessed clay groove (for details see Mason 1986:395). This symbolic combination of the recessed and the vertical is elaborated on some of the door curbs at Olifantspoort through the insertion of rows of acacia thorns set into the clay. Trees with thorns invariably connote maleness (Schapera 1971:92). Furthermore, women are integral to completing the process of construction by closing off the hut by plastering the walls and floors and thatching the roof. In so doing, women continue their connection with the earth.

So far the articulation of the third-phase archaeology, its accompanying historical context, and its ethnography has emphasized male control. Still further detail from Olifantspoort and other similar sites indicates that male labor also shifted and escalated during the third phase. At Olifantspoort hide and metal work are prominent toward the end of the occupation (Mason 1986), and at Mabyanamatshwaana (Pistorius 1995:57), the "large-scale introduction of iron forging" also intensified at approximately the same time. This intensification is entirely consistent with the historical context of greater trade in these commodities. These male crafts were also spatially elaborated in discrete areas of the settlement. Returning to Figure 13.3, the enclosures marked 2 and 3 were specifically for hide and metal forging, respectively (Mason 1986). Enclosure 2 was littered with large kidney-shaped hornfels flakes, with severe attrition on the working surfaces. Microwear analysis indicates a hide-working function (Binneman 1987). Other aggregated third-phase sites in the western Highveld preserve abundant evidence for similar activities (Mason 1969). Hide working, wood working, and metal working were male activities that equated with "refined social accomplishment" (Comaroff 1985:70). This contrasts with the low-value, mundane work of women, constrained as it was to the domestic periphery. However, these activities were spatially linked to the chief (Figure 13.3, enclosure 1) and the court. This close connection to the chief indicates control over prestige commodities and implies that men also occupied positions of power and subordination within their own ranks.

The parallel intensification and segmentation of both female and male activities in the third phase raises the question of time allocation to tasks. It is possible that toward the end of the 18th century women had to invest considerably more time on agriculture than was the case during the first-phase settlements. Even if maize was viable on the western Highveld, and even if it did boost the amount of cereal harvested, the logistics of agriculture in the context of large, aggregated towns may have been considerably more difficult for women at this time. High-density aggregated living must have reduced the availability of suitable agricultural land that was conveniently close to towns and, coupled with the environmental imperative for dispersed fields, required considerable travel time to those fields, or even permanent residence there when weeding and bird scaring became critical as the harvest approached (Schapera 1971; Comaroff 1985). Campbell (1822, I:181) recorded that the fields of one BaRolong settlement were up to 20 miles (32 km) distant from the town. There is no question that the agricultural cycle for women was long and strenuous, and that this was exacerbated through other work routines (Kinsman 1983; Eldredge 1993:109).

Another factor to consider is that men may have increasingly withdrawn their contribution to agricultural labor as their own priorities shifted to a greater preoccupation with cattle, raiding, defense, and intensifying the acquisition of prestige commodities for trade. Furthermore, as discussed by Guyer for the southern Cameroon (1991:260–261), farming traditional cereals, such as sorghum and millet, is deeply sacred and ritualized and their production is shared between men and women in a sequential set of tasks, and is therefore not the sole prerogative of women. It is with the introduction of New World staples, such as maize and cassava, that the ethnographic picture of almost exclusive female farming assumes prominence in Africa, and though an important food, there is a negative attitude toward maize. Richards noted that preparing land for maize "was considered hard and unromantic work by the Bemba, quite unlike millet cultivation" (Richards 1939:304 from Guyer 1991). The rejection of maize beer in favor of millet beer for ritual occasions also underscores that maize is cognitively marginal compared to the traditional cereals. If maize, however, was as important to some Southern Bantu toward the end of the 18th century as has been suggested (Marks 1967; Huffman 1996), then studies such as Guyer's alert us that its introduction in the third phase from about 1750 must have had implications for the organization of labor.

It seems overly simplistic, however, that the secular status of maize is only a function of its relatively shallow time depth within southern Bantu agriculture. If it was important as a staple food, why is that not reflected in its integration into local cosmologies? There are many examples that show how valued innovations are rapidly embedded. Although speculative, it is possible that men, as the pivots of ritual sanction, actively marginalized maize in ritual because it was so important. The inverse proposition that actual importance is not reflected in ritual refocuses attention on the male control of labor and on male anxieties about the real power of women, as well as the critical importance of agriculture in the aggregated and aggressively competitive context of the 18th century.

The arguments so far have been based on a consideration of spatial organization and change between the first and third phases. I have inferred from the increase in the compartmentalization of space a concomitant segmentation and control of female labor that possibly reflects the development of asymmetrical power relations with men. I now add to and elaborate these arguments through a consideration of the ceramic sequence.

Ceramic Change

It has been noted that pottery from the first and second phases of the Sotho sequence is elaborately and richly decorated (Mason 1986:723; Hanisch 1979; Hall 1981, 1985). In some assemblages, over 50 percent of the vessels are decorated with combinations of textured designs that cover large areas. Decoration is combined with a rich use of red ochre and black graphite coloring. In comparison, pottery from the aggregated third phase is decoratively bland. Motifs are simple and the majority of decorated vessels have only a single band of nicking on the rim. This general trend is widespread and is not specific to one cultural group.

To formally demonstrate this difference in decorative intensity between the AD 1400 to 1700 first and second phases, and the post–AD 1700 third phase, I reanalyzed all reasonably sized published collections. This analysis follows the multivariate system advocated by Huffman (1980), which combines profile with decorative position to produce multivariate classes. Class definitions are given in Table 13.1, their distribution through the sequence are given in Table 13.2, and Figures 13.4 and 13.5 illustrate pottery from each phase.

Fifteen ceramic classes account for all the ceramic stylistic variability in the sequence, and it is usual for first- and second-phase assemblages to have over 50 percent of these classes. Of note in these assemblages is the relatively high number of bowl classes, and the fact that from sites with good samples, well over 50 percent of the bowls are decorated (Mason 1986). Third-phase assemblages have much less stylistic complexity, and a maximum of five classes occurred in only one assemblage. Bowls occur in low frequencies and decoration is minimal. It should be noted that the placement of ochre and graphite was not used in the definition of classes, but is nevertheless a highly visible and extensive attribute of first- and second-phase ceramics, though infrequent on third-phase pots.

This pattern of declining decorative intensity, especially in the post–AD 1700 aggregated phase is clear. There is a simple correlation between first- and second-phase small and dispersed homesteads and high decoration, while low decorative intensity correlates with large third-phase aggregated ward clusters. More specifically, in the first phase, large numbers of pots were recovered from within the hut, while vessels were more scattered around third-phase households. Interpretation of this ceramic trend focuses, first, on the symbolic role of pottery and decoration in mediating boundaries between men and women, and, second, on a brief consideration of changes in the organization of ceramic production.

Pottery Decoration and Boundaries

The starting point for a symbolic interpretation comes from a principle developed from ethnoarchaeological work on African pottery. For the Azande, Braithwaite (1982) has shown that pottery used in spaces where men and women interact tends to be decorated, while vessels that are used in private contexts are not. She suggests

Table 13.1. Definitions for the fifteen Moloko ceramic classes.

Class 1   recurved jar decorated with a single band immediately below the rim

Class 2   recurved jar decorated in one zone on the neck

Class 3   recurved jar decorated with a band immediately below the rim and a band low on the neck

Class 4   recurved jar decorated with a band immediately below the rim, a band on the neck, and a band of decoration extending below the neck onto the body

Class 5   recurved jar with multiple bands extending to the base of the neck, a band of arcades on the shoulder, extending onto the body, and isolated triangles low on the body

Class 6   open bowl with a single band of decoration immediately below the rim

Class 7   open bowl with a band of decoration immediately below the rim and a band on top of the rim

Class 8   open bowl with decoration in one zone on the body

Class 9   open bowl with a band of decoration immediately below the rim and a band on the body

Class 10   open bowl with decoration on top of the rim, a band of decoration immediately below the rim, and a band on the body

Class 11   open bowl with multiple bands on the body with a band of chevrons or arcades extending very low on the body

Class 12   open bowl with a wide band of decoration below the rim and which is decorated in the same zone internally, or has alternating bands of graphite and ochre all the way to the bottom

Class 13   constricted pot with a wide band of decoration below the rim

Class 14   constricted pot with a band of decoration immediately below the rim, followed by a wide band of decoration down onto the upper body

Class 15   constricted pot with a single band of decoration immediately below the rim

that decoration "functions" as a low-key ritual and symbolic marker in contexts where breaches in the social order do, or potentially can, occur. The higher intensity of decoration in areas where male and female encounters take place expresses a concern about the overlap of boundaries, and consequently, those boundaries have to be defined. In general, elaborate decoration correlates with high vessel visibility because it communicates information about social categories, roles, and status.

The ethnography underscores the suitability of pottery to "patrol" boundaries because of the fundamental notion that pots are conceptually equivalent to people (David et al. 1988). It is through this link that pots can be actively manipulated in a wide range of social and ritual contexts in order to communicate meaning about "everyday social life," where "differences of form and decoration help create categories of time and persons" (Barley 1994:116; and see Herbert 1993:200 ff. for a review of African potting). Among the eastern-Tswana Pedi, this homology is clear. Pottery production is analogous to procreation because successful manufacture requires that "fertile" clay (women) and strong water (semen/male) need only lie together for one

	No walling / Dispersed homesteads					Walling / Dispersed h'steads					Walling / Aggregated wards							
CL	IC	R3	RF	OL	AF	TF	IR	$R4^1$	$R4^2$	$R4^3$	GI	GII	MK	PB	KR	SB	SC	OL^4
1	X	X			X			X	X	X		X	X	X	X	X	X	X
2		X	X	X	X	X	X	X	X		X	X	X	X	X		X	X
3	X	X	X	X	X	X	X	X	X	X	X	X	X	X	X		X	X
4	X		X	X	X	X	X											
5								X										
6	X	X		X			X	X	X			X	X	X	X	X	X	X
7	X	X		X			X											
8	X	X		X	X	X												
9	X	X			X	X	X	X	X	X	X							
10	X	X	X	X														
11	X	X		X			X	X	X									
12				X														
13				X										X				
14								X	X	X								
15										X								
CL	9	9	4	10	6	5	7	8	7	5	3	4	4	5	4	2	3	4

IC-Icon (Hanisch 1979); R3-Rooiberg unit 3 (Hall 1981); RF-Retiefs Farm (Mason 1986); OL-Olifantspoort 29/72 (Mason 1986); AF-Afsaal (Mason 1986); TF-Tafelkop (Mason 1986); IR-Irrigasie (Lathey 1995); $R4^{1-2}$-Rooikrans 131/78 & 3/79 (Hall 1985); $R4^3$-Rhenosterkloof 101/78 (Hall 1985); GI & II-Group I & II (Taylor 1979); MK-Mmakgame [Mason 1986) incorrectly identified this site as Kaditshwene (Boeyens pers. comm.)];PB-Platberg, KR-Kliprivviersberg, SB-Suikerbosrand, SC-Sun City (Mason 1986; OL^4-Olifantspoort 20/71 (Mason 1986). (see Figure 1 for locations).

Table 13.2. Distribution of ceramic classes through the Moloko.

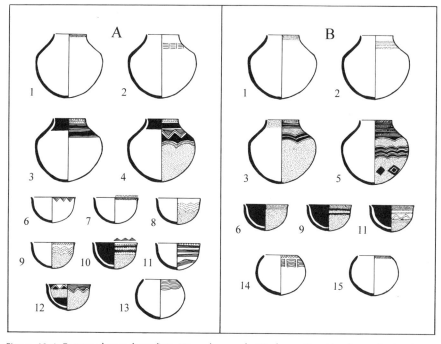

Figure 13.4. Pottery classes from first- (A) and second- (B) phase sites. Numbers refer to classes, which are defined in Table 13.1.

night to be fruitful (Krause 1985:68). Further afield, the Thonga liken a child to a cooling pot after firing, and both must be carefully weaned to maize and water (Junod 1912:100). Shona pottery, "the women's weapons," are symbols of female reproductive organs and can be manipulated to communicate a range of intent, including sexual rejection of her husband through the inversion of her pots (Aschwanden 1982:199).

Furthermore, the motifs used on Tswana pottery are described in terms of female clothing and allude to female fertility (Figures 13.4 and 13.5). Triangles and arcades are described as the tips of the notched rear skirt (*ntepa*) of an initiated women (Vogel 1983), while the chevron is likened to the vulva (Evers and Huffman 1988:740). Other terms for these motifs include the swallow (*peolane*), the moon (*kgwedi*), and the snail (*kgopa*), and through their association with rain and agriculture, also refer to women (Krause 1985). The moon and snail are depicted as full circles, and often decorate the foreskirt (*thetho*) of initiated or married women, which are made and decorated by men (Vogel 1983). These same motifs adorn a wide range of other artifacts, including beadwork, wooden porridge and meat dishes, drums, and mural art. Pottery is also decorated with the red-white-black color triad, which is an explicit symbol in rites of transformation through potentially harmful periods of liminality.

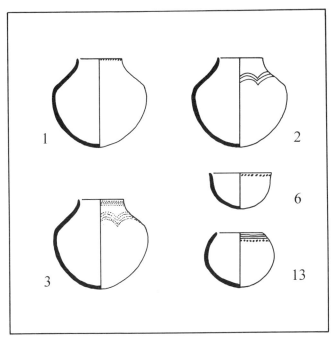

Figure 13.5. Pottery classes from third-phase sites. Numbers refer to classes, which are defined in Table 13.1.

White, therefore, purifies, cools, and cleanses, while red intensifies and consolidates, and black strengthens and protects (Hammond-Tooke 1981:137).

In general, decoration "discourses" on life states, roles, and status. Through its public display and manipulation, decorated pottery draws attention to the sexual power and ambivalence of women, but at the same time it also marks off that ambivalence. In the Tswana world the sexual ambiguity of women and, as Comaroff states, their "lack of closure" (1985:71) is an explicit concern for men that often manifests itself as the undesirable state of heat (*go fisa*), or pollution, that disrupts social order. While women are the prime purveyors of polluting heat, it is generally not a condition that is consciously encouraged or passed on malevolently. It is something that inheres frequently in women because of the perpetual cycle of liminality they experience. Consequently, women with "hot blood" could pollute men through sexual intercourse. Similarly, women who are pregnant, menstruating, or in childbirth are "hot". Women who have suffered a miscarriage can be "hot" for a year after the event (Vogel 1983:395).

As already noted, the potential of women to pollute creates obvious spatial constraints on them. An obvious example is their general confinement to the domestic periphery, and the wild, liminal area beyond the boundary of the homestead, but away from the "cool" judicial domain of the male court and the associated central cattle byres. There are also taboos against their spatial proximity to the male world of iron smelting (see Herbert 1993). Many other cases could be cited. Temporal constraints also affect women. The taboo against making pots during summer has already been mentioned. As a consequence, women "required confinement, they could not extend themselves in physical or social space" (Comaroff 1985:71).

This background provides rich interpretive potential for the disparity between the decorated first- and second-phase pottery and the mundane third-phase pottery. In the relative spatial intimacy of first-phase settlements, symbolic boundaries assume more importance than in third-phase settlements, where physical boundaries controlled, directed, and regulated encounters between men and women. Vessel visibility is high in the first phase, but with spatial segmentation in the third phase, vessel visibility declines. A further impetus to this trend is the possibility, as noted in the ethnography of the Pedi (Mönnig 1967) and the Venda (Stayt 1968), that men eat alone.

A closer examination of changes in both the decorative intensity and the frequency of bowls through the sequence suggests an additional factor in vessel visibility. As noted (Tables 13.1 and 13.2), out of the 15 classes that account for all stylistic variability, 6 are open bowls. In first- and second-phase assemblages, there are at least 5 bowl classes represented, in contrast to third-phase assemblages, where only 1 class occurs. Furthermore, in some first-phase collections, bowls account for over 50 percent of total vessel counts, while in the third phase, this figure drops below 10 percent (Hanisch 1979; Hall 1981; Mason 1986). Historically, bowls were used for serving food, particularly porridge (Quin 1959), and there is no reason why this function was different in the past. In terms of the symbolic mediation discussed above, the transformation of cereal through cooking and its transferral across boundaries between women and men, suggest why the vessel of transferral carries a high symbolic load. This is certainly the case in the first phase, where the spatial evidence indicates that cooking, serving, and eating took place within one confined space. The sharp decline in bowl frequency and the near absence of decoration in the third-phase assemblages implies the opposite. Spatial compartmentalization indicates that the dynamics of food transfer changed. The isolation of food preparation and cooking in discrete spaces is one factor in this. Another is that men stopped using clay bowls to transfer food because they began to manufacture their own wooden bowls and meat trays. As noted above, Tswana men work wood and, specifically, carve wooden porridge bowls and meat dishes (Vogel 1983). The implication is that in the third phase, men were making the wooden porridge bowls and meat trays on which they were served. The use by men of their own personal porridge bowls is also noted in the ethnography of the Pedi (Mönnig 1967). The low frequency of clay bowls in the third phase possibly reflects their substitution by archaeologically less visible wooden bowls. Men, consequently, asserted some control over the transfer of food. Furthermore, ethnographic examples of wooden porridge bowls and meat trays show that men decorated them with the same symbol set found on pottery. Men manipulated material culture that symbolically categorized the fertility of women, and in so doing, actively defined boundaries between them.

In general, the manipulation of space and the possible male intervention in the nature of food transfer constitute strategies developed to order social interaction in the high-density living conditions of large third-phase settlements. A brief digression into the ethnography of Tswana marriage patterns and witchcraft beliefs provides examples of other social strategies that embellish this point.

Tswana marriage is unique among southern Bantu-speakers, with its emphasis on cross-cousin partners. As pointed out by many ethnographers, endogamous marriage (Sansom 1972; Preston-Whyte 1974; Hammond-Tooke 1981; Kuper 1982) creates a high degree of introversion in Tswana kinship. With little ideological constraint over marriage partners, kinship is confounded and creates overlaps in kinship categories so that agnates may also be affines. This kin ambiguity, particularly among women, further emphasizes a concern for boundary definition. In contrast to the strongly exogamous marriage rules among the dispersed homesteads of Nguni-speakers, where there is no ambiguity about the category "women", Tswana wives are not necessarily outsiders, and there is less distinction between "our women" and "their women" (Sansom 1972:205; Hammond-Tooke 1981). Consequently, it is possible that the Tswana emphasis on endogamy developed as aggregation proceeded, and therefore is a relatively recent development. Furthermore, the preference in elite marriage is for a cross-cousin on the agnatic side. Again, this preference may have been emphasized more as aggregation progressed as a strategy by elite men to recirculate cattle within their own line, thereby centralizing the medium of political power.

Turning to witchcraft, Sansom's (1972) discussion of the Pedi suggests that public denunciation seldom occurs. In this regard, there is "a congruence between the lack of ideological limitation on the identity of either a marriage partner or a witch" (Sansom 1972:205). A category of "witch" cannot be defined through clear-cut kin categories or from gender, because these categories are ambiguous. Everyone potentially could be a witch, but to publicly denounce would be disruptive for aggregated town living. In contrast with the nature of witchcraft accusations in small dispersed settlements, the notion of malevolent and personally directed affliction is not emphasized among the Tswana, and female pollution, for example, is not maliciously or consciously imparted. It is impersonal, and its ritual purification is communal. I have mentioned these aspects of social organization because, if contextually specific to the third phase, they add circumstantial significance to the interpretations made above.

The Organization of Ceramic Production

One last factor that requires brief mention in relation to the ceramic trend is possible changes to the organization of production. The combination of archaeological and historical evidence points to male intensification of craft production during the third phase that is tied to the centralization of chiefly power, premised on an increasingly specialized economy through trading opportunities. Although a parallel shift in pottery production would be inconsistent with the argument that women were steadily constrained physically and socially, it is possible that women collaborated among themselves in changing production. Discussion of this is circumstantial, however, and requires archaeological evidence on the actual locales of ceramic production and studies of regional trace elements (see Hall and Grant 1995). It is, however, worth considering relationships between changes in the time allocation to tasks such as potting, and the influence this can have on the nature of production and the character of the pottery (Costin and Hagstrum 1995 give a general summary of labor investment and other factors).

Another way of describing the third-phase assemblages is that they are relatively standardized in terms of the repetitive nature of motifs and their limited simplicity (Figures 13.4 and 13.5). Standardization relates to more efficient labor and time costs. As mentioned, the trend toward simpler and blander pottery on the western Highveld crosscuts cultural boundaries. If women generally had to reapportion time allocation to tasks in the third phase, or use time more efficiently in fulfilling other tasks, then simplification in ceramic production may have contributed one saving. It is also possible that the factor of time investment could have shifted the scale of production from the individual or homestead level to more specialized workgroups that supplied pottery over a much larger area or region. In contrast to first-phase pottery, it is logical to infer less labor investment for the third-phase vessels. There are also other hidden costs in ceramic production, such as the collection and preparation of ochre and graphite (Eldredge 1993:107) for decoration, which is such a prominent feature of first-phase assemblages but is conspicuously absent on third-phase vessels. It is also of interest that ceramic changes at Great Zimbabwe perhaps provide a comparison. Evers and Huffman (1988:740) note that pottery production appears to have become narrowly standardized and also stylistically limited in terms of shape and decoration. While each case must be individually investigated, correlations between ceramic standardization and changes in social organization suggest that there may be some common process at work.

A further aspect of the Tswana social system that could also have impacted ceramic production is the flexibility and fluidity of personnel in the ward system of aggregated towns. Although a village or ward may originate as an agnatic group, "unrelated individuals or groups may be added to the *kgoro*, making it a heterogeneous group surrounding the homogeneous core" (Mönnig 1978:219). This receptivity to outsiders must also have developed during the 18th century as a strategy that encouraged dislocated people to centralize with other chiefs. Fluidity in personnel of different cultural backgrounds could have loosened the need for ethnic expression through material culture (Hodder 1979), and standardization and simplification of style could have been one other strategy for "getting along" in aggregated towns. These ideas about the relationship between women, their labor time, and the nature of ceramic production are speculative, but indicate that a closer examination of this dynamic is warranted.

Conclusion

In this paper I have tried to rework old data with new questions and other perspectives on what this data could mean in terms of social and, specifically, gender correlates. I have "fragmented" the Tswana sequence into a series of historically discrete parts, each of which has a contextually specific set of implications for the nature of gender interactions. The outcome has been an interpretation that recognizes two periods with different emphases in the way gender relations were managed.

The first is characterized by small dispersed homesteads, in which gender interactions were separated, bounded, and defined through symbolic mediation. Although spatial evidence for this early phase of the sequence is poor, I have inferred that the spatial or architectural segmentation of gender and gendered activity was relatively low. I have also suggested that economic and social power was more symmetrical. In sharp contrast, the evidence from the third phase, from AD 1700, suggests changes in the form of social interactions. Spatial segmentation is elaborated through physical boundaries and, as a consequence, there is less uncertainty and more predictability about the nature of encounters. It is suggested that the value of pottery as a medium that facilitates social distinction and interaction declines as spatial separation increases. The circumscription and constraint of women within the domestic zone suggests that there was a more rigid division of labor, and more structural control over productive and reproductive processes that lay at the core of social security. In contrast to the first phase, third-phase gender relations may be described more in terms of hierarchy and asymmetry, where there was more direct male control.

It is clear that the interpretations are more detailed for the third phase than for the first. The variable quality of the data contributes to this, but another critical influence has been a growing wariness of extrapolating Tswana social and gender relations beyond the historical circumstances of its generation (see Lane 1996). Gender matters aside, working with this sequence has drawn attention to the fact that the details of Tswana ethnography are analogically appropriate for the recent period, from the early part of the 18th century. In this regard, I have drawn attention to aspects of Tswana social form that are most probably responses to the economic and political circumstances that prevailed and intensified at that time. For the first phase there are general structural features that are common within Southern Bantu ethnography, but, as outlined at the start, imputing detailed meaning through the ethnography would be misleading. The way these principles are contextually managed can be very different. Indeed, the privilege of time means that the archaeology can provide an independent commentary on the ethnography by contributing toward an understanding of its generative context, and its appropriate temporal use.

At the start of this paper I emphasized the house as the unit of analysis, one that provided a setting that actively "tuned" people to a social logic. It needs to be reemphasized that this logic can be many-sided, depending on whose minds and bodies are being tuned. For men, the domain of women may be seen as dangerous, and it is, therefore, constrained, bounded, and marginalized because it can upset the social order at the center of their power. The intention of this paper, however, has not been to portray active men and passive women. Boundaries obviously acknowledge that the power to impose structure recognizes equally the potential of abutting powers to alter that structure. For women, the house and its symbolic boundaries flaunt productive and reproductive power as reminders of their fundamental importance for social continuity. The house and its symbolic boundaries, therefore, mediate many sides of social power, and the tension between them always holds the potential for change.

Notes

1. Sotho is a term for one of the four main languages spoken in South Africa. Tswana is a variation of Sotho. Although these terms have their origins in the colonial categorization of indigenous society, I still use them as convenient labels for the period from AD 1400, when the first "Sotho"-speakers can be archaeologically identified, and after which there is undoubted continuity.

2. In this paper "house" refers to all the component parts of a domestic unit, comprising courtyards, storage areas, cooking areas, sleeping areas, and so on. "Hut" is used simply as a convenient label to distinguish the roofed area of a "house."

■ *Part Three* ■

Commentaries and Perspectives

Chapter Fourteen

Toward an Archaeology of Gender in Africa

Introduction

It was perhaps inevitable that sooner or later archaeologists working in Africa would become active participants in the ongoing exploration of gender in the archaeological past. This volume is an indication that issues of gender can no longer be ignored in African archaeology and that issues of gender have become an ingredient in our outlook on both the prehistory and the protohistory of Africa.

In this contribution, I aim to present some of my own views on the scope of an archaeology of gender, with specific reference to Africa and the topics discussed by other contributors to this volume. It is not difficult to be overcritical at this point in the development of this new subject, but I think it may be more constructive to focus on the road ahead and the range of possibilities explored in this volume.

Africa, a vast continent with great cultural and historical diversity, provides a broad archeological canvas with unlimited potential for archaeological inquiries. With specific reference to gender, African archaeology provides a situation that can enable us to look at the past from different settings, and perhaps through different eyes, than that of the master (Euro-American) narrative of archaeological inquiry. The industrial revolution and the commercial transformation of Europe have generated hegemonic visions of civilization, ethnicity, nationalism, and an epistemic prism that makes it difficult to examine our past from other vantage points and within other cultural narratives. Africa, like many other continents, has been hit by the commercial and industrial European tsunami. Colonialism (see Feierman 1995) has been a major force in the transformation of the African cultural landscape (see Stahl and Cruz, Chapter 11, for one example). However, African traditions and cultures have not been totally submerged or destroyed. The voices of the ancestors still resound in many parts of Africa, and if we listen carefully they may lead us in new directions. Gender as constituted in western narratives may or may not be analogous to that of Africa. However, in our exploration of the archaeological dimensions of gender we cannot rely solely on the totalizing, stereotypical views of women and men developed and perpetuated within the Judeo-Christian-Islamic tradition and the commercial-industrial experience.

As we must avoid the danger of viewing the African past from exclusively European eyes, we must also guard against making a facile projection of Africa's present to its past. This is a topic that justifiably preoccupies many of the contributors to this volume. However, as important as this is, we must not lose sight of the ultimate objectives of our inquiry. Our concern for methodological rigor should not interfere with a concern for, first, a clarification and an explanation of the current position and status of women and the power differential between men and women in many societies; second, the role of gender as a key ingredient in social transactions and dynamics; and third, the role of gender as a basic constituent of thought and cultural symbolism.

An exploration of these issues, as many contributions in this volume reveal (see below), is under way. In the later prehistory of Africa, these issues are inseparable from the fundamental transformations that have influenced the lineaments and physiognomy of most African societies. Paramount among such transformation was the transition from foraging to the management of livestock and pastoralism, the acquisition of iron-making technology, the rise of chiefdoms, kingdoms, and empires, and the impact of colonialism.

This volume will have succeeded if it stirs the interest of a new generation of archaeologists in exploring the issues raised here on a much better footing and with fresh outlook, untainted like ours with the earlier tradition of archaeological practice and discourse. However, it will succeed at even a higher level if it alerts the archaeological community to the need to engage archaeology in the social and cognitive domains of the archaeological past. Gender is only one of many social issues (such as age, rank, occupation, and ethnicity) that cry out for our attention. A turn in archaeology in this direction will address current concerns at a time when the world is undergoing a rapid, radical reconfiguration. It will also provide archaeology with a new platform far from either the fetishistic preoccupation with typologies, historical periodization, dating, subsistence, and adaptation or the populist portrayal of archaeology in the media and the recreation industry in terms of treasure hunting and exotica.

The Rise of Gendered Archaeology

As archaeologists, we have not come to consider "gender" as the logical outcome of our previous endeavors. "Gender" erupted in the intellectual milieu in the 1970s and 1980s as women were caught up in the rhetoric and tactics of rebellions and revolutions that had swept the world in the 1950s and 1960s.

The revolts and resistance to colonial regimes in the Middle East, Africa, Asia, and Latin America not only led to independence and liberation, but they also created a climate of protest and defiance that fueled civil rights and student protest movements, as well as the women's liberation movement. In the 1960s some women in the

United States actively protested against their perception of gender inequality and discrimination. In the 1970s, feminist organizations in the United States mobilized women to gain political and economic equality, and "gender" became a public issue (Nielson 1990).

In the 1980s and thereafter, gender issues began to make inroads into archaeology, in part as a result of the entry of more women into the profession and their incorporation in the various echelons of academia, albeit not at the same level or pay as their male counterparts (Institute of Field Archaeologists 1991), but the emergence of gender in archaeology was the result of a theoretical turn that acknowledged subjectivity, discourse, emotions, the body, and alterity (the "other" or "otherness"). In a series of contributions, the paradigmatic "man the hunter" was challenged (Dahlberg 1981; Burtt 1987; Fagan 1992). The sexist language or archeology was debated (Evans 1990; Chippindale 1991); gender was explored (Claassen 1992; Conkey and Spector 1984); prehistory was rewritten with woman in mind (Ehrenberg 1989; Gero and Conkey 1991), and the big picture (biased interpretations of gender) was exposed (Hurcombe 1995).

In the meantime, in the hedges of archaeology certain advocates of feminism began to resurrect *Mutterrecht* from the dustbin of anthropology. Goddesses became fashionable (see critical review by Meskell 1995; see also Haaland and Haaland 1995).

Archaeologists engaged in the study of Africa's past cannot afford to ignore either what is happening in their discipline elsewhere, or the propagation of certain notions of gender and feminism in the popular mind. More importantly, they should not stand back at a time when differential treatment and persistent prejudices against women continue to degrade them and deprive them of their basic human rights in many societies. But they also should not stand back as the current state of affairs hampers endeavors aimed at alleviating the misery and misfortune of many peoples in the world (especially in the domains of population planning, education, economic development, and health projects).

Archaeology can change us by showing that neither biology nor history is destiny. This simple, yet most profound, aspect of archaeology decenters the present and disconnects us from the web of current preoccupations as we situate ourselves in a distant time, where we are forced to deal with snatches of information that may have no place, significance, or utility in our own world. We may defeat ourselves by insisting on an isomorphism between past and present and thus reduce the past to nothing more than a pale image of our own lives. This is one of the great temptations in archaeology because we so loathe the ambiguity and murkiness of the unknown that we often proceed most willingly from the known to the unknown. We are lured to see the present in the past in order to legitimate and justify our cultural present. As Lane (Chapter 10) remarks, the position of women, and for that matter men, in past non-Western and Western societies, has been assumed implicitly to have resembled those of women and men in contemporary Western society, *as understood from a male perspective.*

Archaeology has long been engrossed by the act of defining others; not realizing that we cannot fully *know* others until we know how we actively construe others and recognize the common basis that can make our knowledge possible. We have also been concerned with the simple act of collecting, organizing, and interpreting *things*. As such we have only recently become aware of the behavioral modes that generate and animate things. We are even still far removed from probing more deeply into the underlying forces and principles of thinking and feeling that shape and structure human behavior, as well as the integrative relays between thinking, feeling, acting, and regarding things. In this volume, Parkington (Chapter 2) notes that the emergence of an awareness of the role of social relations in the archaeological past has led to a recognition of the need to clarify the role of "people" in past societies, and further to "resolve" (deconstruct) this undifferentiated notion of "people" into men and women, as well as into other categories of social actors. To this observation, I add that there is also a need to recognize the cognitive, symbolic, and emotive dimensions of social relations. We can discern, for example, as Parkington does, the association of men in Western Cape rock art with bows and women with weighted digging sticks. Beyond the probable association between this and a gendered division of labor, the symbolic and emotive significance of such associations are rich with information on the way social categories are created, contrasted, complemented, and integrated. In their analysis of gender and craft production in Ghana, Stahl and Cruz (Chapter 11) conclude that the production of textiles, for example, was important in creating and maintaining social relations because textiles were invested with more than the function of clothing bodies. This is invoked as an explanation of why women were content to rely on extra-household labor to produce pots, while production of textiles appears to have been a household activity. Stahl and Cruz also observed that before the new (19th century) Islamic state regime in the western Sudan, the production of indigo cloth took place within the household. Husbands cultivated cotton while wives grew indigo.

We may wish to inquire why certain crafts or activities are so gendered. In her discussion of gendered technologies, MacLean (Chapter 9) concludes that iron production technology is strictly gendered, not only in the Interlacustrine Region, but throughout Africa and indeed in many other societies around the world. Smelters and smiths, without exception, were and still are male. By contrast, the cooking of food in the Interlacustrine Region is generally a female activity. MacLean attributes the latter to the extension of breast-feeding to the larger feeding of the family. She also explains the symbolism of iron smelting as it inherently resembles the human reproductive process. I doubt, on epistemological grounds, that there is any such thing as an "inherent" resemblance. I suggest instead that certain resemblances are invoked because of dominant, potent "schemata" that are either transcultural (e.g. intercourse, birth, death) or culturally specific (e.g., progress, mechanical function, dynamics). Such schemata facilitate the generation of metaphors (such as the resemblance between the brain and either a switch-blade knife or a computer). Certain metaphors may also develop as a result of historical antecedents; for instance, is it possible that the association between iron smithing and males is a continuation of the link between males and weapons? We should, of course, realize that the attribution of a craft to a specific gender does not imply that other gender affiliations are absent from that craft. In general, the tendency to link a certain craft with one gender or another masks a negotiated range of gender relations. This is clearly the case in the metaphors and rituals of iron smelting (Schmidt, Chapter 8).

The study of gender in archaeology, in my opinion, is not separate from the struggle to improve the conditions and status of women. I do realize that this may be naively interpreted as a single-sided perspective. However, little can be gained from a polarization of positions. Worse still would be the gain if the objective were to allow women to be "like" men. The majority of men and women in many societies are victims of powerlessness. Archaeological inquiries may provide a means for uncovering the dynamics that perpetuate certain modes of social relations, certain images, and certain stereotypical modalities of women and men. Such inquiries may also provide models for gender that do not prevent either men or women (or anything in between) to fulfill and realize their human potential. We will not gain much from simply repeating that women could also hunt, or that they could also make iron. We must explain why, if that is so, certain technologies were gendered, and how this plays in the technology of power. But even beyond that, it would be counterproductive to dwell on power as a matter of competition and opposition. Although we should never overlook the power differential, or its evil consequences, we must examine the complementarity between the sexes and the way by which society creates schemata and icons of integration, complementarity, harmonization, and reconciliation (see, for example, Troy's [1986, 1994, 1996] pioneering examination of Egyptian religion from that perspective).

My worry is that gender may be coopted and neutralizing. Gender inquiries may become no more than a search for the archaeological correlates of what women (or men) do and where, and may become lost in the morass of validating categorical differences, and subsequently lost in a debate of the problems and limitations of analogy or the direct, historical approach. What is needed is a penetrating analysis of the ideology and social technology that generated and perpetuated a most striking asymmetry between men and women, and an explanation why some of those asymmetrical relations (regardless of their specific form) are common among many cultures. As archaeologists, we must also seek to trace the genealogy of the social, psychological, and cognitive differentials between men and women, and to uncover the impact of major cultural transformations of the conceptual constructs of women and men, as well as their roles and status in society.

My worries are shared by Lane (Chapter 10), who notes (after Wylie 1991) that if we do not develop an alternative archaeological epistemology on the basis of insights from gender analysis, there is a real risk that the issues of danger will be simply assimilated within the current master narrative of archaeology.

Many contributors in this volume address gender from the division of labor, taking that as a starting point. Others explore the implications of the division of labor on the spatial loci of gendered activities and technologies. Many have been careful to discuss other aspects of culture, such as information and communication (Casey, Chapter 5), as well as metaphors (Parkington, Chapter 2; MacLean, Chapter 9; and Schmidt, Chapter 8). I sincerely hope that we will not ignore such ecological and economical subjects, such as those key to the arguments by Gifford-Gonzalez (Chapter 7) on early pastoralism in Kenya and northern Tanzania. At the same time, we need to continue to explore the rich and vibrant dimensions of the embodiment and experience of gendered metaphors as expounded in some detail by Schmidt (see also Csordas 1994).

My hope is that an analysis of gender in archaeology will force us to rethink not only the deeper forces that shape social relations but also those forces that make us who we are—a prelude to an archaeology of self. In such an analysis, instead of examining ecology as a domain separate from symbolism, or self as opposed to society, or man as a category antithetical to women, we may choose to operate within a theoretical framework that explores the way the self is interactive with others; the manner by which ideas, actions, and communication are constitutive elements of artifacts and human endeavors; and the means by which the categories of man and woman are interwoven into the fabric of human thinking, behavior, and the material world.

Gender in Theory: From Self to Archaeology

The traditional distinction between men and women as a matter of "sex" (male/female) was found to be wanting: some biologically constituted males are considered as women in certain societies (see discussion in Nielson 1990:147–168). Although women and men as cultural categories are social constructions, their modalities and attributes vary from one society to another. "Sex" also grounded the identity of men or women in sexuality as if this were the primary defining parameter. Theories that provide an explanation of gender tend to attribute it to biological essentialism, social learning (socialization), cognitive development, ecological functionalism, or exploitation of reproductive function and social conflict (reviewed by Nielson 1990:147–241).

Gender categorization has evolutionary, historical, and regional dimensions that are dynamic and active. It is neither fixed nor final. Gender may be viewed as the outcome of cultural processes that involve the interaction between different biologically constituted individuals in different circumstances. These interactions are necessitated by mating, sociality, and food production. Gender is entangled in its ideological, religious, organizational, psychological, behavioral, communicative, and material domains.

The biological capacity of "woman" to bear children and the biological transformation of her body and body-function in association with this biological capability is fundamental. However, it is neither essential for either gender definition or female functions. To search for an essence of "woman," or for that matter of "man," is futile. Society fabricates categories that may or may not select, ignore, emphasize, or deemphasize biological attributes and functions. These categories are interwoven with appearances (presentation) of such categories, and a language, as well as modes of behavior and materiality that vary in their rigidity, but are never too rigid to prevent change and transmutation (Beall 1993).

Gender categories, regardless of their original context and raison d'être, are constantly modified and reformulated. The magnitude of change may vary at times. When the change is too slow or imperceptible, the categories appear as if they were essential, primordial, and fixed. Conservation of the status quo by a beneficiary elite may promote and bolster gender essentialism by an appeal to "nature," divine predetermination, or biological predestination. Essentialism is also a means of simplification and embracing comforting taxonomic classification that eliminates distressing fuzziness and disturbing ambiguities.

A biological function such as sex may be a source of indulgence or abstinence. It may be tightly controlled or licentious. Pregnancy may be considered a blessing or a disaster. Children may be a source of pride or misery. Biological attributes can be ignored, highlighted, or covered up. Breasts may be enlarged or tightly bandaged. Hair may be fashioned in elaborate styles or shaved, partially or completely. A "tan" may be a mark of a poor women who labors in the fields, or a wealthy, healthy, indulgent, and sportive lifestyle.

Mature individuals make choices from the range of social possibilities on the basis of their cultural/social/psychological background, which shapes their perceptions and aspirations, as well as from a calculus (not necessarily deliberate or consciously explicit) of payoffs and penalties. They can also create innovative models of self and act on them, thus creating new modes in societies for imitation, acceptance, or rejection. By rejecting certain innovative behavior or images, people as individuals or as groups may strengthen their own codes and norms, while stressing and affirming both boundaries and limits of tolerance.

Social learning contributes to the formulation of a self as an input that interacts with and is internally organized and retained with and within preexisting, biological cognitive and psychological structures (Fast 1993; Lott and Maluso 1993). Socialization is thus a cognitive-developmental process. The notions of self, including those of gender, are incorporated and substantiated (or altered) within each encounter, in a series of additions, ruptures, transformations, and deletions. In this developmental process certain principles, schemata, and structures emerge as fundamental organizational parameters that form a distinct core of personality, character, or identity. Guarded by concealment and denial (of murmurings that disturb or undermine its integrity) and reenforced by bodily representation and external behavior, as well as language, it becomes a phenotypical "cartoon," a "proxy" that mediates between others and "inner-self" and between "inner-self" and "outer-self."

Archaeologists, whose endeavors are more often than not enmeshed in the world of things, can thus contribute to the study of gender by focusing on its material and iconographic correlates—but, it is hoped, can do so without losing sight of the network of psychological, cognitive, and behavioral associations that bind materiality with self and society (see Gilchrist 1993; Bourdieu 1977). Lane (Chapter 10) explores this domain in some detail. I consider this subject essential for any careful elaboration of the formation and maintenance of gender identities and relations. Embodied experiences and inherited schemata are actively engaged in the creation of gendered identities, and such identities, in turn, are involved in subsequent embodied experiences. The tendency to dichotomize, categorize, and classify is often resisted by the malleability of embodied experiences and social encounters, as well as by the creative dynamics of segregating and recombining traits from preestablished categories or classes. Gender may be thus viewed as a "fuzzy" set of characteristics or behaviors, and individuals are never exclusively one gender or the other. The flux of events that may augment or undermine certain gender notions is well exemplified by Stahl and Cruz's account (Chapter 11) of the changing conditions of textile production in Mali. Demand for indigo cloth worn by the elite increased in the 19th century. Husbands, who traditionally cultivated cotton and wove, would deploy slaves, instead of their wives, to cultivate indigo. Women were increasingly confined to their households and did not take part in cultivating indigo or controlled the finished products as they did in the past. All this changed when the slaves left their masters early in the colonial period, and changed again when cheap imported cloth undermined the local textile industry.

Of particular interest is the argument put forward by Hall (Chapter 13) on the changes in the spatial loci of gendered activities in three successive phases in the later manifestations of the iron technocomplex of the Western Highveld, South Africa, from AD 1300 to the present. In the final phase, for example, the practice of cattle raiding, creation of wealth in cattle, and control of female agricultural production are intertwined with notions of conquest, domination, and sexuality. In the house, signs of female sexuality and procreative functions are incorporated in a scheme of male control. Everyday practices like entering the house thus become a microcosm of the greater social order, while the social order itself becomes the outcome of such daily acts. "This metaphor is explicitly rendered by the Tswana phrase *go tsena mo tlung* ('enter the house'), which refers to sexual relations within marriage (Comaroff 1985:56) (Lane, Chapter 10)."

Self, Sex, and Gender

It is significant that sex (as in sexuality) is inseparable in our own public discourse (e.g. advertisements and television commercials) from women. By contrast, men in public discourse are uncoupled from sexuality (except when public figures are engaged in illicit or sleazy affairs). The male world is often one of work, political power, religious piety, and leadership.

The association between sex and gender is basic. Although gender is a social/cultural construct, it is also predicated on differences between the sexes. The attribution of sex tends to rely primarily on genitals, among both humans and nonhuman primates (Miller 1993:4). The relationship is not of equivalency, homology, or even a wire-frame and an outer overlay. It is not one of veneer or a dressing and an essential core (see discussion by Laqueur 1990; Yates 1993; Butler 1993; Moore 1994; Meskell 1996). Sexuality is clearly manifest in the homologies of penis and arrow, semen and poison, the blood of the kill and the blood of birth (McCall 1973, cited in Parkington, Chapter 2). Parkington (Chapter 2) also suggests that "the regular depiction of penises on men and buttocks on women [in Western Cape rock art] draws attention to the sexual potential of these people and underlines the relationship between the paintings and sexual tensions and metaphors." Schmidt (Chapter 8) also discusses in detail the sexual dimensions of iron smithing (see also MacLean, Chapter 9; Collett 1993; Rowlands and Warnier 1993).

Gender categories are neither contrastive bodies nor disembodied discursive fantasies (see Grosz 1994). One of the problems in the sex–gender debate is that we have to examine gender as gendered entities ourselves, and we can only examine it through language and introspection in social categories that are already preformed. One problem lies in the masculinist language of discourse (as in Lacan's phallic theory of language), which creates a problem both for women who must speak as men (Irigaray 1984) and for men who cannot approach women except from within the prism of sexist language. The insidious messages of "man the hunter," "the emergence of man," or "man the tool-maker" that once were uncritically accepted, appear now in a different light (see especially Wadley's treatment, in Chapter 4, of gender stereotypes among hunter-gatherers; and Kent 1995). However, the deeper and pervasive schemata of language that permeate thinking may not be as transparent as such examples and are thus more difficult to weed out or exterminate.

Archaeological discourse is permeated with concepts that are related to the domain that in the 19th century was assigned to the male gender (see, for example, Lane, Chapter 10). Our basic units of observation, analysis, and interpretation, as well as our tools, industries, technology, technocomplexes, linear evolutionary schemes, and production—to name only a few—are manifestly androcentric. In our archaeological discourse have we ever focused adequately on households, domesticity, life cycles, growth and development, social nurturance, art, creativity, imagination, or expressive activities?

The significance of these differences cannot be easily explained in terms of stereotypical views of male and female domains informed by our current social conceptions and master narratives. The formulation of differences, a function of our criteria and statistical tests, specifies phenomenal forms. As such it may mask unconceptualizable differences (see Derrida 1967) even as it obscures the implications of such differences. The differences as detected do not constitute *the* identity of women, nor do they define *the* difference between the *identity* of men and women; they only point to certain dimensions of males and females and the potential (symbolic) significance(s) of these differences.

Gender as a category subverts women into becoming grounded and tethered to sex: an inescapable vector. As an individual, a woman may be identified primarily by criteria that are not grounded in the size of her hips or the function of her womb, inasmuch as a man's identity may not be primarily a function of his anatomy either. To the extent that anatomy is employed in iconography it cannot be ignored, but the challenge is not to assume a universality of gendered sex, or a sexed gender, but rather to explore the spectrum and ambiguity by which sex is gendered and gender is sexed. Parkington's (Chapter 2) reference to the regular depiction of penises on men and buttocks on women in the Western Cape Rock, as he suggests, was an attempt to draw attention to the sexual potentials of these people. Sexual attributes were used as a sign for gender (sex) of the persons depicted. While this may be true (it may also be a sign for something else: an attribute of a potentiality rather than identity, for example), the scenes of sexuality in Saharan Rock art, some involving "bestiality" (Figure 14.1), might reveal an equivalence between hunting and sexual intercourse, as Parkington also notes. From ethnographic information in South Africa, a man has two wives, his human wife and his eland or gemsbok. We need to probe more deeply into the meanings of sexuality and explore the possibility that this concept may not be only about aggressive men and women as prey, but also about complementarity in acts of procreation, as well as serving as a metaphor for unions between the human world and the animal world, and even an embodiment of cosmic orders that transcend the identities of the individuals involved (see also Barich, Chapter 6, on the representations of family ritual in the Tassili rock art).

Politicizing Gender

The social fabrication of gender is not separable from sociopolitical machination, manipulation, and control. It would be wrong to neutralize gender and dissociate it from this political context. The changes in South Africa during the last 700 years are marked by several transitions involving variations in women's access to political power. Changes in the use of space suggest a pattern indicative of egalitarian, mobile hunter-gatherers to less egalitarian pastoralists. In contrast to the formers' sites, the pastoralists' sites (dating from AD 1300 to 1500, associated with the early manifestations of iron technology) exhibit signs of spatial segregation (Kent, Chapters 1 and 3). The sequence in the Western Highveld, South Africa, reveals that from AD 1700, a sharp asymmetry in gender relations occurred, whereby female labor increasingly came under intensified male control (Hall, Chapter 13). During that phase, major settlement expansion takes place through the aggregation of homesteads in a chiefdom

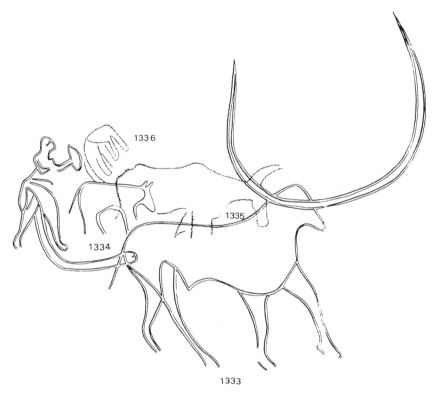

Figure 14.1. Rock art scene from the Tassili-n-Ajjer, Bubaline style; from Lhote 1975:382–383.

into large ward clusters. The choice of broken and higher ground for the settlements suggests that defense was a determining factor. Aggression tended to focus on land and grazing. Cattle raiding figured prominently, as a means to create wealth in order to accumulate wives and garner their labor through bridewealth (Hall, Chapter 13).

Segobye (Chapter 12) suggests that viewing the process of complex social formation as an intrinsically male-directed process ignores the potential contribution that women made, and more specifically the diversity they enjoyed in their forms of social organization and social relations. She also regards as oversimplistic the view that women were valuable only insofar as they were able to reproduce surplus labor and to bear daughters who could in turn be married off, thus creating social or political alliances. Women presumably negotiated power and social identity in more ingenious ways.

Segobye is justified in pointing out the need to approach the past from a different perspective and in emphasizing the need for acknowledging the diversity of social relations and organizations. She is also justified in noting the necessity of highlighting the women who *resisted* control and indicating how they devised ingenious ways of maintaining and perpetuating both their identities and their power. Nevertheless, it is also important not to overlook salient lineaments in the course of the later prehistory of Africa and the subordination of women in public political domains. Pastoralism does indeed seem to have generated and perpetuated a power asymmetry (Ingold 1980). While we must not overlook the local or culture-specific manifestation of such an asymmetry or underestimate the creative, positive contributions of women in such societies, we would be remiss if we ignored the saliency of power asymmetry in such societies and overlooked its implication for women's status in many African societies today.

Domesticating Gender

Our current concepts of gender are deeply situated in the schemata generated and perpetuated in remote and recent antiquity. The advent of food production either as the cultivation of plants or as herding was associated with major transformations of both sex roles and the images of men and women. As we undergo major social and political transformations today, we are actively involved in the remaking of these images. Many of these "traditional" (inherited) images are clothed in the sanctity of religion, even as the inertia of cultural legacies is pervasive in many societies. The inherited images and schemata have influenced the domains and language of archaeology (see Hurcombe 1995).

In Africa, the cultural developments in later prehistory differed significantly from those in Southwest Asia, because of the delay in the advent of food production, as well as basic differences in the modes of food production (see Bower 1995 for a recent, perceptive overview of early food production in Africa). One of the major consequences of intensive agriculture in Southwest Asia, especially, was the emphasis on men's labor as a means of generating "income." This was particularly important with the development of the "state" as the most powerful organizational frame of social interactions. The imposition of taxes, levied on families to support the ruling elite, placed a high demand for male labor. This meant that women had to bring to life more babies. In general, a long child-spacing period of four to five years is necessary in hunting-gathering societies and horticultural communities, to maintain the health of the female. To increase the number of offspring, women who in general entered sexual activity early in life are likely to have been "forced" to abandon or relax birth-control practices. Even the decision to keep or abandon a newborn infant was left to the mother. In an agrarian society in Southwest Asia, it became the concern of males, especially those in power, who benefited from having more male laborers. With high infant mortality through infections and epidemics in an agrarian, sedentary context, even more children had to be born per female. With a high frequency of births, women were also more subject to death during childbirth.

Nevertheless, women in Africa—burdened by pregnancy, birthing, nursing, and raising children, in addition to performing their domestic chores and work in the field—were not likely to participate in the public life of males, who were not so burdened. Men also guarded women as a commodity and token of capital wealth. Women were controlled so that they would not "elope" with strangers. They were pushed away from public view and restricted to deep space within the house, together with stored grain—a situation that still prevailed when I undertook ethnoarchaeological work with Christine Plimpton on domestic activities in Egyptian villages (Plimpton and Hassan 1987).

By contrast with Southwest Asia, in most areas of Africa the situation was different. Following the emergence of cattle keeping in northeast Africa during the 10th or at the latest the 9th millennium bp (Wendorf et al. 1987; Wendorf and Schild 1994), successive arid spells apparently led to the dispersal of cattle keepers and foragers, who kept some livestock (sheep, goats, or cattle), in a series of moves that eventually brought livestock to all parts of Africa.

Initially, cattle keeping spread to the Acacus area. Subsequently, the droughts of 7500–7000 bp are likely to have led to population movements that spread managed cattle to the well-watered areas of central Sahara and the Sahel (Hassan in press b). Although specialized pastoralism might have emerged at about that time in the Acacus region (see Barich, Chapter 6), the spread of cattle to the coastal area of the Maghreb and Libya, as well as farther west from the central Sahara and even into Central Sudan after 7000 bp, was perhaps a result of the movement either of hunter-gatherers who kept some livestock and/or hunter-gatherers on the periphery of livestock keepers who acquired livestock through food exchange. Domestication of local varieties of cattle is also probable. However, goats and sheep are not indigenous to Africa, and must have been adopted as domesticates. Sheep and goats entered Africa shortly before 7000 bp (see, for example, Vermeersch et al. 1996) and then spread rapidly into North Africa.

Cattle and livestock were introduced to the western Sahara, the Sahel, and East Africa by 5000–4000 bp. Early domestic cattle remains in these areas are often found in association with remains of generalized hunting-fowling-fishing subsistence regimes. Small groups apparently moved rapidly during the drought years and mingled with the local hunting-gathering communities.

Domestic carprines appear in East Africa at Enkapune Ya Muto Rock Shelter in a level dating to 4900–3000 radiocarbon years bp (Marean 1992a; Gifford-Gonzalez, Chapter 7). By that time the Sahara was changing rapidly into the current desert conditions, which were established between 4500 and 3000 bp (see Hassan 1996 for a review of Holocene climatic change in Africa).

According to Bower (1995), specialized forms of pastoralism similar to those prevailing today probably did not appear until ca. 3000 bp. By 2000 bp, or perhaps a few centuries earlier, parts of East Africa (Kenya, Tanzania, and Uganda) were occupied by iron makers who kept livestock and cultivated plants. From this area, iron-making technology and agropastoralism spread rapidly southward (Bower:137).

In both East Africa and West Africa the first attempts to cultivate plants were probably under way during the 4th millennium bp. The earliest reports are of cultivated pearl millet at Dhar Tichitt in the 11th century BC in southern Mauritania (Munson 1976) and pearl millet from Neterso in northern Ghana dated to 1250 BC. Other reports of domesticated plants before these dates have not been substantiated (Harlan 1992:60–61). In a more recent account, pot sherds with impressions of cultivated *Pennisetum* pear millet has been dated to 3500 bp at Dhar Tichitt (Amblard 1996).

The shift to specialized pastoralism in East Africa and cultivation (of millet) in Mauritania might have been triggered by droughts at ca. 3700 bp. Further spread of such cultivation southward might have started either at that time or later during the dry spells at ca. 3000 and 2500 bp (Hassan 1996). It was possible during these spells to penetrate the tsetse fly zone.

Cattle with sheep reached the eastern Cape by the 4th century AD and are recorded from many Iron Technocomplex sites (Kinahan 1996; see also Segobye, Chapter 12). According to Klein (1984:285), people herding sheep and perhaps also cattle first appeared in the southern Cape Province between 2000 and 1700 bp. A revised chronology for pastoralism in southernmost Africa (Henshilwood 1996:945) indicates that sheep were present at Blombos Cave, southernmost Cape, at 2000 bp. However, the route by which livestock were introduced is still controversial (Henshilwood 1996:945).

The growth of farming and pastoralism south of the equator is the subject of a recent volume published in *Azania* (Sutton 1996). Several contributors to the present volume (Lane, Chapter 10; Segobye, Chapter 12; Hall, Chapter 13) address the change in gender relations related to iron-making agropastoralists in South Africa. According to Hall, the evidence from the Western Highveld indicates that the change to spatial segmentation did not occur until AD 1700. At that time, he hypothesizes, women were spatially and ideologically constrained and men were in control to some extent over most aspects of production and reproduction. Segobye notes that societies in the Limpopo-Shashe basin and eastern Botswana hardveld by the 10th century AD depended on mixed farming. Politically these societies were characterized by ranking on the basis of age, patrilineage, and gender. Incipient state formation might have occurred in certain cases in east-central Botswana between the 7th and 13th centuries AD. Capitals were positioned on hilltops. Lane suggests that early iron makers were more transient than their successors (the Late Iron Technocomplex). He implies that the appearance of more fixed and bounded spatial units was associated with increased concern with controlling female sexuality and reproduction. On the basis of an exemplary study of spatial organization of herders in the Upper Karoo region of South Africa, Sampson (1996) recognizes a system of grazing territories dating back to AD 700, with growing cross-valley ties across the northern end of the study area by AD 1150, followed by a breakdown perhaps caused by drought or overgrazing at AD 1650.

Segobye (Chapter 12), using ethnographic data, discusses probable gender relations in herding communities. She questions the male-centered explanations of spatial and social organization and the overemphasis on cattle. She notes, however, that community leaders are presumed to have been males and the societies were most likely patrilineal. Ranking was probably in order of descent among different male heads.

Segobye suggests that in the face of recurring droughts, either male political leaders increased their control over resources and made more elaborate rituals, or, in a different scenario, communities came together with less differentiation on the basis of ethnicity or gender—the pattern adopted after the Mfecane wars.

The data from South Africa suggest that changes in asymmetric (hierarchical or rank-order) political organization and, by association, gender relations were not synchronous with the early appearance of livestock or farming, and further that such developments were most likely indigenous developments over 700 to 1,000 years. We may recall here that evidence of provincial state societies in Egypt suggests that they developed at the earliest during Nagada I (3800 BC) and were established by 3500 BC, about 1,500 years following the first evidence of farming in the Delta (ca. 5000 BC) and 600 to 900 years after the Badarian (Hassan 1988).

The political events leading to a spectacular nation-state in Egypt began earlier than elsewhere in Africa, in part as a function of the early introduction of farming in the Nile Valley and in part resulting from its advantageous ecological setting and proximity to Southwest Asia, allowing the cultivation of wheat and barley from a large strip of land. In the rest of Africa, a vast continent with varied ecological opportunities, the adoption of pottery making, pastoralism, and iron smithing by different groups at different times with a whole spectrum of subsistence and technological strategies negates any attempt to arrive at a monolithic model of political systems and gender relations that can be said to be Pan-African. The two contrastive examples of gender relations among agropastoralist ironmakers in Kenya (the Abagusii and Agikuyu), reported by Kiriama (1993), should dispel any hopes for a homology with any single ethnographic case study.

MacLean's search (Chapter 9) for general modalities of gender relations associated with certain technologies, rather than an overarching model of gender relations related to phases or cultural modes, may serve as a first step toward an understanding of gender relations in the archaeological past on the basis of certain combinations of gender-specific activities or patterns. Each society may be different from the other in its gender relationships, inasmuch as a certain combination of gender-specific traits may prevail in that society but not in another. Clearly, neither simplistic ethnographic homologies (as most so-called analogies really are) nor direct historical retrodictions are adequate. Instead, attention to context and inferences from archaeological data are highly desirable.

It does seem that pastoralism created the potential for the emergence of societies where males can acquire a special status or rank on the basis of violent activities, through either defending territories or raiding. Pastoralism, as well as farming, also provided the potential for accumulating wealth. And farming and pastoralism both held the potential for expansion through control of land and labor. However, a distinction must be made between horticulture and intensive agriculture (involving plows or great investment in land preparation or irrigation); the first is often associated with female labor, the second with male labor (Nielson 1990:32–45). In horticultural societies, women contribute significantly to food production, and there appear to be three kinship patterns: matrilineal descent with matrilocal residence, matrilineal descent with avunculocal residence, and patrilineal descent with patrilocal residence. Historically, patriliny often followed matrilineal forms (Nielson 1990:32). Polygyny is practiced in slightly more than half of horticultural societies (Nielson 1990:36). By contrast, herding societies are predominantly patrilineal and patrilocal and polygenous, suggesting low status for women (Nielson 1990:41).

As a general model, we may posit that in the initial stages of the transition from hunting-gathering to food production we may be able to recognize a range of different hunting-gathering-fishing-fowling strategies, coupled with either livestock keeping or horticulture or both. In these societies, gender relations are likely to be predominantly egalitarian with perhaps a slight shift in favor of women, as they are likely to engage in horticultural and probably household livestock keeping. This may also be marked by the emergence of ideological beliefs related to the role of women in the cosmic cycle, on account of their association with growing plants and raising animals, an extension of their life-giving and breast-feeding (that is, biological) endowments.

In a subsequent stage livestock keeping may develop, in favorable habitats (e.g., central Sahara, East Africa, and West Africa, and later in South Africa), into specialized herding (pastoralism), perhaps in response to droughts. The emergence of this strategy may have developed independent of farming (e.g., central Sahara), together with horticulture (e.g., East Africa) or in symbiosis with farming (see Gifford-Gonzalez, Chapter 7). In all cases, hunting-gathering-fishing societies continued to coexist wherever conditions permitted in a regional mosaic of different subsistence strategies (see, for example, Smith 1996). Where cattle represented the fundamental livestock, and where large herds can be raised, the effects of episodic droughts would have necessitated territoriality, the demarcation of boundaries, and a marked divergence of the activities of men and women. Matrilineal or bilateral patterns are likely to have developed into patrilineal kinship with a marked asymmetry in the role and status of women. Although the symbolic and ideological role of women might have been maintained, men's control over cattle and their access to higher status through warfare (in raiding or defense) are likely to have led to the tendency to accumulate women as a source of both progeny and political alliances.

With greater demand for farming land to overcome the effects of droughts or in response to the demands of status-seeking pastoralists, more intensive farming involving land clearance might develop, tipping the balance of farming activities in favor of men. Shoenbrun (1993b, cited in Lane, Chapter 10), using archaeological, ecological, and linguistic data, links deforestation and clearance with new territorial conceptions of land use, perhaps as carryovers from the pastoralist sense of territoriality. In the western Great Lakes, Schoenbrun (1993b) recognizes significant changes, including new terms of leadership in the Karagwe Depression. The changes emphasizing cattle were associated with a reduced position of women. Reid (1996:626), in his examination of the Ntusi political organization (a chiefdom?) in Uganda, remarks that both cattle and agricultural production were practiced and that "women were still able to use their ability to grow crops as a platform for negotiation of power."

According to Herbert (1996), the rise of state societies ruled by men (or were they?) at Great Zimbabwe was associated with a strong relationship between royals (male) and smiths (male) in a power pact.

My own work on the beginnings of Egyptian civilization suggests that the rock art at ca. 3500 BC in Nubia, associated with Nagada II ceramics (Hassan 1993), reveals a marked distinction between a schema of women as nursing mothers (more typically as a cow or less often an ostrich) and another for men as hunters (with bows or arrows, sometimes with dogs chasing gazelles or antelopes). I have also gathered evidence (Hassan 1992) in support of early religious beliefs in Predynastic Egypt (ca. 3500 BC) of an association between females and life after death (and an association with water, grain, and cows). In a more recent examination of the textual data on early Egyptian goddesses (in press a), women as goddesses in association with a royal ideology linked with giving birth, nursing, and protection. These traits are probably inherited from a Neolithic past when women in cattle-keeping societies were bestowed with a life-giving role in a developing religious system. It also appears that men were identified with bulls, lions, and dogs as well as hunting and warfare activities consistent with their role as warriors in a specialized pastoralist economy.

Final Remarks

Investigations of gender relations in African archaeology have hardly begun. In the voluminous *Archaeology of Africa: Food, Metals and Towns* (Shaw et al. 1993) there are no more than three entries in the index on gender (one on Kenyan iron makers, another on Tiv farming, and the third on East African Islamic societies). Papers from the 10th Congress of the PanAfrican Association for Prehistory and Related studies (Pwiti and Soper 1996) are equally bereft of studies of gender relations, except for passing references by Smith (1996:474) and Reid (1996:626). This is symptomatic of a general neglect of social issues and an overriding preoccupation with technology, typology, periodization, and site reports in African archaeology. The current volume, by emphasizing gender as a subject, may be regarded more as a step toward a social archaeology of Africa than just another book on gender in archaeology.

The contributions to this volume highlight the need to use ethnographic analogy and historical approaches cautiously, critically, and with discrimination. They also warn against the use of such aids as a substitute for archaeological data and contextual information.

Africa provides a vast reservoir of archaeological riches that defy oversimplistic notions of linear evolution and ethnic encapsulations. The vibrancy of experiences as peoples met, and their inventiveness in crafts, ideology, and social organization that show both fluidity and ingenuity, are truly worthy of clarification and exposition.

Gender is one of many issues that vie for our attention. Other issues should be equally addressed. Social inequalities are closely linked with certain political orders that are marked not only by the degradation of women, but also by slavery, warfare, even genocide. Inequalities that exploit differences in genitals and reproductive functions, also exploit differences in color, religion, dialect, and national origin. Gender issues should not lead us to think that the quarrel is between men and women or that it is simply a matter of biological difference that has engendered inequalities.

OFER BAR-YOSEF AND ANNA BELFER-COHEN ■

Chapter Fifteen

Views of Gender in African Prehistory from a Middle Eastern Perspective

Uncovering evidence for gender-related domains in archaeological contexts is almost a "mission impossible." This statement is especially true if we adopt current attitudes and reject the typecasting of "stereotypic" male–female roles in human societies of the past according to the documentation of present-day ethnographic studies (e.g., Gero and Conkey 1991; and see Wadley, Chapter 4). However, as much as this is sound advice, in reality most archaeologists, including many of the authors in this volume, do use ethnographic data in order to decipher male–female activities from archaeological remains.

In our discussion, we limited ourselves to the Late Paleolithic (mostly referred to as the Epi-Paleolithic) and the Early Neolithic of the Middle East. We chose this time period (from ca.18,000 to 8000 BP), because it seems to be the most comparable to the late Late Stone Age and Early Iron Age in sub-Saharan Africa in terms of cultural complexity. As a result, we were only able to discuss articles in the present volume that deal with hunter-gatherers and early herders and farmers. Nonetheless, it is important to stress that the African archaeological entities are chronologically later in time than those of the Middle East.

There is a growing awareness among Middle Eastern prehistorians of the need to try to decipher the internal dynamics of prehistoric societies. These societies preceded the emergence of urban societies, metallurgy, writing systems, complex bureaucratic organizations, and, later on, empires, all of which occurred very early in that part of the world. The archaeological studies of the Neolithic phenomena in this region indicate that this early florescence is indeed linked closely to social complexity. It is therefore amazing that topics related to the current discussion of social issues, past and present, have not become the focus of prehistoric investigations. Still, a noticeable change has been observed in recent years (e.g., Henry 1985; Bar-Yosef and Belfer-Cohen 1989a,b; Kuijt 1996; Garfinkel 1994; Gopher and Orelle 1996; Cauvin 1994).

Lessons from African Archaeology

One of the main strengths of African prehistory is the presence of rock art (see Parkington, Chapter 2; Barich, Chapter 6) as well as ethnohistorical records depicting foragers and herders and their interactions (e.g., Lane, Chapter 10; Gifford-Gonzalez, Chapter 7; Casey, Chapter 5). In addition, a greater variability of archaeological information is available in African sites in comparison to sites in the Middle East. For example, the ceramic component, considered to be an important source of information concerning production, function, gender, and repertoire of symbols, is missing from the Late Paleolithic–early Neolithic entities of the Middle East. Here, pottery was introduced first to farming communities in the later Neolithic (from ca. 8400 to 7800 BP). It was adopted by forager groups in the semiarid belt only some 2,000 years later, when these groups were on the verge of either becoming herders or being replaced by them. In the Middle East, the period of coexistence of foragers and incipient farmers was of shorter duration than in African regions discussed in the present volume, because of the rapid cultural changes and acculturation processes that brought about the emergence of urban societies some 6,000 years ago.

We agree with Kent (Chapter 3), who warns that it is only in socially/politically complex societies that different gender-specific roles are visible and identifiable. Among hunter-gatherer societies, even when they were sedentary (as in the Natufian culture of the Levant), the division of labor according to gender either did not exist or is impossible to recognize archaeologically.

Even though there are large skeletal samples from the Late Paleolithic and Early Neolithic sites, there is no information concerning the deferential ratio of stable carbon isotopes in male versus female skeletons similar to that used by Parkington (Chapter 2) and Wadley (Chapter 4). This is attributable to several causes, but prominent among them are postburial diagenesis and the antiquity of burials.

In sum, the lack of several lines of evidence from the relevant prehistoric periods in the Middle East precludes gender analyses similar to those presented in other chapters in this volume. Thus, the available archaeological data from the Middle East enable us to explore gender-related issues on a more limited scale.

Middle Eastern Comparisons

As Wadley describes in her article (Chapter 4), a broad-spectrum subsistence strategy prevailed in the Middle East beginning about 20,000 years ago (e.g., Flannery 1973; Hillman et al. 1989; Bar-Yosef and Belfer-Cohen 1992; Kislev et al. 1992). The sizes of Late Paleolithic sites documented in the Middle East, especially in the Levant (e.g., Goring-Morris 1988), reflect the presence of small groups of humans. In the desertic areas, most of the small sites are undoubtedly the remains of short-term hunting camps. The elongated, narrow-pointed microliths, which constitute a major part of the lithic toolkit, are interpreted as indicating the presence of bows and arrows. This interpretation is strengthened in later Natufian contexts (12,800–10,300 BP, uncalibrated) by the presence of shaft straighteners that bear the same burning marks as the typical historical examples known from North America.

If we *do* use ethnographic data, we can suggest that gathering, trapping, and snaring were probably female activities. Unfortunately, plant remains are scarce, with the exception of two well-preserved sites (Ohallo II and the Epi-Paleolithic at Abu Hureyra). In contrast, faunal assemblages are rich in bones of small mammals, reptiles, birds, and sometimes also fish (Tchernov 1975, 1993; Campana and Crabtree 1990; Davis at al. 1994; Garrard et al. 1996). It should be noted that the study of past faunas of the Middle East revealed an absence of large mammals since at least the early Upper Paleolithic. As a result, plant food and small game in such environments were of paramount importance. The hunt of small and medium-sized mammals by male task groups was probably quite important within the social realm, but it was the females who provided the basic subsistence ingredients that assured survival.

The Natufian is the cultural entity that has provided most of the known Late Paleolithic graves, and much literature has been published reporting the various aspects of these burials (e.g., Garrod and Bate 1937; Wright 1978; Byrd and Monahan 1995; Belfer-Cohen 1995; Valla 1995; Tchernov and Valla 1997). Natufian graveyards contain the relics of adult males, adult females, and children of both sexes. Graves were mostly dug pits, some of them lined with stones, and were rarely covered with stone slabs. In a few sites, the graves were marked by small cup-holes or upright, deep, breached mortars. A great variety is observed in the position (flexed or extended), composition (single or multiple), or nature (primary and secondary) of the burials. However, none of these varieties can be attributed to differential treatment according to gender or age. In the Early Natufian (12,800–11,000 BP, uncalibrated), about 10 percent of the dead were decorated, though no patterns have been observed in the choice of the individual to be decorated. The same statement holds true for the Late Natufian custom of skull removal.

The study of the skeletal material demonstrated that 60 percent of the Natufian adults can be identified by gender (Belfer-Cohen et al. 1991). Of these, about 69 percent are males. In many cases, the sexing of the remains, owing to the fragmentary state of the bones (e.g., absence of complete basins), was based on the skulls and the general robusticity of limb bones, which means a bias in identifying male remains. Hence it seems that among the 40 percent of unidentified adults, the number of females is probably quite high. This observation casts doubts on Henry's proposal (1989) that the Natufians practiced female infanticide.

While incipient sedentism is observed among Natufian communities, fully sedentary villages are recorded in the later cultural entities of the Pre-Pottery Neolithic period (10,300–7800 BP, uncalibrated). The Neolithic interaction spheres, where farmers and foragers had mutualistic relationships, has already been noted (Bar-Yosef and Belfer-Cohen 1989a). The need for the meat of wild game in farming communities led to the establishment of game drives in the neighboring steppic belt during the Pre-Pottery Neolithic B period (9300–7800 BP, uncalibrated; Bar-Yosef and Belfer-Cohen 1989a). These drives, known in the Middle East as "desert kites," consist of two converging, low-lying stone walls that lead to an enclosure that served as the killing area (Meshel 1974; Helms and Betts 1987). This organized, communal hunt of gazelles by foragers could be explained as designed to fulfill the demand created by the large farming villages such as Ain Ghazal, where an area of some 12 hectares (Rollefson et al. 1992) accommodated an estimated population of 1,000 to 1,500 people. It is therefore interesting to note that Casey (Chapter 5), considering the importance of protein obtained from game, arrived at similar explanations. She correctly emphasizes that neither sedentism nor animal domestication necessarily reduced the need for wild protein.

Additional similarities can be drawn from Casey's description of what is generally defined as an interaction sphere. In a previous study (Bar-Yosef and Belfer-Cohen 1989a), we indicated that the spread of the same arrowhead types across the Levant (a region of about 200,000 km^2) could indicate interaction among hunters who were either farmers or foragers. Conversely, mundane, or domestic, stone tools such as adzes-axes were produced locally and do vary in their morphology. Most likely, they designate delineated territories within this Neolithic interaction sphere. Indeed, the idea of distinct, well-made projectile points serving as "little packages" of social information is clearly expressed in the finely made Kintampo Late Stone Age projectiles. The African case indicates (Casey, Chapter 5) that these projectiles had a very important function in transmitting information, and that they persist in assemblages alongside less elaborate tools that were used to perform most daily tasks. We agree with Casey's proposal that "people who go into the far bush, or hunt at night, risk coming into contact with supernatural beings, wild animals, and other humans whose territories abut the forests on the other side. . . . Hunting and trapping in the farms and fields is . . . more pedestrian[; it is] not worthy of the elaborate preparations that a 'real' hunter must make when he ventures beyond the limits of the village's fields" (Casey, Chapter 5).

Unfortunately, no parallels for a ceramic industry, such as that of the Kintampo or other Late Stone Age African cultures (Barich, Chapter 6; Casey, Chapter 5; MacLean, Chapter 9), existed in the Early Neolithic context of the Middle East. Thus, it is difficult to weave a tale about only males producing and using elaborate arrowheads while only females were making and using pottery. We can perhaps substitute the ceramics with the rich assemblages of ground-stone utensils, such as mortars, pestles, handstones, bowls, and the like, which are associated with domestic chores of food preparation.

Another point of difference between the Early Neolithic of the Middle East and that of the Kintampo Stone Age industries is reflected in the quality of flaked lithic tools. Although standardization of the Neolithic production of lithics is lower than in preceding Late Paleolithic cultures, and while the microlithic component is absent, there is still more standardization than that observed in the Kintampo assemblages. Perhaps this disparity reflects not only social differences regarding the status of and need for the lithic tools, but also the availability of raw material and local African traditions.

Ample evidence exists from the Middle Eastern Neolithic for the emergence of pyrotechnology for the production of lime plaster (Kingery et al. 1988). This process required the use of special pits, the accumulation of firewood and limestone fragments, and the keeping of fire burning for many hours. Researchers consider this technology as a precursor of copper smelting, which began around 6500 BP, uncalibrated) (Najjar 1994; Levy 1995). It is not impossible that labor division and symbolic connotations involved in the production of lime plaster were similar to those related to metallurgical activities and their social context, as described by McLean (Chapter 9).

The plastering of Neolithic houses enabled the inhabitants to keep them clean. Sections through the floors reveal that they were occasionally renewed. Perhaps the renewal of surface plastering occurred in ritual contexts (Goring-Morris: personal communication). The special treatment of houses during the Neolithic may reflect what Watkins (1990) called the transformation from *house* to *home*. However, when sites were abandoned, floors were often cleaned, and thus the interesting proposal (Lane, Chapter 10) to identify the internal organization of house space with either women or men is impossible to accomplish.

Neolithic plaster was used not only for covering the floors of some of the houses, but also for modeling selected skulls and creating human statues, such as those currently well known from the caches discovered in Ain Ghazal (Rollefson 1983, 1990). The plastered skulls are generally interpreted as the "cult of the ancestors" (e.g., Cauvin 1994). Morphometric descriptions of the skulls indicate that the measurements obtained best fit male skulls (Arensburg and Hershkovitz 1988). Still, definite determinations are as yet unavailable, and treatment of female skulls could have taken place as well. It is worth noting that a large number of the human statues are also genderless. In this respect they differ from the small clay figurines, common since the very early Neolithic, which are mostly female (Bar-Yosef in press a).

In such a Neolithic society, women were probably involved in the following activities: house construction, food preparation, water and wood gathering, planting fields, tending crops, taking care of domesticated animals (which were introduced since 9500 BP; Legge 1996), harvesting, as well as cleaning and refuse disposal, as suggested by Gifford-Gonzalez (Chapter 7). Archaeologists have spent a lot of energy first exposing and later observing and describing house construction and daily activities (both secular and ritual) inside the houses, in the village, and in the fields. During the incipient phase of village communities (10,300–9300 BP), early farmers expressed a level of social differentiation between adults, whose skulls were removed (males and females alike), and children, whose skeletons were left untouched (Bar-Yosef et al. 1991).

We agree entirely with Gifford-Gonzalez (Chapter 7), who notes that "Heightened disease vulnerabilities, combined with lower stock densities for herd-replacement through pastoral alliances, may have made ties to local hunting and gathering peoples a considerably more important risk-reduction strategy for pastoralists. . . . Local foraging groups could offer labor during good years for livestock and local knowledge of exploitable wild foods during bad." A similar explanation was offered by one of us (Bar-Yosef in press b) with respect to the situation during the early part of the Pre-Pottery Neolithic B period (9300–7800 BP). During this time, sedentary farmers relied on local foragers for meat supplies and other commodities obtained in the steppic and semidesertic belt of the Middle East. The possibility that farmers and foragers at that time shared the same mating network is perhaps reflected in the great similarity among lithic assemblages, regardless of the ecological zone in which the sites are located.

Conclusions

In sum, it seems that we have fewer means for determining gender activities in the prehistoric context of the Middle East than African archaeologists who face the same task. Still, the issue cannot be reduced to the simple identification of activity differentiation by gender. Indeed, like Kent (Chapter 3), we believe that not all societies—either past or present—separate space according to gender or function. We also agree entirely when she asks, "What does the ability to state conclusively that men sat here and women there at a prehistoric site tell us about gender during the Stone Age or after it?"

Still, studying the role of the individual, whether male or female, in various social contexts is a new and exciting challenge for archaeologists. As noted by Parkington (Chapter 2), it reflects a transformation in archaeological thought and a shift toward accepting not only ecological or environmental but also social explanations for the changes observed in the archaeological record.

Chapter Sixteen

Reflections on Gender Studies in African and Asian Archaeology

Engendering the past is no simple task, as the preceding chapters have demonstrated with varying amounts of sophistication. This book opens a Pandora's box of questions, releasing not ills, but rather a swarm of nascent possibilities mixed with difficulties. The chapters show that what is interesting about gender, in any place and time, is the variations in possible gender relationships. The "problem" of gender in African pre-history is not "solved" by these chapters—because there is no single explanation, no evolutionary trajectory to help fill in the gaps, no necessary gender arrangements. This situation requires that actual archaeological data be used to discuss gender, and all these chapters respond to that need.

I am far too ignorant about the details of African archaeology to comment on the specifics of the preceding chapters. Rather, I would like to stand back from the content and discuss the ways that gender is approached by these authors, and then offer a few opinions, observations, and comparisons of my own—especially comparisons with gendered work that has been attempted in Asia, where I do much of my work. But it is clear to me that, if intentional archaeological gender studies in Africa are just beginning to be conceived (Gifford-Gonzalez, Chapter 7), then the archaeology of gender in Asia is somewhere near inconceivable (not to say inscrutable).

It is interesting, however, that approaches to archaeology in Africa (at least as exemplified by these chapters) are more similar to Asian archaeological approaches than either are to Americanist or European archaeology. The need to place all sites and cultures in lattices of spatio-temporal frameworks is certainly active in both regions, as is an emphasis on historical frameworks in addition to anthropological ones. This situation can actually work in favor of a gendered archeology, for attention to differences in time and place allow us to engender archaeological sites in a multitude of ways, eschewing evolutionary assumptions about the gender arrangements of both simple and complex societies.

In China and in North Korea, steeped as they have been in historical Marxism, the assumption that matriarchies precede patriarchies is applied to the data whether it fits or not; or more precisely, there is no attempt to verify the assumption and discover whether or not it fits a given site. This practice, while it results in attention to social structure, can hardly count as awareness of gender (for an equally un-gender-aware but otherwise cogent critique, see Pearson 1981). A very small amount of "finding the women" has been done to good effect in Thailand (Higham and Bannanurag 1990; Higham and Thosarat 1994); differences in burial goods have been noted for South Asia (Kenoyer 1995); and some awareness of the masculinist twist to standard explanations has been underlined for Korea (Nelson 1991, 1993). In general, however, it is hard to find *any* kind of theoretical perspective on gender in Asia. An exception is an earlier and rather innocent paper of mine regarding a site nicknamed the "Goddess Temple" in northeast China, which reached for theory but fell short (Nelson 1991). I made a more complex but less gendered argument later (Nelson 1995). These few examples fail to fit into the same categories as those I have extracted from the chapters in this book to discuss.

Therefore, this discussion takes themes raised by the Africa chapters and considers how they might be applied in Asia, given a consciousness of gender issues. Let me say at the outset that I have four specific criteria for adequate gendered archaeology, which have developed as I have read as much as possible about gendered archaeology and have attempted to put gendered archaeology into practice. While some of my own work has breached these four "rules," nevertheless they are useful to articulate as a standard by which to evaluate gender studies in archaeology.

First, gender roles should not be attached to or reduced to biological differences, either real (e.g., women bear and nurse babies) or imagined (e.g., women are passive while men are active, or women are more amenable to boring jobs, or men are natural leaders). Essentializing gender roles cannot reveal anything about cultural differences. To begin by supposing that men always did *X* and women always did *Y*, in all times and cultures, is to sell short both archaeology and gender. If the answers to gendered questions are known ahead of time without any excavations, then why bother to do any archaeology at all? That is simply reading present prejudices into the past. Any kind of statement about the eternal nature of men and women, or about sex differences, is therefore a barrier to discovering gender in the past, rather than an opening wedge. It may *seem* to be a beginning of thinking about gender, but in fact it turns out to be a dead end.

Second, whether or not a division of labor by sex even exists—and, if it does exist, how much flexibility is built into the system—should be built into the question, not used as an assumption about the way the world works. Citing means or tendencies from the Human Relations Area Files is the least likely way to lead to any nuanced understanding of gender in a particular site; instead, it merely imposes an *a priori* solution.

Third, the notion of women as inside persons and men as outside persons (to use the Korean terminology), or the private/public dichotomy to phrase this common assumption another way, is not necessarily a worldwide phenomenon, and it should not be applied to archaeological sites without evidence. Assuming that household objects are associated with women and that external relationships and objects belong to men is failing to ask about the *way* gender works in whatever particular site or culture is under consideration. Examples of women as long-distance traders are not hard to find, as well as instances of women occupying many other public and private roles. If particular activities are to be ruled out for women in a particular archaeological site or culture, reasons relating to that site need to be strictly adduced.

Finally, homogenizing all the women and all the men of any particular culture may approach gender relations after a fashion, but the result is likely to be too simplistic to reach the realities of the past. The possibilities for negotiating gender roles are as interesting as the gender "rules." Questions come to a wondering mind . . . Are specific talents more important than gender? Does age have an effect? How does class cross-cut gender, and which takes precedence? Are different ethnicities represented in this site or that group of sites—and if so, how do they affect gender?

If the above four types of assumptions about biological differences, the division of labor, the pubic/private split, and gender as an absolute category must be problematized, where is it possible even to begin? If the natures of men and women, artifacts, and space cannot be called on to engender archaeology, what can? I agree that artifacts and space can be used, but they need to fit into a theory that is aware of the gender traps and tries to avoid them. This task is not easy, and a certain amount of floundering is to be expected before archaeologists learn how to relinquish the gender assumptions of their own cultures and actually examine the workings of gender in particular past societies. To begin the discussion, a summary of the ways that gender is addressed in the preceding chapters might be helpful.

Finding Women . . . or Finding Gender?

The chapters in this volume address the problem of engendering African prehistory in various ways. A basic question about the way to begin doing gendered archaeology divides these chapters. Answering that the first task must be to find the women, on the one hand (Parkington, Chapter 2), or that is not necessary to know which gender did which activities in order to engender archaeology (Gifford-Gonzalez, Chapter 7), on the other, creates fundamentally different approaches.

John Parkington argues that it is absolutely necessary to know specific details of women and men in order to be able to discuss gender. He therefore looks for definite evidence of sex, in burials and rock art. Barbara Barich (Chapter 6) follows the same strategy *without* making explicit the notion that finding the women must precede a study of gender.

Diane Gifford-Gonzalez (Chapter 7), on the contrary, looks for gender as an organizing principle of the pastoralist societies she studies, and makes a thorough critique of the implicit engendering of archaeology that has occurred in the past—especially the disparagement and/or neglect of whatever artifacts or technologies are presumed to be associated with women.

Other paths of entry into the problem include universalist or "statistically likely" approaches, ethnographic analogy, the direct historical approach, depictions of women (especially in rock art), and burials. References to the Human Relations Area

Files (HRAF) may fall into either the "universalist" or the "statistically likely" category. Rachel MacLean (Chapter 9) relies on the HRAF for her assertion of a universally clear gender distinction in the division of labor, which, as noted above, I find problematic. Since the HRAF data are based on gender-unaware research, they are a frail reed indeed to lean on, as noted by Lyn Wadley (Chapter 4).

Ethnographic Analogy

The use of ethnographic analogy is widely called into play in these chapters. It is used both with and without explicit acknowledgment of potential problems with "reading" ethnography into the past. Some relevant and useful caveats are those by Gifford-Gonzalez (Chapter 7), who sounds a caution about colonial influences on pastoralist societies, and by Wadley (Chapter 4), who points out that new technology, such as guns and horses used for hunting, may fundamentally alter the gender construction of at least that specific activity, whether or not repercussions reverberate throughout the society.

While ethnographies must be used cautiously, they can certainly help steer the wary archaeologist away from overgeneralizing. For example, the detailed recital of the variations in hunting practices, and the possible contributions of women to hunting in these societies, takes a giant step away from the tiresome "man the hunter"/ "woman the gatherer" cliches. Hunting, after all, is more than the simple act of killing an animal, and the ethnographic accounts drawn together by Wadley (Chapter 4) effectively demonstrate the wide variety of ancillary activities that are considered part of hunting by various groups, from sewing to meat sharing to generous behavior. The work of Kent (1995) in the Kalahari has contributed a great deal to this more-nuanced understanding of the overlapping and permeable roles of men and women as hunters and gatherers. I am especially charmed by Kent's report of a Kutse woman using her husband's spear to stir the dinner pot, a delightful example of unexpected overlap of tool function—and one that could not be observed archaeologically. Wadley (Chapter 4) argues for snaring and trapping in the Middle Stone Age of Africa, based on the distribution of both animal bones and projectile points. She suggests that, owing to the small size of settlements, women must have been needed as participants in game drives, a common means of hunting in Africa. Lack of attention to snares and nets used to obtain meat is noted by Kehoe (1990) for Upper Paleolithic sites in France, where only the presence of projectile points is interpreted as evidence of hunting.

Susan Kent (Chapter 3) interestingly reverses the process of searching ethnographies for analogues to archaeological sites. She has revealed a great deal about specific gender dynamics in her own ethnoarchaeological work in Africa, and on the basis of that work she describes what one might find archaeologically in similar contexts, and goes on to interpret some archaeological sites with specific spatial patterns. It is interesting that she disagrees that the Dunefield Midden site was gender segregated (as has been argued by others) and notes that associating hearths with women's work cannot be substantiated ethnographically. Her observations about the lack of gender segregation or its limitations are particularly important.

Rachel MacLean (Chapter 9) uses ethnographic analogy to show which technologies are specifically gendered in Africa, and suggests from this comparison that iron production is reliably male and pot cooking reliably female. She associates pot cooking with women as an extension of breast-feeding, with no archaeological evidence—an unsatisfying and ultimately unconvincing methodology. Her explanations of those genderings are universalist, positing pan-human symbolism, to which I object because archaeological data do not support the idea that universal or pan-human symbolism exists. Rather, the diversity of symbolic meanings in various times and places is as important as the diversity in gender roles.

Other appeals to ethnographic analogy are less specific. Barbara Barich (Chapter 6) assumes that in the Saharan region women are the primary food providers because plant food, shellfish, fish, and small game are more visible in the archaeological record than is the hunting of large animals. She also appears to assume that women are biologically more able to recognize plant species and their growth patterns, by appeal to "ethnographic observation," referenced only with a very general prehistory of women (Ehrenberg 1989) rather than with any specific group or particular observation. Pottery production, too, she genders as female by appeal to ethnographic analogy, in this case using African groups in similar environments, while Rachel MacLean (Chapter 9), on the other hand, also examining African ethnography, finds a more mixed assortment of men and women potters.

The Direct Historical Approach

A full gamut of attitudes toward using history is found in the preceding chapters. Ann Stahl and Maria das Dores Cruz (Chapter 11) use ethnographic analogy to some extent, but argue cogently that historical differences and individual choice have important effects on the outcome of the division of labor. Their nuanced scenario in the Banda area of west-central Ghana is accomplished with the aid of historic documents, and so perhaps is not directly applicable to prehistoric research, though it is exemplary nonetheless. It is particularly notable that Stahl and Cruz make no attempt to gender any whole industry as male or female, but rather note that men and women tend to cooperate in both cloth production and potting, with particular aspects of the production often (but not exclusively) allocated by sex. It is also notable that in some instances, parts of the production are individual, while other parts are cooperative. The shift in location of potting activities is placed into the whole context of endemic warfare and the effects this would have had on women's movements, both to acquire clay and to buy and sell finished pots.

Peter Schmidt (Chapter 8) follows a strategy similar to Wadley's, in examining a number of groups in detail. However, since his selected groups are all African, he is using the direct, historical approach. Schmidt is interested in rituals relating to iron smelting and the gendered ideology expressed through these rituals. He suggests differences through time in both the gender symbolism and the gender relationships in economic activities, and also indicates the specific ways he would expect to encounter these rituals in an archaeological site.

Rachel MacLean (Chapter 9) uses the direct historical approach to gender both pot cooking and ironworking in East Africa, and she finds that the former is consistently female and the latter consistently male. On the other hand, Alinah Segobye (Chapter 12) seems to be suggesting that too much can be made of historic cultures, in this case in reference to animal herding in southern Africa, and demanding that other variables should be taken into account as well.

Diane Gifford-Gonzalez (Chapter 7) makes a critique of the direct historical approach more explicit, pointing out that it is a special case of arguing by analogy, and that the relevant analogues must be delineated clearly. In particular, she notes that the social and ecological environment of the early farmers and herders in Africa was quite different from those that can be observed archaeologically. Furthermore, she asserts, some strategies used by recent pastoralists for smoothing the effects of occasional ecological difficulties were not available to the first pastoralists who came into the area, for the more recent strategies require greater density of pastoralists. Strategies instead would be based on relationships with the local hunting and gathering groups. The local groups might well have found their own subsistence strategies enhanced by the use of containers for cooking, especially the possibility of boiling food.

This suggestion has an echo in the pottery of Incipient Jomon in Japan, dated to 12,000 BP, in which the ceramic containers appear to have been made for cooking purposes long before any evidence of plant domestication (Imamura 1996). Female figurines are made by the Middle Jomon period, and it is surprising that there is as yet little gender work on it, except by Nagamine (1986), who is more interested in the sex of the figurines than their gendered meanings.

Changes in Gender Through Time

It is heartening that most of the chapters in this volume do not expect gender arrangements to be unchanging and eternal, but instead offer several cases of gender change through time, basing their interpretations on both historical and archeological evidence. Parkington (Chapter 2) and Wadley (Chapter 4) suggest changes in southern Africa, based on skeletal evidence, from more similar food habits in men and women to differentiated ones. I will comment more on the differences in their interpretations below.

Segobye (Chapter 12) argues for change in gender relationships in the 7th to 10th centuries AD, as the hunting-gathering pattern of the previous inhabitants in southern Africa succumbed to the intrusive herders. This point of view leads to a more detailed analysis of the likely position of women in societies that follow the Central Cattle Pattern of circular enclosures, thus raising the possibility of diverse gender relations through time. Some sites in the Mokgware Hills, with activity areas for making pottery and smelting iron, suggest that women as potters may have been able to negotiate power better there than in sites where there was no alternative to cattle raising.

Wadley (Chapter 4) makes another important point in noting how change has occurred recently, especially with the introduction of guns and horses, which fundamentally alters the organization of hunting labor. Hall (Chapter 13) notes that the introduction of New World crops had an effect on the values of gendered work in agriculture. Thus it is changes in various circumstances that lead to changes in gender relationships—a much richer approach than a static view of culture can produce.

An Appeal to Agency

Agency has become almost a catchword in postprocessual archaeology, and is appealed to in several chapters, though it is not clear that the authors always mean the same thing. However, as Gifford-Gonzalez (Chapter 7) points out, it is important to consider agency, if for no other reason than that *all* agency has been traditionally accorded to men. Regarding women also as potential actors is necessary for a balanced consideration of gender. Ethnographic accounts of African pastoralist societies, such as that of the Nuer, are said to contain more observations about the cattle than about the women. It is therefore not surprising that two of the chapter titles contain the word "invisible" (Kent, Chapter 3; Wadley, Chapter 4). Barich (Chapter 6) assumes that males were in charge of the herds when animal domestication became important, reducing women to a marginal role. In direct contrast, Gifford-Gonzalez (Chapter 7), also discussing pastoralism, points out the androcentrism inherent in the supposition that women's work in herding societies is only marginal, and goes on to cite studies that demonstrate women as agents in these societies. This is a good example of the difference between *finding women* and *discussing gender*. Barich further supposes, without adducing evidence, that task groups are divided into male and female. Even if there were archaeological evidence for task groups (and it would be germane to know what the evidence is), what reason is there to suppose that they were assigned along gender lines—rather than, say, age or talent or acquired ability? This is not to say that she is wrong, but that the reader needs more information.

Social Organization

Gender can hardly be denied as a part of social organization, hence it is remarkable that it was seldom mentioned in social archaeology before the 1970s, and, as Barich (Chapter 6) notes, social archaeology as practiced at that time managed to thrive without any attention to gender issues. One of the most frequent assumptions has been that of increasing control by men over female labor, without even asking why this should be the case, let alone demonstrating that it exists.

Furthermore, the complementarity of men's and women's roles and activities has been often overlooked, but is a topic specifically addressed in some of these chapters.

Gifford-Gonzalez (Chapter 7) uses sites containing both wild fauna and Nderit pottery to consider social organization and its gendered consequences. Noting two alternative explanations for this phenomenon and suggesting a third, she explicitly teases out the consequences of each. These explanations involve hunter-gatherers who exchanged some products of the wild for pots made elsewhere, groups with mixed economies, and the presence of women from pottery-making groups resident among the hunter-gatherers. Finding that the data are most compatible with the last, she suggests that the groups were relatively equal, and infers that both had much to gain from the closer relationships caused by intermarriage.

The Interpretation of Burial Data

Both Wadley and Parkington note studies that show more positive ^{13}C values for men after 3000 BP. Both of them interpret this as indicating that men consumed more marine food, but Parkington's scenario is based on shellfish, while Wadley suggests sea mammals and fish. These marine sources require quite different means of obtaining the food, though both authors conclude that division of labor by sex must have been operating to produce the bone ^{13}C differential. Wadley believes that shellfish collectors could have been both men and women, but were not likely to have been exclusively male because of the seasonality conflicts with the hunting season (which had to be undertaken in the dry season owing to equipment requirements). Parkington supposes, on the contrary, that the shell mounds were created by men alone. It is interesting that the same data can lead to such different interpretations. Further refinement of the question can lead to even better gender studies.

Depictions of Women and Men

Barich uses the rock art associated with the Saharan sites, called "round head" art, to discuss the activities of men and women. She argues that the diversity demonstrated in the depictions reflects a complex and changing society, and asserts that men and women are shown doing different things, and that women are more often represented than men. Furthermore, the motifs associated with women are the same ones used to decorate pots. A switch to depictions of cattle and a lessening of the number of females in the drawings is said to coincide with the pastoral economy and to demonstrate the importance of herd animals. Parkington also uses rock art, pointing out that the depictions are usually definitive about the sex of the participants in the activities shown, and arguing that therefore this must have been an important category. He then goes on to assume that where men are shown more often than women, they more commonly performed that activity. He interprets the "processional" scenes as rituals with mostly males, including references to trance states, which lead to understanding shamans as being men.

Spatial Patterning

Susan Kent (Chapter 3) demonstrates that the distribution of artifacts and the interpretation of spatial patterning cannot result in a direct attribution of the exclusive use of space by men or women. Intervening variables of storage spaces rather than activity areas, multiple uses by men and women of the same artifacts, and overlapping uses of space make such attributions too simplistic. Rather, Kent advocates careful horizontal excavations followed by interpretations that are sensitive to many possible permutations. Based on these observations, she suggests that not all hunter-gatherer sites will exhibit gender-specific activity areas because not all hunter-gatherer cultures divide space by gender, while Iron Age sites will contain interpretable, gender-specific areas.

Simon Hall (Chapter 13) likewise considers spatial analysis an important key to gender analysis of archaeological sites, and adds to it the way gender boundaries were "symbolically patrolled" by pottery. He marks a specific time period (1700 AD) when women's work increasingly began to be controlled by men. He notes that the Central Cattle Pattern, in which men control the central spaces where women are not allowed, has dominated the interpretation of Iron Age sites in Africa. Women, in contrast, occupy the outer circle, which has domestic uses. Hall's analysis of the change is based on the introduction of low stone walls, physically marking off space, which gradually includes more and more elaborated household space, in turn indicating the separation of gendered work. The control by men over women's work is asserted on the basis of historical causes. It is not clear whether *all* men or only *some* men were thus in control, or whether *some* men (the chiefs?) also had control over some other men's labor. The intensification of male labor and its segregation into workshops suggests the latter.

Gender Symbolism

Interpreting certain motifs as symbolic of men or women is always a risky business, but it can be more convincing when tied to a specific culture by means of the direct historical approach. Even then it can be problematic. Hall (Chapter 13) repeats uncritically the notion that wooden "hut" doors, carved by men, represent women's subordination because they allude to female fertility. An alternate interpretation, not considered by Hall, could be that women celebrate their own fertility, and use it as a counterpoise to men's economic domination—if indeed that exists as thoroughly or as consistently as is often portrayed. Since men carve the doors, it is even possible that men and women have different interpretations of them. Gifford-Gonzalez (Chapter 7) proposes that this notion needs further examination.

Hall also notes differences in the elaboration of pottery decoration, changing from complex painted pottery to much simpler and "bland" motifs. He uses the Azande case in which decorated pottery tends to be used in spaces where both genders are found to suggest a similar meaning to the changes in decoration in the archaeological assemblages. It seems odd to me that the motifs, which he demonstrates are related to women, are interpreted as indicating that women are ambivalent and polluting. This is an example of a male view masquerading as a view of the whole society, for I have never seen it alleged that women pollute each other, and their "ambivalence" comes strictly from a male point of view that perceives women as instruments rather than as *persons*. I find Hall's suggestion that the changing allocation of women's time caused a standardization (and simplification) of pottery decoration to be a more compelling argument, and one that does not depend on an androcentric interpretation, but rather adduces forces that apply everywhere.

Another example of androcentrism is Hall's assertion that men "appropriated the manufacture" of wooden porridge bowls and meat trays, therefore taking control of the space occupied by both men and women, while women taking up new productive work (farming) is *also* interpreted as men's control over women. Change in work patterns cannot be interpreted both ways, depending on which sex is doing it. Furthermore, one might interpret the fact that the wooden artifacts contain the same motifs as the pottery to suggest that women's symbolism was dominant. Instead, Hall interprets the similar motifs as demonstrating men's concern for boundary definition.

Joanna Casey (Chapter 5) escapes this problem of shifting meaning by considering both formal bifacial tools (projectile points) and decorated pottery as carriers of symbolic meaning. She suggests, interestingly, that projectile points are made in specific patterns because they are more likely than any other form of shaped stone to be lost—either misfired at an animal or embedded in an animal that was hit but able to escape the hunter. These points become "calling cards" that can be "read" by other groups utilizing or passing through the same area. Pottery is briefly mentioned as possibly encoding the internal symbolic communication within larger sedentary communities.

Conclusion

Attempts to engender archaeology, as shown by the chapters in this book, result in more rigorous archeology, as noted by Gifford-Gonzalez. For example, these chapters pay closer attention to space, tool usage, food preparation, food acquisition, and productive activities. An awareness of gender creates less homogenizing of the culture and of the sites described. More-nuanced questions lead to a search for more detail in the data. The data may have existed all along—but we have not thought to look for them. Diane Gifford-Gonzalez's expression "methodological androcentrism" is a useful concept for perceiving the blinders that our own gender attitudes have placed on our vision, affecting both what we see as data and (especially) research studies that we view as appropriate. The studies in this book demonstrate that seeking gender creates better archaeology.

Bibliography

Aldiss, D.
1987   A record of stone axes near Tswaane Borehole, Ghanzi District. *Botswana Notes and Records* 19:41–43.

Almagor, U.
1978   *Pastoral partners: Affinity and bond partnership among the Dassanetch of southeastern Ethiopia.* Manchester, England: Manchester University Press.

Amblard, S.
1996   Agricultural evidence and its interpretation on the Dhars Tichitt and Oulalata, south-eastern Mauritania. In *Aspects of African archaeology*, ed. by G. Pwiti and R. Soper, pp. 421–427. Harare: University of Zimbabwe Publications.

Ambrose, S. H.
1980   Elmenteitan and other Late Pastoral Neolithic adaptations in the central highlands of East Africa. In *Proceedings of the VIIIth Panafrican Congress of Prehistory and Quaternary Studies*, ed. by R. E. Leakey and B. A. Ogot, pp. 279–282. Nairobi: International Louis Leakey Memorial Institute for African Prehistory.
1982   Archaeological and linguistic reconstructions of history in East Africa. In *The archaeological and linguistic reconstruction of African history*, ed. by C. E. and M. Posnansky, pp. 104–157. Berkeley: University of California Press.
1984a Holocene environments and human adaptations in the central Rift Valley, Kenya. Ph.D. dissertation, University of California–Los Angeles.
1984b Introduction of pastoral adaptations to the highlands of East Africa. In *From hunters to farmers*, ed. by J. D. Clark and S. Brandt, pp. 212–239. Berkeley: University of California Press.

Ambrose, S. H., and M. J. DeNiro
1986   Reconstruction of African human diet using bone collagen carbon and nitrogen isotope ratios. *Nature* 319:321–324.

Ambrose, S. H., F. Hivernel, and C. M. Nelson
1980   The taxonomic status of the Kenya Capsian. In *Proceedings of the VIIIth Panafrican Congress of Prehistory and Quaternary Studies*, ed. by R. E. Leakey and B. A. Ogot, pp. 248–252. Nairobi: International Louis Leakey Memorial Institute for African Prehistory.

Ameyaw, K.
1965   Tradition of Banda. In *Traditions from Brong-Ahafo*, nos. 1–4. Legon, University of Ghana: Institute of African Studies.

Anderson, G. C.
1990   *Andriesgrond revisited: Material culture, ideologies and social change.* Unpublished B.A. honors dissertation, Department of Archaeology, University of Cape Town.

Anquandah, J.
1976   Boyasi Hill—A Kintampo "Neolithic" village site in the forest of Ghana. *Sankofa* 2:92.

Arensburg, B., and I. Hershkovitz
1988   Nahal Hemar Cave: Neolithic human remains. *'Atiqot* 18:50–58.

Arhin, K. , ed.
1974   *The papers of George Ekem Ferguson: A Fanti official of the government of the Gold Coast, 1890–1897.* African Social Research Documents, vol. 7. Cambridge: African Studies Centre.

1976–77 The pressure of cash and its political consequences in Asante in the colonial period. *Journal of African Studies* 3:453–468.

1979 *West African traders in Ghana in the nineteenth and twentieth centuries.* London: Longman.

1985 Pastoral man in the Garden of Eden: The Maasai of the Ngorongoro Conservation Area, Tanzania. Uppsala Research Reports in Cultural Anthropology no. 3. University of Uppsala, Department of Cultural Anthropology in cooperation with the Scandinavian Institute of African Studies, Uppsala.

1987 Savanna contributions to the Asante political economy. In *The golden stool: Studies of the Asante center and periphery*, ed. by E. Schildkrout, pp. 51–59. Anthropological Papers, vol. 65, part 1. American Museum of Natural History, New York.

1995 Monetization and the Asante state. In *Money Matters: Instability, values and social payments in the modern history of West African communities*, ed. by J. I. Guyer, 97–110. Portsmouth, N.H.: Heinemann.

Arnold, D., H. Neff, and R. Bishop
1991 Compositional analysis and "sources" of pottery: An ethnoarchaeological approach. *American Anthropologist* 93:70–90.

Ascher, R.
1961 Analogy in archaeological interpretation. *Southwestern Journal of Anthropology* 17:317–325.

Aschwanden, H.
1982 *Symbols of life: An analysis of the consciousness of the Karanga.* Zimbabwe: Mambo Press.

Ashton, H.
1952 *The Basuto.* London: Oxford University Press.

Aumassip, G.
1984 Ti-n-Hanakaten, Tassili-n-Ajjer, Algerie, Bilan de 6 campagnes de fouilles. *Libyca* 28–29:115–127.

Bailey, R. C.
1988 The significance of hypergyny for understanding subsistence behavior among contemporary hunters and gatherers. In *Diet and subsistence: Current archaeological perspectives (Proceedings of the 19th Annual Chacmool Conference)*, ed. by B. V. Kennedy and G. M. LeMoine, pp. 57–65. Proceedings of the Annual Chacmool Conferences. University of Calgary Archaeological Association, Calgary.

1989 Significance of the social relationships of Efe pygmy men in the Ituri forest, Zaire. *American Journal of Physical Anthropology* 78:495–507.

Bailey, R. C., and I. DeVore
1989 Research on the Efe and Lese populations of the Ituri forest, Zaire. *American Journal of Physical Anthropology* 78:459–471.

Bar-Yosef, O.
in press a Symbolic expressions in later prehistory of the Levant: Why are they so few? In *Beyond art: Pleistocene image and symbol*, ed. by M. D. Conkey, O. Soffer, and D. Stratman.

in press b Holocene forager-farmer interactions in the Near East. In *From Jomon to Star Carr*, ed. by P. Rowley-Conwy.

Bar-Yosef, O., and A. Belfer-Cohen
1989a The Levantine "PPNB" interaction sphere. In *People and culture in change*, ed. by I. Hershkovitz, pp. 59–72. Oxford: BAR International Series 508(i).

1989b The origins of sedentism and farming communities in the Levant. *Journal of World Prehistory* 3(4):447–498.

1992 From foraging to farming in the Mediterranean Levant. In *Transitions to agriculture in prehistory*, ed. by A. B. Gebauer and T. D. Price, pp. 21–48. Madison, Wis.: Prehistory Press.

Bar-Yosef, O., A. Gopher, E. Tchernov, and M. E. Kislev
1991 Netiv Hagdud—An early Neolithic village site in the Jordan Valley. *Journal of Field Archaeology* 18(4):405–424.

Barich, B. E.
1974 La serie stratigrafica dell'Uadi Ti-n-Torha (Acacus, Libia)—Per una interpretazione delle facies a ceramica saharo-sudanesi. *Origini* viii:7–184.
1990 Rock art and archaeological context: The case of the Tadrart Acacus (Libya). *Libyan Studies* 21:1–8.
1992 The botanical collections from Ti-n-Torha/Two Caves and Uan Muhuggiag (Tadrart Acacus, Libya)—An archaeological commentary. *Origini* xvi:109–23.

Barley, N.
1994 *Smashing pots: Feats of clay from Africa*. London: British Museum Press.

Barnard, A., and T. Widlock
1996. Nharo and Hai//om settlement patterns in comparative perspective. In *Cultural diversity among twentieth century foragers: An African perspective*, ed. by S. Kent, pp. 87–107. Cambridge: Cambridge University Press.

Barndon, R.
1992 *Traditional iron working among the Fipa: An ethnoarchaeological study from southwestern Tanzania*. M.A. thesis, University of Bergen.
1996 Fipa ironworking and its technological style. In *The culture and technology of African iron working*, ed. by P. R. Schmidt, pp. 58–73. Gainesville: University Press of Florida.

Barrow, J.
1801–04 *An Account of travels into the interior of southern Africa in the years 1797 and 1798*. Two vols. London: Cadell and Davies.

Barthelme, J. W.
1985 Fisher-hunters and Neolithic pastoralists in east Turkana, Kenya. BAR International Series 254. British Archaeological Reports, Oxford, England.

Bassett, T. J.
1995 The uncaptured corvée: Cotton in Côte d'Ivoire, 1912–1946. In *Cotton, colonialism, and social history in Sub-Saharan Africa*, ed. by A. Isaacman and R. Roberts, pp. 247–267. Portsmouth, N.H.: Heinemann.

Bates, D. A.
1962 Geology. *In agriculture and land use in Ghana*, ed. by J. B. Wills, pp. 51–61. London: Oxford.

Beall, A. E.
1993 A social constructionist view of gender. In *The Psychology of gender*, ed. by A. B. Beall and R. J. Sterberg, pp. 127–147. New York: Gilford Press.

Beaumont, P. B.
1978 Border Cave. Unpublished M.A. thesis, University of Cape Town.

Bednarick, R. G.
1990–91 Epistemology in palaeoart studies. *Origini* xv:57–78.

Belfer-Cohen, A.
1995 Rethinking social stratification in the Natufian. In *The archaeology of death in the ancient Near East*, ed. by S. Campbell and A. Green, pp. 9–16. Manchester, England: Oxbow Monograph 51.

Belfer-Cohen, A., A. Schepartz, and B. Arensburg
1991 New biological data for the Natufian populations in Israel. In *The culture in the Natufian Levant*, ed. by O. Bar-Yosef and F. R. Valla, pp. 411–424. Ann Arbor, Mich.: International Monographs in Prehistory.

Bender, B.
1979   Gatherer-hunter to farmer: A social perspective. *World Archaeology* 10:204–219.
1985   Prehistoric developments in the American midcontinent and in Brittany, northwest France. In *Prehistoric hunter-gatherers: The emergence of cultural complexity*, ed. by T. D. Price and J. A. Brown, pp. 21–57. New York: Academic Press.

Berglund, A. I.
1976   *Zulu thought-patterns and symbolism*. Uppsala: Swedish Institute for Missionary Thought.

Bernhard, F. O.
1962   Two types of iron smelting furnaces on Ziwa Farm (Inyanga). *South African Archaeological Bulletin* 17(68):235–236.

Berns, M. C.
1993   Art, history, and gender: Women and clay in West Africa. *African Archaeological Review* 11:29–148.

Biesele, M.
1993   *Women like meat: The folklore and foraging ideology of the Kalahari Ju/'hoansi*. Bloomington: University of Indiana Press.

Binford, L. R.
1967   Smudge pits and hide smoking: Use of analogy in archaeological reasoning. *American Antiquity* 32:1–12.
1973   Interassemblage variability—The Mousterian and the "functional" argument. In *The explanation of culture change: Models in prehistory*, ed. by C. Renfrew, pp. 227–254. London: Duckworth.
1980   Willow smoke and dogs' tail: Hunter-gatherer settlement systems and archeological site formation. *American Antiquity* 45(1):4–20.
1981   *Bones: Ancient men and modern myths*. New York: Academic Press.
1987a Researching ambiguity: Frames of reference and site structure. In *Method and theory for area research: An ethnoarchaeological approach*, ed. by S. Kent, pp. 448–512. New York: Columbia University Press.
1987b Searching for camps and missing the evidence? Another look at the Lower Paleolithic. In *The Pleistocene Old World*, ed. by O. Soffer, pp. 17–31. New York: Plenum Press.
in press *Hunter-gatherers of the past*. Princeton: Princeton University Press.

Binneman, J.
1987   Microwear analysis of eight stone tools from Kruger Cave and Olifantspoort. In *Report on the excavation of Kruger Cave*, prepared for the Human Sciences Research Council, ed. by R. J. Mason, pp. 139–57. Johannesburg: Archaeological Research Unit.
in press Naturally-backed knives: A case study in stone tool analysis. In *Eland's Bay Cave: A view on the past*, ed. by J. E. Parkington.

Binneman, J., and J. Deacon
1986   Experimental determination of use wear on stone adzes from Boomplaas Cave, South Africa. *Journal of Archaeological Science* 13:219–228

Bjerke, S.
1981   *Religion and misfortune: The Bachwezi Complex and other spirit cults of the Zinza of northwestern Tanzania*. Oslo: Universitetsforlaget.

Blackburn, R. H.
1982   In the land of milk and honey: Okiek adaptations to their forests and neighbors. In *Politics and history in band societies*, ed. by E. Leacock and R. Lee, pp. 283–305. Cambridge: Cambridge University Press.
1996   Fission, fusion, and foragers in East Africa: Micro- and macroprocesses of diversity and integration among Okiek groups. In *Cultural diversity among twentieth century foragers: An African perspective*, ed. by S. Kent, pp. 188–212. Cambridge: Cambridge University Press.

Blackman, M. J., S. Mery, and R. P. Wright
1989 Production and exchange of ceramics on the Oman Peninsula from the perspective of Hili. *Journal of Field Archaeology* 16:61-77.

Blackman, M. J., G. J. Stein, and P. M. Vandiver
1993 The standardization hypothesis and ceramic mass production: Technological, compositional, and metric indexes of craft specialization at Tell Leilan, Syria. *American Antiquity* 58:60–80.

Bleek, D. F.
1924 *The mantis and his friends*. Cape Town: Maskew Miller.
1931 Customs and beliefs of the /Xam Bushmen 1: Baboons. *Bantu Studies* 5:167–169.
1932a Customs and beliefs of the /Xam Bushmen 2: The lion, *Bantu Studies* 6:47–63.
1932b Customs and beliefs of the /Xam Bushmen 3: Game animals. *Bantu Studies* 6:233–249.
1932c Customs and beliefs of the /Xam Bushmen 4: Omens, wind-making, clouds. *Bantu Studies* 6:321–342.
1933a Beliefs and customs of the /Xam Bushmen 5: The rain. *Bantu Studies* 7:297–312.
1933b Beliefs and customs of the /Xam Bushmen 6: Rain-making. *Bantu Studies* 7:375–392.
1935 Beliefs and customs of the /Xam Bushmen 7: Sorcerors. *Bantu Studies* 9:1–47.
1936 Beliefs and customs of the /Xam Bushmen 8: More about sorcerors and charms. *Bantu Studies* 10:131–162.

Blier, S. P.
1987 *The anatomy of architecture*. Cambridge: Cambridge University Press.

Bodenhorn, B.
1990 "I'm not the great hunter, my wife is": Inupiat and anthropological models of gender. *Etudes/Inuit Studies* 14(1–2):55–74.

Boesch-Achermann, H., and C. Boesch
1994 Hominization in the rainforest: The chimpanzee's piece of the puzzle. *Evolutionary Anthropology* 3(1):9–16.

Boeyens, J. C. A.
1997 Die latere ystertidperk in Suid-en Sentraal Marico. Unpublished Ph.D. dissertation, University of Pretoria, South Africa.

Bollong, C., and G. Sampson
1996 Hunter-forager and herder pottery from the Seacow Valley, South Africa: A technological and functional assessment. Paper given at the Society for Paleoanthropology, New Orleans.

Bollong, C. A., and G. Sampson
n.d. Later Stone Age herder-hunter interactions: A ceramic perspective. In *Technological strategies of African hunter-gathers and herders*, ed. by B. Bouseman. Manuscript submitted to publisher.

Booyens, J. H.
1985 Aetiology as social comment on life amongst Tswana-speaking urbanites. *African Studies* 44: 137–157.

Bourdieu, P.
1977 *Outline of a theory of practice*. Cambridge: Cambridge University Press.
1990 *The logic of practice*. Cambridge: Polity Press.

Bourque, B.
1995 *Diversity and complexity in prehistoric maritime societies: A Gulf of Maine perspective*. New York: Plenum Press.

Bower, J. R. F.
1973 Seronera: Excavations at a stone bowl site in the Serengeti National Park. *Azania* 8:78–104.
1986 Further excavation of Pastoral Neolithic sites in Serengeti. *Azania* 21:129–133.

1991 The Pastoral Neolithic of East Africa. *Journal of World Prehistory* 5:49–82.

1995 Early food production in Africa. *Evolutionary Anthropology* 4:130–139.

Bower, J. R. F., and A. Grogan-Porter

1981 Prehistoric cultures of the Serengeti National Park. *Iowa State University Papers in Anthropology* no. 3.

Bower, J. R. F., and C. M. Nelson

1978 Early pottery and pastoral cultures of the central Rift Valley, Kenya. *Man* 13:554–566.

Bower, J. R. F., C. M. Nelson, A. F. Waibel, and S. Wandibba

1977 Later Stone Age/Pastoral Neolithic comparative study in central Kenya: An overview. *Azania* 12:119–146.

Bozzoli, B.

1983 Marxism, feminism and South African studies. *Journal of Southern African Studies* 9:139–171.

Braithwaite, M.

1982 Decoration as ritual symbol: A theoretical proposal and an ethnographic study in southern Sudan. In *Symbolic and Structural Archaeology*, ed. by I. Hodder, pp. 80–88. Cambridge: Cambridge University Press.

Brandt, S.

1996 Introduction to symposium on the ethnoarchaeology of flaked stone tool use: Gender and ethnicity. Paper given at the 61th Annual Meeting of the Society for American Archaeology, New Orleans.

Brandt, S., G. Hindie, A. Talibi, and N. Walters

1992 Exploratory investigations into the origins and evolution of food producing systems in southwestern Ethiopia. Paper presented at the Society of Africanist Archaeologists Conference, Los Angeles.

Bravmann, R.

1972 The diffusion of Ashanti political art. In *African art and leadership*, ed. by D. Fraser and H. M. Cole, pp. 153–171. Madison: University of Wisconsin.

Brooks, A.

1984 San land use patterns, past and present: Implications for southern African prehistory. In *Frontiers: Southern African archaeology*, ed. by M. Hall, D. M. Avery, M. Wilson, L. Today, and A. J. B. Humphreys, pp. 40–52. Oxford: BAR 207.

Brooks, A., and J. Yellen

1987 The preservation of activity areas in the archaeological record: Ethnoarchaeological and archaeological work in northwest Ngamiland, Botswana. In *Method and theory for activity area research: An ethnoarchaeological approach*, ed. by S. Kent, pp. 63–106. New York: Columbia University Press.

Bruhns, K.

1991 Sexual activities: Some thoughts on the sexual division of labor and archaeological interpretation. In *The archaeology of gender*, ed. by D. Walde and N. Willows, pp. 420–429. Calgary: Chacmool Archaeological Association of the University of Calgary.

Brumbach, H., and R. Jarvenpa

1997 Woman the hunter: Ethnoarchaeological lessons from Chipewyan life-cycle dynamics. In *Women in prehistory: North America and Mesoamerica*, ed. by C. Claassen and R. Joyce, pp. 17–32. Philadelphia: University of Philadelphia Press.

Brumfiel, E. M.

1992 Distinguished lecture in archaeology: Breaking and entering the ecosystem—Gender, class, and faction steal the show. *American Anthropologist*. 94:551–567.

Buchanan, W. F.
1988   *Shellfish in prehistoric diet: Eland's Bay, S.W. Cape Coast, South Africa*. Cambridge: British Archaeological Reports International Series.

Burchell, W. J.
1953 [1822]   *Travels in the interior of southern Africa*. 2nd ed. London: Batchworth.

Burtt, F.
1987   "Man the hunter": Bias in children's archaeology books. *Archaeological Review from Cambridge* 6(2):157–74.

Butler, J.
1993   *Bodies that matter: On the discursive limits of sex*. New York: Routledge.

Butzer, K. W.
1971   Recent history of an Ethiopian delta: The Omo River and the level of Lake Rudolf. *University of Chicago Department of Geography Research Paper* no. 136. Chicago: University of Chicago Press.

Butzer, K. W., G. L. Isaac, J. L. Richardson, and C. K. Washbourne-Kamau
1972   Radiocarbon dating of East African lake levels. *Science* 175:1069–1076.

Byrd, B. F., and C. M. Monahan
1995   Death, mortuary ritual, and Natufian social structure. *Journal of Anthropological Archaeology* 14(3):251–287.

Cameron, C. M., and S. A. Tomka, eds.
1993   *Abandonment of settlements and regions: Ethnoarchaeological and archaeological approaches*. Cambridge: Cambridge University Press.

Campana, D. V., and P. J. Crabtree
1990   Communal hunting in the Natufian of the southern Levant: The social and economic implications. *Journal of Mediterranean Archaeology* 3(2):223–243.

Campbell, A., C. van Waarden, and G. Holmberg
1996   Variation in the Early Iron age of SE Botswana. *Botswana Notes and Records* 28:1–22.

Campbell, J.
1822   *Travels in South Africa undertaken at the request of the London Missionary Society: Being the narrative of a second journey in the interior of that country*. London: Westley.

Camps, G.
1969   *Amekni, Neolithique ancien du Hoggar*. Paris: Mem. du CRAPE X, Arts et Metiers Graphiques.
1974   *Les civilisations prehistoriques de l'Afrique du Nord et du Sahara*. Paris: Doin.
1982   Beginnings of pastoralism and cultivation in north-west Africa and the Sahara: Origins of the Berbers. In *The Cambridge history of Africa, vol.I: From the earliest times to c. 500 BC*, ed. by J. D. Clark, pp. 548–623. Cambridge: Cambridge University Press.

Carsten, J., and S. Hugh-Jones
1995   Introduction. In *About the house*, ed. by J. Carsten and S. Hugh-Jones, pp. 1–46. Cambridge: Cambridge University Press.

Carter, P. L., and C. A. Flight
1972   Report on the fauna from the sites of Ntereso and Kintampo Rock Shelter Six in Ghana with evidence for the practice of animal husbandry during the second millennium, BC. *Man* 7:277–282.

Casey, J.
1993   The Kintampo Complex in northern Ghana: Late Holocene human ecology on the Gambaga Escarpment. Unpublished Ph.D. dissertation. Department of Anthropology, University of Toronto.
1994   Geometric microliths from northern Ghana and notes for a tentative morphological typology. *Nyame Akuma* 40:23–39.

Cauvin, J.
1994 Naissance des divinités, naissance de l'agriculture. Empreintes. Paris: CNRS.

Celis, G., and E. Nzikobanyanka
1976 *La métallurgie traditionelle au Burundi*. Turvuren: Musée Royale de L'Afrique Centrale.

Chang, C., and H. Koster
1994 *Pastoralists at the periphery: Herders in a capitalist world*. Tucson: University of Arizona Press.

Chang, K. C.
1967 *Rethinking archaeology*. New York: Random House.

Chapman, S.
1967 Kantsyore Island. *Azania* 2:165–191.

Chief Commissioner, Ashanti
1926 Tour of inspection in Jaman and Banda Divisions and French Frontier. 22nd February. File 491, Provincial Commissioner's Report, Ghana National Archives, Kumase.

Childs, S. T.
1988 Clay resource specialization in ancient Tanzania: Implications for cultural process. In *Ceramic ecology revisited, 1987: The technology and socioeconomics of pottery*, part 1, ed. by C. C. Kolb, pp. 1–31. British Archaeological Reports, International Series, no. 436.
1991 Style, technology and iron smelting furnaces in Bantu-speaking Africa. *Journal of Anthropological Archaeology* 10:332–359.

Childs, S. T., and D. Killick
1993 Indigenous African metallurgy: Nature and culture. *Annual Review of Anthropology* 22:317–37.

Chippindale, C.
1991a Sexist language in archaeological discourse: A reply. *Archaeological Review from Cambridge* 10(1):102–104.
1991b Editorial. *Antiquity* 65(248):439–445.

Claassen, C. P.
1991 Gender, shellfishing, and the Shell Mound Archaic. In *Engendering archaeology*, ed. by J. M. Gero and M. W. Conkey, pp. 276–300. Oxford: Blackwell.
1992a ed. *Exploring gender through archaeology: Monographs in world archaeology*, Madison, Wis.: Prehistory Press.
1992b Questioning gender: An introduction. In *Exploring gender through archaeology—Selected papers from the 1991 Boone Conference, Monographs in world archaeology*, ed. by C. P. Claassen, pp. 1–9. Madison, Wis.: Prehistory Press.

Claassen, C. P., and R. Joyce, eds.
1997 *Women in prehistory: North America and Mesoamerica*. Philadelphia: University of Pennsylvania Press.

Clark, J. D., J. L. Phillips, and P. S. Staley
1974 Interpretations of prehistoric technology from ancient Egyptian and other sources. Part 1: Ancient Egyptian bows and arrows and their relevance for African prehistory. *Paleorient* 2:323–388.

Cline, W.
1937 *Mining and metallurgy in Negro Africa*. Menasha, Wis.: George Banta Publishing Co.

Close, A. E.
1995 Few and far between: Early ceramics in North Africa. In *The emergence of pottery, technology and innovation in ancient societies*, ed. by W. K. Barnett and J. W. Hoopes, pp.23–37. Washington: Smithsonian Institution Press.

Cobbing, J.
1988 The *Mfecane* as alibi: Thoughts on Dithakong and Mbolompo. *Journal of African History* 29:487–519.

Coetzee, J. A.
1987   Palynological intimations on the East African mountains. In *Paleoecology of Africa*, ed. by J. A. Coetzee, pp. 231–244, vol. 18. Rotterdam: A. A. Balkema.

Collett, D. P.
1982   Ruin distributions in the stone-walled settlements of eastern Transvaal. *South African Journal of Science* 78:39–40.
1985   The spread of early iron-producing communities in eastern and southern Africa. Unpublished Ph.D. dissertation, Department of Archaeology, University of Cambridge.
1993   Metaphors and representations associated with precolonial iron-smelting in eastern and southern Africa. In *The archaeology of Africa: Food, metals and towns*, ed. by T. Shaw, P. Sinclair, B. Andah, and A. Okpokp, pp. 499–511. London and New York: Routledge.

Collett, D. P., and P. T. Robertshaw
1983a   Pottery traditions of early pastoral communities in Kenya. *Azania* 18:107–125.
1983b   Problems in the interpretation of radiocarbon dates: Dating the Pastoral Neolithic of East Africa. *African Archaeological Review* 1:57–74.

Collier, J. F., and M. Z. Rosaldo
1981   Politics and gender in simple societies. In *Sexual meanings: The cultural construction of gender and sexuality*, ed. by S. B.Ortner and H. Whitehead, pp. 275–329. Cambridge: Cambridge University Press.

Comaroff, J.
1985   *Body of power, spirit of resistance: The culture and history of a South African people*. Chicago: University of Chicago Press.

Comaroff, J., and J. L. Comaroff
1981   The management of a marriage in a Tswana chiefdom. In *Essays on African marriage in southern Africa*, ed. by E. J. Krige and J. L. Comaroff, pp. 29–49. Cape Town: Juta.
1991   *Of revelation and revolution: Christianity, colonialism and consciousness in South Africa*. London: University of Chicago Press.
1992   *Ethnography and the historical imagination*. Boulder, Colo.: Westview.

Conkey, M. W.
1989   The structural analysis of Palaeolithic art. In *Archaeological thought in America*, ed. by C. C. Lamberg-Karlovsky, pp. 135–154. Cambridge: Cambridge University Press.
1993   Metaphors and representations associated with precolonial iron-smelting in eastern and southern Africa. In *The archaeology of Africa*, ed. by T. Shaw, P. Sinclair, B. Andah, and A. Okpoko, pp. 499–511. London: Routledge.

Conkey, M. W., and J. Spector
1984   Archaeology and the study of gender. In *Advances in archaeological method and theory 7*, ed. by M. B. Schiffer, pp. 1–38. London: Academic Press.

Constantine, S.
1984   *The making of British colonial development policy 1914–1940*. London: Frank Cass.

Copi, I.
1982   *Introduction to logic*. 6th ed. New York: MacMillan.

Costin, C. L.
1996   Exploring the relationship between gender and craft in complex societies: Methodological and theoretical issues of gender attribution. In *Gender and archaeology*, ed. by R. P. Wright, pp. 111–140. Philadelphia: University of Pennsylvania Press.

Costin, C. L., and M. B. Hagstrum
1995   Standardization, labour investment, skill, and the organization of ceramic production in Late Prehispanic Highland Peru. *American Antiquity* 60:619–639.

Courtin, J.
1969 Le neolithique du Borkou, Nord-Tchad: Actes du Premier Colloque International d'Archeologie Africaine, Fort-Lamy, Decembre 1966, Inst. Nat. Tcha. Scien. Hum., Fort-Lamy, pp.147–159.

Crabtree, D.
1972 An introduction to flintworking. Pocatello: *Occasional Papers of the Idaho State Museum* no. 28.

Cronk, L.
1991 Wealth, status, and reproductive success among the Mukogodo of Kenya. *American Anthropologist* 93:345–360.

Crossland, L. B.
1989 Pottery from the Begho-B2 Site, Ghana. *African Occasional Papers* no. 4. Calgary: University of Calgary Press.

Crossland, L. B., and M. Posnansky
1978 Pottery, peoples and trade at Begho, Ghana. In *The spatial organization of culture*, ed. by I. Hodder, pp. 77–89. Pittsburgh: University of Pittsburgh Press.

Cruz, M. D.
1996 Ceramic production in the Banda area (west-central Ghana): An ethnoarchaeological approach. *Nyame Akuma* 45:30–37.
n.d. Production, exchange and consumption: A multi-scale analysis of ceramics from the Banda area, Ghana. Ph.D. dissertation, Department of Anthropology, State University of New York, Binghamton.

Csordas, T.
1994 *Embodiment and experience: The existential ground of culture and self.* Cambridge: Cambridge University Press.

D'Andrade, R. G.
1974 Sex differences and cultural conditioning. In *Culture and personality*, ed. by R. A. Levine, pp. 16–37. Chicago: Aldine.

Dahl, G., and A. Hjort
1976 Having herds: Pastoral herd growth and household economy. *Stockholm Studies in Social Anthropology* no. 2. Department of Anthropology, University of Stockholm.

Dahlberg, F. ed.
1981 *Woman the gatherer*. New Haven: Yale University Press.

Damm, C.
1991 From burials to gender roles: Problems and potentials in post-processual archaeology. In *The archaeology of gender*, ed. by D. Walde and N. Willows, pp.130–135. Proceedings of the Twenty-Second Annual Conference of the Archaeological Association of the University of Calgary. Calgary: University of Calgary Archaeological Association.

David, N., and I. Robertson
1996 Competition and change in two traditional African iron industries. In *The culture and technology of African iron production*, ed. by P. R. Schmidt, pp. 128–144. Gainesville: University of Florida Press.

David, N., J. Sterner, and K. Gavua
1988 Why pots are decorated. *Current Anthropology* 29:365–79.

Davidson, P.
1988 The social use of domestic space in a Mpondo homestead. *South African Archaeological Bulletin* 43:100–108.

Davies, O.
1966   The invasion of Ghana from the Sahara in the Early Iron Age. *Actas del V Congreso Panafricano de Prehistoria y Estudio del Cuaternario*, ed. by Luis Diego Cuscoy, pp. 27–42. Tenerife, Spain: Museo Arqueologico Santa Cruz de Tenerife.
1967   *West Africa before the Europeans*. London: Methuen.
1980   The Ntereso culture in Ghana. In *West African culture dynamics*, ed. by B. K. Swartz and R. A. Dumett, pp. 205–225. The Hague: Mouton.

Davis, S. J. M., O. Lernau, and J. Pichon
1994   The animal remains: New light on the origin of animal husbandry. In *Le Gisement de Hatoula en Judée Occidentale, Israel*, ed. by M. Lechevallier and A. Ronen, pp. 83–100. Memoires et Travaux du Centre de Recherche Français de Jerusalem, 8. Paris: Association Paléorient.

Deacon, H. J.
1976   *Where hunters gathered: A study of Holocene Stone Age people in the eastern Cape*. South African Archaeological Society Monograph Series no. 1. Stellenbosch.

Deacon, J.
1984a   Later Stone Age people and their descendants in southern Africa. In *Southern African prehistory and palaeoenvironments*, ed. by R. G. Klein. Rotterdam: A. A. Balkema.
1984b   *The Later Stone Age of southernmost Africa*. Oxford: British Archaeological Reports International Series.
1996   Archaeology of the flat and grass Bushmen. In *Vocies from the past: /Xam Bushmen and the Bleek and Lloyd Collection*, ed. by J. Deacon and T. Dowson. Johannesburg: Witwatersrand University Press.

Dei, G.
1988   Crisis and adaptation in a Ghanaian forest community. *Anthropological Quarterly* 61(2):63–72.

Denbow, J. R.
1982   The Toutswe tradition: A study in socio-economic change. In *Settlement in Botswana: the historical development of a human landscape*, ed. by R. R. Hitchcock and M. R. Smith, pp. 73–86. Marshalltown, Iowa: Heinemann.
1983   *Iron Age economics: Herding, wealth, and politics along the fringes of the Kalahari Desert during the Early Iron Age*. Unpublished Ph.D dissertation, Indiana University.
1984   Prehistoric herders and foragers of the Kalahari: The evidence for 1500 years of interaction. In *Past and present in hunter-gatherer studies*, ed. by C. Schrire, pp. 175–193. Orlando, Fla.: Academic Press.
1986   A new look at the later prehistory of the Kalahari. *Journal of African History* 27:1–25.
1990a   Comment on foragers, genuine or spurious? *Current Anthropology* 31(2):124–126.
1990b   Congo to Kalahari: Data and hypotheses about the political economy of the western stream of the Early Iron Age. *African Archaeological Review* 8:139–175.

Denbow, J. R., and E. N. Wilmsen
1986   Advent and course of pastoralism in the Kalahari. *Science* 234:1509–1515.

Deng, F. M.
1972   *The Dinka of the Sudan: Case studies in cultural anthropology*. New York: Holt, Rinehart, and Winston.

Derrida, J.
1967   *Writing and difference*, trans. by Alan Bass. Chicago: Chicago University Press.

Dewey, W., and S. T. Childs
1996   Forging memory. In *Memory: Luba art and the making of history*, ed. by M. N. Roberts and A. F. Roberts, pp. 61–83. New York: Museum of African Art.

Digombe, L., P. R. Schmidt, V. Mouleingui, J.-B. Mombo, and M. Locko
1988 The development of an Early Iron Age prehistory in Gabon. *Current Anthropology* 29(1):179–184.

Dobres, M. A.
1995a Gender in the making: Late Magdalenian social relations of production in the French Pyrenees. Ph.D. dissertation, University of California, Berkeley.
1995b Gender and prehistoric technology: On the social agency of technical strategies. *World Archaeology* 27(1):25–49.

Dombrowski, J.
1976 Mumute and Bonoase—Two sites of the Kintampo industry. *Sankofa* 2:64–71.
1980 Earliest settlements in Ghana: The Kintampo industry. In *Proceedings of the VIIIth Panafrican Congress of Prehistory and Quaternary Studies*, ed. by R. E. Leakey and B. A. Ogot, pp. 261–262. Nairobi: International Louis Leakey Memorial Institute for African Prehistory.

Dorst, J., and P. Dandelot
1970 *A field guide to the larger mammals of Africa*. Boston: Houghton Mifflin.

Douglas, M.
1995 *Purity and danger: An analysis of the concepts of pollution and taboo*. London and New York: Routledge.

Dowson, T. A., and D. Lewis-Williams, eds.
1994 *Contested images: Diversity in southern African rock art research*. Johannesburg: Witwatersrand University Press.

Draper, P.
1975a Cultural pressure on sex differences. *American Ethnologist* 2:602–616.
1975b !Kung women: Contrasts in sexual egalitarianism in foraging and sedentary contexts. In *Toward an anthropology of women*, ed. by R. R. Reiter, pp. 77–109. New York: Monthly Review Press.
1976 Social and economic constraints on child life among the !Kung. In *Kalahari Hunter Gatherers*, ed. by R. B. Lee and I. DeVore, pp. 200–217. Cambridge: Harvard University Press.
1992 Room to maneuver: !Kung women cope with men. In *Sanctions and sanctuary: Cultural perspectives on the beating of wives*, ed. by D. Counts, J. Brown, and J. Campbell, pp. 43–61. Boulder, Colo.: Westview Press.

Draper, P., and E. Cashdan
1988 Technological change and child behavior among the !Kung. *Ethnology* 27:339–365.

Draper, P., and M. Kranichfeld
1990 Coming in from the bush: Settled life by the !Kung and their accommodation to Bantu neighbors. *Human Ecology* 18(4):363–384.

Dreyer, J.
1995 Late Iron Age sites in the Magaliesberg Valley: Jones (1935) stone structures revisted. *Southern African Field Archaeology* 1:50–57.

Dunn, E. J.
1873 Through Bushmanland. *Cape Monthly Magazine* 6:31–42.
1931 *The Bushmen*. London: Charles Griffin.

Dupuis, J.
1966 [1824] *Journal of a residence in Ashantee*. 2d ed. London: Frank Cass.

Dupuy, C.
1993 Primauté du masculin dans les arts graves du Sahara. Nomadisme pastoral et societé. In *L'homme mediterraneen, melanges offerts a Gabriel Camps*, ed. by R. Chenorkian, pp. 193–207. Publ. de l'Université de Provence, Aix-en-Provence.

Dutour, O.
1989   *Les hommes fossiles du Sahara: Peuplements holocenes du Mali septentrional.* Paris: CNRS.

Dyson-Hudson, R., and N. Dyson-Hudson
1970   The food production system of a semi-nomadic society: The Karimojong, Uganda. In *African food production systems: Cases and theory*, ed. by P. F. M. McLoughlin, pp. 91–124. Baltimore: Johns Hopkins Press.
1980   Nomadic pastoralism. *Annual Review of Anthropology*, pp. 15–61.

Earle, T. K.
1987   Specialization and the production of wealth: Hawaiian chiefdoms and the Inka empire. In *Specialization, exchange and complex societies*, ed. by E. M. Brumfiel and T. K. Earle, pp. 64–75. Cambridge: Cambridge University Press.

Ehrenberg, M.
1989   *Women in prehistory.* Norman: University of Oklahoma Press.

Ehret, C.
1967   Cattle-keeping and milking in eastern and southern African history: The linguistic evidence. *Journal of African History* 8:1–17.
1974   *Ethiopians and East Africans: The problem of contacts.* Nairobi: East African Publishing House.

Eldredge, E. A.
1993   *A South African kingdom: The pursuit of security in nineteenth-century Lesotho.* Cambridge: Cambridge University Press.

Eliade, M.
1962   *The forge and the crucible.* Trans. by S. Corrin. London: Rider and Co.

Engels, F.
1942 [1884]   *The origins of the family, private property and the state.* 2d ed. New York: International Publishers.

Erlandson, Jon
1994   *Early hunter-gatherers of the California coast.* New York: Plenum Press.

Estioko-Griffin, A., and P. B. Griffin
1981   Woman the hunter: The Agta. In *Woman the gatherer*, ed. by F. Dahlberg, pp. 121–151. New Haven: Yale University Press.

Etienne, M.
1977   Women and men, cloth and colonization: The transformation of production-distribution relations among the Baule (Ivory Coast). *Cahiers d'Études Africaines* 17(65):41–64.

Evans, K.
1990   Sexist language in archaeological discourse. *Archaeological Review from Cambridge* 9(2):252–261.

Evans-Pritchard, E. E.
1940   *The Nuer, a description of the modes of livelihood and political institutions of a Nilotic people.* Oxford: Clarendon Press.

Evers, T. M.
1981   The Iron Age in the eastern Transvaal. In *Guide to archaeological sites in the northern and eastern Transvaal*, ed. by E. A. Voigt, pp. 65–109. Pretoria: Transvaal Museum.
1983   "Oori" or "Moloko"? The origins of the Sotho-Tswana on the evidence of the Iron Age of the Transvaal, reply to R. J. Mason. *South African Journal of Science* 79:261–64.
1984   Sotho-Tswana and Moloko settlement patterns and the Bantu cattle patterns. In *Frontiers: Southern African archaeology today*, ed. by M. Hall, G. Avery, D. M. Avery, M. L. Wilson, and A. J. Humphreys, pp. 236–247. Oxford: British Archaeological Reports, International Series, no. 207.

Evers, T. M., and T. N. Huffman
1988   On why pots are decorated the way they are. *Current Anthropology* 29:739–40.

Fagan, B. M.
1992   A sexist view of prehistory. *Archaeology* 45(2):14–16, 18, 66.

Fast, I.
1993   Aspects of early gender development: A psychodynamic perspective. In *The psychology of gender*, ed. by A. B. Beall and R. J. Sterberg, pp. 173–193. New York: Gilford Press.

Feierman, S.
1995   Africa in history: The end of universal narratives. In *After colonialism: Imperial histories and postcolonial displacements*, ed. by G. Prakash, pp. 40–65. Princeton: Princeton University Press.

Fell, T. E.
1913   Notes on the history of Banda. Rattray Papers, MS101:7, paper 7. London: Royal Anthropological Society.

Ferguson, G. W.
1894   Mr Ferguson to the Governor, Enclosure 1 in no. 57, W. B. Griffith to Marquess of Ripon. CO 879/41, no. 479, African (West) Correspondence respecting the mission of Mr G. E. Ferguson and the extent of British influence in the hinterland of the Gold Coast Colony. Colonial Office, Sept. 1895. London: Public Records Office.

Flannery, K. V.
1973   The origins of agriculture. *Annual Review of Anthropology* 2:271–310.

Flenniken, J. J.
1981   Replicative systems analysis: A model applied to the vein quartz artifacts from the Hoko River Site. Pullman: *Washington State University Laboratory of Anthropology, Reports of Investigations* no. 59. Hoko Archaeological Project Contribution no. 2.

Fowler, I.
1990   Babungo: A study of iron production, trade, and power in a nineteenth-century Ndop Plain chiefdom (Cameroons). Ph.D. dissertation, University of London.

Frank, B. E.
1993   Reconstructing the history of an African ceramic tradition: Technology, slavery and agency in the region of Kadiolo (Mali). *Cahiers d'Études Africaines* 33(131):381–401.

Fratt, L.
1991   A preliminary analysis of gender bias in the sixteenth and seventeenth century Spanish colonial documents of the American Southwest. In *The archaeology of gender*, ed. by D. Walde and N. Willows, pp. 245–251. Calgary: Chacmool Archaeological Association of the University of Calgary.

Freeman, L. G., Jr.
1968   A theoretical framework for interpreting archaeological materials. In *Man the Hunter*, ed. by R. B. Lee and I. DeVore, pp. 262–267. Chicago: Aldine.

Freeman, R. A.
1967 [1898]   *Travels and life in Ashanti and Jaman.* London: Frank Cass.

Gabriel, B.
1977   Zum okologischen Wandel im Neolithikum der Ostliken Zentralsahara, *Berliner Geographische Abhand* 27, Inst. für physische Geogr. der Universitat, Berlin.
1984   Great plains and mountain areas as habitats for the Neolithic man in the Sahara. In *Origin and early development of food-producing cultures in north-eastern Africa*, ed. by L. Krzyzaniak and M. Kobusiewicz, pp. 391–398. Poznan, Poland: Poznan Archaeological Museum.

1987 Palaeoecological evidence from Neolithic fireplaces in the Sahara. *African Archaeological Review* 5:93–103.

Galaty, J. G.
1977 In the pastoral image: The dialectic of Maasai identity. Ph.D. dissertation, University of Chicago.
1982 Being Maasai; being people-of-cattle: Ethnic shifters in East Africa. *American Ethnologist* 1:25–39.
1991 Pastoral orbits and deadly jousts: Factors in the Maasai expansion. In *Herds, warriors, and traders: Pastoralism in Africa*, ed. by J. G. Galaty and P. Bonte, pp. 171–198. Boulder, Colo.: Westview Press.

Gallay, A., E. Huysecom, A. Mayor, and G. de Ceuninck
1996 *Hier et aujourd'hui, des poteries et des femmes. Ceramiques traditionelles du Mali*. Université de Geneve, Geneva.

Garfinkel, Y.
1994 Ritual burial of cultic objects: The earliest evidence. *Cambridge Archaeological Journal* 4(2):159–188.

Garrard, A., S. Colledge, and L. Martin
1996 The emergence of crop cultivation and caprine herding in the "marginal zone" of the southern Levant. In *The origins and spread of agriculture and pastoralism in Eurasia*, ed. by D. Harris, pp. 204–226. London: UCL Press.

Garrod, D. A. E., and D. M. Bate
1937 *The Stone Age of Mount Carmel, vol. I*. Oxford: Clarendon Press.

Gautier, A.
1981 Late Pleistocene and recent climatic changes in the Egyptian Sahara: A summary of research. In *The Sahara: Ecological change and early economic history*, ed. by J. A. Allen, pp. 29–34. London: Menas.

Gay, L. O.
1956 The geology of the Bui hydro-electric project. *Gold Coast Geological Survey Bulletin* no. 22.

Gero, J. M.
1985 Socio-politics and the woman-at-home ideology. *American Antiquity* 50:342–350.
1989 Assessing social information in material objects: How well do lithics measure up? In *Time, energy and stone tools*, ed. by R. Torrence, pp. 92–105. Cambridge: Cambridge University Press.
1991 Genderlithics: Women's roles in stone tool production. In *Engendering archaeology: Women and prehistory*, ed. by J. M. Gero and M. W. Conkey, pp. 163–193. Oxford: Blackwell Publishers.

Gero, J. M., and M. W. Conkey, eds.
1991 *Engendering archaeology: Women and prehistory*. Oxford: Blackwell Publishers.

Giddens, A.
1979 *Central problems in social theory*. London: Macmillan.
1984 *The constitution of society*. Cambridge: Polity Press.

Gifford, D. P.
1981 Taphonomy and paleoecology: A critical review of archaeology's sister disciplines. *Advances in Archaeological Method and Theory* 4:77–101.
1991 Bones are not enough: Analogues, knowledge, and interpretive strategies in zooarchaeology. *Journal of Anthropological Archaeology* 10:215–254.
1993 Gaps in zooarchaeological analyses of butchery: Is gender an issue? In *Bones to behavior: Ethnoarchaeological and experimental contributions to the interpretation of faunal remains*, ed. by J. Hudson, pp. 181–199. Carbondale: Southern Illinois University Press.

Gifford, D. P., G. L. Isaac, and C. M. Nelson
1980   Evidence for predation and pastoralism at Prolonged Drift, a Pastoral Neolithic. *Azania* 15:57–108.
1981   Evidence for predation and pastoralism at a Pastoral Neolithic site in Kenya. *Azania* 15:57–108.

Gifford-Gonzalez, D. P., and J. Kimengich
1984   Faunal evidence for early stock-keeping in the central Rift of Kenya: Preliminary findings. In *The development and spread of food-producing cultures in northeastern Africa*, ed. by L. Krzyzaniak, pp. 457–471. Poznan: Polish Academy of Science.

Gilbert, C., J. Sealy, and A. Sillen
1994   An investigation of barium, calcium and strontium as paleodietary indicators in the south-western Cape, South Africa. *Journal of Archaeological Science* 21:173–184.

Gilchrist, R.
1991   Women's archaeology? Political feminism, gender theory and historical revision. *Antiquity* 65:495–501.

Gold Coast Colony
1910   Annual reports: *Gold Coast government departments*, CO 98/18. London: Public Records Office.
1918   Report on Ashanti, 1918. *Gold Coast Colony departmental reports for 1918*, CO 98/30. London: Public Records Office.

Goodale, J.
1971   *Tiwi wives*. Seattle: University of Washington Press.

Goody, J. R.
1965   Introduction. In *Ashanti and the Northwest*, ed. by J. R. Goody and K. Arhin, pp. 1–110. Research Review Supplement no. 1, Institute of African Studies. Legon: University of Ghana.

Gopher, A., and E. Orrelle
1996   An alternative interpretation for the material imagery of the Yarmukian, a Neolithic culture of the sixth millenium BC in the southern Levant. *Cambridge Archaeological Journal* 6(2):255–279.

Goring-Morris, A. N.
1988   Trends in the spatial organization of terminal Pleistocene hunter-gatherer occupations as viewed from the Negev and Sinai. *Paléorient* 14(2):231–244.

Goucher, C. L., and E. W. Herbert
1996   The blooms of Banjeli: Technology and gender in West African iron making. In *The Culture and technology of African iron production*, ed. by P. R. Schmidt, pp. 40–57. Gainesville: University of Florida Press.

Gould, R. A.
1978   Beyond analogy in ethnoarchaeology. In *Explorations in ethnoarchaeology*, ed. by R. A. Gould, pp. 249–293. Albuquerque: University of New Mexico Press.
1980   *Living archaeology*. Cambridge: Cambridge University Press.

Gould, R. A., and P. J. Watson.
1982   A dialogue on the meaning and use of analogy in ethnoarchaeological reasoning. *Journal of Anthropological Archaeology* 1:355–381.

Grace, P.
1996   Pottery-making in the Kigorobya area. In *Kibiro*, ed. by G. Connah, pp. 175–183. London: British Institute in Eastern Africa.

Greenfield, H., and T. Jongsma
1997   Ndondonwane revisited: New perspectives on the southern African central cattle pattern. Paper presented at the 62nd Annual Conference for the Society of American Archaeology, Nashville, Tenn.

Griaule, G.
1955 Notes sur l'habitation du plateau central Nigerien. *Bulletin de l'Institute Français d'Afrique Noire Ser. B*, 17:477–499.

Griaule, M.
1949 L'image du monde au Soudan. *Journal de la Societé des Africanistes* 19:81–87.

Grier, B.
1981 Underdevelopment, modes of production, and the state in colonial Ghana. *African Studies Review* 24:21–47.

Grosz, E.
1994 *Volatile bodies: Toward a corporeal feminism*. Bloomington: Indiana University Press.

Guenther, M.
1996 Diversity and flexibility: The case of the Bushmen of southern Africa. In *Cultural diversity among twentieth century foragers: An African perspective*, ed. by S. Kent, pp. 65–86. Cambridge: Cambridge University Press.

Gulliver, P. H.
1955 *The family herds: A study of two pastoral tribes in East Africa, the Jie and Turkana*. International Library of Sociology and Social Reconstruction. London: Routledge and Kegan Paul.

Guy, J.
1990 Gender oppression in southern Africa's precapitalist societies. In *Women and gender in southern Africa to 1945*, ed. by C. Walker, pp. 33–47. Cape Town: David Philip.

Guyer, J. I.
1991 Female farming in anthropology and African history. In *Gender at the crossroads of knowledge: Feminist anthropology in the postmodern era*, ed. by M. di Leonardo, pp. 257–277. Los Angeles: University of California Press.
1995 Introduction: The currency interface and its dynamics. In *Money matters: Instability, values and social payments in the modern history of West African communities*, ed. by J. I. Guyer, pp. 1–33. Portsmouth, N.H.: Heinemann.

Haaland, G., and R. Haaland
1995 Who speaks the Goddess's language? Imagination and method in archaeological research. *Norwegian Archaeological Review* 28:105–121.

Habicht-Mauche, J. A.
1987 Southwestern-style culinary ceramics on the southern Plains: A case study of technological innovation and cross-cultural interaction. *Plains Anthropologist* 32(116):175–189.
1991 Evidence for the manufacture of southwestern-style culinary ceramics on the southern Plains. In *Farmers, hunters, and colonists: Interaction between the Southwest and the southern Plains*, ed. by K. A. Spielmann, pp. 51–70. Tucson: University of Arizona Press.

Haight, B.
1981 Bole and Gonja. Contributions to the history of northern Ghana. Ph.D. dissertation, Department of History, Northwestern University.

Hakansson, N. T.
1994 Grain, cattle, and power: Social processes of intensive cultivation and exchange in precolonial western Kenya. *Journal of Anthropological Research* 50:249–276.

Hall, M.
1976 Dendroclimatology, rainfall and human adaptation in Natal and Zululand. *Annals of the Natal Museum* 22:693–703.
1984 The myth of the Zulu homestead: archaeology and ethnography. *Africa* 54:65–71.
1987 Archaeology and modes of production in pre-colonial southern Africa. *Journal of Southern African Studies* 14:1–17.

1990   *Farmers, kings, and traders: The people of southern Africa.* Chicago: University of Chicago Press.

Hall, M., and T. Maggs
1979   Nqabeni, a later Iron Age site in Zululand. *South African Archaeological Society, Goodwin Series,* 3:159–176.

Hall, S.
1981   Iron Age sequence and settlement in the Rooiberg, Thabazimbi area. M.A. thesis, University of the Witwatersrand.
1985   Excavations at Rooikrans and Rhenosterkloof, Late Iron Age sites in the Rooiberg area of the Transvaal. *Annals of the Cape Provincial Museums* 1:131–210.
1990   Hunter-gatherer-fishers of the Fish River Basin: A contribution to the Holocene prehistory of the eastern Cape. Unpublished Ph.D.dissertation, University of Stellenbosch.
1995   Indicators of stress in the western Transvaal region between the 17th and 19th centuries. In *The Mfecane aftermath: Reconstructive debates in southern African history,* ed. by C. Hamilton. Johannesburg and Pietermaritzburg: University of the Witwatersrand Press and University of Natal Press.

Hall, S., and M. Grant
1995   Indigenous ceramic production in the context of the colonial frontier in the Transvaal, South Africa. In *Proceedings of the VIIIth CIMTEC: The ceramics cultural heritage,* ed. by P. Vincenzini, pp. 465–473. Faenza: Techna srl.

Hamilton, A. C.
1982   *Environmental history of East Africa.* London: Academic Press.

Hamilton, C., ed.
1995   *The Mfecane aftermath: Reconstructive debates in southern African history.* Johannesburg and Pietermaritzburg: University of the Witwatersrand Press and University of Natal Press.

Hammond-Tooke, W. D.
1981   *Boundaries and belief: The structure of a Sotho worldview.* Johannesburg: Witwatersrand University Press.
1993   *The Roots of black South Africa.* Johannesburg: Jonathan Ball.

Handsman, R. G.
1991   Who made the art at Lepenski Vir? In *Engendering archaeology,* ed. by J. M. Gero and M. W. Conkey. Oxford: Routledge.

Hanisch, E. O. M.
1979   Excavations at Icon, northern Transvaal. *South African Archaeological Society Goodwin Series* 3:72–79.

Harako, R.
1976   The Mbuti as hunters: A study of ecological anthropology of the Mbuti pygmies. *Kyoto University African Studies* 10:37–99.

Harlan, J. R.
1992   Indigenous African agriculture. In *The origins of agriculture: An international perspective,* ed. by C. W. Cowan and P. J. Watson, pp. 59–70. Washington, D.C.: Smithsonian Institution Press.

Harpending, H.
1991   Review of *Land filled with flies,* by E. Wilmsen. *Anthropos* 86:313–315.

Hassan, F. A.
1988   The predynastic of Egypt. *Journal of World Prehistory* 2:135–185.
1992   Primeval goddess to divine king: The mythogenesis of power in the early Egyptian state. In *The followers of Horus: Studies dedicated to Michael Allen Hoffman,* ed. by R. Friedman and B. Adams, pp. 307–321. Oxford: Oxbow Books.

1993   Rock art—Cognitive schemata and symbolic interpretation: A matter of life and death. In *Memorie della Società Italiana di Scienze Naturali e del Museo Civico di Storia Naturale di Milano*. Vol. 26, pp. 269–282. Milan: Societê Italiana di Scienze Naturali e Museo Civico di Storia Naturale di Milano corso Venezia.

1996   Abrupt climatic events in Africa. In *Aspects of African archaeology*, ed. by G. Pwiti and R. Soper, pp. 83–89. Harare: University of Zimbabwe Publications.

in press a   The earliest goddesses of Egypt: Divine mothers and royal consorts. In *Ancient goddesses*. London: British Museum.

in press b   Climate and cattle in North Africa. In *African livestock: The new synthesis; Archaeology, linguistics and DNA*, ed. by R. M. Blench and K. C. McDonald. London: University College London Press.

Hastenrath, S., and J. E. Kutzbach
1983   Paleoclimatic estimates from water and energy budget of East African lakes. *Quaternary Research* 19:141–153.

Hastorf, C. A.
1991   Gender, space and food in prehistory. In *Engendering archaeology*, ed. by J. M. Gero and M. W. Conkey, pp. 132–159. Oxford: Blackwell.

Hawkins, A., J. Casey, A. C. D'Andrea, and D. I. Godfrey-Smith
1997   A Middle Stone Age component at the Birimi Site, Northen Ghana, West Africa. Forthcoming in *Nyame Akuma*.

Hayden, B.
1973   Analysis of a "Taap" composite knife. *Archaeology and Physical Anthropology in Oceania* 8:116–126.
1977   Stone tool functions in the Western Desert. In *Stone tools as cultural markers*, ed. by R. V. S. Wright, pp. 178–188. Australian Institute of Aboriginal Study, Canberra.
1992a   Contrasting theories of domestication. In *Transitions to agriculture through prehistory*, ed. by A. B. Gebauer and D. T. Price, pp. 11–20. Madison, Wis.: Prehistory Press.
1992b   Observing prehistoric women. In *Exploring gender through archaeology*, ed. by C. Claassen, pp. 33–47. Monographs in World Archaeology no. 11. Madison, Wis.: Prehistory Press.

Haynes, G.
1977   Reply to Sollberger and Patterson. *Newsletter of Lithic Technology* 6(1–2):5–6.

Headland, T., and L. Reid
1991   Holocene foragers and interethnic trade: A critique of the myth of isolated independent hunter-gatherers. In *Between bands and states*, ed. by S. Gregg, pp. 333–340. Center for Archaeological Investigations, Ocassional Paper no. 9. Carbondale: Southern Illinois University.

Helms, S., and A. Betts
1987   The desert "kites" of Badiyat Esh-Sham and North Arabia. *Paléorient* 13(1):41–67.

Hendrickson, H., ed.
1996   *Clothing and difference: Embodied identities in colonial and post-colonial Africa*. Durham, N.C.: Duke University Press.

Henry, D. O.
1985   Preagricultural sedentism: The Natufian example. In *Prehistoric hunter-gatherers: The emergence of complex societies*, ed. by T. C. Price and J. A. Brown, pp. 365–384. New York: Academic Press.
1989   *From foraging to agriculture: The Levant at the end of the Ice Age*. Philadelphia: University of Pennsylvania Press.

Henshilwood, C.
1990   Home is where the hearth is: An interpretation of hearth associated activity areas and domestic organization at the Dunfield's Midden site, Eland's Bay. Unpublished honors B.A. thesis, Department of Anthropology, University of Cape Town.

1996   A revised chronology for pastoralism in southernmost Africa: New evidence of sheep at c. 2000 BP from Blombos Cave, South Africa. *Antiquity* 70:945–949.

Henshilwood, C., Nilssen, P., and Parkington, J.
1994   Mussel drying and food storage in the Late Holocene, SW Cape, South Africa. *Journal of Field Archaeology* 21:103–109.

Herbert, E. W.
1993   *Iron, gender and power: Rituals of transformation in African societies.* Bloomington and Indianapolis: Indiana University Press.
1996   Metals and power in Great Zimbabwe. In *Aspects of African archaeology*, ed. by G. Pwiti and R. Soper, pp. 641–647. Harare: University of Zimbabwe Publications.

Hesse, M.
1966   *Models and analogies in science.* Notre Dame, Ind.: University of Notre Dame Press.

Higham, C., and R. Bannanurag
1990   The princess and the pots. *New Scientist* 26 May: 50–55.

Higham, C., and R. Thosarat
1994   Thailand's good mound. *Natural History* 12(94):60–66.

Hillman, G. C., S. Colledge, and D. R. Harris
1989   Plant food economy during the Epi-Palaeolithic period at Tell Abu Hureyra, Syria: Dietary diversity, seasonality and modes of exploitation. In *Foraging and farming: The evolution of plant exploitation*, ed. by G. C. Hillman and D. R. Harris, pp. 240–266. London: Hyman Unwin.

Hills, R. C.
1978   The organisation of rainfall in East Africa. *Journal of Tropical Geography* 47:40–50.

Hivernel, F.
1983   *Archaeological excavation and ethnoarchaeological interpretation: A case study in Kenya* 2(2):27–36.

Hodder, I.
1979   Economic and social stress and material culture patterning. *American Antiquity* 44:446–454.
1982   *Symbols in action.* Cambridge: Cambridge University Press.
1986   *Reading the past.* Cambridge: Cambridge University Press.
1989, ed.   *The meanings of things.* London: Unwin Hyman.
1990   *The domestication of Europe.* London: Blackwell.
1993   Style as historical quality. In *The uses of style in archaeology*, ed. by M. W. Conkey and C. Hasdorf, pp. 44–51. Cambridge: Cambridge University Press.

Holden, J.
1970   The Samorian impact on Buna: An essay in methodology. In *African perspectives. Papers in the history, politics and economics of Africa presented to Thomas Hodgkin*, ed. by C. Allen and R. W. Johnson, pp. 83–108. Cambridge: Cambridge University Press.

Holl, A.
1989   Social issues in Saharan prehistory. *Journal of Anthropological Archaeology* 8:313–354.
1995   Pathways to elderhood. Research on past pastoral iconography: The paintings from Tikadouine (Tassili-n-Ajjer). *Origini Preistorica e Protostoria delle Civiltà Antiche* 18:69–113.

Homewood, K. M., and W. A. Rogers
1991   *Maasailand ecology: Pastoralist development and wildlife conservation in Ngorongoro, Tanzania.* Cambridge: Cambridge University Press.

Hopkins, A. G.
1970   The creation of a colonial monetary system: The origins of the West African Currency Board. *African Historical Studies* 3:101–132.

Huffman, T. N.
1978   The Iron Age of the Buhwa District, Rhodesia. *Occasional Papers of the National Museums and Monuments of Rhodesia* A4(3):81–100.
1980   Ceramics, classification and Iron Age entities. *African Studies* 39:123–174.
1982   Archaeology and ethnohistory of the African Iron Age. *Annual Review of Anthropology* 11:133–50.
1984a Expressive space in the Zimbabwe culture. *Man (N.S.)* 19:593–612.
1984b Where you are the girls gather to play: The Great Enclosure at Great Zimbabwe. In *Frontiers: Southern African archaeology today*, ed. by M. Hall, G. Avery, D. M. Avery, M. L. Wilson, and A. J. Humphreys, pp. 252–265. British Archaeological Reports, International Series, no. 207.
1986   Archaeological evidence and conventional explanations of southern Bantu settlement patterns. *Africa* 56:280–298.
1989   *Iron Age migrations: The ceramic sequence in southern Zambia.* Johannesburg: Witwatersrand University Press.
1990   Broederstroom and the origins of cattle-keeping in southern Africa. *African Studies* 49:1–12.
1993   Broederstroom and the central cattle pattern. *South African Journal of Science* 89:220–226.
1996a Archaeological evidence for climatic change during the last 2000 years in southern Africa. *Quaternary International* 33:55–60.
1996b Gender and the central cattle pattern. Unpublished paper presented at the Society for African Archaeology Biennial Conference, Poznan, Poland, September 1996.
1996c *Snakes and crocodiles: Power and symbolism in ancient Zimbabwe.* Johannesburg: Witwatersrand University Press.

Huffman, T.N., and E. Hanisch
1987   Settlement Hierarchies in the northern Transvaal: Zimbabwe ruins and Venda history. *African Studies* 46:79–116.

Hugh-Jones, C.
1979   *From the Milk River: Spatial and temporal processes in northwest Amazonia.* Cambridge: Cambridge University Press.

Hurcombe, L.
1995   Our own engendered species. *Antiquity* 69(262):87–100.

Ichikawa, M.
1983   An examination of the hunting-dependent life of the Mbuti Pygmies, eastern Zaire. *African Studies Monographs* 4:55–76.

Idiens, D.
1980   An introduction to traditional African weaving and textiles. In *Textiles of Africa*, ed. by D. Idiens and K. G. Ponting, pp. 5–21. Bath, England: The Pasold Research Fund.

Ingold, T.
1980   *Hunters, pastoralists, and ranchers.* Cambridge: Cambridge University Press.

Institute of Field Archaeologists
1991   Women in British archaeology—The equal opportunities in archaeology. Working Report 1991, *Field Archaeologist* 15:280–82.

Irigaray, L.
1984   *Ethique de la différence sexualle.* Paris: Minuit.

Isaac, G. L., H. V. Merrick, and C. M. Nelson
1972   Stratigraphic and archaeological studies in the Lake Nakuru Basin, Kenya. *Paleoecology of Africa* 6:225–232.

Isaacman, A., and R. Roberts
1995   Cotton, colonialism, and social history in Sub-Saharan Africa: Introduction. In *Cotton, colonialism, and social history in Sub-Saharan Africa*, ed. by A. Isaacman and R. Roberts, pp. 1–39. Portsmouth, N.H.: Heinemann.

Jacobson, L.
1990   Comment on foragers, genuine or spurious? *Current Anthropology* 31(2):131.

Jacobson-Widing, A.
1991   Subjective body, objective space. In *Body and space: Symbolic models of unity and division in African cosmology and experience*, ed. by A. Jacobson-Widing, pp. 15–48. Uppsala: Uppsala Studies in Cultural Anthropology 16.

Jarvenpa, R. and H. J. Brumbach
1995   Ethnoarchaeology and gender: Chipewyan woman as hunters. *Research in Economic Anthropology* 16:39–82.

Jerardino, A., and R. Yates
1996   Preliminary results from excavations at Steenboksfontein Cave: Implications for past and future research. *South African Archaeological Bulletin* 51:7–16.
1997   Excavations at Mike Taylor's Midden: A summary report and implications for a re-characterisation of Megamiddens. *South African Archaeological Bulletin* 51.

Jochim, M. A.
1989   Optimization and stone tool studies: Problems and potential. In *Time, energy and stone tools*, ed. by R. Torrence, pp. 106–111. Cambridge: Cambridge University Press.

Johnson, M.
1980   Cloth as money: The cloth strip currencies of Africa. In *Textiles of Africa*, ed. by D. Idiens and K. G. Ponting, pp. 193–202. Bath, England: The Pasold Research Fund.

Johnson, T. C., C. A. Scholz, M. R. Talbot, K. Keits, R. D. Ricketts, G. Ngobi, K. Beuning, I. Ssemmanda, and J. W. McGill
1996   Late Pleistocene desiccation of Lake Victoria and rapid evolution of cichlid fishes. *Science* 273:1091–1093.

Jolly, P.
1996   Symbiotic interaction between African rock art studies, ethnographic analogy, and hunter-gatherer cultural identity. *Current Anthropology* 37(3):277–305.

Jones, P.
1978   An approach to stone settlement typology of the Late Iron Age: Stone walling on the Klip River, 27°10′S 29°10′E *African Studies* 37:83–97.

Jones, T. L.
1996   Mortars, pestles, and division of labor in prehistoric California: A view from Big Sur. *American Antiquity* 61(2):243–264.

Jones, T. R.
1935   Prehistoric stone structures in the Magaliesberg Valley, Transvaal. *South African Journal of Science* 32:528–536.

Joyce, R., and C. Claassen
1997   Women in the ancient Americas: Archaeologists, gender, and the making of prehistory. In *Women in prehistory: North America and Mesoamerica*, ed. by C. Claassen and R. Joyce, pp. 1–14. Philadelphia: University of Pennsylvania Press.

Junod, H.
1912   *The life of a South African tribe*. Neuchatel, Switzerland: Attinger.

Kaplan, J.
1987   Settlement and subsistence at Renbaan Cave. In *Papers in the prehistory of the Western Cape, South Africa*, ed. by J. E. Parkington and M. Hall, pp. 350–372. Oxford: British Archaeological Reports International Series.

Katz, R.
1982   *Boiling energy: Community healing among the Kalahari !Kung*. Cambridge: Harvard University Press.

Kehoe, A.
1990   Points and lines. In *Powers of observation: Alternative views in archeology*, ed. by S. M. Nelson and A. B. Kehoe, pp. 25–38. Archeological Paper no. 2. Washington, D.C.: American Anthropological Association.

Kelly, R.
1995   The foraging spectrum: Diversity in hunter-gatherer lifeways. Washington, D.C.: Smithsonian Institution Press.

Kenoyer, J. M.
1995   Ideology and legitimation in the Indus State as revealed through public and private symbols. *Pakistan Archaeologists Forum* 1995(3).

Kense, F. J.
1992   Settlement and livelihood in Mampurugu, northern Ghana: Some archeological reflections. In *An African commitment: Papers in honour of Peter Lewis Shinnie*, ed. by J. Sterner and N. David, pp. 143–155. Calgary: University of Calgary Press.

Kent, S.
1984   *Analyzing activity areas: An ethnoarchaeological study of the use of space*. Albuquerque: University of New Mexico Press.
1987   Understanding the use of space—An ethnoarchaeological perspective. In *Method and theory for activity area research—An ethnoarchaeological approach*, ed. by S. Kent, pp. 1–60. New York: Columbia University Press.
1989a   Cross-cultural perceptions of farmers as hunters and the value of meat. In *Farmers as hunters—The implications of sedentism*, ed. by S. Kent, pp. 1–17. Cambridge: Cambridge University Press.
1989b   And justice for all: The development of political centralization among newly sedentary foragers. *American Anthropologist* 91(3):703–711.
1990a   A cross-cultural study of segmentation, architecture, and the use of space. In *Domestic architecture and the use of space: An interdisciplinary cross-cultural study*, ed. by S. Kent, pp.127–152. Cambridge: Cambridge University Press.
1990b   Activity areas and architecture: An interdisciplinary view of the relationship between use of space and domestic built environments. In *Domestic architecture and the use of space—An interdisciplinary cross-cultural study*, ed. by S. Kent, pp. 1–8. Cambridge: Cambridge University Press.
1990c   Invisible foragers: The archaeological visibility of prehistoric hunter-gatherers. Paper given at the Society for Africanist Archaeology Conference, Gainesville, Fla.
1991a   Partitioning space: Cross-cultural factors influencing domestic spatial configuration. *Environment and Behavior* 23(4):438–473.
1991b   The relationship between mobility strategies and site structure. In *The interpretation of spatial patterning within Stone Age archaeological sites*, ed. by E. Kroll and T. D. Price, pp. 33–59. New York: Plenum Publishing Corporation.
1992a   The current forager controversy: Real versus ideal views of hunter-gatherers. *Man: Journal of the Royal Anthropological Institute* 27(1):40–65.
1992b   Studying variability in the archaeological record: An ethnoarchaeological model for distinguishing mobility patterns. *American Antiquity* 57(4):635–660.

1993a Models of abandonment and material culture frequencies. In *Abandonment processes: Seasonal variation and regional mobility*, ed. by C. Cameron and S. Tomka, pp. 54–73. Cambridge: Cambridge University Press.

1993b Sharing in an egalitarian Kalahari community. *Man: Journal of the Royal Anthropological Institute* 28:479–519.

1993c Invited comment on "Egalitarian behavior and reverse dominance hierarchy" by C. Boehm. *Current Anthropology* 34(3):243.

1995 Does sedentism promote gender inequality? A case study from the Kalahari. *Journal of the Royal Anthropological Institute* (NS) 1:513–536.

1996a Cultural diversity among African foragers. In *Cultural diversity among twentieth century foragers: An African perspective*, ed. by S. Kent, pp. 1–18. Cambridge: Cambridge University Press.

1996b Hunting variation in a recently sedentary Kalahari village. In *Cultural diversity among twentieth century foragers*, ed. by S. Kent, pp. 125–156. Cambridge: Cambridge University Press.

1997 Moving to sedentism and aggregation: Implications and ramifications. Paper presented at the 62nd Annual Conference for the Society for American Archaeology, Nashville, Tenn..

in press a Which came first: Residential sedentism or residential segregation? In *Residual residences: Investigating domestic architecture in an archaeological context*, ed. by S. Steadman and T. Matney.

in press b Egalitarianism, equality, and equitable power. In *Gender and interpretations of power*, ed. by T. Sweely. London: Routledge.

n.d. How egalitarian are highly egalitarian societies?—Variation among Kalahari foragers. Manuscript submitted to journal for review.

Kent, S., and H. Vierich
1989 The myth of ecological determinism—Anticipated mobility and site organization of space. In *Farmers as hunters—The implications of sedentism*, ed. by S, Kent, pp. 96–133. Cambridge: Cambridge University Press.

Kinahan, J.
1996 A new archaeological perspective on nomadic pastoralist expansion in south-western Africa. In *The growth of farming communities in Africa from the equator southwards*, ed. by J. E. G. Sutton. *Azania*: 29–30:211–226.

Kingery, W. D., P. B. Vandiver, and M. Prickett
1988 The beginnings of pyrotechnology, part II: Production and use of lime and gypsum plaster in the pre-pottery Neolithic Near East. *Journal of Field Archaeology* 15:219–244.

Kinsman, M.
1983 Beasts of burden: The subordination of southern Tswana women, ca. 1800–1840. *Journal of Southern African Studies* 10:39–54.

Kiriama, H. O.
1984 Fabric analysis of Nderit ware. M.A. thesis, University of Nairobi.

1993 The iron-using communities in Kenya. In *The archaeology of Africa: Food, metals and towns*, ed. by T. Shaw, P. Sinclair, B. Andah, and A. Okpoko, pp. 484–498. London: Routledge.

Kislev, M. E., D. Nadel, and I. Carmi
1992 Epi-Palaeolithic (19,000 BP) cereal and fruit diet at Ohalo II, Sea of Galilee, Israel. *Review of Palaeobotany and Palynology* 71:161–166.

Kitson, A. E.
1924 Report on the geological survey. *Government of the Gold Coast Departmental Reports, 1923–1924*, CO98/40. London: Public Records Office.

Kjekshus, H.
1977 *Ecology control and economic development in East African History*. Berkeley: University of California Press.

Klein, R. G.
1981 Stone Age predation on small African bovids. *South African Archaeological Bulletin* 36:55–65.
1984 The prehistory of Stone Age herders in South Africa. In *From hunters to farmers: Causes and consequences of food-production in Africa*, ed. by J. D. Clark and S. A. Brandt, pp. 281–289. Berkeley: University of California Press.

Kleindienst, M. R.
1992 Discussion: Expedient technology in global context. Canadian Archaeology Association Conference, London, Ontario.

Klima, G. J.
1970 *The Barabaig: East African cattle-herders.* New York: Holt, Rinehart and Winston.

Koch, C. P.
1994 The Jaragole mortuary tradition: New light on Pastoral Neolithic burial practices. Paper presented at the South African Archaeological Association Annual Meetings.

Koponen, J.
1988 People and production in Late Precolonial Tanzania: History and structures. *Monographs of the Finnish Society for Development Studies* no. 2. Scandinavian Institute of African Studies, Uppsala, Sweden.

Kratz, C. A.
1981 Are the Okiek really Masai? or Kipsigis? or Kikuyu? *Cahiers d'Etudes Africaines* 78(20):3355–3368.

Krause, R. A.
1985 *The clay sleeps: An ethnoarchaeological study of three African potters.* Athens: University of Alabama Press.

Kriger, C.
1993 Textile production and gender in the Sokoto Caliphate. *Journal of African History* 34:361–401.

Kuijt, I.
1996 Negotiating equality through ritual: A consideration of Late Natufian and pre-pottery Neolithic, a period mortuary practices. *Journal of Anthropological Archaeology* 15:313–336.

Kuper, A.
1970 *Kalahari village politics: An African democracy.* Cambridge: Cambridge University Press.
1980 Symbolic dimensions of the southern Bantu homestead. *Africa* 50:8–23.
1982 *Wives for cattle: Bridewealth and marriage in southern Africa.* London: Routledge and Keegan Paul.

Kureishi, H.
1990 *Buddha of suburbia.* London: Faber and Faber.

Lamprey, R., and R. Waller
1990 The Loita-Mara region in historical times: Patterns of subsistence, settlement and ecological change. In *Early pastoralists of south-western Kenya*, ed. by P. T. Robertshaw. Nairobi: British Institute in Eastern Africa.

Lane, P. J.
1994 The temporal structuring of settlement space among the Dogon of Mali: An ethnoarchaeological study. In *Architecture and order*, ed. by M. P. Pearson and C. Richards, pp. 196–216. London: Routledge.
1994–95 The use and abuse of ethnography in Iron Age studies of southern Africa. *Azania* 29–30:51–64.
1996 The use and abuse of ethnography in the study of the southern African Iron Age. *Azania* 29–30:51–64.

Langdale-Brown, I., H.A. Osmaston, and J.G. Wilson
1964 *The vegetation of Uganda and its bearing on land use.* Entebbe: Government Press.

Langdon, J., and P. T. Robertshaw
1985   Petrographic and physico-chemical studies of early pottery from south-western Kenya. *Azania* 19–20:1–28.

Laqueur, T.
1990   *Making sex: Body and gender from the Greeks to Freud.* Cambridge: Harvard University Press.

Larsson, A.
1990   *Modern houses for modern life: The transformation of housing in Botswana.* Lund, Sweden: University of Lund, School of Architecture.

Lathey, G.
1995   Excavations at Irrigasie on the Springbok Flats. Honours project, Department of Archaeology, University of the Witwatersrand.

Leach, M.
1992   Women's crops in women's spaces: Gender relations in Mende rice farming. In *Bush base: Forest farm*, ed. by E. Croll and D. Parkin, pp. 76–96. London: Routledge.

Leakey, L. S. B.
1931   *The Stone Age cultures of Kenya Colony.* Cambridge: Cambridge University Press.
1935   *The Stone Age races of Kenya Colony.* Oxford: Oxford University Press.

Leakey, M. D.
1971   *Olduvai Gorge III.* Cambridge: Cambridge University Press.

Leakey, M. D., and L. S. B. Leakey
1950   *Excavations at the Njoro River Cave.* Oxford: Clarendon Press.

Ledger, H. K.
1968   Body composition as a basis for a comparative study of some East African mammals. Symposium Zoological Society, London, 21:289–310.

Lee, R. B.
1968   What hunters do for a living, or, how to make out on scarce resources. In *Man the hunter*, ed. by R. B. Lee and I. DeVore, pp. 30–48. Chicago: Aldine.
1969   !Kung Bushmen subsistence: An input-output analysis. In *Environment and cultural behavior*, ed. by A. P. Vayda, pp. 47–79. New York: Natural History Press.
1972   Population growth and the beginnings of sedentary life among the !Kung Bushmen. In *Population growth: Anthropological implications*, ed. by B. Spooner. Cambridge, Mass.: MIT Press.
1979   *The !Kung San: Men, women and work in a foraging society.* Cambridge: Cambridge University Press.
1982   Politics, sexual and non-sexual, in egalitarian societies. In *Politics and history in band societies*, ed. by E. Leacock and R. B. Lee, pp. 83–102. Cambridge and New York: Cambridge University Press.
1993   *The Dobe Ju/'hoansi.* 2d ed. New York: Harcourt, Brace.

Lee, R. B., and M. Guenther
1991   Oxen or onions? The search for trade (and truth) in the Kalahari. *Current Anthropology* 32(5):592–603.
1993   Problems in Kalahari historical ethnography and the tolerance of error. *History in Africa* 20:185–235.

Lee Thorp, J. A., J. C. Sealy, and N. J. Van Der Merwe
1989   Stable carbon isotope ratio differences between bone collagen and bone appatite, and their relationship to diet. *Journal of Archaeological Science* 16:585–599.

Legge, T.
1996   The beginning of caprine domestication in southwest Asia. In *The origins and spread of agriculture and pastoralism in Eurasia*, ed. by D. Harris, pp. 238–262. London: UCL Press.

Lemonnier, P.
1989   Bark capes, arrowheads and concorde: On social representations technology. In *The Meanings of things*, ed. by I. Hodder, pp. 156–171. London: Unwin Hyman.

Lepionka, L.
1977   Excavations at Tautswemogala. *Botswana Notes and Records* 9:1–16.

Leroi-Gourhan, A.
1968   *The art of prehistoric man in Western Europe*. London: Thames and Hudson.

Levy, T.
1995   Cult, metallurgy and rank societies—Chalcolithic period (ca. 4500–3500 BCE). In *The archaeology of society in the Holy Land*, ed. by T. Levy, pp. 226–244. London: Leicester University Press.

Lewin, T. J.
1978   *Asante before the British: The Prempean years, 1875–1900*. Lawrence, Kans.: Regents Press of Kansas.

Lewis-Williams, J. D.
1981   *Believing and seeing: Symbolic meanings in southern San rock painting*. London: Academic Press.
1982   The economic and social context of southern San rock art. *Current Anthropology* 23(4):429–449.
1984   Ideological continuities in prehistoric southern Africa: The evidence of rock art. In *Past and present in hunter-gatherer studies*, ed. by C. Schrire, pp. 225–252. New York: Academic Press.
1989   *Images of power: Understanding Bushman rock art*. Johannesburg: Southern Book Publishers.
1993   Southern African archaeology in the 1990s. *South African Archaeological Bulletin* 48:45–50.

Lewis-Williams, J. D., and T. A. Dowson
1988   Signs of all times: Entoptic phenomena in Upper Paleolithic art. *Current Anthropology* 29(2):201–245.
1989   *Images of power: Understanding Bushmen rock art*. Johannesburg: Southern Book Publishers.

Lhote, H.
1976   Les gravures rupestres de l'oued Djerat (Tassili-n-Ajjir). Tome II. *Mem. du Centre de Recherches Anthropologiques Prehistoriques et Ethnographiques* XXV, Alger.

Lightfoot, R.
1993   Abandonment processes in prehistoric pueblos. In *Abandonment of settlements and regions: Ethnoarchaeological and archaeological approaches*, ed. by C. M. Cameron and S. A. Tomka, pp. 164–190. Cambridge: Cambridge University Press.

Livingstone, D.
1858   *Missionary Travels and Researches in South Africa*. New York: Harper and Brothers.

Livingstone, D. A.
1975   Late Quaternary climatic change in Africa. *Annual Review of Ecology and Systematics* 6:249–280.
1980   Environmental changes in the Nile headwaters. In *The Sahara and the Nile*, ed. by M. A. J. Williams and H. Faure, pp. 339–359. Rotterdam: A. A. Balkema.

Llewelyn-Davies, M.
1979   Two contexts of solidarity among pastoral Maasai women. In *Women united, women divided: Comparative studies of ten contemporary cultures*, ed. by P. Caplan and J. M. Bujra. Bloomington: Indiana University Press.

Lloyd, L.
1911   *Specimens of Bushmen folklore*. London: Allen.

Lonsdale, R. L.
1882   Short report on the mission to Ashanti and Gaman 1882. Dated August 2, Enclosure 2 in no. 26. CO879/19 no. 249. *Further correspondence regarding affairs of the Gold Coast.* London: Public Records Office.
1883   West Africa. The roads traversed by Capt. R. LaT. Londsdale. Map Reference MPGG 80. London: Public Records Office.

Lott, B. and Maluso, D.
1993   The social learning of gender. In *The psychology of gender,* ed. by A. B. Beall and R. J. Sterberg, pp. 99–123. New York: Gilford Press.

Loubser, J. H. N.
1985   Buffelshoek: An ethnoarchaeological consideration of a Late Iron Age settlement in the southern Transvaal. *South African Archaeological Bulletin* 40:81–87.
1993   Ndondondwane: The significance of features and finds from a ninth century site on the lower Thukela River, Natal. *Natal Museum Journal of Humanities* 5:109–151.

Lupo, K. D.
1995   Hadza bone assemblages and hyena attrition: An ethnographic example of the influence of cooking and mode of discard on the intensity of scavenger ravaging. *Journal of Anthropological Archaeology* 14(3):288–314.

MacCalman, H. R., and B. J. Grobelaar
1965   Preliminary report on two Ova Tjumba groups in the northern Kaokoveld of South West Africa. *Cimbebasia* 13:1–39.

MacLean, M. R.
1996a   The social impact of the beginnings of iron technology in the western Lake Victoria basin: A district case study. Unpublished Ph.D. dissertation, Department of Archaeology, University of Cambridge.
1996b   Recognizing the social dimension in the Early Iron Age of East Africa. *Archaeological Review from Cambridge* 13(1):61–73.
1996c   Late Stone Age and Early Iron Age settlement in the Interlacustrine region: A district case study. *Azania* 29–30:296–302.
1996d   Socio-political developments in the Early Iron Age of the Interlacustrine region. In *Aspects of African archaeology: Papers from the Tenth Congress of the Pan-African Association for Prehistory and Related Studies,* ed. by G. Pwiti and R. Soper, pp. 497–503. Harare: University of Zimbabwe Press.

Maggs, T.
1976   *Iron Age communities of the southern Highveld.* Pietermaritzburg: Natal Museum.
1980   Msuluzi confluence: A seventh century Early Iron Age site on the Tugela River. *Annuals of the Natal Museum* 24:111–145.
1984   The Iron Age south of the Zambezi. In *Southern African prehistory and palaeoenvironments,* ed. by R. Klein, pp. 329–360. Rotterdam: A. A. Balkema.
1993   Sliding doors at Mokgatle's, a nineteenth century Tswana town in the central Transvaal. *South African Archaeological Bulletin* 48:32–36.
1994–95   The Early Iron Age in the extreme south: Some patterns and problems. *Azania* 29–30:171–178.

Maier, D. J. E.
1995   Persistence of precolonial patterns of production: Cotton in German Togoland, 1800–1914. In *Cotton, colonialism, and social history in Sub-Saharan Africa,* ed. by A. Isaacman and R. Roberts, pp. 71–95. Portsmouth, N.H.: Heinemann.

Manhire, A. H.
1981   Rock art of the Sandveld. Unpublished honours thesis, Department of Archaeology, University of Cape Town.

Manson, A.
1995   Conflict in the western highveld/southern Kalahari c. 1750–1820. In *The Mfecane aftermath: Reconstructive debates in southern African history*, ed. by C. Hamilton, pp. 351–361. Johannesburg and Pietermaritzburg: University of the Witwatersrand Press and University of Natal Press.

Mapunda, B. B.
1995   An archaeological view of the history and variation of iron working in southwestern Tanzania. Ph.D. dissertation, University of Florida.

Marean, C. W.
1990   Late Quaternary paleoenvironments and faunal exploitation in East Africa. Ph.D. dissertation, University of California.
1992a Hunter to herder: Large mammal remains from the hunter-gatherer occupation at Enkapuna Ya Muto rock-shelter, central Rift, Kenya. *African Archaeological Review* 10:65–128.
1992b Implications of Late Quaternary mammalian fauna from Lukenya Hill (south-central Kenya) for paleoenvironmental change and faunal extinctions. *Quaternary Research* 37:239–255.

Marean, C. W., and D. Gifford-Gonzalez
1991   Late Quaternary extinct ungulates of East Africa and paleoenvironmental implications. *Nature* 350:418–420.

Marks, S.
1967   The rise of the Zulu kingdom. In *The middle ages of African history*, ed. by R. Oliver, pp. 85–91. London: Oxford University Press.

Marquardt, W. H.
1985   Complexity and scale in the study of fisher-hunter-gatherers: An example from the eastern United States. In *Prehistoric hunter-gatherers: The emergence of cultural complexity*, ed. by T. D. Price and J. A. Brown, pp. 59–98. New York: Academic Press.

Marshall, F. B.
in press The origins and spread of domestic animals in East Africa. In *African livestock: The new synthesis, archaeology, linguistics, DNA*, ed. by K. MacDonald and R. Blench.

Marshall, F. B., and P. T. Robertshaw.
1982   Preliminary report on archaeological research in the Loita-Mara region, southwest Kenya. *Azania* 17:173–180.

Marshall, L.
1957   N!ow. *Africa* 27:232–40
1976   *The !Kung of Nyae Nyae*. Cambridge: Harvard University Press.

Masao, F. T.
1982   On the possible use of unshaped flakes: An ethno-historical approach from central Tanzania. *Ethnos* 47:262–270.

Mason, R. J.
1968   Transvaal and Natal Iron Age settlement revealed by aerial photography and excavation. *African Studies* 27:167–180.
1969   Iron Age artefacts from Olifantspoort, Rustenburg District and Kaditshwene, Zeerust District. *South African Journal of Science* 65:41–44.
1972   Locational models of Transvaal Iron Age settlements. In *Models in archaeology*, ed. by D. L. Clarke, pp. 871–885. London: Methuen.
1981   Early Iron Age settlement at Broederstroom 24/73, Transvaal, South Africa. *South African Journal of Science* 77:401–416.
1983   "Oori" or "Moloko"? The origins of the Sotho-Tswana on the evidence of the Iron Age of the Transvaal. *South African Journal of Science* 79:261.

1986 Origins of Black people of Johannesburg and the southern western central Transvaal, AD 350–1880. Johannesburg: *Occasional Paper 16 of the Archaeological Research Unit*, University of the Witwatersrand.
1988 Kruger Cave. Johannesburg: *Occasional Paper 17 of the Archaeological Research Unit*, University of the Witwatersrand.

Matumo, Z. I.
1993 *Setswana-English-Setswana dictionary*. Gaborone: Macmillan Boleswa.

Maurer, B.
1991 Feminist challenges to archaeology: Avoiding an epistemology of the "other." In *The archaeology of gender*, ed. by D. Walde and N. Willows, pp. 414–419. Calgary: Chacmool Archaeological Association of the University of Calgary.

Mazel, A. D.
1987 The archaeological past from the changing present: Towards a critical assessment of South African Later Stone Age studies from the early 1960's to the early 1980's. In *Papers in the prehistory of the Western Cape, South Africa*, ed. by J. E. Parkington and M. Hall, pp. 504–529. Oxford: British Archaeological Reports International Series.
1989 People making history: The last ten thousand years of hunter-gatherer communities in the Thukela Basin. *Natal Museum Journal of Humanities* 1:1–168.

Mazel, A. D., and J. E. Parkington
1981 Stone tools and resources: A case study from southern Africa. *World Archaeology* 13(1):16–30.

McCabe, J. T., J. Weinpahl, and N. Dyson-Hudson
1982 The role of goats in the South Turkana nomadic subsistence system. In *Proceedings of the Third International Conference on Goat Production and Disease*, ed. by J. L. Ayers and W. C. Foote, p. 573. Scottsdale, Ariz.: Dairy Goat Journal.

McCall, D. F.
1970 Wolf courts girl: The equivalence of hunting and mating in Bushman thought. *Ohio University Papers in International Studies, Africa Series*, 7.

McIntosh, R.
1976 Finding lost walls on archaeological sites—The Hani model. *Sankofa* (The Legon Journal of Archaeological and Historical Studies, University of Ghana) 2:45–53.

McIntosh, S. K., and R. J. McIntosh.
1983 Current directions in West African prehistory. *Annual Review of Anthropology* 12:215–258.

Meeker, M. E.
1989 *The pastoral son and the spirit of patriarchy: Religion, society, and person among East African stock keepers*. Madison: University of Wisconsin Press.

Mehlman, M. J.
1989 Late Quaternary archaeological sequences in northern Tanzania. Ph.D. dissertation, University of Illinois.

Merrick, H. V., and F. H. Brown
1984 Obsidian sources and patterns of source utilization in Kenya and northern Tanzania. *African Archaeological Review* 2:129–152.

Merrick, H. V., and M. C. Monaghan
1984 The date of cremated burials in Njoro River Cave. *Azania* 19:7–11.

Meshel, Z.
1974 New data about the "desert kites." *Tel Aviv* 1:129–143.

Meskell, L.
1995 Goddesses, Gimbutas and "new age" archaeology. *Antiquity* 69:74–86.

Miller, B. D.
1993 ed.   *Sex and gender hierarchies.* Cambridge: Cambridge University Press.

Miller, D.
1995   *Material culture and mass consumption.* Oxford: Blackwell.

Miller, D. E., and N. J. van der Merwe
1994   Early metal working in Sub-Saharan Africa: A review of recent research. *Journal of African History* 35(1):1–36.

Mitchell, P.
1988   The Late Pleistocene early microlithic assemblages of southern Africa. *World Archaeology* 20:27–39.

Mogapi, K.
1990   *Ngwao ya Setswana* (Setswana culture). Mabopane, South Africa: L. Z. Sikwane Publishers.

Monnig, H. O.
1967   *The Pedi.* Pretoria: Van Schaik.

Moore, H.L.
1982   The interpretation of spatial patterning in settlement residues. In *Symbolic and structural archaeology*, ed. by I. Hodder, pp. 74–79. Cambridge: Cambridge University Press.

1986   *Space, text and gender: An anthropological study of the Marakwet of Kenya.* Cambridge: Cambridge University Press.

1991   Epilogue. In *Engendering archaeology: Women and prehistory*, ed. by J. M. Gero and M. W. Conkey, pp. 407–411. Oxford: Blackwell.

1994   *A passion for difference: Essays in anthropology and gender.* Bloomington: Indiana University Press.

Moore, H. L., and M. Vaughan
1994   *Cutting down trees: Gender, nutrition, and agricultural change in the Northern Province of Zambia, 1890–1990.* Portsmouth, N.H.: Heinemann.

Mori, F.
1971   Proposta per una attribuzione alla fine del pleistocene delle incisioni della fase più antica dell'arte rupestre sahariana. *Origini* v:7–20.

Muhammed, A.
1977   The Samorian occupation of Bondoukou: An indigenous view. *International Journal of African Historical Studies* 10:242–258.

Muhly, F., and P. R. Schmidt
1988   Film script for *The tree of iron.* Gainesville, Fla.: Foundation for African Prehistory and Archaeology.

Munson, P. J.
1976   Archaeological data on the origin of cultivation in the southwestern Sahara and their implications for West Africa. In *Origins of African plant domestication*, ed. by J. R. Harlan, J. M. de Wet, and A. Stemler, pp. 197–209. The Hague: Mouton.

Murdock, G. P., and C. Provost
1973   Factors in the division of labour by sex: A cross-cultural analysis. *Ethnology* 12:203–225.

Mushi, E. Z., and F. R. Rurangirwa
1981   Epidemiology of bovine malignant catarrhal fevers, a review. *Veterinary Research Communications* 5(2):127–142.

Myers, A.
1989   Reliable and maintainable technologies in the Mesolithic of mainland Britain. In *Time, energy and stone tools*, ed. by R. Torrence, pp. 78–91. Cambridge: Cambridge University Press.

Nagamine, M.
1986 Clay figures and Jomon society. In *Windows on the Japanese past*, ed. by R. J. Pearson. Ann Arbor: Center for Japanese Studies, University of Michigan.

Najjar, M.
1994 Ghwair I, a Neolithic site in Wadi Feinan, the Near East. *Antiquity* iv:75–85.

Nelson, C. M.
1980 The Elmenteitan lithic industry. In *Proceedings of the VIIIth Panafrican Congress of Prehistory and Quaternary Studies*, ed. by R. E. Leakey and B. A. Ogot, pp. 275–278. Nairobi: International Louis Leakey Memorial Institute for African Prehistory.

Nelson, S. M.
1991 The "Goddess Temple" and the status of women at Niuheliang, China. In *The archaeology of gender*, ed. by N. Walde and D. Willows, pp. 220–225. Proceedings of the Twenty-Second Annual Conference of the Archaeological Association of the University of Calgary. Calgary: University of Calgary Archaeological Association.
1993 Gender hierarchies and the queens of Silla. In *Sex and gender hierarchies*, ed. by Barbara D. Miller, pp. 297–315. Cambridge: Cambridge University Press.
1995 Ritualized pigs and the origins of complex society: Hypotheses regarding the Hongshan culture. *Early China* 20:1–16.
1997 *Gender in Archaeology: Analyzing Power and Prestige*. Walnut Creek, Calif.: AltaMira Press.

Neville, D. E.
1996 European impacts of the Seacrow River valley and its hunter-gatherer inhabitants, AD 1770–1900. Unpublished M.A. thesis, Department of Archaeology, University of Cape Town.

Nielson, J. M.
1990 *Sex and gender in society: Perspective on stratification*. Prospect Heights, Ill.: Waveland Press.

Northcott, H. P.
1899 *Report on the northern territories of the Gold Coast*. Intelligence Division, War Office. London: Her Majesty's Stationery Office.

O'Brien, M. J.
1977 Intrasite variability in a Middle Mississippian community. Ph.D. dissertation, University of Texas.

O'Brien, P.
1990 Evidence for the antiquity of gender roles in the central plains tradition. In *Powers of observation: Alternative views in archaeology*, ed. by S. Nelson and A. Kehoe, pp. 61–72. Archaeological Papers of the American Anthropological Association, no. 2, Washington, D.C.

O'Connell, J. F., K. Hawkes, and N. Blurton-Jones
1988 Hadza hunting, butchering, and bone transport and their archaeological implications. *Journal of Anthropological Research* 44(2):113–161.

Odell, G.
1979 A new and improved system for the retrieval of functional information from microscopic observations of chipped stone tools. In *Lithic use-wear analysis*, ed. by B. Hayden, pp. 229–233. New York: Academic Press.

Odell, G., and F. Odell-Vereecken
1980 Verifying the reliability of lithic use wear assessment by "blind tests": The low-power approach. *Journal of Field Archaeology* 7(1):87–120.

Odner, K.
1972 Excavations at Narosura, a stone bowl site in the southern Kenya Highlands. *Azania* 6:25–92.

Okeke, C. S.
1980   Use of traditional textiles among the Aniocha Igbo of mid-western Nigeria. In *Textiles of Africa*, ed. by D. Idiens and K. G. Ponting, pp. 108–118. Bath, England: The Pasold Research Fund.

Orpen, J. M.
1974   A glimpse into the mythology of the Maluti Bushmen. *Cape Monthly Magazine* (n.s.) 9(49):1–3.

Osaki, M.
1984   The social influence of change in hunting technique among the central Kalahari San. *African Study Monographs* 5:49–62.

Parkington, J. E.
1972   Seasonal mobility in the Later Stone Age. *African Studies* 31:223–243.
1977   Soaqua: Hunter-fisher-gatherers of the Olifants River, western Cape. *South African Archaeological Bulletin* 32:150–157.
1980   Time and place: Some observations on spatial and temporal patterning in the Later Stone Age sequence in southern Africa. *South African Archaeological Bulletin* 35:73–83.
1984   Soaqua and Bushmen: Hunters and robbers. In *Past and present in hunter gatherer studies*, ed. by C. Shrire, pp. 151–174. New York: Academic Press.
1986   Comment on J. Sealy and N. J. van der Merwe. Isotope assessment and the seasonal mobility hypothesis in the southwestern Cape of South Africa. *Current Anthropology* 27(2):145–146.
1988   The Pleistocene/Holocene transition in the western Cape, South Africa: Observations from Verlorenvlei. In *Prehistoric cultures and environments in the Late Quaternary of Africa*, ed. by J. Bower and D. Lubell. Oxford: British Archaeological Reports International Series 405:197–206.
1991   Approaches to dietary reconstruction in the western Cape: Are you what you have eaten? *Journal of Archaeological Science* 18:331–342.
1996   What is an eland? N/ao and the politics of age and sex in the rock paintings of the western Cape. In *Miscast: Negotiating the presence of the Bushmen*, ed. by P. Skotnes. Cape Town: University of Cape Town Press.
in press ed.   *Eland's Bay Cave: A view on the past.*

Parkington, J., and M. Cronin
1979   The site and layout of Mgungundlovu. *South African Archaeological Society, Goodwin Series* 3:133–148.

Parkington, J., and A. H. Manhire
1991   Reading San images: Paintings as domestic artefacts. In *Current perspectives in South African art and architecture*, ed. by S. Klopper and M. Pissarra, pp. 121–131.

Parkington, J., and R. Yates
in press   Stone tool assemblages. In *Eland's Bay Cave: A view on the past*, ed. by J. E. Parkington.

Parkington, J., R. Yates, A. Manhire, and D. Halkett
1986   The social impact of pastoralism in the southwestern Cape. *Journal of Anthropological Archaeology* 5:313–329.

Parkington, J, P. Nilssen, C. Reeler, and C. Henshilwood
1992   Making sense of space at Dunefield Midden campsite, Western Cape, South Africa. *Southern African Field Archaeology* 1:63–70.

Parkington, J., C. Poggenpoel, W. F. Buchanan, T. S. Robey, A. H. Manhire, and J. Sealy
1988   Holocene coastal settlement patterns in the western Cape. In G. Bailey and J. Parkington, eds. *The Archaeology of prehistoric coastlines*. Cambridge: Cambridge University Press.

Parry, W. J., and R. L. Kelly
1987   Expedient core technology and sedentism. In *The organization of core technology*, ed. by J. K. Johnson and C. A. Morrow, pp. 285–304. Boulder, Colo.: Westview.

Parsons, N.
1995 Prelude to Difaqane in the interior of southern Africa c. 1600–c. 1822. In *The Mfecane aftermath: Reconstructive debates in southern African history*, ed. by C. Hamilton, pp. 323–350. Johannesburg and Pietermaritzburg: University of the Witwatersrand Press and University of Natal Press.

Patterson, L., and J. B. Sollberger
1976 The myth of bipolar flaking industries. *Newsletter of Lithic Technology* 5(3):40–42.

Pavilish, L., R. G. V. Hancock, and J. Casey
1989 INAA of chert and quartzite materials from archaeological and potential quarry outcrops in northern Ghana. *University of Toronto SLOWPOKE Reactor Facility Annual Report*, p. 44.

Paynter, R.
1989 The archaeology of equality and inequality. *Annual Review of Anthropology* 18:369–399.

Pearson, M., and C. Richards
1994 Ordering the world: Perceptions of architecture, space, and time. In *Architecture and order: Approaches to social space*, ed. by M. Pearson and C. Richards, pp. 1–37: London: Routledge.

Pearson, N.
1995 Archaeological research at Modipe Hill, Kgatleng District, Botswana: Survey and excavation, 1992–1995. *Nyame Akuma* 44:2–15.

Pearson, R.
1995 Social complexity in Chinese coastal Neolithic sites. *Science* 213:1078–1086.

Petit-Maire, N., and Riser, J.
1983 Sahara ou Sahel? *Quaternaire Recent du Bassin de Taoudenni (Mali)*. CNRS, Marseille.

Phillipson, D. W.
1977 *The later prehistory of eastern and southern Africa*. London: Heinemann.
1980 Some speculations on the beginnings of backed-microlith manufacture. *Proceedings of the VIIIth Panafrican Congress of Prehistory and Quaternary Studies*, ed. by R. E. Leakey and B. A. Ogot, pp. 229–30. Nairobi: International Louis Leakey Memorial Institute for African Prehistory.

Picton, J.
1980 Women's weaving: The manufacture and use of textiles among the Igbirra people of Nigeria. In *Textiles of Africa*, ed. by D. Idiens and K. G. Ponting, pp. 63–88. Bath, England: The Pasold Research Fund.

Pistorius, J. C. C.
1992 *Molokwane, an Iron Age Bakwena village: Early Tswana settlement in the western Transvaal*. Johannesburg: Perskor Printers.
1995 Rathateng and Mabyanamatshwaana: Cradles of the Kwena and Kgatla. *South African Journal of Ethnology* 18:49–64.

Plimpton, C., and F. A. Hassan
1987 Social space: A determinant of house architecture. *Environmental Planning B Issue of Planning and Design* 14:439–449.

Plowright, W.
1965a Malignant catarrhal fever in East Africa I: Behaviour of the virus in free-living populations of blue wildebeest. *Research on Veterinary Science* 6:56–68.
1965b Malignant catarrhal fever in East Africa II: Observation on wildebeest calves at the laboratory and contact transmission of the infection to cattle. *Research on Veterinary Science* 6:69–83.

Posnansky, M.
1976 West African trade project, Report for 1976. Unpublished manuscript. Department of Archaeology. Legon: University of Ghana.
1980 How Ghana's crisis affects a village. *West Africa* no. 3306 (1 December 1980):2418–2420.
1984 Hardships of a village. *West Africa* no. 3506 (29 December 1984):2161–2163.
1987 Prelude to Akan civilization. In *The golden stool: Studies of the Asante center and periphery*, ed. by E. Schildkrout, pp. 14–22. Anthropological Papers, vol. 65, part 1. New York: American Museum of Natural History.

Potgieter, E. F.
1955 *The disappearing Bushmen of Lake Chrissie: A preliminary survey*. Pretoria: J. L. van Schaik.

Pratt, D. J., and M. D. Gwynne
1977 *Rangeland management and ecology in East Africa*. London: Hodder and Stoughton.

Preston-Whyte, E.
1974 Kinship and marriage. In *The Bantu-speaking peoples of southern Africa*, ed. by W. D. Hammond-Tooke. London: Routledge Kegan Paul.

Prezzano, S.
1997 Warfare, women and household: The development of Iroquois culture. In *Women in prehistory: North American Mesoamerica*, ed. by C. Claassen and R. Joyce, pp. 88–99. Philadelphia: University of Pennsylvania Press.

Price, T. D., and J. A. Brown
1985 *Prehistoric hunter-gatherers: The emergence of cultural complexity*. New York: Academic Press.

Price, T. D., and G. M. Feinman, eds.
1995 *Foundations of social inequality*. New York: Plenum Press.

Prins, F. E., and Granger, J. E
1993 Early farming communities in northern Transkei: The evidence from Ntsitsana and adjacent areas. *Natal Museum Journal of Humanities* 5:153–174

Pwiti, G., and R. Soper, eds.
1996 *Aspects of African archaeology*. Harare: University of Zimbabwe Publications.

Quin, P. J.
1959 *Foods and feeding habits of the Pedi*. Johannesburg: Witwatersrand University Press.

Raum, O. F.
1973 *The social functions of avoidances and taboos among the Zulu*. Berlin: Walter De Gruyter.

Raymaekers, J., and F. Van Noten
1986 Early iron furnaces with "bricks" in Rwanda: Complementary evidence from Mutwarubona. *Azania* 21:65–84.

Reeler, C.
1992 Spatial patterns and behaviour at Dunefield Midden. Unpublished M.A. thesis, Department of Archaeology, University of Cape Town.

Reid, Adam
1996 Ntusi and the development of social complexity in southern Uganda. In *Aspects of African archaeology*, ed. by G. Pwiti and R. Soper, pp. 621–627. Harare: Univeristy of Zimbabwe Publications.

Reid, Andrew, K. Sadr, and N. Hanson-James
1996 Herding traditions in Botswana. Paper presented at the Archaeology in Botswana Symposium, University of Botswana, Gaborone.

Reid, D. A. M., and J. Njau
1994 Archaeological research in Karagwe District. *Nyame Akuma* 41:68–73.

Renfrew, C.
1984 *Approaches to social archaeology.* Cambridge: Harvard University Press.

Renfrew, C., and J. F. Cherry, eds.
1986 *Peer polity interaction and socio-political change.* Cambridge: Cambridge University Press.

Rice, P.
1991 Women and prehistoric pottery production. In *The archaeology of gender,* ed. by D. Walde and
N. Willows, pp. 436–443. Calgary: Chacmool Archaeological Association of the University of
Calgary.

Richards, A. E.
1939 *Land, labour and diet in northern Rhodesia.* London: Oxford University Press.

Richardson, J. L.
1972 Paleolimnological records from Rift lakes in central Kenya. *Palaeoecology of Africa* 6:131–136.

Richardson, J. L., and A. E. Richardson
1972 The history of an East Africa Rift lake and its paleoclimatic implications. *Ecological Monographs* 42:499–534.

Robbins, L.
1984 Toteng, a Late Stone Age site along the Nghabe River, Ngamiland. *Botswana Notes and
Records* 16:1–6.

Roberts, R.
1984 Women's work and women's property: Household social relations in the Maraka textile industry of the nineteenth century. *Comparative Studies in Society and History* 26:229–250.
1992 Guinée cloth: Linked transformations within France's empire in the nineteenth century.
Cahiers d'Études Africaines 32(128):597–627.

Robertshaw, P. T.
1988 The Elmenteitan: An early food-producing culture in East Africa. *World Archaeology* 20:57–69.
1989 The development of pastoralism in East Africa. In *The walking larder: Patterns of domestication,
pastoralism, and predation,* ed. by J. Clutton-Brock, pp. 207–212. London: Unwin Hyman.
1990, ed. *Early pastoralists of south-western Kenya.* Nairobi: British Institute in Eastern Africa.
1991 Gogo Falls: Excavations at a complex archaeological site east of Lake Victoria. *Azania* 26:63–195.
1994 Lake Victoria and eastwards: Urewe, its antecedents and its neighbors. Paper presented at the
Growth of Farming Communities in Africa from the Equator Southwards Conference. The
British Institute in Eastern Africa in association with the African Studies Centre, University
of Cambridge, Cambridge.

Robertshaw, P. T., and D. Collett.
1983a The identification of pastoral peoples in the archaeological record: An example from East
Africa. *World Archaeology* 15:67–78.
1983b A new framework for the study of early pastoral communities in East Africa. *Journal of
African History* 24:289–301.

Robertshaw, P. T., D. Collett, D. Gifford-Gonzalez, and M. B. Nube
1983 Shell middens on the shores of Lake Victoria. *Azania* 18:1–43.

Rollefson, G. O.
1983 Ritual and ceremony at Neolithic 'Ain Ghazal (Jordan). *Paléorient* 9(2):29–38.
1990 The uses of plaster at Neolithic 'Ain Ghazal, Jordan. *Archeomaterials* 4(1):33–54.

Rollefson, G. O., A. H. Simmons, and Z. Kafafi
1992 Neolithic cultures at 'Ain Ghazal, Jordan. *Journal of Field Archaeology* 19:443–470.

Roosevelt, A.
1997 Human ecology, organization, and gender imagery in Amazon prehistory. Paper presented in the symposium Culture and Nature: Married or Divorced? The Impact of Gender Upon Sustainability, at the Annual Meetings of the American Association for the Advancement of Science in Seattle, February 14.

Rosemond, C. C. de
1943 Iron smelting in the Kahama district. *Tanganyika Notes and Records* 16:79–84.

Rowlands, M.
1989 The archaeology of colonialism and constituting the African peasantry. In *Domination and resistance*, ed. by D. Miller, M. Rowlands, and C. Tilley, pp. 261–283. London: Unwin Hyman.

Rowlands, M., and J.-P. Warnier
1993 The magical production of iron in the Cameroon grassfields. In *The archaeology of Africa: Food, metals, and towns*, ed. by T. Shaw, B. Andah, P. Sinclair, and A. Okpoko, pp. 512–550. London: Unwin Hyman.

Roy, K. J.
1902 Monthly reports. Kintampo District for 1902 by the Officer Commanding Kintampo. April. File ADM56/1/457. Ghana National Archives, Accra.

Rudner, J.
1979 The use of stone artifacts and pottery among the Khoisan people in historic and protohistoric times. *South African Archaeology Bulletin* 34:3–17.

Russell, A. C.
1931a District Commissioners Diary for the month of July 1931. File 2063, Ghana National Archives, Kumasi, and Towns.
1931b Report on a tour of inspection, 6 July to 23 July of Banda area. Banda Native Affairs, File 168, Ghana National Archives, Kumasi.

Sackett, J. R.
1973 Style, function and artifact variability in Paleolithic assemblages. In *Explanation of culture change*, ed. by C. Renfrew, pp. 317–325. London: Duckworth.
1977 The meaning of style in archaeology. *American Antiquity* 42:369–80.
1982 Approaches to style in lithic archeology. *Journal of Anthropological Archaeology* 1:59–112.
1985 Style, ethnicity and stone tools. In *Status, structure and stratification: Current archaeological reconstructions*, Proceedings of the Sixteenth Annual Chacmool Conference, ed. by M. Thompson, M. T. Marcia, and F. J. Kense, pp. 277–282. Calgary: University of Calgary Press.
1989 Statistics, attributes and the dynamics of Burin typology. In *Alternative applications in lithic analysis*, ed. by D. O. Henry and G. Odell, pp. 51–82. Archaeological Papers of the American Anthropological Association 1.
1993 Style and ethnicity in archaeology: The case for Isochrestism. In *The uses of style in archaeology*, ed. by M. Conkey and C. Hasdorf, pp. 32–43. Cambridge: Cambridge University Press.

Sadr, K.
1997 Kalahari archaeology and the Bushman debate. *Current Anthropology* 38:104–112.

Saitoti, T. O.
1986 *The worlds of a Maasai warrior: An autobiography*. Berkeley: University of California Press.

Saitoti, T. O., and C. Beckwith
1980 *Maasai*. New York: H. N. Abrams.

Sampson, C. G.
1968 The Middle Stone Age industries of the Orange River Scheme Area. *Memoirs of the National Museum at Bloemfontein*, no. 4. Bloemfontein, South Africa: OFS.

1988 *Stylistic boundaries among mobile hunter-foragers.* Washington, D.C.: Smithsonian Institution Press.
1996 Spatial organization of Later Stone Age herders in the Upper Karoopp. In *Aspects of African archaeology,* ed. by G. Pwiti and R. Soper, pp. 316–326. Harare: University of Zimbabwe Publications.

Sanders, W. T., and B. Price
1968 *Mesoamerica: The evolution of a civilization.* New York: Random House.

Sansom, B.
1972 When witches are not named. In *The allocation of responsibility,* ed. by M. Gluckma. Manchester, England: University Press.
1974 Traditional economic systems. In *The Bantu-speaking peoples of southern Africa,* ed. by W. D. Hammond-Tooke. London: Routledge Kegan Paul.

Sansoni, U.
1994 *Le piú antiche pitture del Sahara: L'arte delle Teste Rotonde.* Milan: Jaca Book.

Sassaman, K. E.
1992 Lithic technology and the hunter-gatherer sexual division of labor. *North American Anthropologist* 13(3):249–262.

Schapera, I.
1935 The social structure of the Tswana ward. *Bantu Studies* 9:203–224.
1938 *A handbook of Tswana law and custom.* London: Oxford University Press.
1952 *The Ethnic Composition of Tswana Tribes.* London School of Economics: Monographs on Social Anthropology, No. 11.
1971 *Rainmaking rites of Tswana tribes.* Leiden: Afrika-Studiecentrum.
1978 Some Kgatla theories of procreation. In *Social system and tradition in southern Africa,* ed. by J. Argyle and E. Preston-Whyte, pp. 165–182. Cape Town: Oxford University Press.

Schepartz, L. A.
1988 Who were the later Pleistocene eastern Africans? *African Archaeological Review* 6:57–72.

Schmidt, E.
1992 *Peasants, traders and wives: Shona women in the history of Zimbabwe, 1870–1939.* London: James Currey.

Schmidt, P. R.
1978 *Historical archaeology: A structural approach in an African culture.* Westport, Conn.: Greenwood Press.
1980 Early Iron Age settlements and industrial locales in West Lake. *Tanzania Notes and Records* 84–85:77–94.
1983 An alternative to a strictly materialist perspective: A review of historical archaeology, ethnoarchaeology, and symbolic approaches in African archaeology. *American Antiquity* 48(1):62–81.
1996a Cultural representations of African iron production. In *The culture and technology of African iron production,* ed. by P. R. Schmidt, pp. 1–28. Gainesville: University Press of Florida.
1996b Reconfiguring the Barongo: Reproductive symbolism and reproduction among a work association of iron smelters. In *The culture and technology of African iron production,* ed. by P. R. Schmidt, pp. 74–127. Gainesville: University Press of Florida.
1997a *Iron production in East Africa: Symbolism, science, and archaeology.* Bloomington: University of Indiana Press.
1997b Archaeological views on a history of landscape change in East Africa. *Journal of African History* 38:260–288.

Schmidt, P., and D. Avery
1978 Complex iron-smelting and prehistoric culture in Tanzania. *Science* 201(4361):1085–1089.

Schmidt, P. R., and S. T. Childs
1985   Innovation and industry during the Early Iron Age in East Africa: The KM2 and KM3 sites of northwest Tanzania. *African Archaeological Review* 3:53–94.

Schmidt, P. R., and B. B. Mapunda
1997   Ideology and the archaeological record in Africa: Interpreting symbolism in iron smelting technology. *Journal of Anthropological Archaeology* 16:128–157.

Schmidt, P. R., and T. Patterson
1995   From constructing to making alternative histories. In *Making alternative histories: The practice of archaeology and history in nonwestern cultures*, ed. by P. R. Schmidt and T. Patterson, pp. 1–24. Santa Fe, N.M.: School of American Research.

Schmidt, P. R., L. Digombe, M. Locko, and V. Mouleingui
1985   Newly dated Iron Age sites in Gabon. *Nyame Akuma* 22:16–18.

Schoenbrun, D. L.
1990   Early history in eastern Africa's Great Lakes region: Linguistic, ecological, and archaeological approaches, ca. 500 B.C. to ca. A.D. 1000. Ph.D. dissertation, Department of History, University of California, Los Angeles.
1993a   Cattle herds and banana gardens: The historical geography of the western Great Lakes region, ca. AD 800–1500. *African Archaeological Review* 11:39–72.
1993b   We are what we eat: Ancient agriculture between the Great Lakes. *Journal of African History* 34:1–31.
1996   Social aspects of agricultural change between the Great Lakes, AD 500 to 1000. *Azania* 29–30:270–282.

Schrire, C.
1984a ed.   *Past and present in hunter-gatherer studies*. Orlando, Fla.: Academic Press.
1984b   Wild surmises on savage thoughts. In *Past and present in hunter-gatherer studies*, ed. by C. Schrire, pp. 1–25. Orlando, Fla.: Academic Press.

Sealy, J. C.
1992   Diet and dental caries among Later Stone Age inhabitants of the Cape Province, South Africa. *American Journal of Physical Anthropology* 88:123–134.

Sealy, J. C., and A. Sillen
1988   Sr and Sr/Ca in marine and terrestrial foodwebs in the southwestern Cape, South Africa. *Journal of Archaeological Science* 15:1–14.

Sealy, J. C., N. J. van der Merwe, J. A. Lee Thorp, and J. L. Lanham
1987   Nitrogen isotopic ecology in southern Africa: Implications for environmental and dietary tracing. *Geochimica et Cosmochimica Acta* 51:2707–2717.

Sealy, J. C., and N. J. van der Merwe
1985   Isotope assessment of Holocene human diets in the southwestern Cape, South Africa. *Nature* 315:138–140.
1986   Isotope assessment and the seasonal-mobility hypothesis in the southwestern Cape of South Africa. *Current Anthropology* 27:135–150.
1987   Reply to J. E. Parkington. *Current Anthropology* 28(1):94–95.
1988   Social, spatial and chronological patterning in marine food use as determined by _13C measurements of Holocene human skeletons from the southwestern Cape, South Africa. *World Archaeology* 20:87–102.

Sealy, J. C., M. K. Patrick, A. G. Morris, and D. Alder
1992   Diet and dental caries among Later Stone Age inhabitants of the Cape Province, South Africa. *American Journal of Physical Anthropology* 88:123–134.

Segobye, A. K.
1993 Representing the past: Anthropological and archaeological discourse in southern Africa. Unpublished paper, presented at the conference Symbols of Change: Transregional Culture and Local Practice in Southern Africa, Berlin.

Shaw, C. T.
1978–79 Holocene adaptations in West Africa: The Late Stone Age. *Early Man News* 3–4:51–82.

Shaw, T., P. Sinclair, B. Andah, and A. Okpoko, eds.
1993 *The archaeology of Africa: Food, metals and towns.* London: Routledge.

Shea, J.
1988 Methodological considerations affecting the choice of analytical techniques in use-wear analysis: Tests, results and application. In *Industries lithiques,* ed. by S. Beyries, pp. 65–82. Oxford: BAR International Series no. 411, vol 2.

Shostak, M.
1981 *Nisa.* New York: Vintage Books.

Silberbauer, G.
1981 *Hunter and habitat in the central Kalahari Desert.* Cambridge: Cambridge University Press.

Sillitoe, P.
1982 The lithic technology of a Papua New Guinea highland people. *Artefact* 7:19–38.

Singer, R., and Wymer, J.
1982 *The Middle Stone Age at Klasies River Mouth in South Africa.* Chicago: Chicago University Press.

Smith, A. B.
1992 *Pastoralism in Africa: Origins and Developmental Ecology.* London: Hurst & Company.
1996 The archaeological evidence of precolonial hunter/herder ethnicity at the Cape, South Africa. In *Aspects of African Archaeology,* ed. by G. Pwiti and R. Soper, pp.469–476. Harare: University of Zimbabwe Publications.

Smith, B. D.
1977 Archaeological inference and inductive confirmation. *American Anthropologist* 79:598–617.

Smith, N. S.
1970 Appraisal of condition estimation methods for East African ungulates. *East African Wildlife Journal* 8:123–129.

Sobania, N.
1991 Feasts, famines and friends: Nineteenth-century exchange in the eastern Lake Turkana region. In *Herds, warriors, and traders: Pastoralism in Africa,* ed. by J. G. Galaty and P. Bonte, pp. 118–142. Boulder, Colo.: Westview Press.

Solomon, A.
1989 *Division of the earth: Gender, symbolism and the archaeology of the southern San.* Unpublished M.A. thesis, Department of Archaeology, University of Cape Town.
1992 Gender, representation and power in San ethnography and rock art. *Journal of Anthropological Archaeology* 11:291–329.
1994 Mythic women: A study in variability in San art. In *Contested images: Diversity in southern African rock art research,* ed. by T. A. Dowson and J. D. Lewis-Williams, pp. 331–372. Johannesburg: Witwatersrand University Press.
1996 Rock art incorporated: An archaeological and interdisciplinary study of certain human figures in San art. Unpublished Ph.D. dissertation, Department of Archaeology, University of Cape Town.

Soper, R. C.
1965 The Stone Age in northern Nigeria. *Journal of the Historical Society of Nigeria* 3(2):175–194.
1969 Radiocarbon dating of "dimple-based ware" in western Kenya. *Azania* 4:149–153.

Soper, R. C., and B. Golden
1969   An archaeological survey of the Mwanza region, Tanzania. *Azania* 4:15–79.

Sparrman, A.
1785   *A voyage to the Cape of Good Hope toward the Antarctic polar circle, and round the world; but chiefly into the country of the Hottentots and Caffers, from the years 1772 to 1776.* London: Colburn.

Spector, J.
1982   Male–female task differentiation among the Hidatsa: Toward the development of an archaeological approach to the study of gender. In *The hidden half: Studies of native Plains women*, ed. by P. Albers and B. Medicine. Washington, D.C.: University Press of America.
1991   What this awl means: Toward a feminist archaeology. In *Engendering archaeology: Woman and prehistory*, ed. by J. M. Gero and. M. W. Conkey, pp. 388–406. Oxford: Blackwell.

Spencer, P.
1965   *The Samburu: A study of gerontocracy in a nomadic tribe.* London: Routledge Kegan Paul.
1988   *The Maasai of Matapato: A study of rituals of rebellion.* International African Library. Bloomington: Indiana University Press.

Speth, J. D.
1990   Seasonality, resource stress, and food sharing in so-called egalitarian societies. *Journal of Anthropological Archaeology* 9:148–188.

Speth, J. D., and Spielmann, K. A.
1983   Energy source, protein metabolism, and hunter-gatherer subsistence strategies. *Journal of Anthropological Archaeology* 2:1–31.

Stahl, A. B.
1985a   The Kintampo culture: Subsistence and settlement in Ghana during the mid-second millennium BC. Unpublished Ph.D. dissertation, Dept. of Anthropology, University of California–Berkeley.
1985b   Reinvestigation of the Kintampo 6 Rockshelter, Ghana: Implications for the nature of culture change. *African Archaeological Review* 3:117–150.
1989   Plant food processing: Implications for dietary quality. In *Foraging and farming: The evolution of plant exploitation*, ed. by D. R. Harris and G. C. Hillman, pp. 171–194. London: Unwin Hyman.
1991   Ethnic styles and ethnic boundaries: A diachronic case study from west central Ghana. *Ethnohistory* 38:250–275.
1992   The culture history of the central Volta basin: Retrospect and prospect. In *An African commitment. Papers in honour of Peter Lewis Shinnie*, ed. by J. Sterner and N. David, pp. 123–142. Calgary: University of Calgary Press.
1993   Concepts of time and approaches to analogical reasoning in historical perspective. *American Antiquity* 58:235–260.
1994a   Change and continuity in the Banda area, Ghana: The direct historical approach. *Journal of Field Archaeology* 21:181–203.
1994b   Valuing the past, envisioning the future: Local perspectives on environmental and cultural heritage in Ghana. In *Proceedings of the International Conference on Culture and Development in Africa*, ed. by I. Serageldin and J. Taboroff, pp. 411–424. Washington, D.C.: The World Bank.
in press   Historical process and the impact of the Atlantic trade on Banda, Ghana, 1800–1920. In *Historical archaeology in West Africa: Culture contact, continuity and change*, ed. by C. R. DeCorse. Washington, D.C.: Smithsonian Institution Press.
n.d.   *A seamless fabric: Historical anthropology and the interpretation of Africa's past.* Book manuscript.

Stahl, A. B., and J. Anane
1989   Family histories from the Banda traditional area, Brong-Ahafo Region, Ghana. Report on file with Ghana National Museum, Institute of African Studies, University of Ghana, and Nafaanra Literacy Project, Banda, Ghana.

Stayt, H.
1968   *The Bavenda*. London: Frank Cass.

Steiner, C. B.
1985   Another image of Africa: Toward an ethnohistory of European cloth marketed in West Africa 1873–1960. *Ethnohistory* 32:91–110.

Stenning, D. J.
1958   Household variability among the pastoral Fulani. In *The development cycle in domestic groups*, ed. by J. Goody. Cambridge: Cambridge University Press.

Steward, J. H.
1942   The direct historical approach to archaeology. *American Antiquity* 7:337–343.

Stirnimann, H.
1976   *Existenzgundlagen und traditionelles Handwerk de Pengwa von SW.-Tansania*. Freiburn: Schweiz.

Strathern, M.
1969   Stone axes and flake tools: Evaluations from two New Guinea highlands societies. *Proceedings of the Prehistoric Society* n.s., 35:311–324.

1987, ed.   *Dealing with inequality: Analysing gender relations in Melanesia and beyond*. Cambridge: Cambridge University Press.

Sussman, C.
1988a   *A microwear analysis of use-wear and polish formation on experimental quartz tools*. Oxford: Bar International Series no. 395.

1988b   Aspects of microwear as applied to quartz. In *Industries Lithiques*, ed. by S. Beyrie, pp. 1–27. Oxford: BAR International Series no. 411, vol 2.

Sutton, J.
1977   The African aqualithic. *Antiquity* 51:25–34.

Sutton, J. E. G.
1966a   The archaeology and early peoples of the highlands of Kenya and northern Tanzania. *Azania* 1:37–58.

1966b   The growth of farming and the Bantu settlement on and south of the equator. In *The growth of farming communities in Africa from the equator southwards*, ed. by J. E. G. Sutton. *Azania* 29–30:2–14.

Swift, J.
1981   Labour and subsistence in a pastoral economy. In *Seasonal dimensions to rural poverty*, ed. by R. Chambers , R. Longhurst, and A. Pacey, pp. 47–93. New York: John Wiley and Sons.

Tanaka, J.
1976   Subsistence ecology of central Kalahari San. In *Kalahari hunter-gatherers: Studies of the !Kung San and their neighbors*, ed. by R. Lee and I. De Vore. Cambridge: Harvard University Press.

Tannahill, R.
1988   *Food in history*. London: Penguin.

Taylor, M. O. V.
1979   Late Iron Age settlements on the northern edge of the Vredefort Dome. M.A. thesis, University of the Witwatersrand.

1984   Southern Transvaal stone walled sites: A spatial consideration. In *Frontiers: Southern African archaeology today*, ed. by M Hall, G. Avery, D. M. Avery, M. L. Wilson, and A. J. Humphreys, pp. 248–251. Oxford: British Archaeological Reports, International Series no. 207.

Tchernov, E.
1975   Rodent faunas and environmental changes in the Pleistocene of Israel. In *Rodents in the desert environments*, ed. by I. Prakash and P. K. Ghosh, pp. 331–362. The Hague: Dr. W. Junk.

1993   Exploitation of birds during the Natufian and Early Neolithic of the southern Levant. *Archaeofauna* 2:121–143.

Tchernov, E., and F. Valla
1997   Two new dogs, and other Natufian dogs, from the southern Levant. *Journal of Archaeological Science* 24(1):65–95.

Tessmann, G.
1913   *Die Pangwe.* Berlin.

Testart, A.
1982   The significance of food-storage among hunter-gatherers: Residence patterns, population densities, and social inequalities. *Current Anthropology* 23(5):523–37.

Thomas E., A.
1982   *The 27th kingdom.* London: Duckworth.

Thomas, E. W.
1950   *Bushman stories.* Cape Town: Oxford University Press.
1965   *Warrior herdsmen.* New York: Knopf.

Thunberg, C. P.
1793–95   *Travels in Europe, Africa and Asia made between the years 1770 and 1779.* London: F & C Rivington.

Tixier, J.
1963   *Typologie de l'épipaléolithique du Maghreb.* Mémoires du Centre de Recherches Anthropologiques, Préhistoriques et Ethnographiques d'Alger. T.II.

Tomenchuk, J.
1983   Predicting the past: Examples from the use-wear study of selected chipped stone tools from two Epi-Paleolithic occupations in Israel. In *Traces d'utilisation sur les outils Néolithiques du Proche-Orient*, ed. by M. Cauvin, pp. 57–76. Travaux de la Maison de l'Orient 5.
1985   The development of a wholly parametric use-wear methodology and its application to two selected samples of Epipalaeolithic chipped stone tools from Hayonim Cave, Israel. Unpublished Ph.D dissertation, Department of Anthropology, University of Toronto.

Tomka, S. A.
1993   Site abandonment behavior among transhumant agropastoralists: The effects of delayed curation on assemblage composition. In *Abandonment of settlements and regions: Ethnoarchaeological and archaeological approaches*, ed. by C. M. Cameron and S. A. Tomka, pp. 11–24. Cambridge: Cambridge University Press.

Torrence, R.
1989   Re-tooling: Towards a behavioral theory of stone tools. In *Time, energy and stone tools*, ed. by R. Torrence, pp. 57–66. Cambridge: Cambridge University Press.

Troy, L.
1986   *Patterns of queenship in ancient Egyptian myth and history.* Boreas 14. Uppsala: Acta Universitatis Upsaliensis.
1994   The first time: Homology and complementarity as structural forces in ancient Egyptian cosmology. *Cosmos, Journal of the Traditional Cosmology Society* 10(1):3–51.
1996   The Egyptian queenship as an icon for the state. Paper presented at the Society of Biblical Literature Annual Meeting, New Orleans. Unpublished manuscript.

Turner, G.
1987   Early Iron Age herders in northwestern Botswana: The faunal evidence. *Botswana Notes and Records* 19:7–23.

Turton, D.
1991 Movement, warfare, and ethnicity in the Lower Omo Valley. In *Herders, warriors, and traders: Pastoralism in Africa*, ed. by J. Bonte. Boulder, Colo.: Westview Press.

Tyson P. D., and J. A. Lindesay
1992 The climate of the last 2000 years in southern Africa. *Holocene* 2:271–278.

Udvardy, M.
1991 Gender, power and the fragmentation of fertility among the Giriama of Kenya. In *Body and space: Symbolic models of unity and division in African cosmology and experience*, ed. by A. Jacobson-Widing, pp. 143–154. Uppsala: Uppsala Studies in Cultural Anthropology 16.

Valla, F.
1995 The first settled societies—Natufian (12,500–10,200 BP). In *The archaeology of society in the Holy Land*, ed. by T. Levy, pp. 169–189. London: Leicester University Press.

Van der Merwe, N., and D. Avery
1987 Science and magic in African technology: Traditional iron smelting in Malawi. *Africa* 57:143–172.

van der Ryst, M.
1996 The Later Stone Age prehistory of the Waterberg, with special reference to Goergap Shelter. Unpublished M.A. thesis, Department of Anthropology, University of the Witwatersrand.

Van Grunderbeek, M. -C.
1988 Essai d'étude typologique de ceramique Urewe de la région des collines au Burundi et Rwanda. *Azania* 23:11–55.
1992 Chronologie de l'âge du fer ancien au Burundi, au Rwanda et dans la région des Grands Lacs. *Azania* 27:53–80.

Van Grunderbeek, M. C., E. Roche, and H. Doutrelepont
1983 *Le premier âge du fer au Rwanda et au Burundi: Archeologie et environment*. Brussels: I.F.A.Q.

Van Neer, W.
1995 Domesticated animals from sites in central Africa. Paper presented at the African Livestock, Archaeology, Linguistics and DNA Conference, London.

Van Neer, W., and H. P. Uerpmann
1989 Palaeoecological significance of the Holocene faunal remains of the B.O.S. Missions. In Forschungen zur Unweltgeschichte der Ostsahara, ed. by R. Kuper, pp. 307–341. Africa Praehistorica vol. 2. Heinrich-Barth-Institut, Köln.

Van Noten, F.
1979 The Early Iron Age in the Interlacustrine Region: The diffusion of iron technology. *Azania* 14:61–80.
1983 Histoire archeologique de Rwanda, Serie in 8⁰, Sciences Humaines, no. 112. Tervuren: Musée Royal de l'Afrique Centrale.

Van Noten, F., and J. Raymaekers
1988 Early iron smelting in central Africa. *Scientific American* 258:84–91.

Van Rijssen, W. J. J.
1980 Ways of seeing: Some aspects of the interpretation of rock paintings. Unpublished honours dissertation, Department of Archaeology, University of Cape Town.

van Schalkwyk, L.
1994–95 Settlement shifts and socio-economic transformations in early agriculturalist communities in the lower Thukela basin. *Azania* 29–30:187–198.

van Waarden, C.
1987 Matanga, a Late Zimbabwe cattle post. *South African Archaeological Bulletin* 42:107–124.

1989   The granaries of Vumba: Structural interpretation of a Khami period commoner site. *Journal of Anthropological Archaeology* 8:131–157.
1992   Pitse (45–D1–9): An Early Iron Age site on the Gaborone-Thamaga-Kanye Road. Unpublished report, commissioned by The Roads Department, Gaborone. Francistown, Botswana: Marope Research.

Vermeersch, P. Van Peer, J. Moeyersons, and W. Van Neer
1996   Sodmein Cave Site, Red Sea Mountains (Egypt). *Sahara* 6: 31–40.

Vincent, A.
1985a   Plant foods in savannah environments: A preliminary report of tubers eaten by the Hadza of northern Tanzania. *World Archaeology* 17(2):131–148.
1985b   Wild tubers as a harvestable resource in the East African savannas: Ecological and ethnographic studies. Ph.D. dissertation, University of California, Berkeley.

Vinnicombe, P.
1976   *People of the Eland: Rock paintings of the Drakensberg Bushmen as a reflection of their life and thought.* Pietermaritzburg: University of Natal Press.

Vogel, C. A. M.
1983   The traditional mural art of the Pedi of Sekhuhkuneland. M.A. thesis, Johannesburg: University of the Witwatersrand.

Vogel, J. O.
1984   An Early Iron Age settlement system in southern Zambia. *Azania* 19:61–78.

Voight, E. A.
1983   *Mapungubwe: An archaeozoological interpretation of an Iron Age community.* Pretoria: Transvaal Museum.
1986   Iron Age herding: Archaeological and ethnoarchaeological approaches to pastoral problems. In *Prehistoric pastoralism in southern Africa*, ed. by M. Hall and A. B. Smith, pp. 13–21. Vlaeberg: South African Archaeological Society.

Wadley, L.
1987   *Later Stone Age hunters and gatherers of the southern Transvaal.* Oxford: Cambridge Monographs in African Archaeology 25.
1993   The Pleistocene Later Stone Age south of the Limpopo River. *Journal of World Prehistory* 7:243–296.
1996   Changes in the social relations of precolonial hunter-gatherers after agropastoral contact: An example from the Magaliesberg, South Africa. *Journal of Anthropological Archaeology* 15: 205–217.
in press a   Pleistocene and Holocene use of space at Rose Cottage Cave. In *Khoison studies*, ed. by Edwin Wilmsen and R. Vossen. Hamburg: Helmut Buske Verlag.
in press b   The use of space in a gender study of two South African Stone Age sites. In *Gender and material culture*, ed. by L. Hurcombe and M. Dondald. MacMillan.

Wadley, L., and J. Binneman
1995   Arrowheads or pen knives? A microwear analysis of mid-Holocene stone segments from Jubilee Shelter, Transvaal. *South African Journal of Science* 91:153–155.

Walde, D., and N. Willows, eds.
1991   *The archaeology of gender.* Proceedings of the 22nd Annual Chacmool Conference. Calgary: University of Calgary.

Walker, C.
1990   Gender and the development of the migrant labour system c. 1850–1930: An overview. In *Women and gender in southern Africa to 1945*, ed. by C. Walker, pp. 168–196. Cape Town: David Philip.

Walker, E.
1901 Monthly report. Kintampo District for July 1901. File ADM 56/1/415. Accra: Ghana National Archives.

Walker, N.
1994 The Late Stone Age of Botswana: some recent excavations. *Botswana Notes and Records* 26:1–36.
1995 *Late Pleistocene and Holocene hunter-gatherers of the Matopos.* Studies in African Archaeology, Uppsala: Societas Archaeologica Upsaliensis.

Waller, R.
1985 Ecology, migration, and expansion in East Africa. *African Affairs* 84:347–370.

Walton, J.
1956 *African village.* Pretoria: Van Schaik.

Wandibba, S.
1980 The application of attribute analysis to the study of Later Stone Age/Neolithic ceramics. In *Proceedings of the VIIIth Panafrican Congress of Prehistory and Quaternary Studies,* ed. by R. E. Leakey and B. A. Ogot, pp. 283–285. Nairobi: International Louis Leakey Memorial Institute for African Prehistory.

Warnier, J. P., and I. Fowler
1979 A nineteenth century Ruhr in central Africa. *Africa* 49: 329–351.

Wasylikowa, K.
1992 Holocene flora of the Tadrart Acacus area, SW Libya, based on plant macrofossils from Uan Muhuggiag and Ti-n-Torha/Two Caves archaeological sites. *Origini* xvi:125–159.

Watkins, T.
1990 The origins of house and home. *World Archaeology* 21:336–347.

Watson, P. J., and M. C. Kennedy
1991 The development of horticulture in the eastern woodlands of North America: Women's role. In *Engendering archaeology: Woman and prehistory,* ed. by J. M. Gero and M. W. Conkey, pp. 255–275. Oxford: Blackwell.

Weissner, P.
1983 Style and social information in Kalahari San projectile points. *American Antiquity* 49(2):253–276.
1990 Comment on foragers, genuine or spurious? *Current Anthropology* 31(2):137–138.
1993 Is there a unity to style? In *The uses of style in archaeology,* ed. by M. Conkey and C. Hasdorf, pp. 105–112. Cambridge: Cambridge University Press.

Welbourn, A.
1984 Endo ceramics and power strategies. In *Ideology, power and prehistory,* ed. by D. Miller and C. Tilley, pp. 17–24. Cambridge: Cambridge University Press.

Wendorf, F., and R. Schild
1980 *Prehistory of the eastern Sahara.* New York: Academic Press.
1994 Are the early Holocene cattle in the eastern Sahara domestic or wild? *Evolutionary Anthropology* 3(4):118–128.
1995 The Saharan Neolithic and the emergence of ranked societies in Egypt. Abstract volume of the First Workshop of the Forum for African Archaeology and Cultural Heritage, Rome, April 1995, p. 27.

Wendorf, F., A. E. Close, and R. Schild
1987 Early domestic cattle in the eastern Sahara. *Palaeoecology of Africa.* 18:441–448.

Wendorf, F., A. E. Close, A. Gautier, and R. Schild
1990 Les debuts du pastoralisme en Egypte. *La recherche* 21(220):436–445.

White, C.
1986 Food shortages and seasonality among the Wo Daa Be communities in Niger. *IDS Bulletin* 17(3):19–26.

White, J. P.
1977 Reply to Patterson and Sollberger. *Newsletter of Lithic Technology* 6(1–2):6–7.

Whitelaw, G.
1993 Customs and settlement patterns in the first millenium AD: Evidence from Nanda, an Early Iron Age site in the Mngeni Valley, Natal. *Natal Museum Journal of Humanities* 5:47–81.
1994 KwaGandaganda: Settlement patterns in the Natal Early Iron Age. *Natal Museum Journal of Humanities* 6:1–64.
1994–95 Towards an Early Iron Age worldview: Some ideas from KwaZulu-Natal. *Azania* 29–30:37–50.

Wienpahl, J.
1984 Women's roles in livestock production among the Turkana of Kenya. *Research in Economic Anthropology* 6:193–215.

Wilks, I.
1975 *Asante in the nineteenth century: The structure and evolution of a political order*. Cambridge: Cambridge University Press.
1982a Wangara, Akan and Portuguese in the fifteenth and sixteenth centuries. I. The matter of Bitu. *Journal of African History* 23:333–349.
1982b Wangara, Akan and Portuguese in the fifteenth and sixteenth centuries. II. The struggle for trade. *Journal of African History* 23:463–472.
1993 *Forests of gold*. Athens: Ohio University Press.

Willey, G. R., and P. Phillips
1958 *Method and theory in American archaeology*. Chicago: University of Chicago Press.

Williams, S.
1987 An "archaeology" of Turkana beads. In *The archaeology of contextual meanings*, ed. by I. Hodder, pp. 31–38. Cambridge: Cambridge University Press.

Williamson, B.
in press Preliminary stone tool residue analysis from Rose Cottage Cave. *Southern African Field Archaeology*.

Wilmsen, E.
1978 Prehistoric and historic antecedents of a contemporary Ngamiland community. *Botswana Notes and Records* 10:5–18.
1989 *Land filled with flies: A political economy of the Kalahari*. Chicago: University of Chicago Press.
1990 Comment on foragers, genuine or spurious? *Current Anthropology* 31(2):136–137.

Wilmsen, E. N., and J. Denbow
1990 Paradigmatic history of San-speaking peoples and current attempts at revision. *Current Anthropology* 31:498–524.

Wilmsen, E. N., and D. Durham
1988 Food as a function of seasonal environment and social history. In *Coping with uncertainty in food supply*, ed. by I. de Garine and G. A. Harrison, pp. 52–87. Oxford: Clarendon Press.

Wobst, H. M.
1977 Stylistic behaviour and information exchange. In *For the director: Research essays in honor of James B. Griffin*, ed. by C. E. Cleland, pp. 317–342. University of Michigan Museum of Anthropology, Anthropological Papers 61. Ann Arbor: University of Michigan Press.

Wolf, E. R.
1982 *Europe and the people without history*. Berkeley: University of California Press.

Wright, G. A.
1978 Social differentiation in the Early Natufian. In *Social archaeology: Beyond subsistence and dating*, ed. by C. L. Redman, M. J. Berman, E. V. Curint, W. T. J. Langhorne, N. M. Versaggi, and J. C. Wanser, pp. 201–233. New York: Academic Press.

Wright, M.
1985 Iron and regional history: Report on a research project in southwestern Tanzania. *African Economic History* 14:147–165.

Wright, R.
1991 Women's labor and pottery production in prehistory. In *Engendering archaeology: Woman and prehistory*, ed. by J. M. Gero and M. W. Conkey, pp. 194–223. Oxford: Blackwell.

1996 ed.   Gender and archaeology. Philadelphia: University of Pennsylvania Press.

Wylie, A.
1982 An analogy by any other name is just as analogical: A commentary on the Gould-Watson dialogue. *Journal of Anthropological Archaeology* 1(14):382–401.

1985 The reaction against analogy. In *Advances in archaeological method and theory vol. 8*, ed. by M. B. Schiffer, pp. 63–111. New York: Academic Press.

1987 The philosophy of ambivalence: Sandra Harding on "the science question in feminism." *Canadian Journal of Philosophy*, Supplementary volume 13:59–73.

1988 "Simple" analogy and the role of relevance assumptions: Implications of archaeological practice. *International Studies in the Philosophy of Science* 2:134–150.

1989 Archaeological cables and tacking: The implications for practice for Bernstein's—Options beyond objectivism and relativism. *Philosophy of Social Science* 19:1–18.

1991 Gender, theory and the archaeological record: Why is there no archaeology of gender? In *Engendering archaeology: Woman and prehistory*, ed. by J. M. Gero and M. W. Conkey, pp. 31–54. Oxford: Blackwell.

1995 Alternative histories: Epistemic disunity and political integrity. In *Making alternative histories*, ed. by P. R. Schmidt and T. Patterson. Santa Fe, N.M.: School of American Research.

Yarak, L.
1979 Dating Asantehene Osei Kwadwo's campaign against the Banna. *Asantesem* 10:58.

Yates, R., J. Golson, and M. Hall
1985 Trance performance: The rock art of Boontjieskloof and Sevilla. *South African Archaeological Bulletin* 40:70–89

Yates, R., and R. Jerardino
1996 A fortuitous fall: Early rock paintings from the west coast of South Africa. *South African Journal of Science* 92:110.

Yates, R., and A. Manhire
1991 Shamanism and rock paintings: Aspects of the use of rock art in the south-west Cape, South Africa. *South African Archaeological Bulletin* 46:3–11.

Yates, T.
1993 Frameworks for an archaeology of the body. In *Reading material culture*, ed. by C. Tilley, pp. 281–347. London: Blackwell.

Yellen, J.
1977 *Archaeological approaches to the present.* New York: Academic Press.
1990a Comment on foragers, genuine or spurious? *Current Anthropology* 31(2):137–138.
1990b The transformation of the Kalahari !Kung. *Scientific American* 262(4):96–105.

Yellen, J., A. Brooks, R. Stuckenrath, and R. Welbourne
1987 A terminal Pleistocene assemblage from Drotsky's Cave, western Ngamiland, Botswana. *Botswana Notes and Records* 19:1–6.

About the Authors

OFER BAR-YOSEF is the MacCurdy Professor of Prehistoric Archaeology, Peabody Museum, Harvard University, Boston. His major projects are dealt with in numerous publications, including *Übeidiya, a Lower Paleolithic Site in the Jordan Valley* (jointly with E. Tchernov), *The Middle, Upper, and Epi-Paleolithic Deposits in Kebara Cave* (with B. Vandermeersch), and *Hayonim Cave* (with E. Tchernov, B. Arensburg, and B. Vandermeersch). He surveyed and excavated Upper and Epi- Paleolithic sites in northern Sinai with J. L. Phillips. His interest in the origins of agriculture led him to initiate the excacations of an Early Neolithic mound in the Jordan Valley (with A. Gopher). Looking for the spatial distribution of socioeconomic entities across the Levant motivated him to carry out a series of salvage excavations of hunter-gatherer sites in southern Sinai (with N. Goring-Morris and A. Gopher). He has published several papers with Anna Belfer-Cohen on the Natufian and Neolithic of the Levant. Recently he has become involved in Paleolithic projects in Turkey, the Republic of Georgia, and China.

BARBARA BARICH is Professor of Prehistorical Ethnography at the Dipartimento di Scienze Storiche, Archeologiche e Antropologiche dell'Antichita', University of Rome "La Spienza." She is Director of two official archaeological missions organized by the University of Rome in Egypt (Farafra Oasis) and Libya (Jebel Gharbi). Her main areas of interest are the early ceramic cultures of the Sahara and Nile Valley. In particular, she has devoted special attention to the theme of the transition from hunting-gathering to food-production societies. Besides her affiliation with many Italian organizations of archaeological and anthropological studies, she takes part in numerous foreign associations and is a member of the Executive Committee of the International Union of Prehistorical and Protohistorical Sciences. She is also the Permanent Secretary of the Forum for African Archaeology and Cultural Heritage. She has contributed articles to Italian and international journals, and is also the author of university textbooks.

ANNA BELFER-COHEN is a senior lecturer in Prehistoric Archaeology at the Institute of Archaeology, Hebrew University, Jerusalem. She received her Ph.D. in 1988 on a study of the Natufian settlement in Hayonim Cave, Western Galilee. She has participated in numerous field projects in Israel and Sinai and is currently involved in a project in the Republic of Georgia. Her areas of interest include the beginnings of agriculture and complex societies, paleoanthropology, prehistoric art, and Levantine prehistory.

JOANNA CASEY has been conducting archaeological and ethnographic research in northern Ghana since 1987. Her interests include the Stone Age, and the origin and nature of food-producing societies in West Africa. Her ethnographic interests concern women's businesses and the procurement and processing of indigenous wild resources. Her doctoral research at the University of Toronto was a study of human ecology during the Ceramic Late Stone Age. Most recently, she has been directing an archaeology project investigating a Kintampo Complex settlement in northern Ghana. She is currently visiting professor of Anthropology at the University of South Carolina.

MARIA DAS DORES CRUZ is a lecturer at Universidade Católica Portuguesa (Viseu, Portugal) and is completing her dissertation in anthropology at the State University of New York–Binghamton. Her interests include African archaeology, ceramic studies, and ethnoarchaeology. She has worked in archaeological projects in Portugal and conducted ethnoarchaeological fieldwork in Ghana, integrating the Banda Research Project.

DIANE GIFFORD-GONZALEZ is Professor of Anthropology at the University of California–Santa Cruz. She received her doctorate from the University of California–Berkeley in 1977 and has served on the Executive Board of the Society for American Archaeology and on the Executive Committee of the Archaeology Division of the American Anthropological Association. She has done ethnoarchaeological research in Kenya and Tanzania since 1972. In addition to analyses of faunas from Holocene East Africa, her publications have dealt with vertebrate taphonomy, ethnoarchaeology, the role of analogy in archaeological reasoning, and representations of age and gender in artists' portrayals of prehistoric humans.

SIMON HALL is a Lecturer in the Department of Archaeology at the University of the Witwatersrand, South Africa. He has research interests in the Later Stone Age hunter-gatherer (Ph.D.) and the agro-pastoralist (M.A.) archaeology of Southern Africa. His current research is an examination of interaction between hunter-gatherers and agropastoralists in the Limpopo Valley.

FEKRI A. HASSAN is the Petrie Professor of Archaeology at the Institute of Archaeology, University College, London. Trained first as a geologist, he later obtained a Ph.D. in anthropology (Egyptian archaeology) from Southern Methodist University, Dallas, Texas. His research focuses on the origins of agriculture and civilization.

SUSAN KENT is Professor of Anthropology at Old Dominion University, Norfolk, Virginia. She has conducted participant-observation and interview fieldwork among the G/wi and G//ana Basarwa (Bushmen or San) and Bakgalagadi of Kutse, Botswana; Navajo Indians of Navajo Mountain, Utah; Hispanics in rural and urban

Colorado; Euroamericans in urban Colorado and rural Oklahoma; and Northwest Coast Indians in Washington. She also has excavated archaeological sites ranging in date from PaleoIndian to historic and in geographical regions from the Northwest Coast and Columbia Plateau to the American Southwest. She plans to co-excavate a Late Stone Age site in southern Africa in order to study gender, activity area function, and the use of space.

PAUL LANE received his Ph.D. from Cambridge University, England. For his dissertation research, he spent approximately 16 months with the Dogon people of Mali, conducting an ethnoarchaeological study of the organization and use of space and time. He has taught at the University of Botswana and the University of Dar es Salaam, Tanzania. He also has directed several archaeological and ethnoarchaeological projects in Africa. His research interests include the Early and Late Iron Age of southern Africa, ethnoarchaeology, historical archaeology, and the sociopolitics of the past.

RACHEL MACLEAN received her Ph.D. in archaeology from the University of Cambridge, England, in 1996. She now holds a British Academy Post-Doctoral Fellowship in the Department of Archaeology at Cambridge. Her interests lie in the social functioning of technologies, and in the development of social archaeology in an African context. The majority of her fieldwork has been concentrated in East Africa, but she has recently worked in West Africa and has begun looking at British material.

SARAH MILLEDGE NELSON is John Evans Professor of Archaeology in the Anthropology Department at the University of Denver. She works in East Asia, especially China and Korea, and specializes in the Neolithic/Bronze Age transition, as well as gender. Her recent books include *Gender in Archaeology: Analyzing Power and Prestige* (1997), *The Archaeology of Northeast China: Beyond the Great Wall* (1995), *Equity Issues for Women in Archaeology* (1994, edited, with Margaret Nelson and Alison Wylie), and *The Archaeology of Korea* (1993).

JOHN PARKINGTON, Professor of Archaeology at the University of Cape Town, is a Palaeolithic archaeologist with an interest in the coastal archaeology of hunter-gatherers, African prehistory in general, and rock art. His work in the Western Cape has included excavations at Elands Bay cave and several other Later and Middle Stone Age sites, as well as the recording of rock paintings. He has recently begun to excavate Middle Stone Age shell middens and late middle Pleistocene hyena lairs.

PETER SCHMIDT has been engaged in Africa archaeology for the last three decades. He has carried out archaeological and ethnoarchaeological research in Tanzania, Uganda, Cameroon, Gabon, and Eritrea. The author of five books and many articles, he most recently wrote *Plundering Africa's Past* (Indiana University Press, 1996), ed.

with R. McIntosh; *Making Alternative Histories* (SAR Press, 1995), ed. with T. Patterson; and *Iron Technology in East Africa: Symbolism, Science, and Archaeology* (Indiana University Press, 1997). He is former Director of the Center for African Studies at the University of Florida, where he is currently Associate Professor of Anthropology.

ALINAH SEGOBYE teaches at the University of Botswana, Gaborone, Botswana. She received her Ph.D. from the University of Cambridge, England. Her dissertation field work was a study of later prehistoric settlement patterns in eastern Botswana. She has presented papers at numerous international and local conferences and is currently working with Swedish archaeologists in northern Botswana. Her interests include the Early and Late Iron Age of southern Africa, particularly Botswana, and paleoenvironmental issues.

ANN B. STAHL is an Associate Professor of Anthropology at the State University of New York–Binghamton, with interests in historical anthropology and African archaeology. Her dissertation focused on the period of early sedentism and the transition to food production in Ghana. Since 1986, she has pursued oral historical, archival, and archaeological research focused on the political economy of Banda, Ghana, ca. 1300–1925 AD. In addition, she has published on the topics of analogy, the history of anthropology, and dietary reconstruction.

LYN WADLEY is Professor of Archaeology in the Department of Archaeology at the University of the Witwatersrand, South Africa. She received her Ph.D. in 1987 from the University of the Witwatersrand. Her research interests are the Later and Middle Stone Age of southern Africa, and gender studies in archaeology. She has excavated Stone Age sites in Zimbabwe, Namibia, and South Africa, where she has a long-term project in the eastern Free State. Rose Cottage, a large cave, is the focus of the research. In addition to establishing the cultural sequence in the cave, she is conducting spatial studies with the aim of examining social change through time.

Index